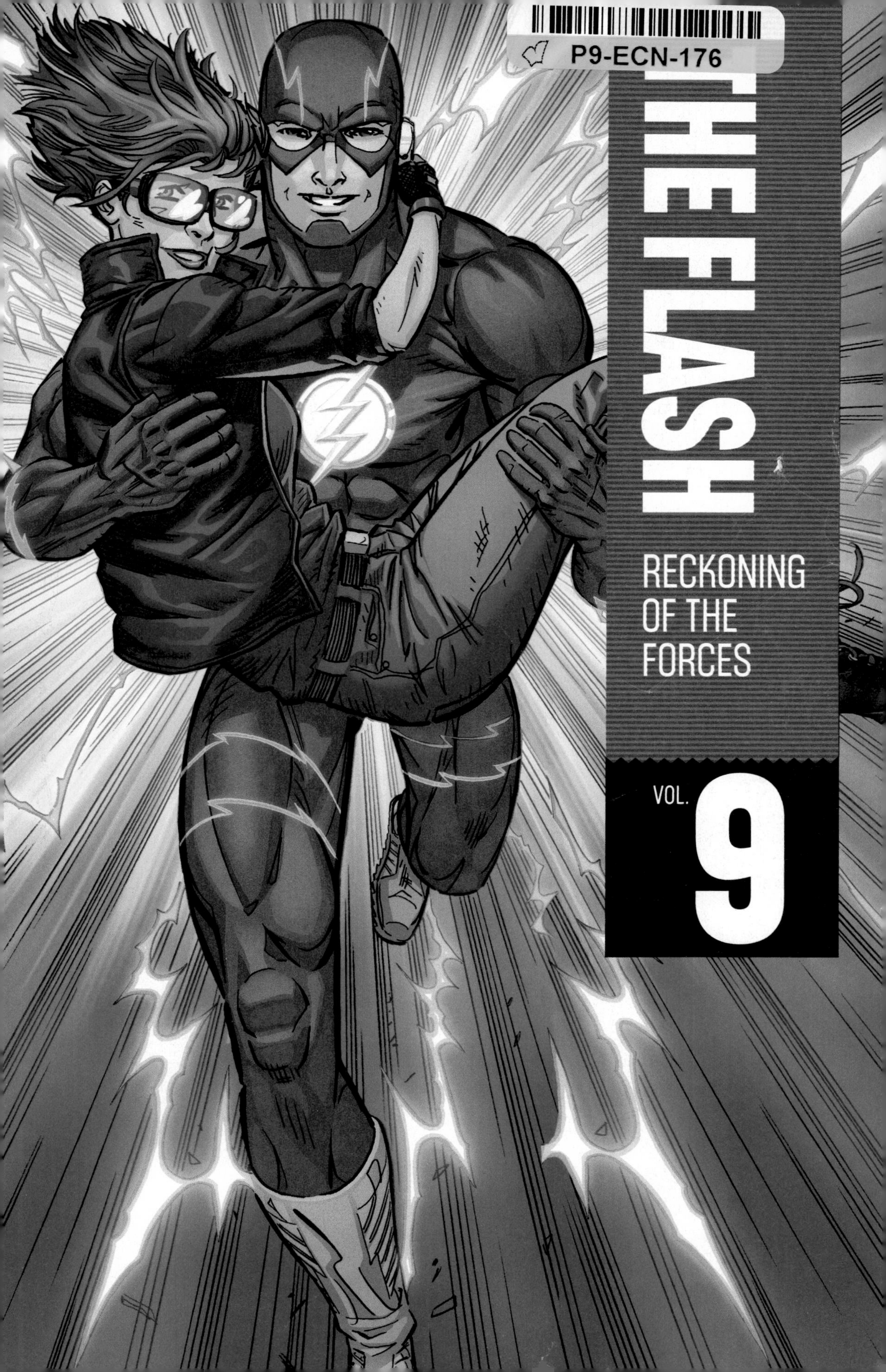
THE FLASH
RECKONING
OF THE
FORCES
VOL.
9

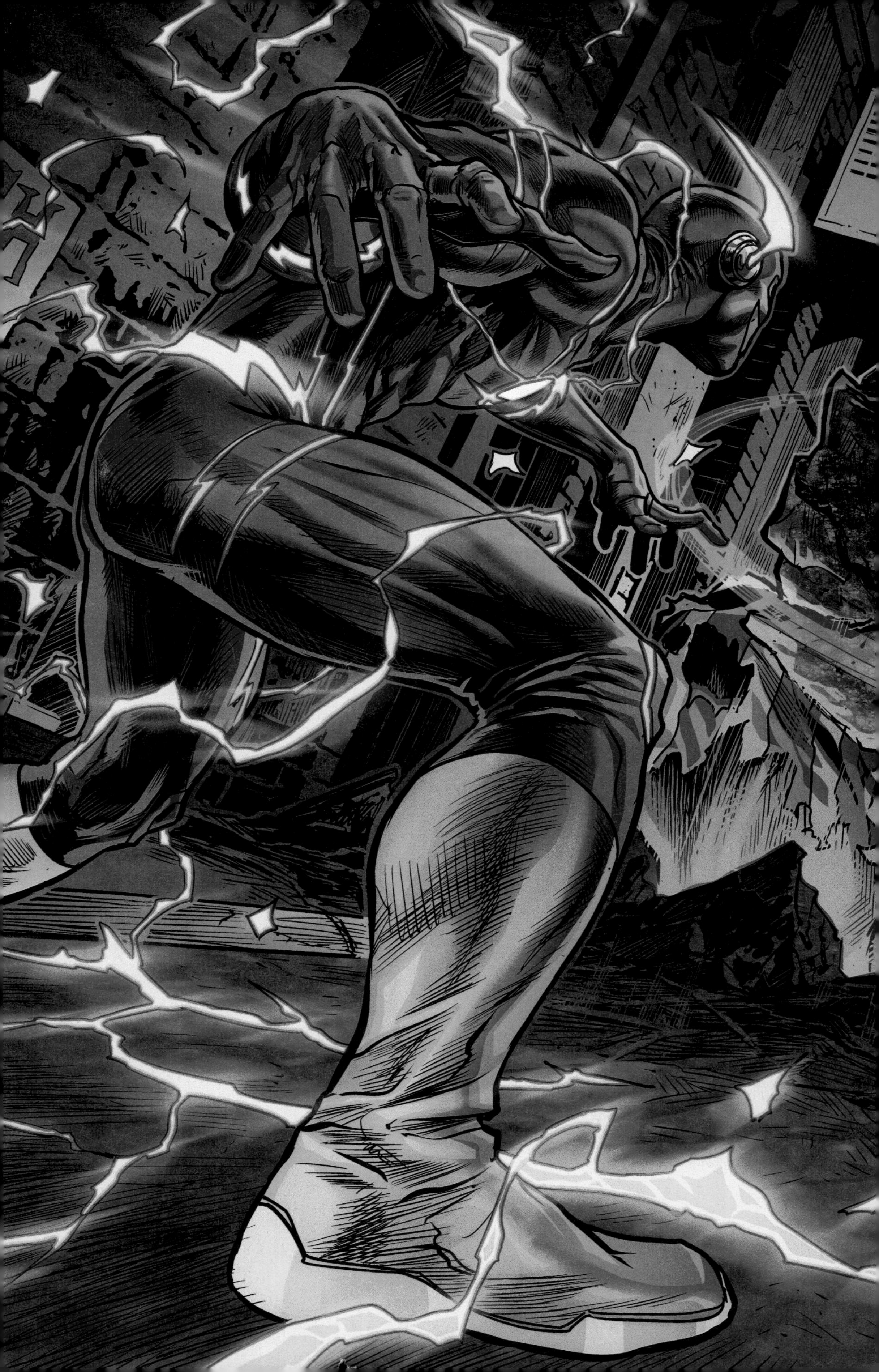

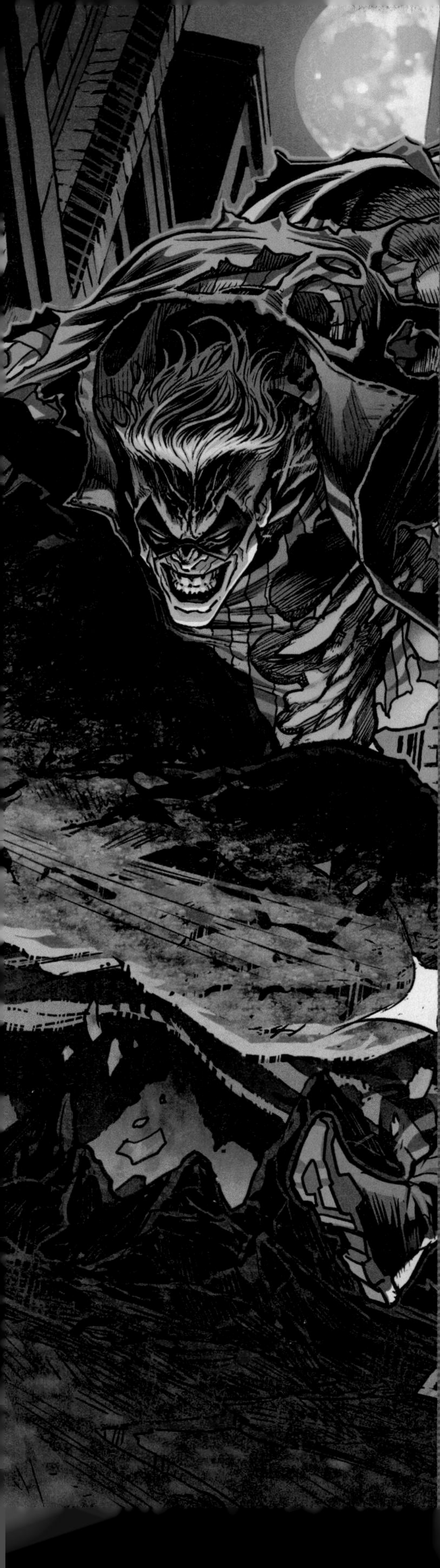

THE FLASH
RECKONING OF THE FORCES

writer
JOSHUA WILLIAMSON

artists
CHRISTIAN DUCE
SCOTT KOLINS

colorist
LUIS GUERRERO

letterer
STEVE WANDS

collection cover artist
DAN MORA

VOL. **9**

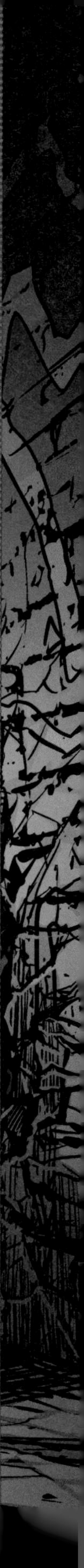

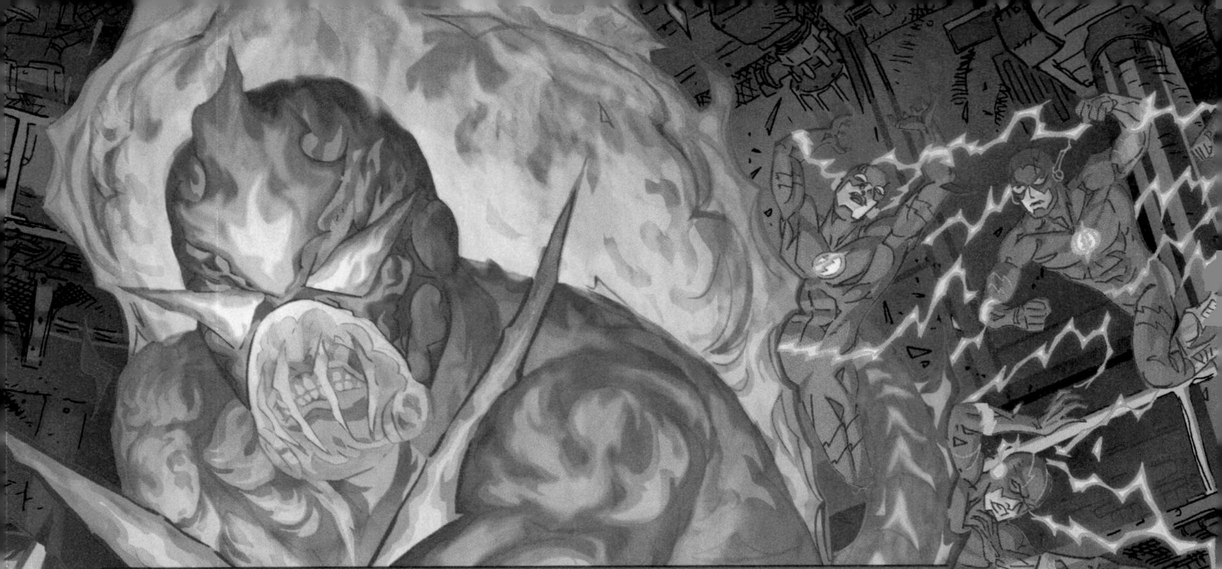

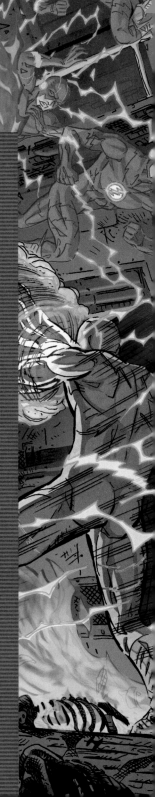

REBECCA TAYLOR Editor – Original Series
ANDREW MARINO Assistant Editor – Original Series
JEB WOODARD Group Editor – Collected Editions
ERIKA ROTHBERG Editor – Collected Edition
STEVE COOK Design Director – Books
CURTIS KING JR. Publication Design

BOB HARRAS Senior VP – Editor-in-Chief, DC Comics
PAT McCALLUM Executive Editor, DC Comics

DAN DiDIO Publisher
JIM LEE Publisher & Chief Creative Officer
AMIT DESAI Executive VP – Business & Marketing Strategy, Direct to Consumer & Global Franchise Management
BOBBIE CHASE VP & Executive Editor, Young Reader & Talent Development
MARK CHIARELLO Senior VP – Art, Design & Collected Editions
JOHN CUNNINGHAM Senior VP – Sales & Trade Marketing
BRIAR DARDEN VP – Business Affairs
ANNE DePIES Senior VP – Business Strategy, Finance & Administration
DON FALLETTI VP – Manufacturing Operations
LAWRENCE GANEM VP – Editorial Administration & Talent Relations
ALISON GILL Senior VP – Manufacturing & Operations
JASON GREENBERG VP – Business Strategy & Finance
HANK KANALZ Senior VP – Editorial Strategy & Administration
JAY KOGAN Senior VP – Legal Affairs
NICK J. NAPOLITANO VP – Manufacturing Administration
LISETTE OSTERLOH VP – Digital Marketing & Events
EDDIE SCANNELL VP – Consumer Marketing
COURTNEY SIMMONS Senior VP – Publicity & Communications
JIM (SKI) SOKOLOWSKI VP – Comic Book Specialty Sales & Trade Marketing
NANCY SPEARS VP – Mass, Book, Digital Sales & Trade Marketing
MICHELE R. WELLS VP – Content Strategy

THE FLASH VOL. 9: RECKONING OF THE FORCES

DC Comics, 2900 West Alameda Ave., Burbank, CA 91505
Printed by LSC Communications, Owensville, MO, USA. 2/22/19. First Printing.
ISBN: 978-1-4012-8855-6

Library of Congress Cataloging-in-Publication Data is available.

PEFC Certified
This product is from sustainably managed forests and controlled sources
PEFC
PEFC/29-31-337
www.pefc.org

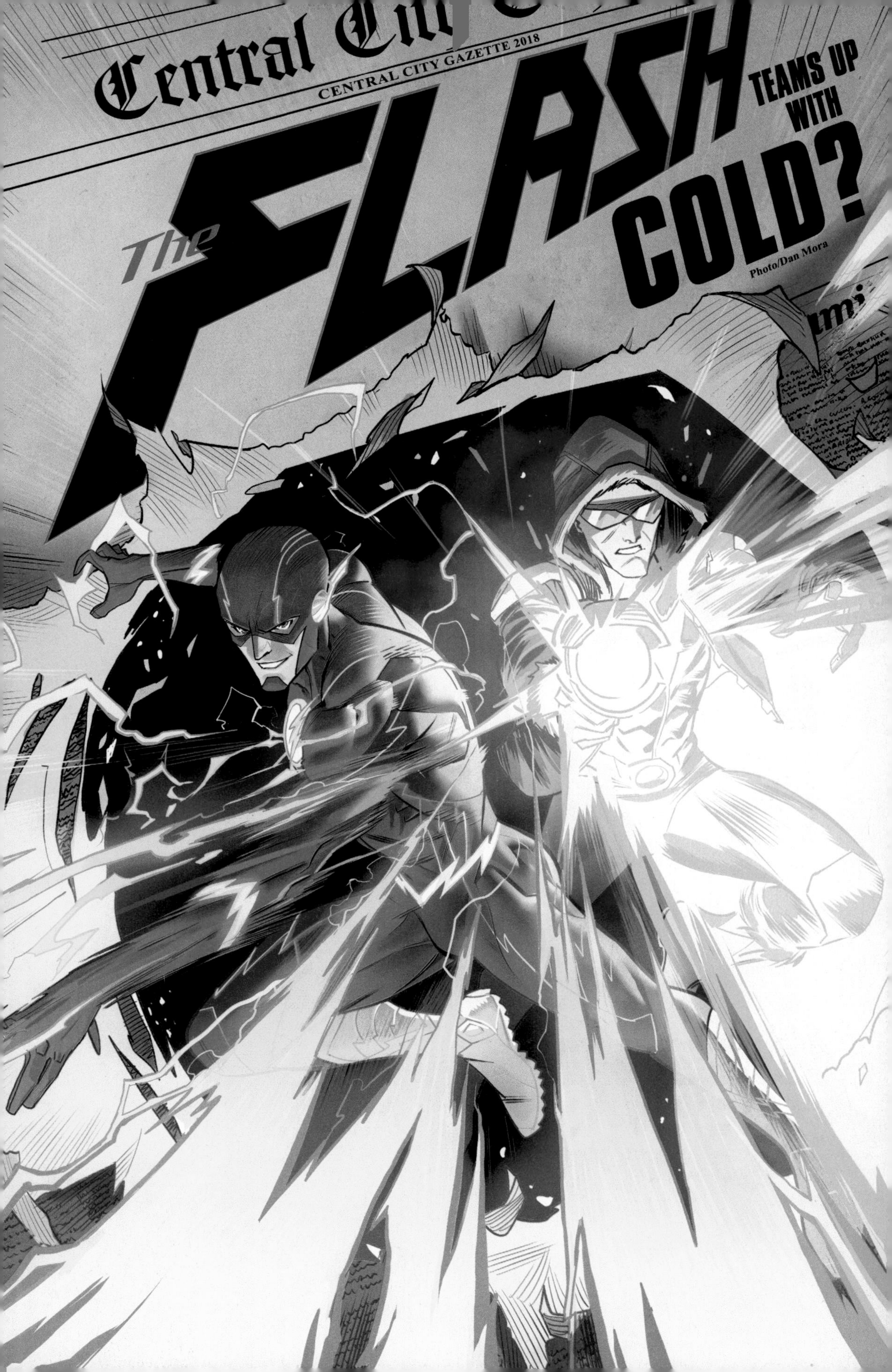
Central Cit
CENTRAL CITY GAZETTE 2018
The FLASH
TEAMS UP WITH
COLD?
Photo/Dan Mora

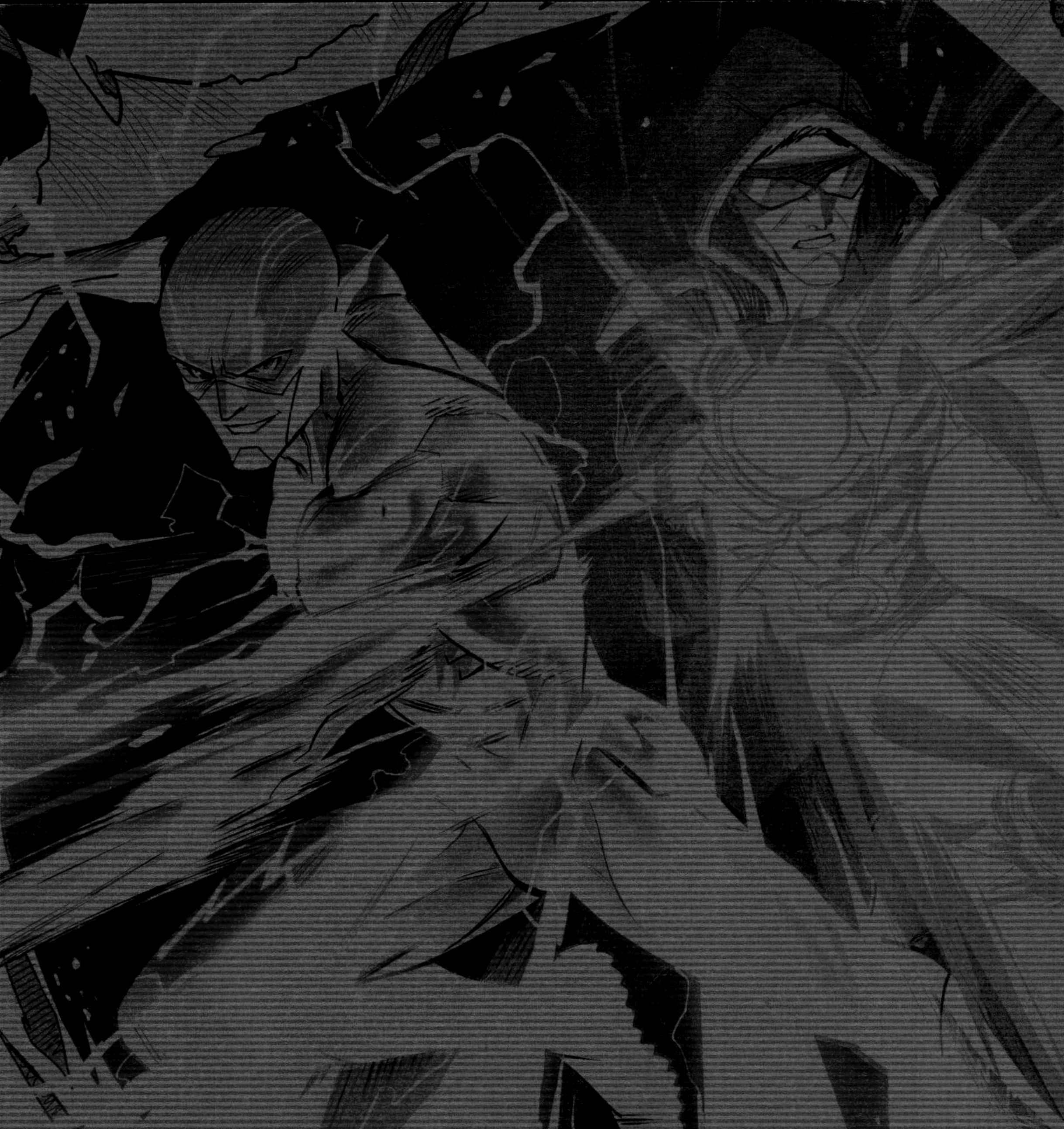

THE FLASH

#52

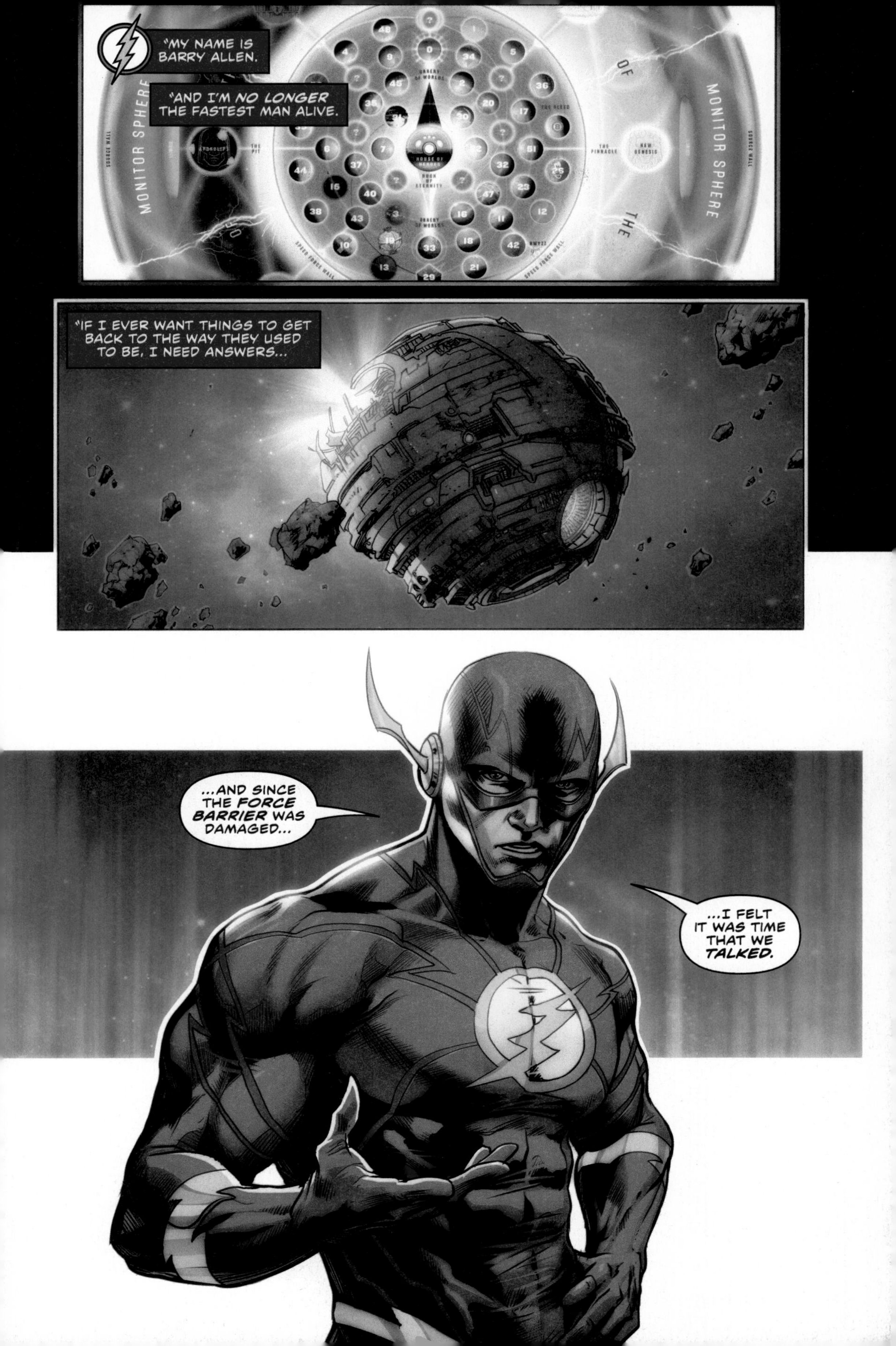
"MY NAME IS BARRY ALLEN.
"AND I'M NO LONGER THE FASTEST MAN ALIVE.
MONITOR SPHERE
OF
THE
MONITOR SPHERE
"IF I EVER WANT THINGS TO GET BACK TO THE WAY THEY USED TO BE, I NEED ANSWERS...
...AND SINCE THE *FORCE BARRIER* WAS DAMAGED...
...I FELT IT WAS TIME THAT WE *TALKED.*

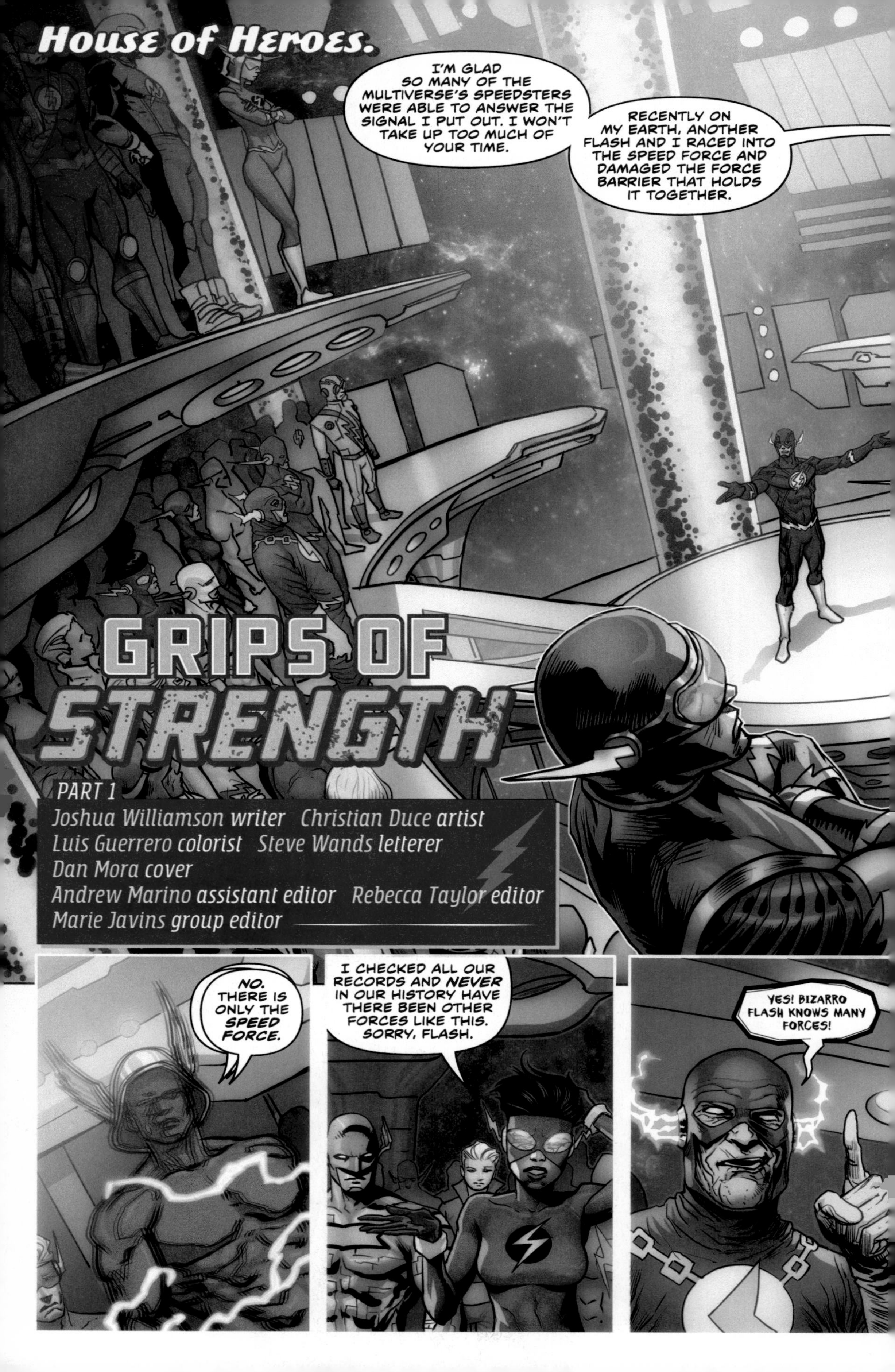
House of Heroes.
I'M GLAD SO MANY OF THE MULTIVERSE'S SPEEDSTERS WERE ABLE TO ANSWER THE SIGNAL I PUT OUT. I WON'T TAKE UP TOO MUCH OF YOUR TIME.
RECENTLY ON MY EARTH, ANOTHER FLASH AND I RACED INTO THE SPEED FORCE AND DAMAGED THE FORCE BARRIER THAT HOLDS IT TOGETHER.
GRIPS OF STRENGTH
PART 1
Joshua Williamson writer Christian Duce artist
Luis Guerrero colorist Steve Wands letterer
Dan Mora cover
Andrew Marino assistant editor Rebecca Taylor editor
Marie Javins group editor
NO. THERE IS ONLY THE SPEED FORCE.
I CHECKED ALL OUR RECORDS AND NEVER IN OUR HISTORY HAVE THERE BEEN OTHER FORCES LIKE THIS. SORRY, FLASH.
YES! BIZARRO FLASH KNOWS MANY FORCES!

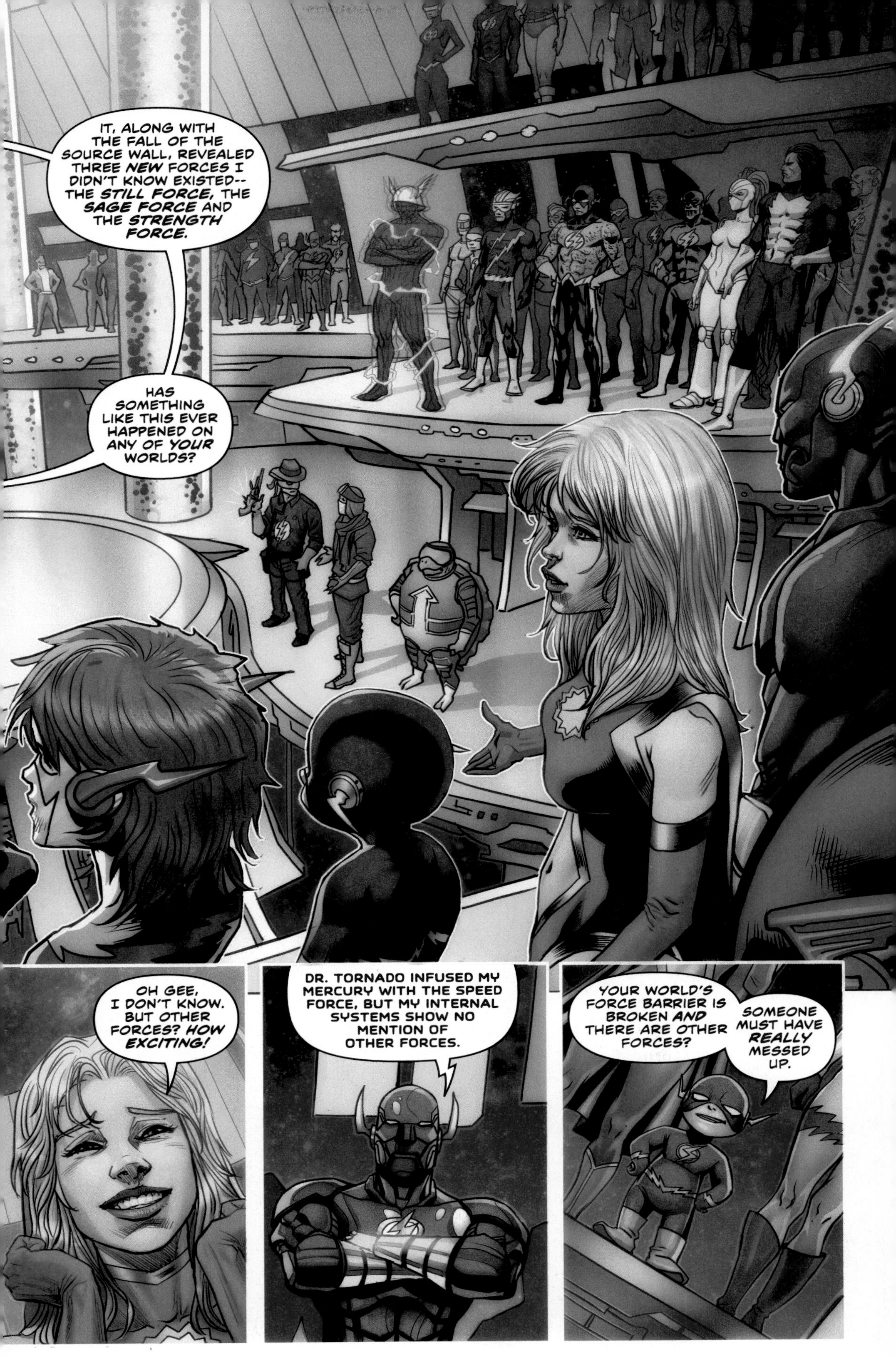
IT, ALONG WITH THE FALL OF THE SOURCE WALL, REVEALED THREE NEW FORCES I DIDN'T KNOW EXISTED-- THE STILL FORCE, THE SAGE FORCE AND THE STRENGTH FORCE.
HAS SOMETHING LIKE THIS EVER HAPPENED ON ANY OF YOUR WORLDS?
OH GEE, I DON'T KNOW. BUT OTHER FORCES? HOW EXCITING!
DR. TORNADO INFUSED MY MERCURY WITH THE SPEED FORCE, BUT MY INTERNAL SYSTEMS SHOW NO MENTION OF OTHER FORCES.
YOUR WORLD'S FORCE BARRIER IS BROKEN AND THERE ARE OTHER FORCES?
SOMEONE MUST HAVE REALLY MESSED UP.

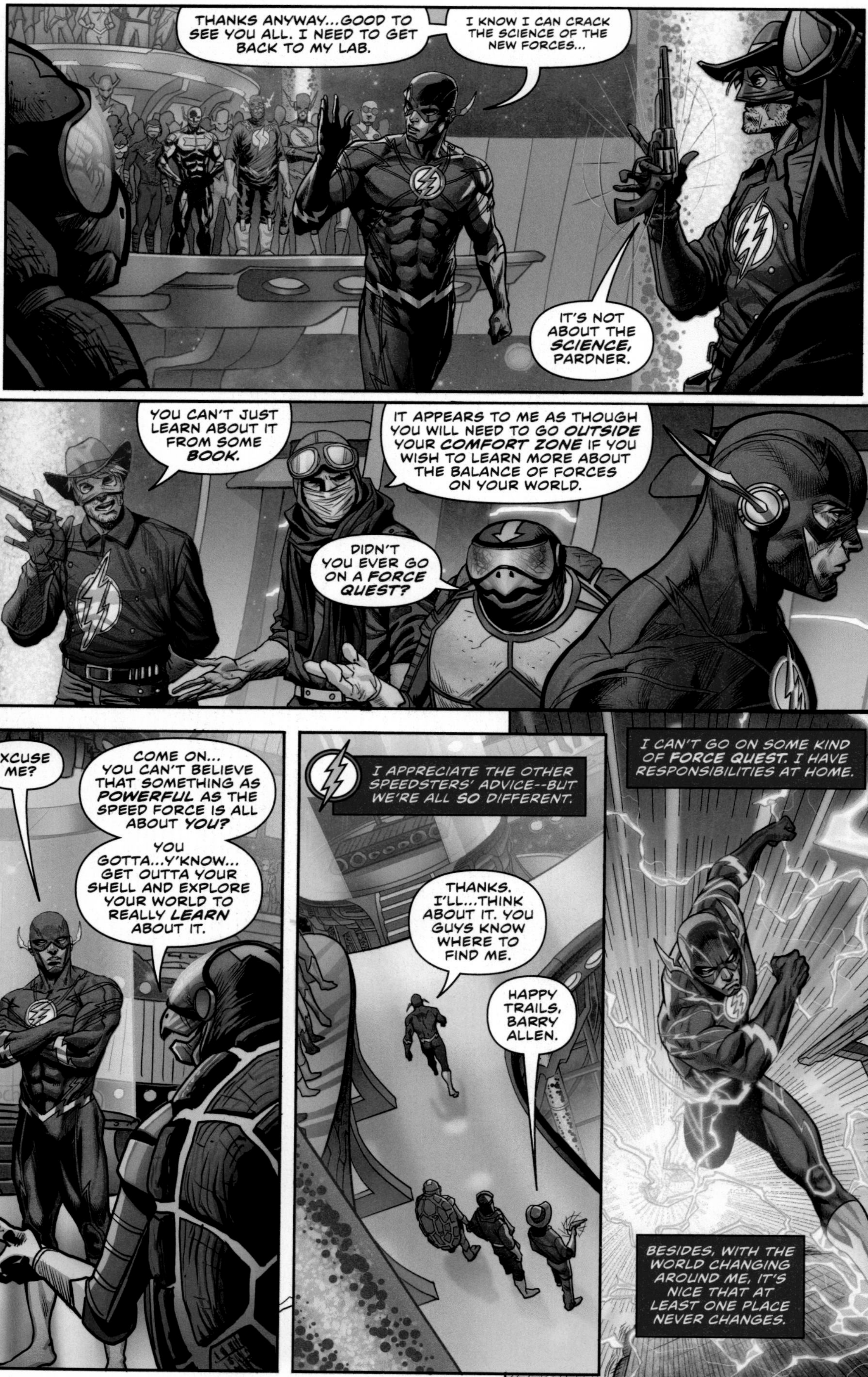
THANKS ANYWAY...GOOD TO SEE YOU ALL. I NEED TO GET BACK TO MY LAB.
I KNOW I CAN CRACK THE SCIENCE OF THE NEW FORCES...
IT'S NOT ABOUT THE SCIENCE, PARDNER.
YOU CAN'T JUST LEARN ABOUT IT FROM SOME BOOK.
IT APPEARS TO ME AS THOUGH YOU WILL NEED TO GO OUTSIDE YOUR COMFORT ZONE IF YOU WISH TO LEARN MORE ABOUT THE BALANCE OF FORCES ON YOUR WORLD.
DIDN'T YOU EVER GO ON A FORCE QUEST?
EXCUSE ME?
COME ON... YOU CAN'T BELIEVE THAT SOMETHING AS POWERFUL AS THE SPEED FORCE IS ALL ABOUT YOU?
YOU GOTTA...Y'KNOW... GET OUTTA YOUR SHELL AND EXPLORE YOUR WORLD TO REALLY LEARN ABOUT IT.
I APPRECIATE THE OTHER SPEEDSTERS' ADVICE--BUT WE'RE ALL SO DIFFERENT.
THANKS. I'LL...THINK ABOUT IT. YOU GUYS KNOW WHERE TO FIND ME.
HAPPY TRAILS, BARRY ALLEN.
I CAN'T GO ON SOME KIND OF FORCE QUEST. I HAVE RESPONSIBILITIES AT HOME.
BESIDES, WITH THE WORLD CHANGING AROUND ME, IT'S NICE THAT AT LEAST ONE PLACE NEVER CHANGES.

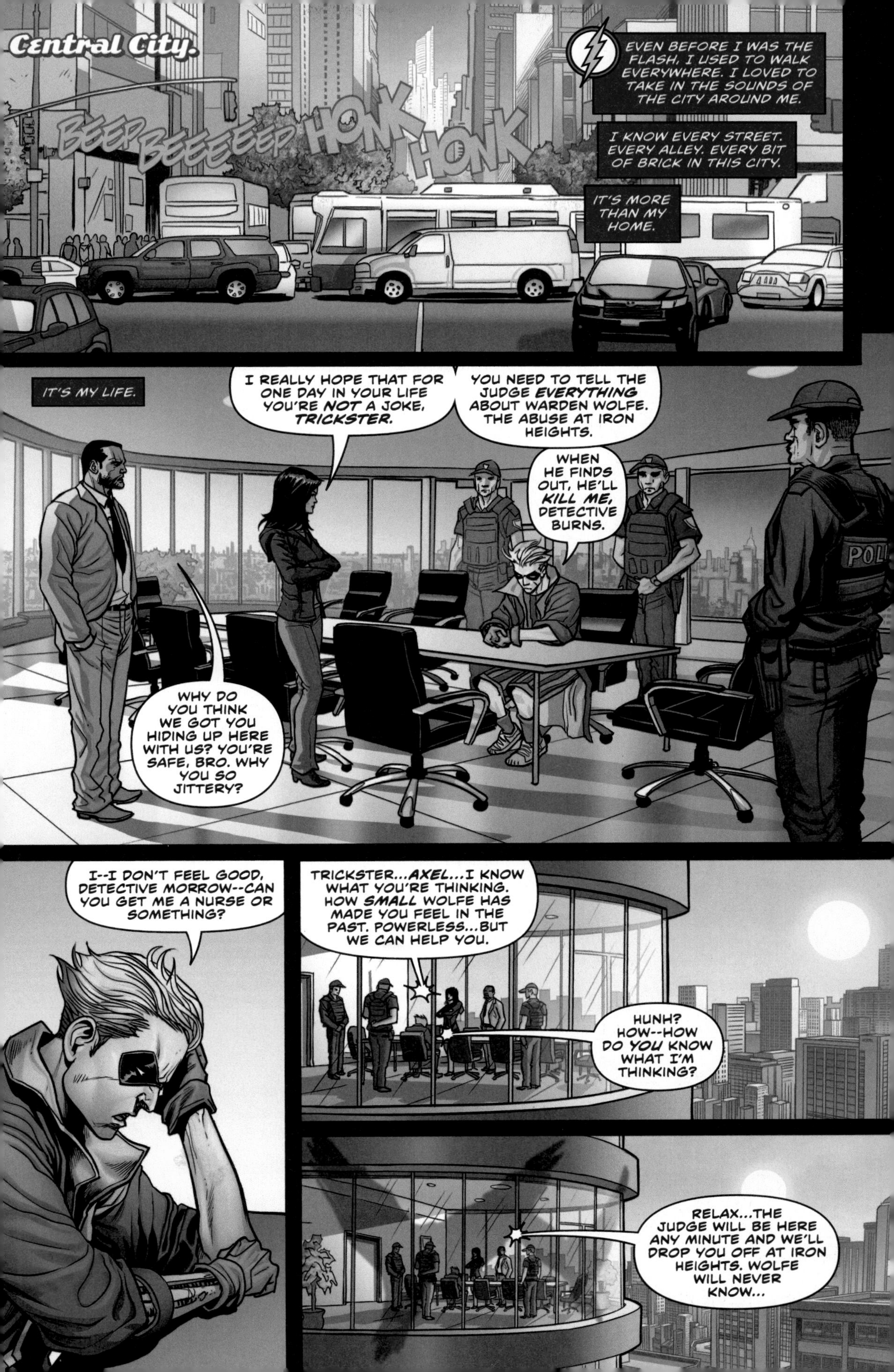

Central City.
EVEN BEFORE I WAS THE FLASH, I USED TO WALK EVERYWHERE. I LOVED TO TAKE IN THE SOUNDS OF THE CITY AROUND ME.
BEEP BEEEEEEP HONK HONK
I KNOW EVERY STREET. EVERY ALLEY. EVERY BIT OF BRICK IN THIS CITY.
IT'S MORE THAN MY HOME.
IT'S MY LIFE.
I REALLY HOPE THAT FOR ONE DAY IN YOUR LIFE YOU'RE NOT A JOKE, TRICKSTER.
YOU NEED TO TELL THE JUDGE EVERYTHING ABOUT WARDEN WOLFE. THE ABUSE AT IRON HEIGHTS.
WHEN HE FINDS OUT, HE'LL KILL ME, DETECTIVE BURNS.
WHY DO YOU THINK WE GOT YOU HIDING UP HERE WITH US? YOU'RE SAFE, BRO. WHY YOU SO JITTERY?
POLI
I--I DON'T FEEL GOOD, DETECTIVE MORROW--CAN YOU GET ME A NURSE OR SOMETHING?
TRICKSTER...AXEL...I KNOW WHAT YOU'RE THINKING. HOW SMALL WOLFE HAS MADE YOU FEEL IN THE PAST. POWERLESS...BUT WE CAN HELP YOU.
HUNH? HOW--HOW DO YOU KNOW WHAT I'M THINKING?
RELAX...THE JUDGE WILL BE HERE ANY MINUTE AND WE'LL DROP YOU OFF AT IRON HEIGHTS. WOLFE WILL NEVER KNOW...

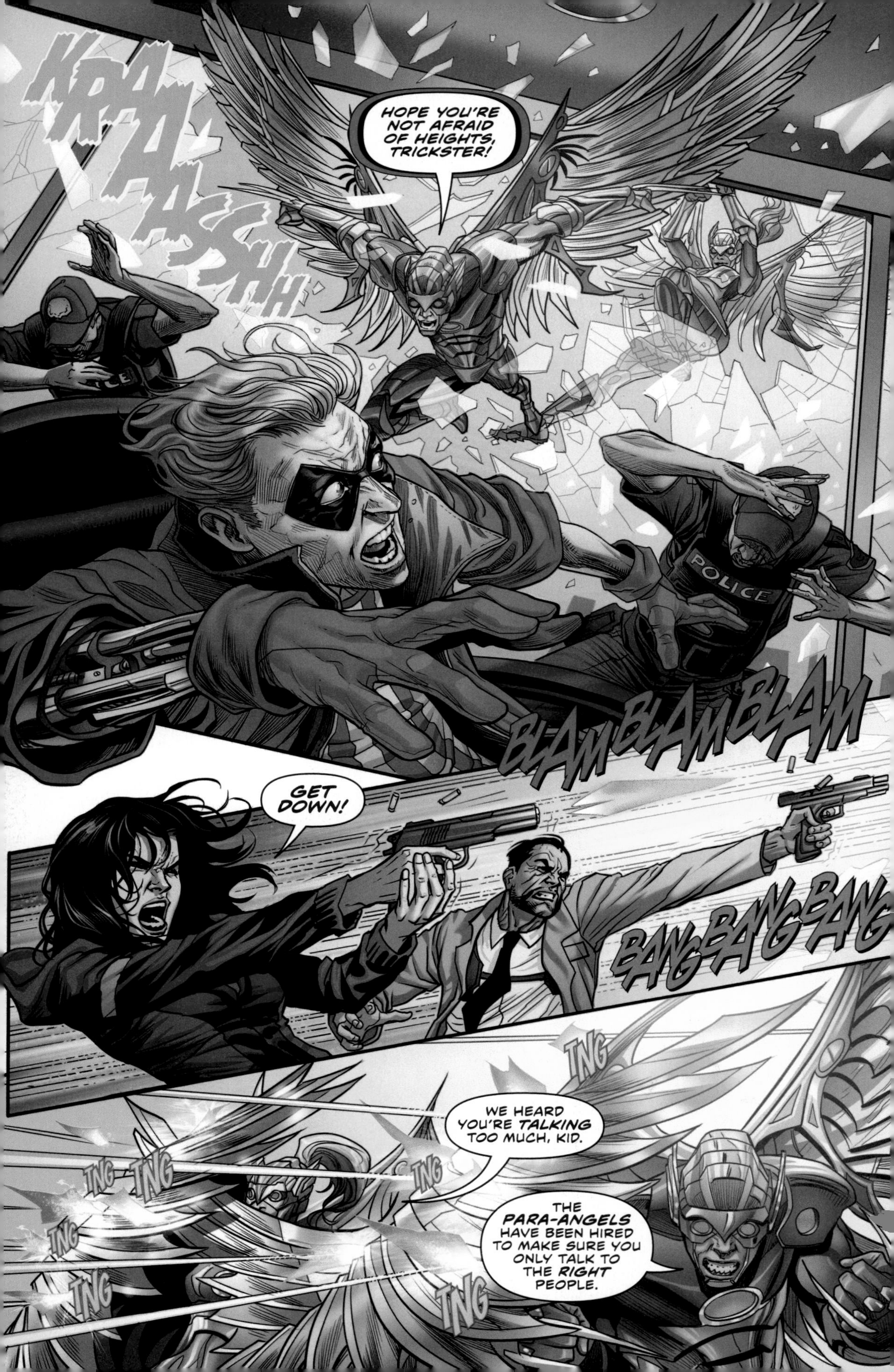
KRAAAASHH
HOPE YOU'RE NOT AFRAID OF HEIGHTS, TRICKSTER!
POLICE
BLAM BLAM BLAM
GET DOWN!
BANG BANG BANG
TNG
WE HEARD YOU'RE TALKING TOO MUCH, KID.
TNG TNG TNG
THE PARA-ANGELS HAVE BEEN HIRED TO MAKE SURE YOU ONLY TALK TO THE RIGHT PEOPLE.
TNG TNG TNG

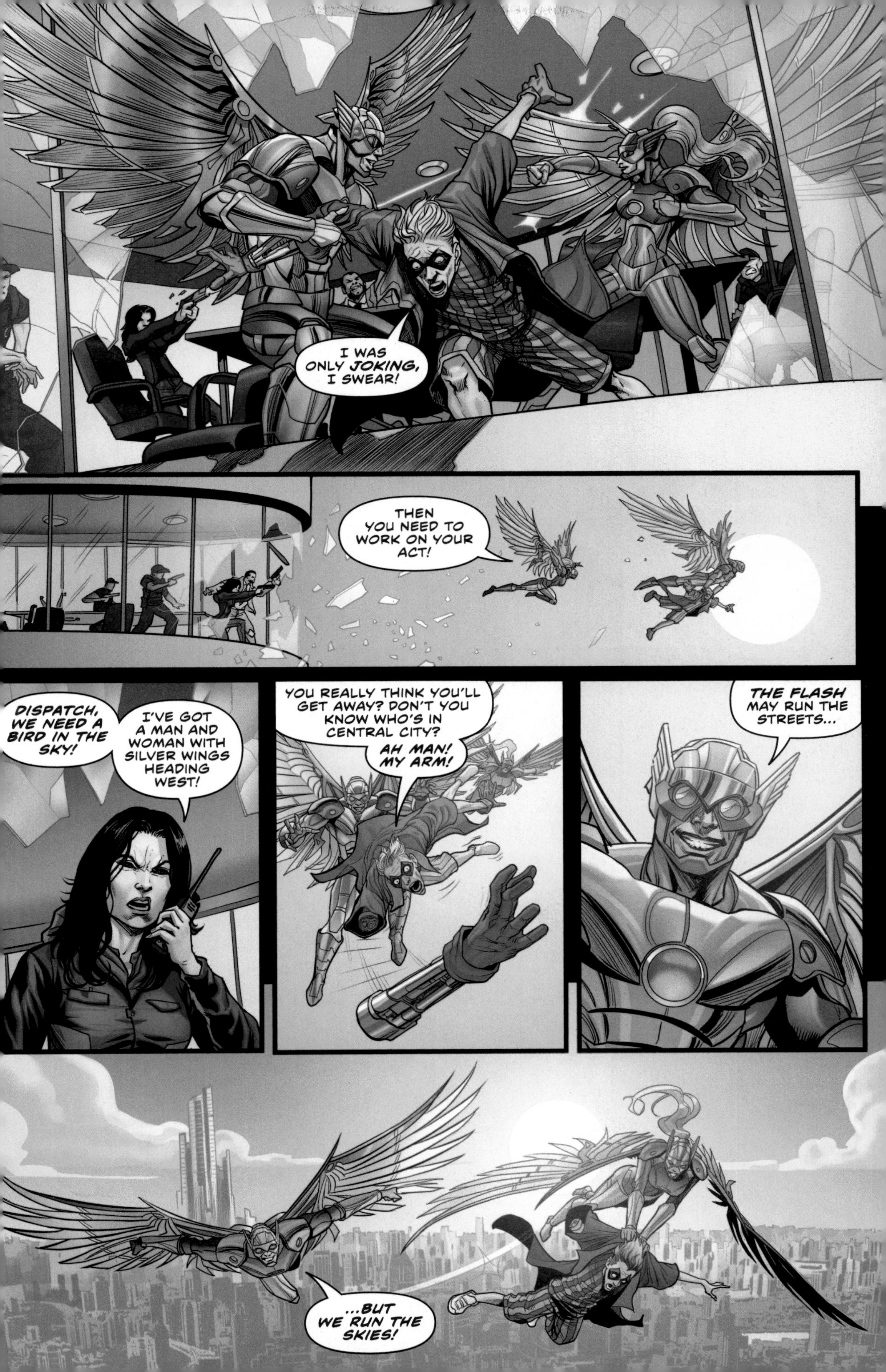
I WAS ONLY JOKING, I SWEAR!
THEN YOU NEED TO WORK ON YOUR ACT!
DISPATCH, WE NEED A BIRD IN THE SKY!
I'VE GOT A MAN AND WOMAN WITH SILVER WINGS HEADING WEST!
YOU REALLY THINK YOU'LL GET AWAY? DON'T YOU KNOW WHO'S IN CENTRAL CITY?
AH MAN! MY ARM!
THE FLASH MAY RUN THE STREETS...
...BUT WE RUN THE SKIES!

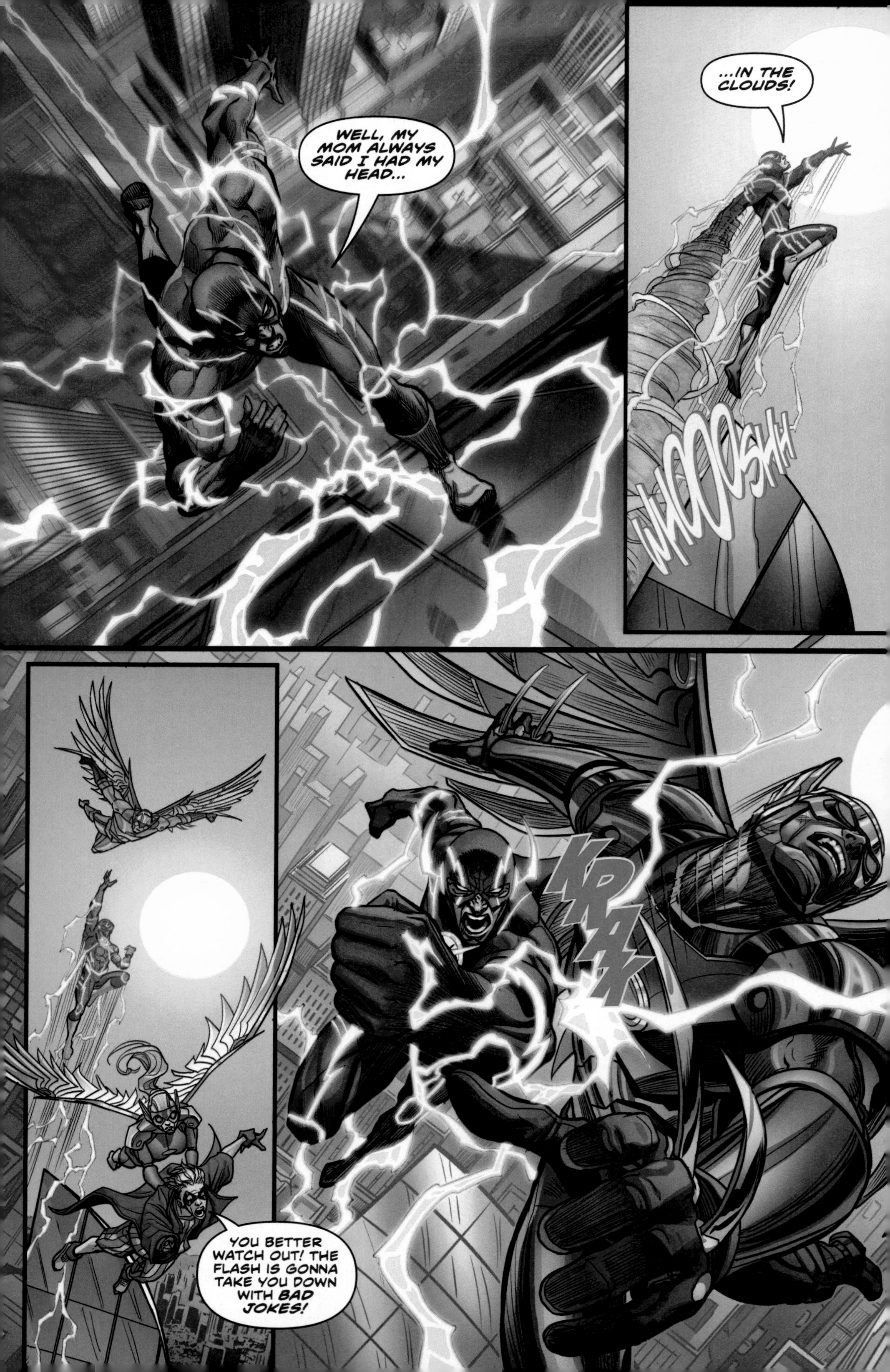
WELL, MY MOM ALWAYS SAID I HAD MY HEAD...
...IN THE CLOUDS!
WHOOOSHH
KRAK
YOU BETTER WATCH OUT! THE FLASH IS GONNA TAKE YOU DOWN WITH BAD JOKES!

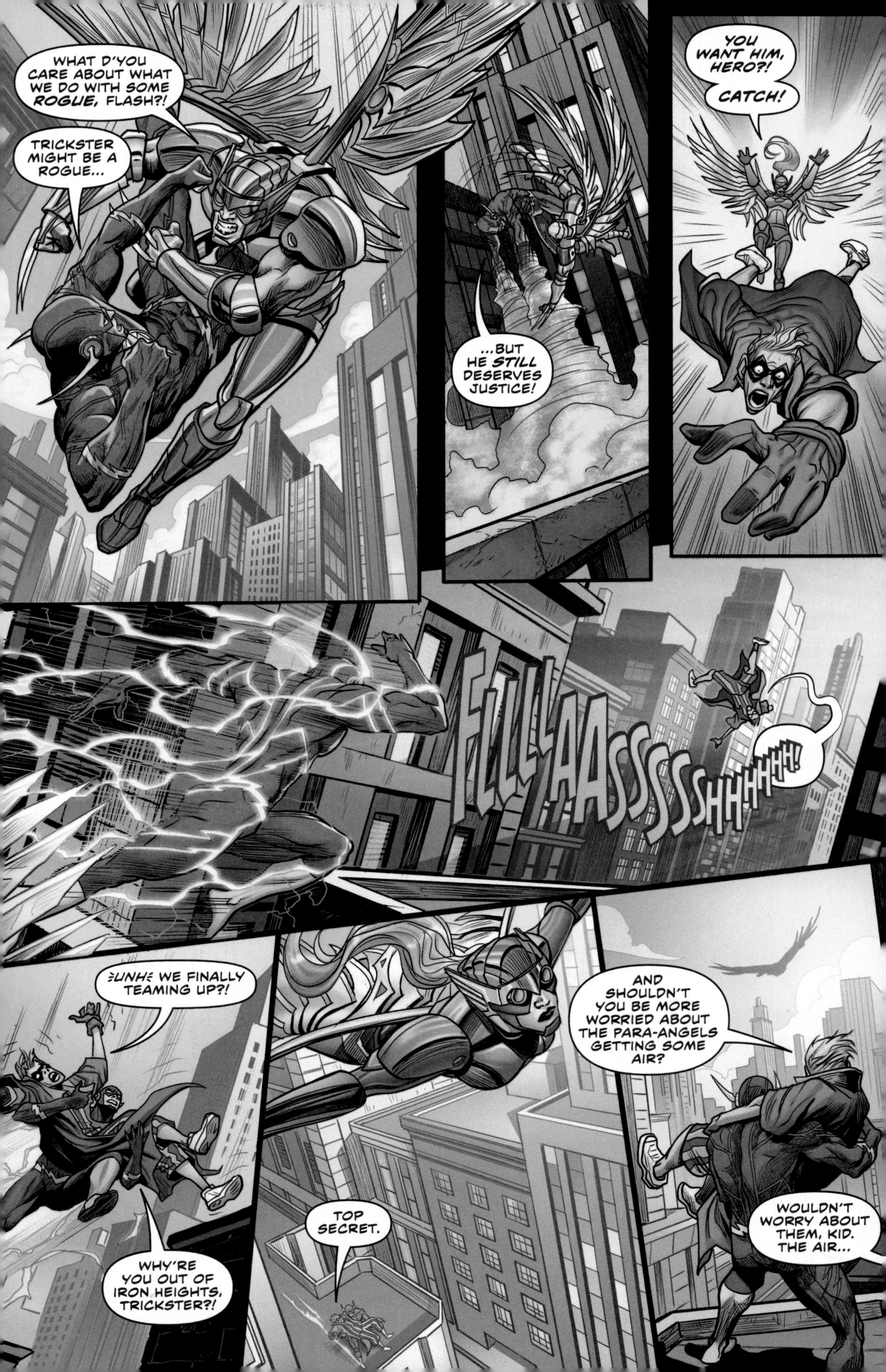
WHAT D'YOU CARE ABOUT WHAT WE DO WITH SOME *ROGUE*, FLASH?!
TRICKSTER MIGHT BE A ROGUE...
...BUT HE *STILL* DESERVES JUSTICE!
YOU WANT HIM, HERO?!
CATCH!
FLLLAASSSSSSHHHHH!
UNH WE FINALLY TEAMING UP?!
WHY'RE YOU OUT OF IRON HEIGHTS, TRICKSTER?!
TOP SECRET.
AND SHOULDN'T YOU BE MORE WORRIED ABOUT THE PARA-ANGELS GETTING SOME AIR?
WOULDN'T WORRY ABOUT THEM, KID. THE AIR...

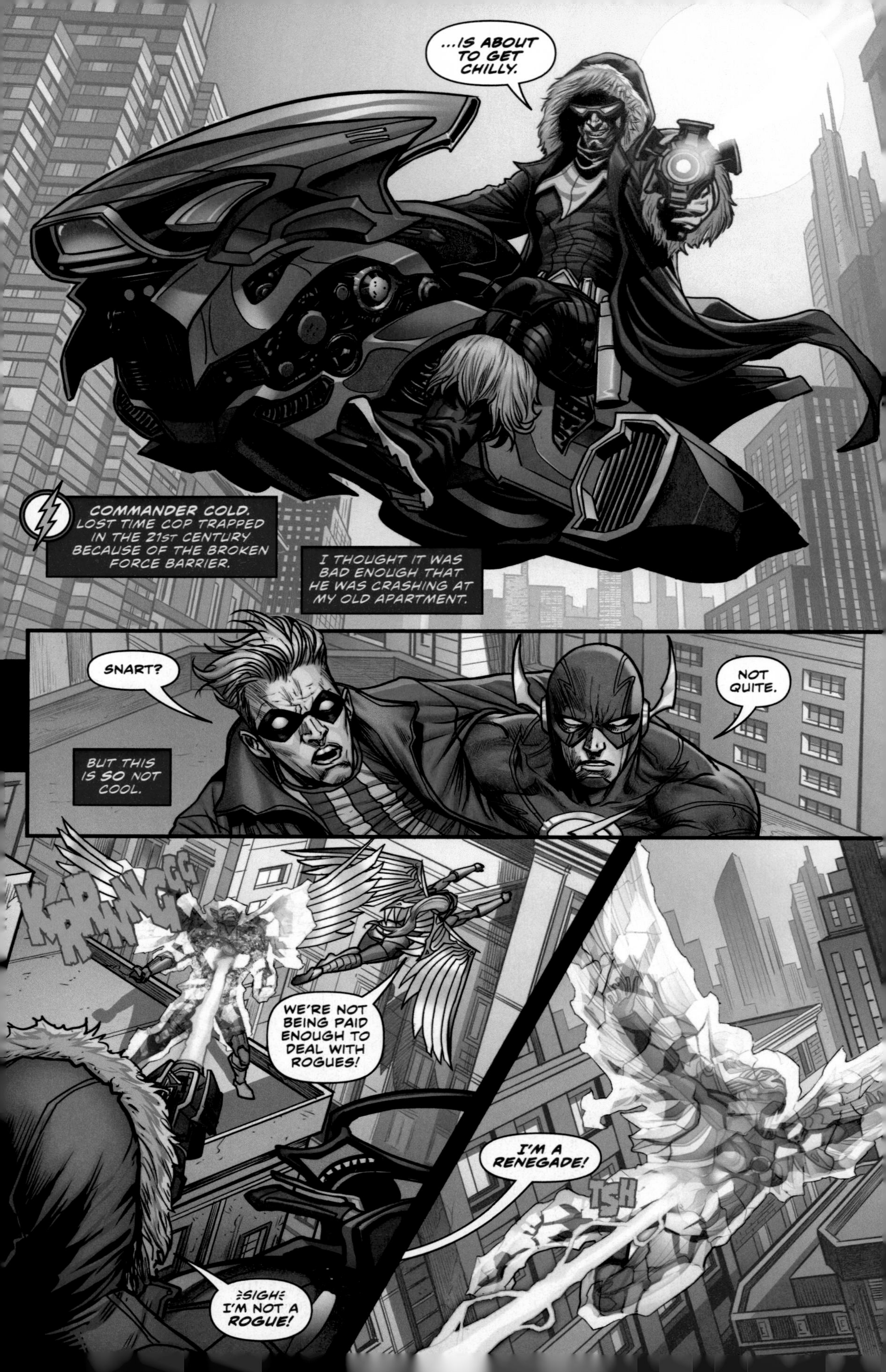
...IS ABOUT TO GET CHILLY.
COMMANDER COLD. LOST TIME COP TRAPPED IN THE 21ST CENTURY BECAUSE OF THE BROKEN FORCE BARRIER.
I THOUGHT IT WAS BAD ENOUGH THAT HE WAS CRASHING AT MY OLD APARTMENT.
SNART?
NOT QUITE.
BUT THIS IS SO NOT COOL.
KRANNGG
WE'RE NOT BEING PAID ENOUGH TO DEAL WITH ROGUES!
SIGH I'M NOT A ROGUE!
I'M A RENEGADE!
TSH

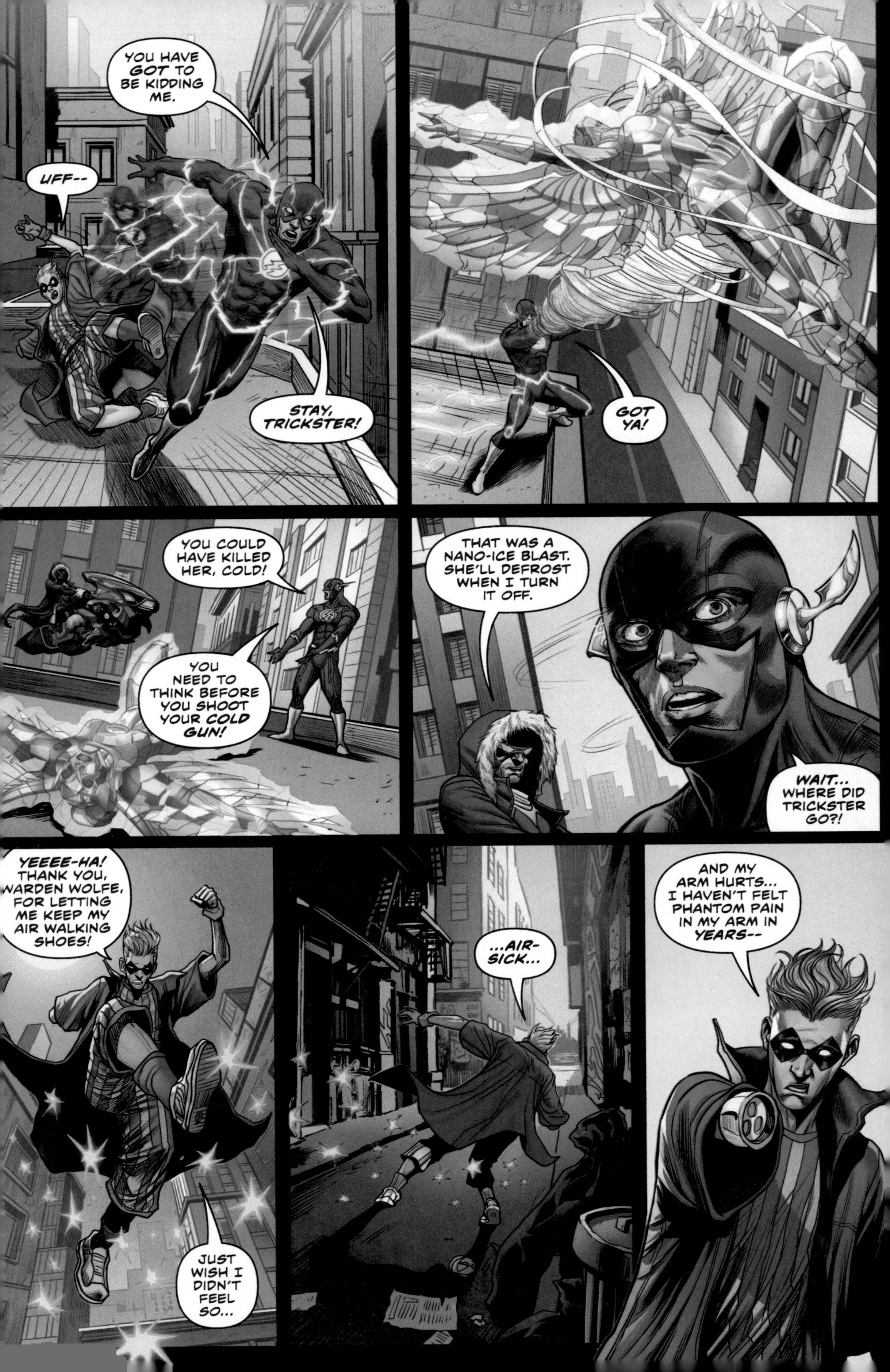
UFF--
YOU HAVE GOT TO BE KIDDING ME.
STAY, TRICKSTER!
GOT YA!
YOU COULD HAVE KILLED HER, COLD!
YOU NEED TO THINK BEFORE YOU SHOOT YOUR COLD GUN!
THAT WAS A NANO-ICE BLAST. SHE'LL DEFROST WHEN I TURN IT OFF.
WAIT... WHERE DID TRICKSTER GO?!
YEEEE-HA! THANK YOU, WARDEN WOLFE, FOR LETTING ME KEEP MY AIR WALKING SHOES!
JUST WISH I DIDN'T FEEL SO...
...AIR-SICK...
AND MY ARM HURTS... I HAVEN'T FELT PHANTOM PAIN IN MY ARM IN YEARS--

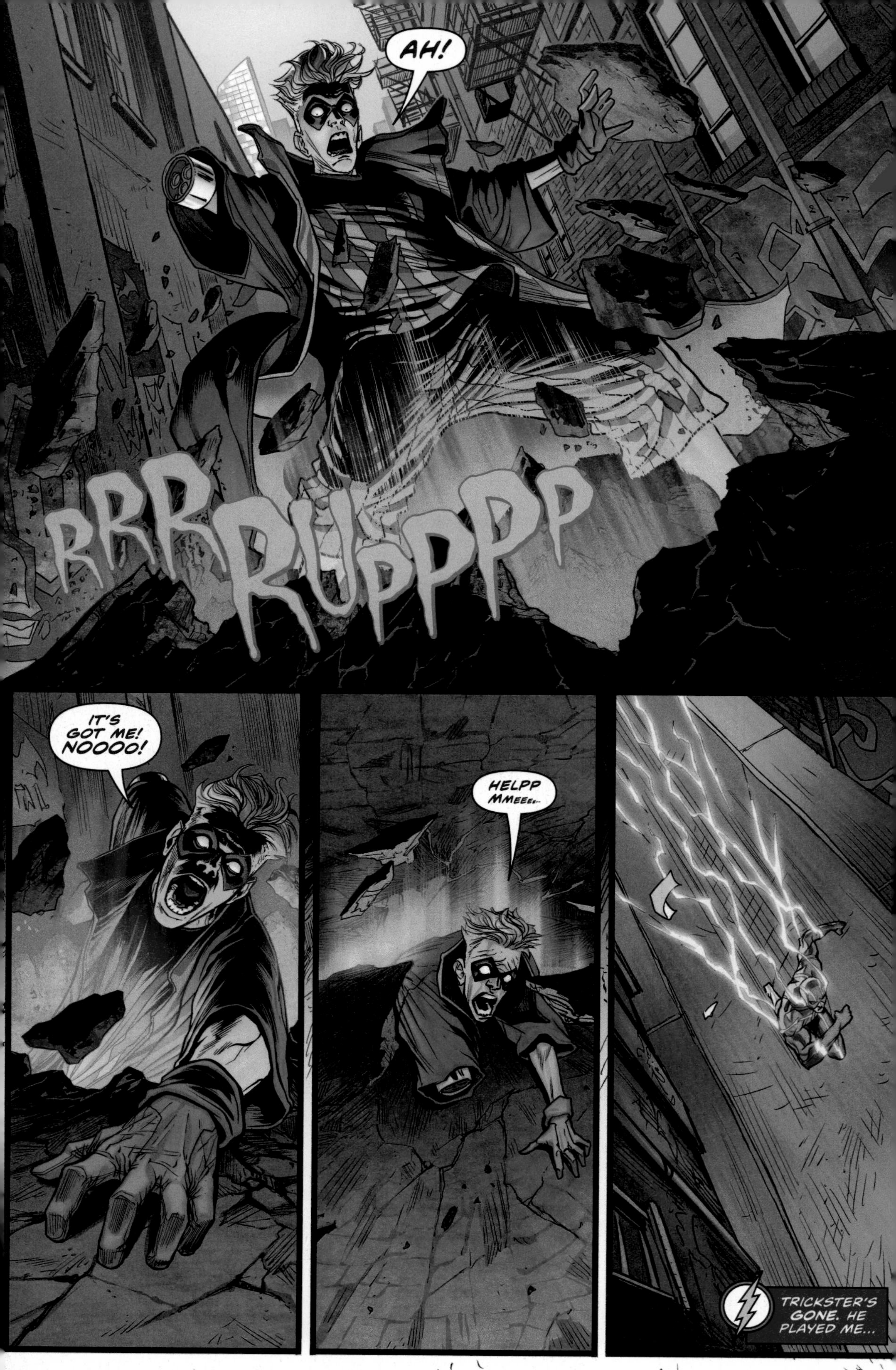
AH!
RRRRUPPPP
IT'S GOT ME! NOOOO!
HELPP MMEEE...
TRICKSTER'S GONE. HE PLAYED ME...

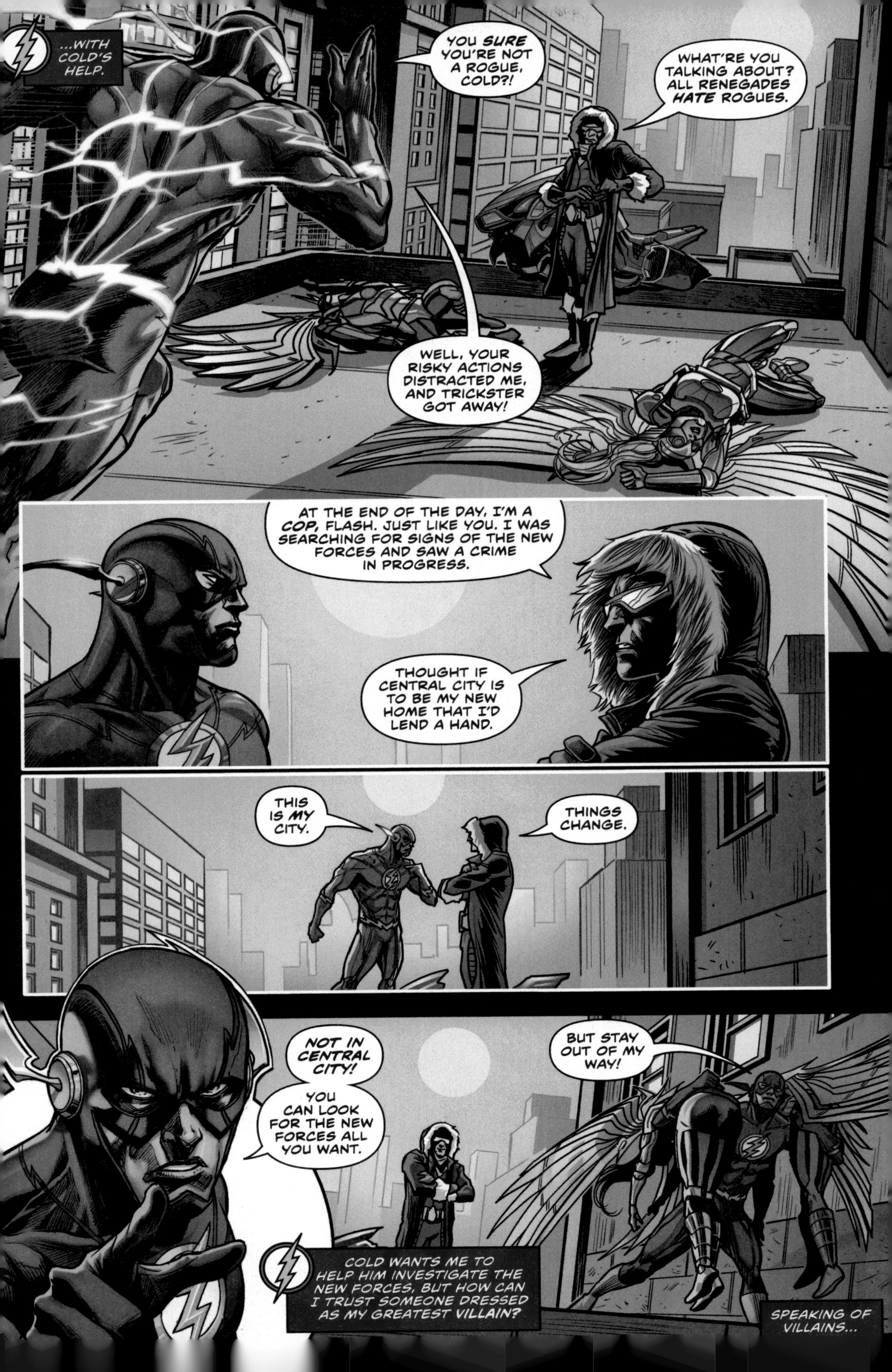
...WITH COLD'S HELP.
YOU SURE YOU'RE NOT A ROGUE, COLD?!
WHAT'RE YOU TALKING ABOUT? ALL RENEGADES HATE ROGUES.
WELL, YOUR RISKY ACTIONS DISTRACTED ME, AND TRICKSTER GOT AWAY!
AT THE END OF THE DAY, I'M A COP, FLASH. JUST LIKE YOU. I WAS SEARCHING FOR SIGNS OF THE NEW FORCES AND SAW A CRIME IN PROGRESS.
THOUGHT IF CENTRAL CITY IS TO BE MY NEW HOME THAT I'D LEND A HAND.
THIS IS MY CITY.
THINGS CHANGE.
NOT IN CENTRAL CITY!
YOU CAN LOOK FOR THE NEW FORCES ALL YOU WANT.
BUT STAY OUT OF MY WAY!
COLD WANTS ME TO HELP HIM INVESTIGATE THE NEW FORCES, BUT HOW CAN I TRUST SOMEONE DRESSED AS MY GREATEST VILLAIN?
SPEAKING OF VILLAINS...

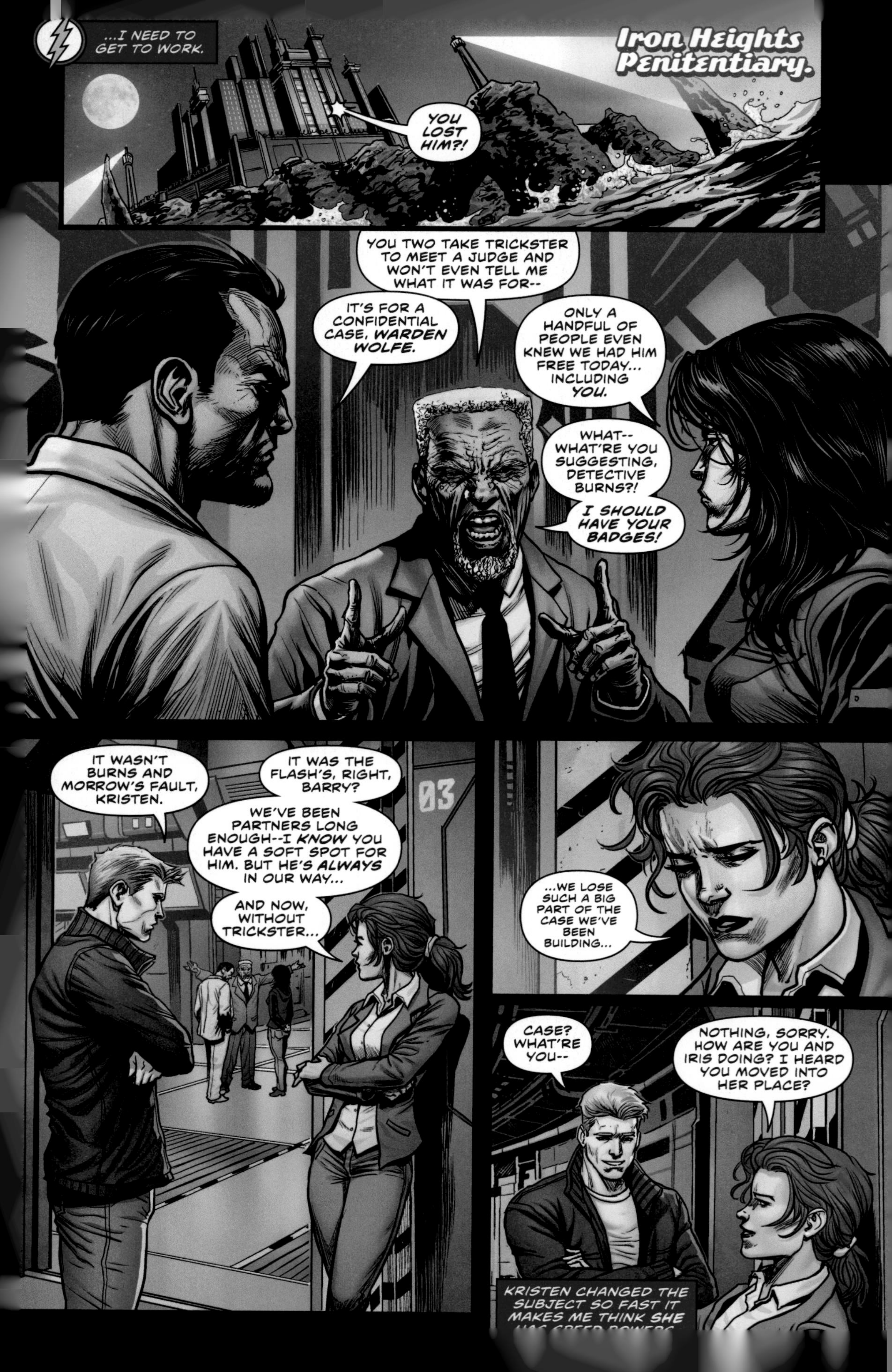
...I NEED TO GET TO WORK.
Iron Heights Penitentiary.
YOU LOST HIM?!
YOU TWO TAKE TRICKSTER TO MEET A JUDGE AND WON'T EVEN TELL ME WHAT IT WAS FOR--
IT'S FOR A CONFIDENTIAL CASE, WARDEN WOLFE.
ONLY A HANDFUL OF PEOPLE EVEN KNEW WE HAD HIM FREE TODAY... INCLUDING YOU.
WHAT-- WHAT'RE YOU SUGGESTING, DETECTIVE BURNS?!
I SHOULD HAVE YOUR BADGES!
IT WASN'T BURNS AND MORROW'S FAULT, KRISTEN.
IT WAS THE FLASH'S, RIGHT, BARRY?
WE'VE BEEN PARTNERS LONG ENOUGH--I KNOW YOU HAVE A SOFT SPOT FOR HIM. BUT HE'S ALWAYS IN OUR WAY...
AND NOW, WITHOUT TRICKSTER...
03
...WE LOSE SUCH A BIG PART OF THE CASE WE'VE BEEN BUILDING...
CASE? WHAT'RE YOU--
NOTHING, SORRY. HOW ARE YOU AND IRIS DOING? I HEARD YOU MOVED INTO HER PLACE?
KRISTEN CHANGED THE SUBJECT SO FAST IT MAKES ME THINK SHE

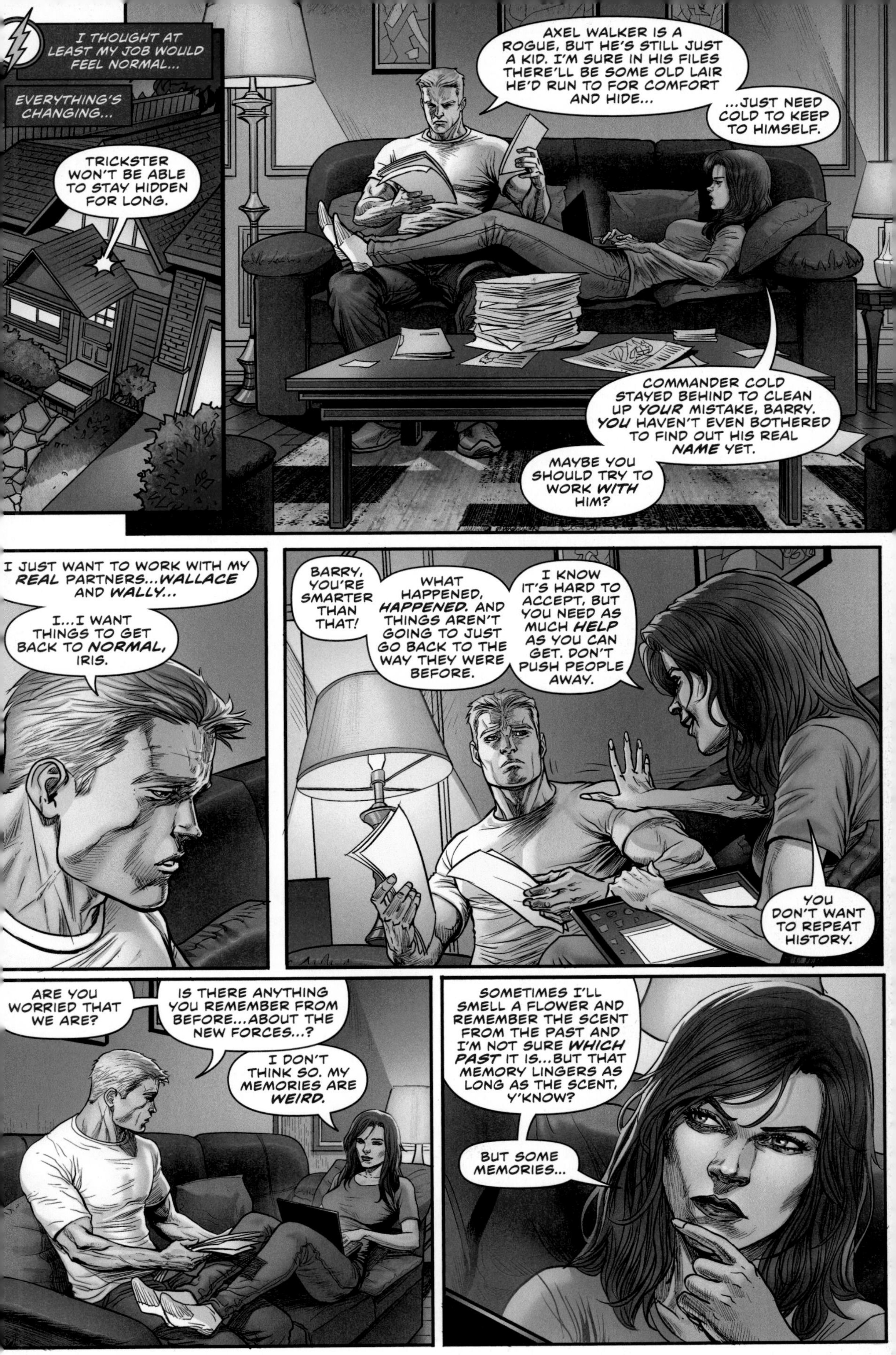
I THOUGHT AT LEAST MY JOB WOULD FEEL NORMAL...
EVERYTHING'S CHANGING...
TRICKSTER WON'T BE ABLE TO STAY HIDDEN FOR LONG.
AXEL WALKER IS A ROGUE, BUT HE'S STILL JUST A KID. I'M SURE IN HIS FILES THERE'LL BE SOME OLD LAIR HE'D RUN TO FOR COMFORT AND HIDE...
...JUST NEED COLD TO KEEP TO HIMSELF.
COMMANDER COLD STAYED BEHIND TO CLEAN UP YOUR MISTAKE, BARRY. YOU HAVEN'T EVEN BOTHERED TO FIND OUT HIS REAL NAME YET.
MAYBE YOU SHOULD TRY TO WORK WITH HIM?
I JUST WANT TO WORK WITH MY REAL PARTNERS...WALLACE AND WALLY...
I...I WANT THINGS TO GET BACK TO NORMAL, IRIS.
BARRY, YOU'RE SMARTER THAN THAT!
WHAT HAPPENED, HAPPENED. AND THINGS AREN'T GOING TO JUST GO BACK TO THE WAY THEY WERE BEFORE.
I KNOW IT'S HARD TO ACCEPT, BUT YOU NEED AS MUCH HELP AS YOU CAN GET. DON'T PUSH PEOPLE AWAY.
YOU DON'T WANT TO REPEAT HISTORY.
ARE YOU WORRIED THAT WE ARE?
IS THERE ANYTHING YOU REMEMBER FROM BEFORE...ABOUT THE NEW FORCES...?
I DON'T THINK SO. MY MEMORIES ARE WEIRD.
SOMETIMES I'LL SMELL A FLOWER AND REMEMBER THE SCENT FROM THE PAST AND I'M NOT SURE WHICH PAST IT IS...BUT THAT MEMORY LINGERS AS LONG AS THE SCENT, Y'KNOW?
BUT SOME MEMORIES...

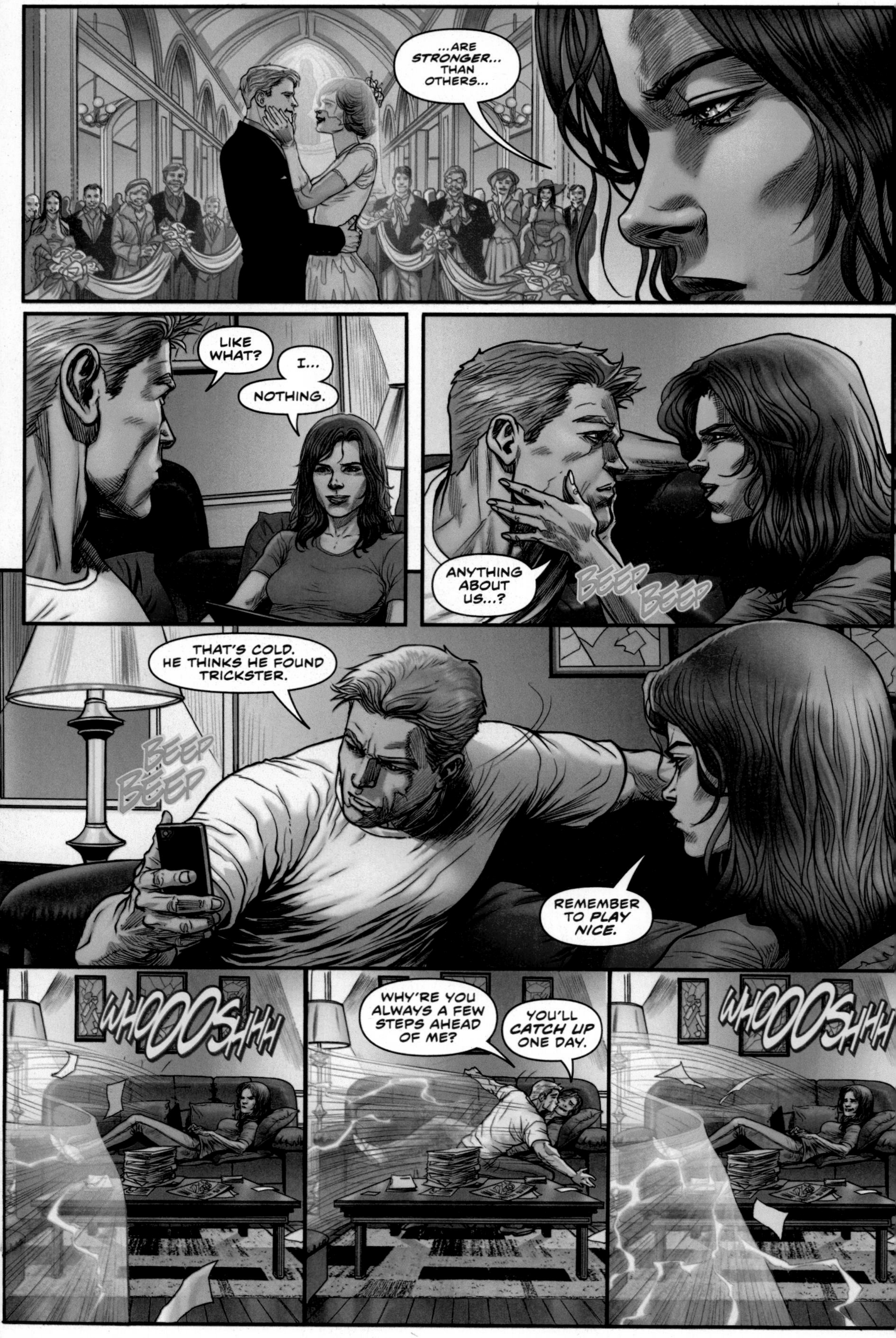
...ARE STRONGER... THAN OTHERS...
LIKE WHAT?
I...
NOTHING.
ANYTHING ABOUT US...?
BEEP BEEP
THAT'S COLD. HE THINKS HE FOUND TRICKSTER.
BEEP BEEP
REMEMBER TO PLAY NICE.
WHOOOSHHH
WHY'RE YOU ALWAYS A FEW STEPS AHEAD OF ME?
YOU'LL CATCH UP ONE DAY.
WHOOOSHHH

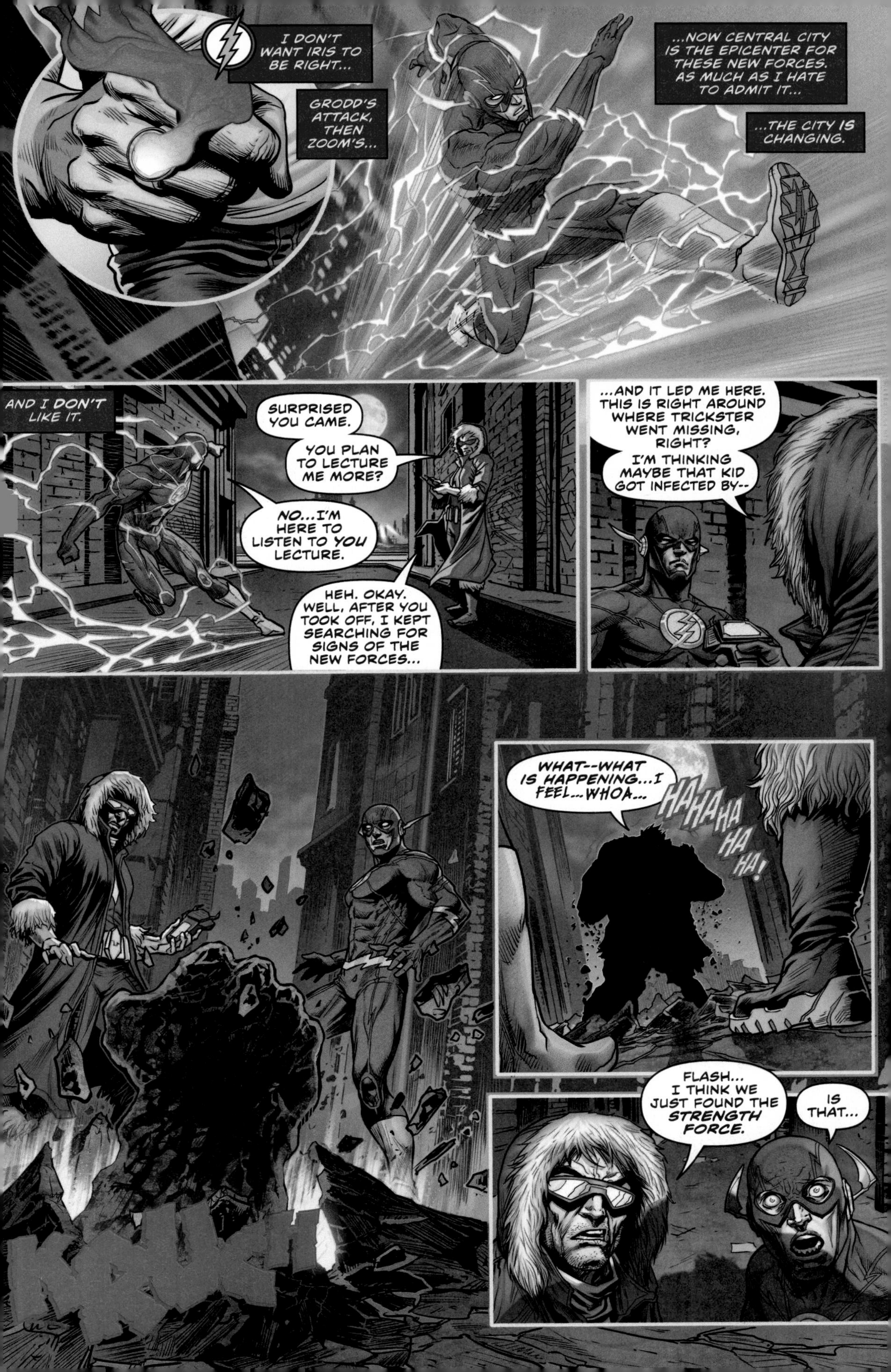
I DON'T WANT IRIS TO BE RIGHT...
GRODD'S ATTACK, THEN ZOOM'S...
...NOW CENTRAL CITY IS THE EPICENTER FOR THESE NEW FORCES. AS MUCH AS I HATE TO ADMIT IT...
...THE CITY IS CHANGING.
AND I DON'T LIKE IT.
SURPRISED YOU CAME.
YOU PLAN TO LECTURE ME MORE?
NO...I'M HERE TO LISTEN TO YOU LECTURE.
HEH. OKAY. WELL, AFTER YOU TOOK OFF, I KEPT SEARCHING FOR SIGNS OF THE NEW FORCES...
...AND IT LED ME HERE. THIS IS RIGHT AROUND WHERE TRICKSTER WENT MISSING, RIGHT?
I'M THINKING MAYBE THAT KID GOT INFECTED BY--
WHAT--WHAT IS HAPPENING...I FEEL...WHOA...
HAHAHAHA HA HA!
FLASH... I THINK WE JUST FOUND THE STRENGTH FORCE.
IS THAT...

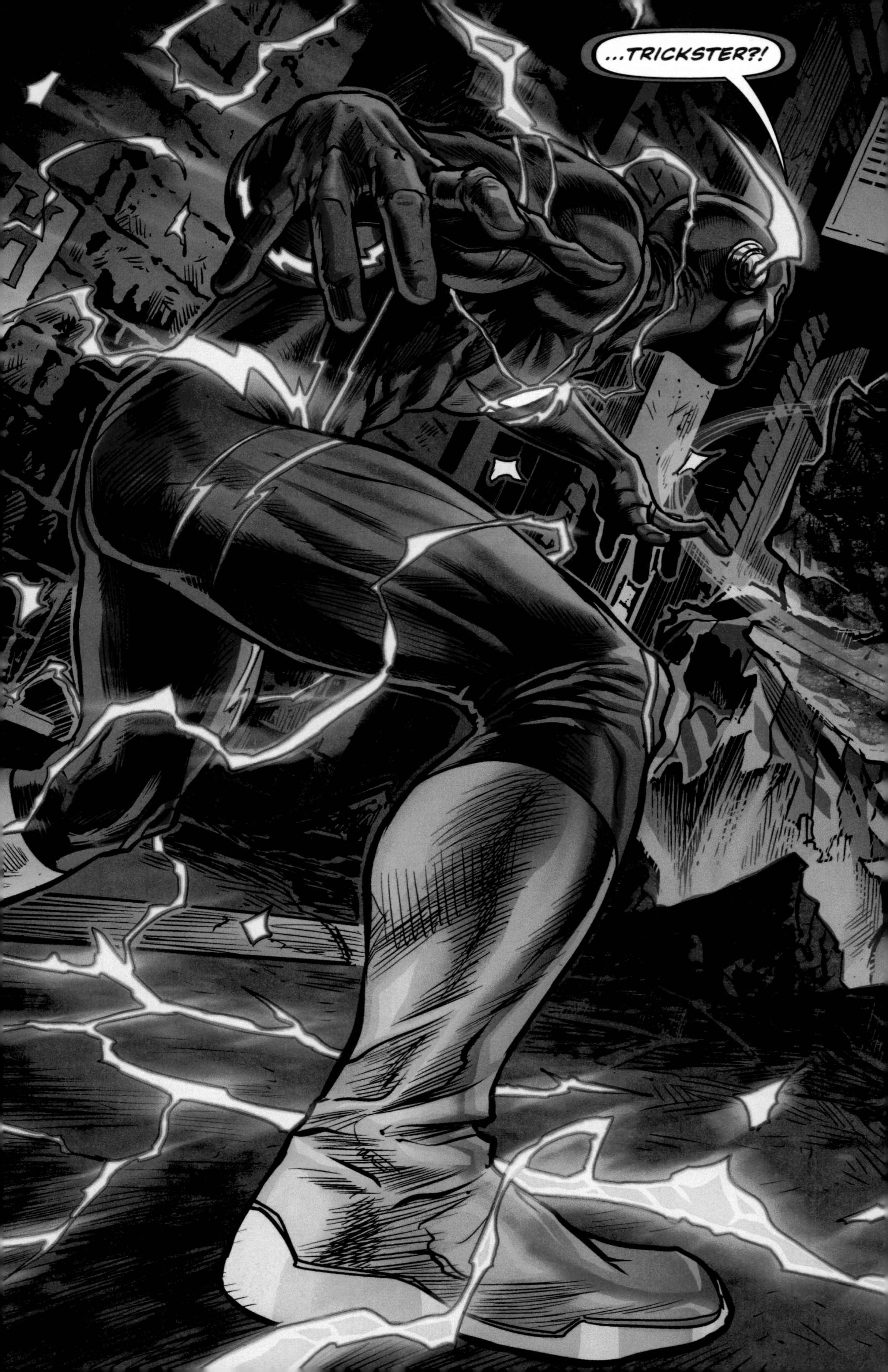
...TRICKSTER?!

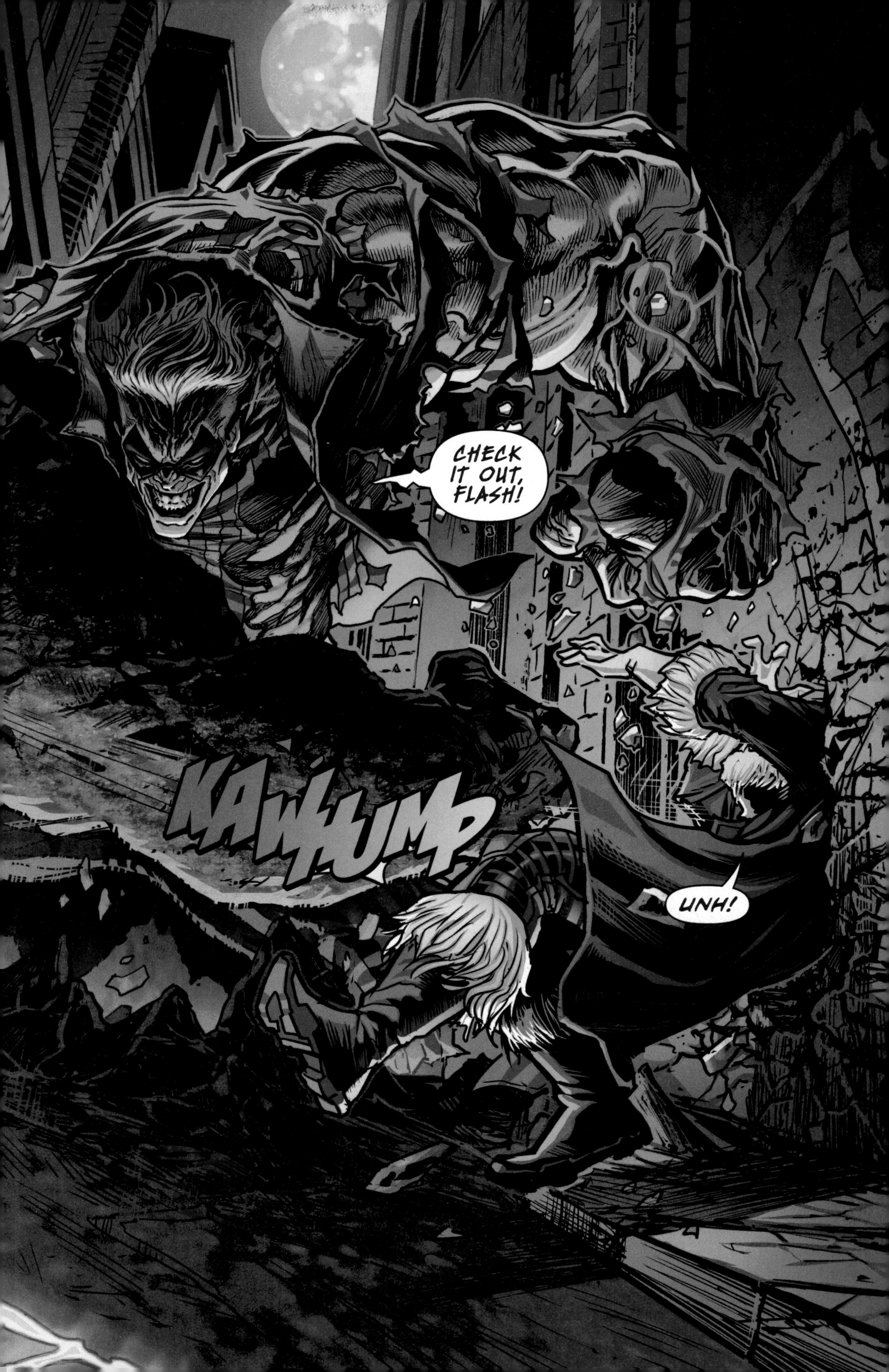
CHECK IT OUT, FLASH!
KAWHUMP
UNH!

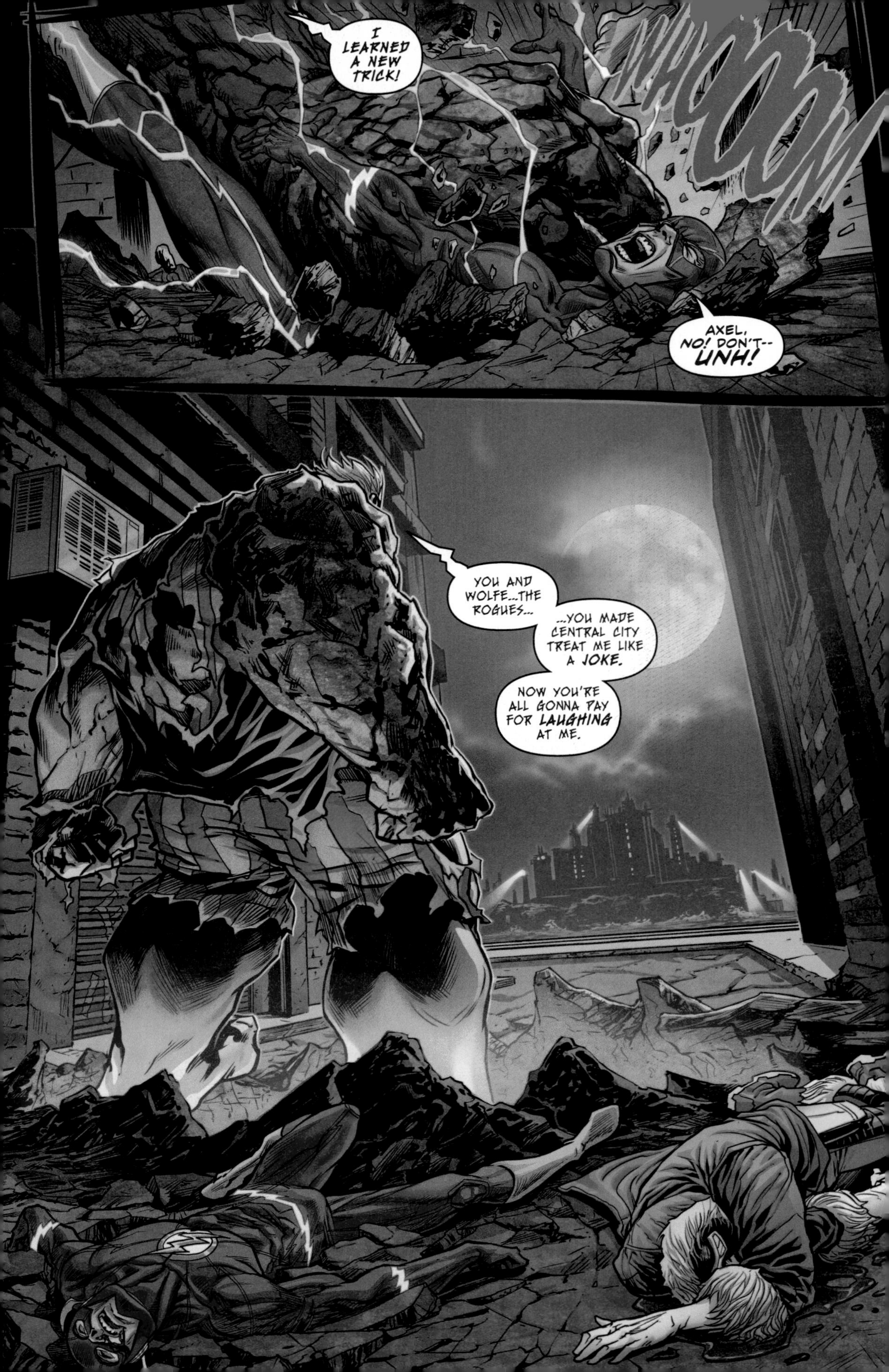
I LEARNED A NEW TRICK!
WHHOOOM
AXEL, NO! DON'T-- UNH!
YOU AND WOLFE...THE ROGUES...
...YOU MADE CENTRAL CITY TREAT ME LIKE A JOKE.
NOW YOU'RE ALL GONNA PAY FOR LAUGHING AT ME.

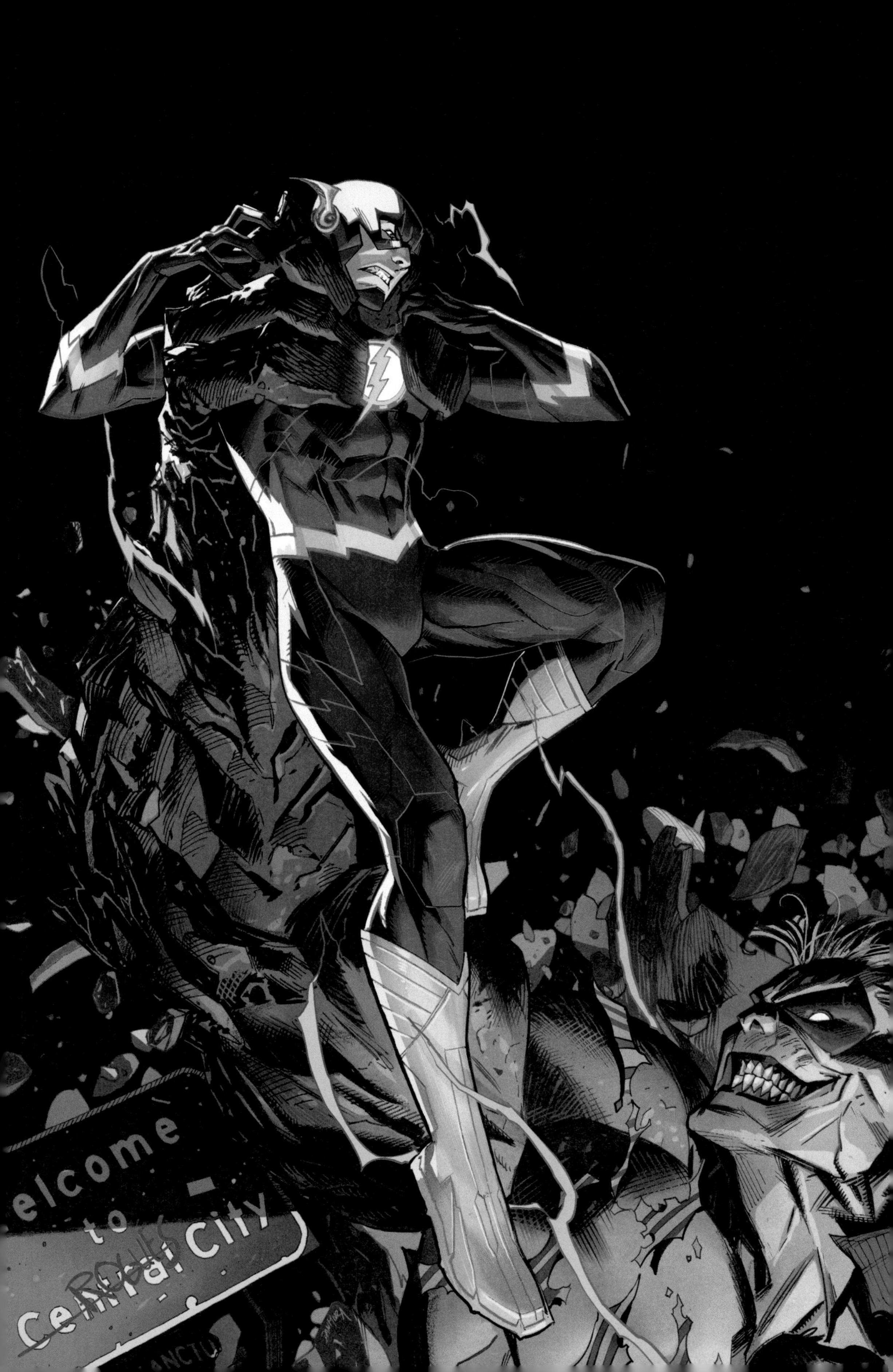
elcome
to
Central City
Rogues

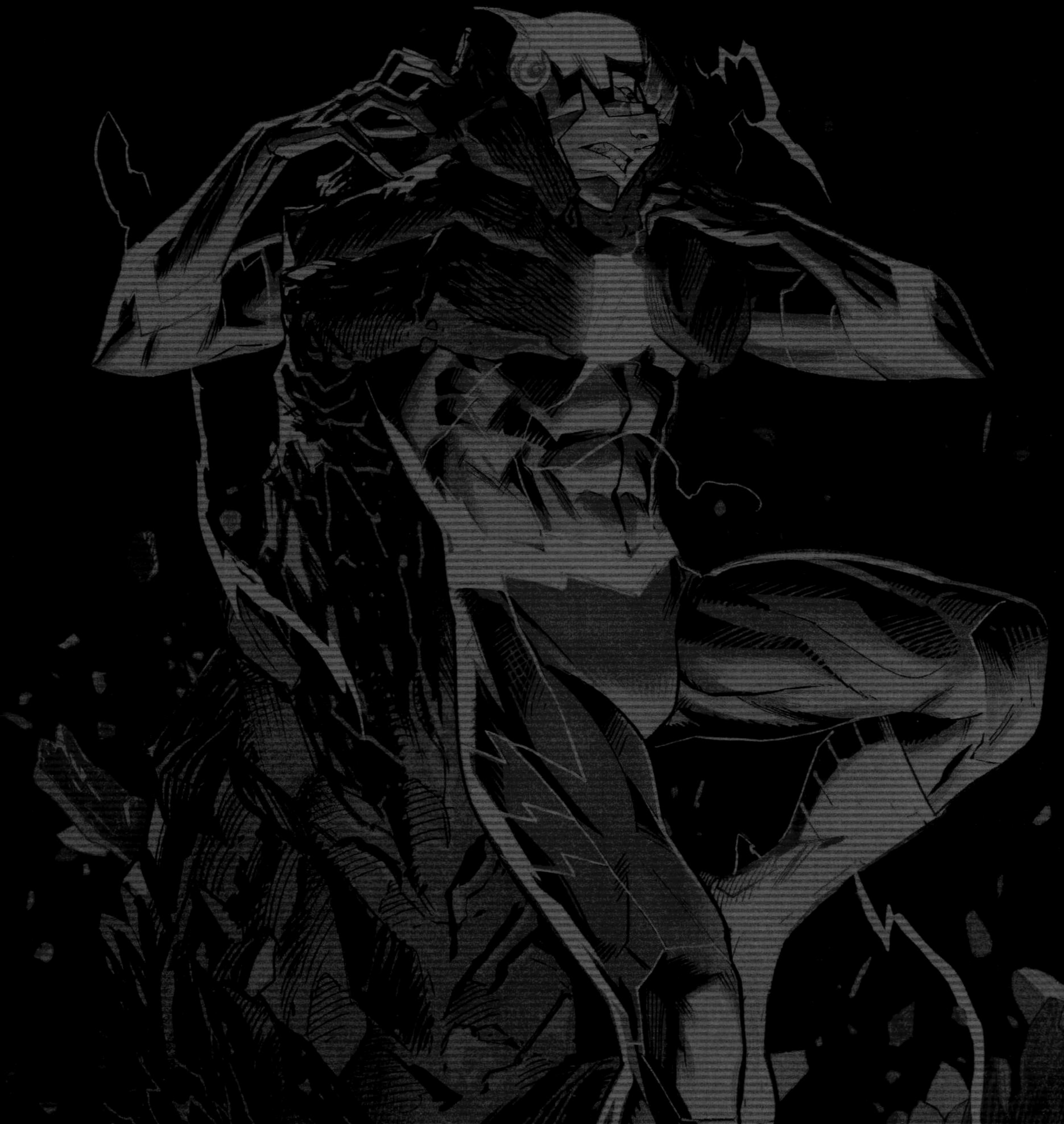

THE FLASH
#53

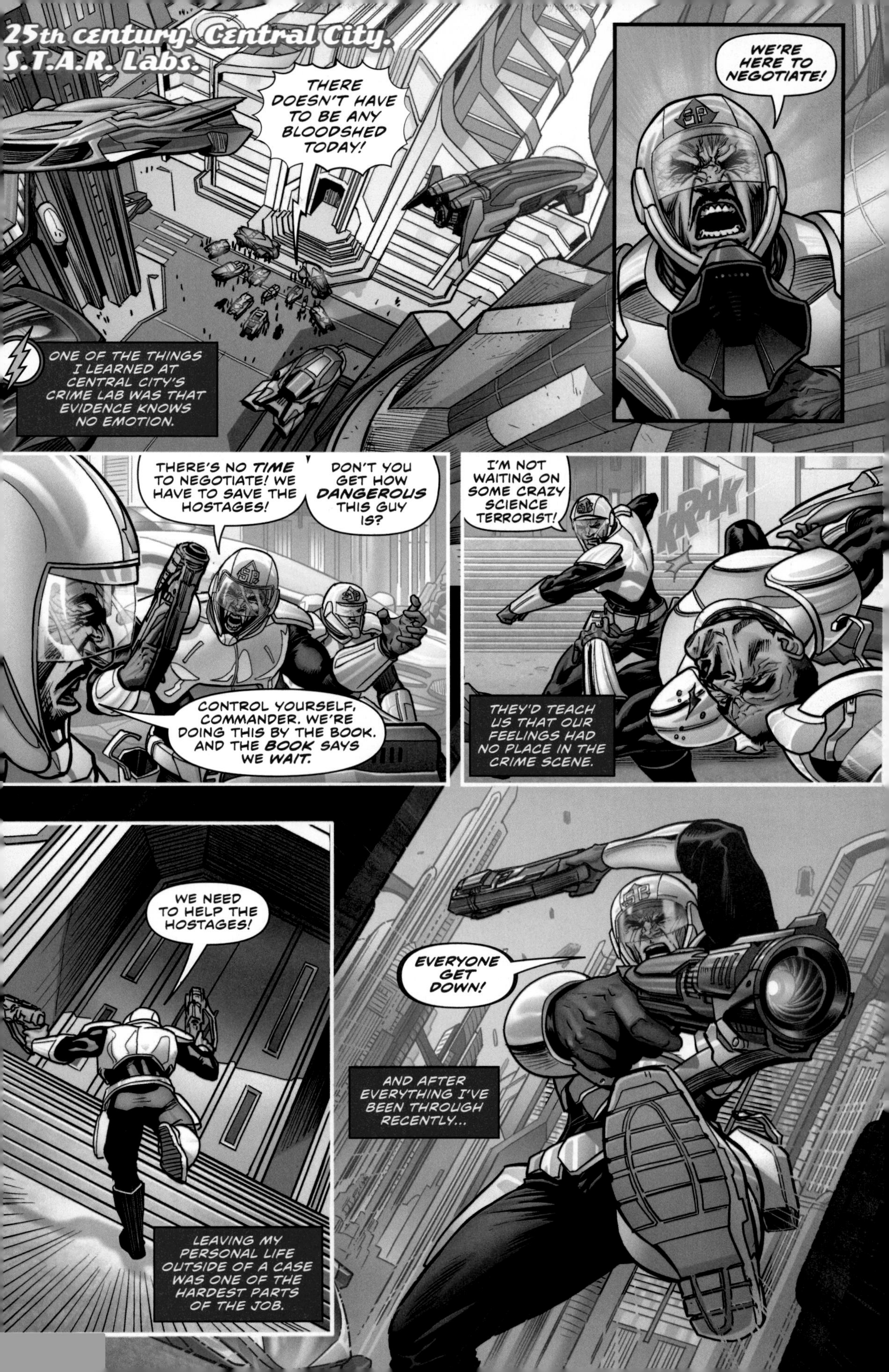
25th century. Central City. S.T.A.R. Labs.
THERE DOESN'T HAVE TO BE ANY BLOODSHED TODAY!
ONE OF THE THINGS I LEARNED AT CENTRAL CITY'S CRIME LAB WAS THAT EVIDENCE KNOWS NO EMOTION.
WE'RE HERE TO NEGOTIATE!
THERE'S NO TIME TO NEGOTIATE! WE HAVE TO SAVE THE HOSTAGES!
DON'T YOU GET HOW DANGEROUS THIS GUY IS?
CONTROL YOURSELF, COMMANDER. WE'RE DOING THIS BY THE BOOK. AND THE BOOK SAYS WE WAIT.
I'M NOT WAITING ON SOME CRAZY SCIENCE TERRORIST!
KRAK
THEY'D TEACH US THAT OUR FEELINGS HAD NO PLACE IN THE CRIME SCENE.
WE NEED TO HELP THE HOSTAGES!
LEAVING MY PERSONAL LIFE OUTSIDE OF A CASE WAS ONE OF THE HARDEST PARTS OF THE JOB.
EVERYONE GET DOWN!
AND AFTER EVERYTHING I'VE BEEN THROUGH RECENTLY...

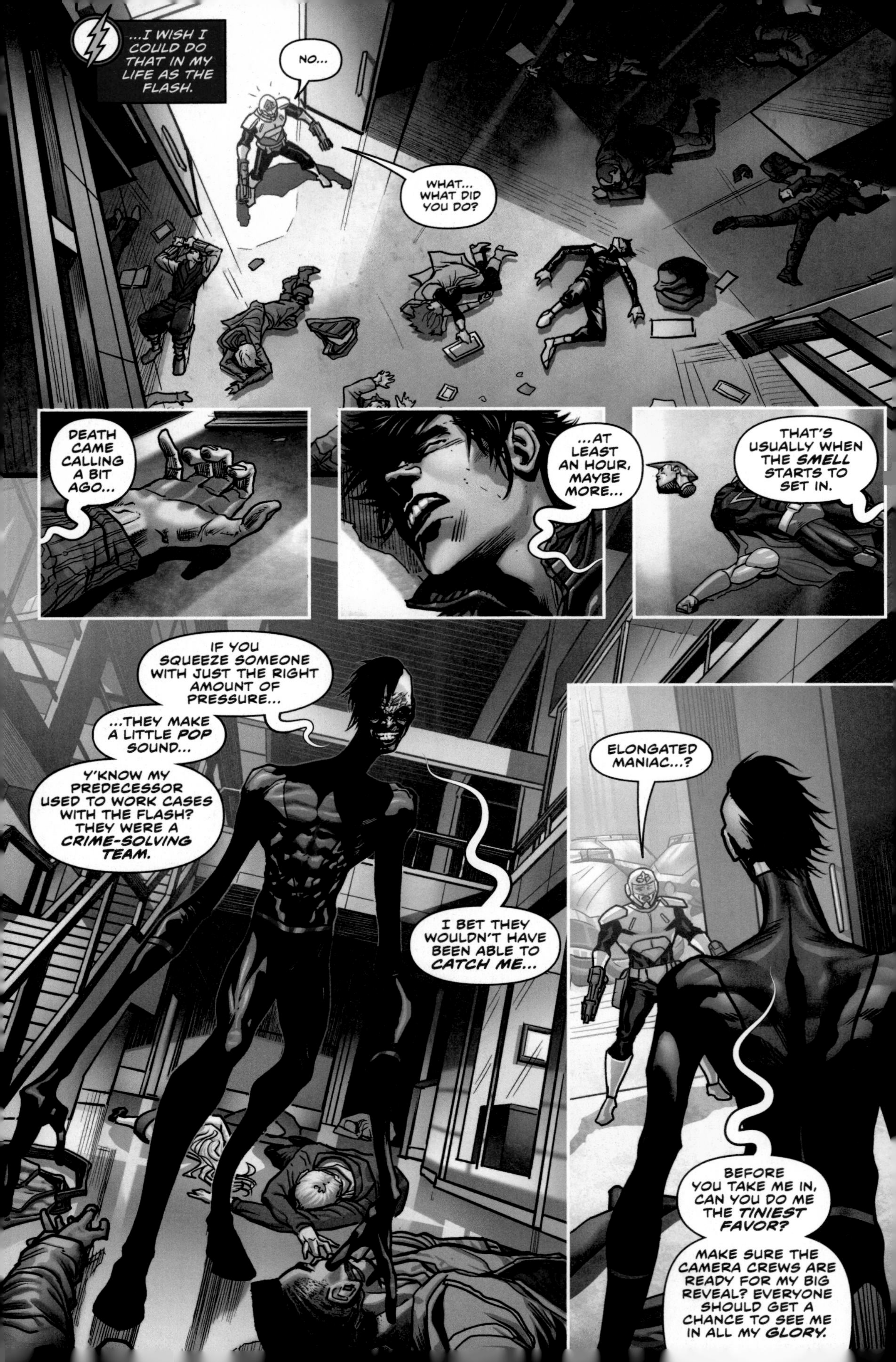
...I WISH I COULD DO THAT IN MY LIFE AS THE FLASH.
NO...
WHAT... WHAT DID YOU DO?
DEATH CAME CALLING A BIT AGO...
...AT LEAST AN HOUR, MAYBE MORE...
THAT'S USUALLY WHEN THE SMELL STARTS TO SET IN.
IF YOU SQUEEZE SOMEONE WITH JUST THE RIGHT AMOUNT OF PRESSURE...
...THEY MAKE A LITTLE POP SOUND...
Y'KNOW MY PREDECESSOR USED TO WORK CASES WITH THE FLASH? THEY WERE A CRIME-SOLVING TEAM.
I BET THEY WOULDN'T HAVE BEEN ABLE TO CATCH ME...
ELONGATED MANIAC...?
BEFORE YOU TAKE ME IN, CAN YOU DO ME THE TINIEST FAVOR?
MAKE SURE THE CAMERA CREWS ARE READY FOR MY BIG REVEAL? EVERYONE SHOULD GET A CHANCE TO SEE ME IN ALL MY GLORY.

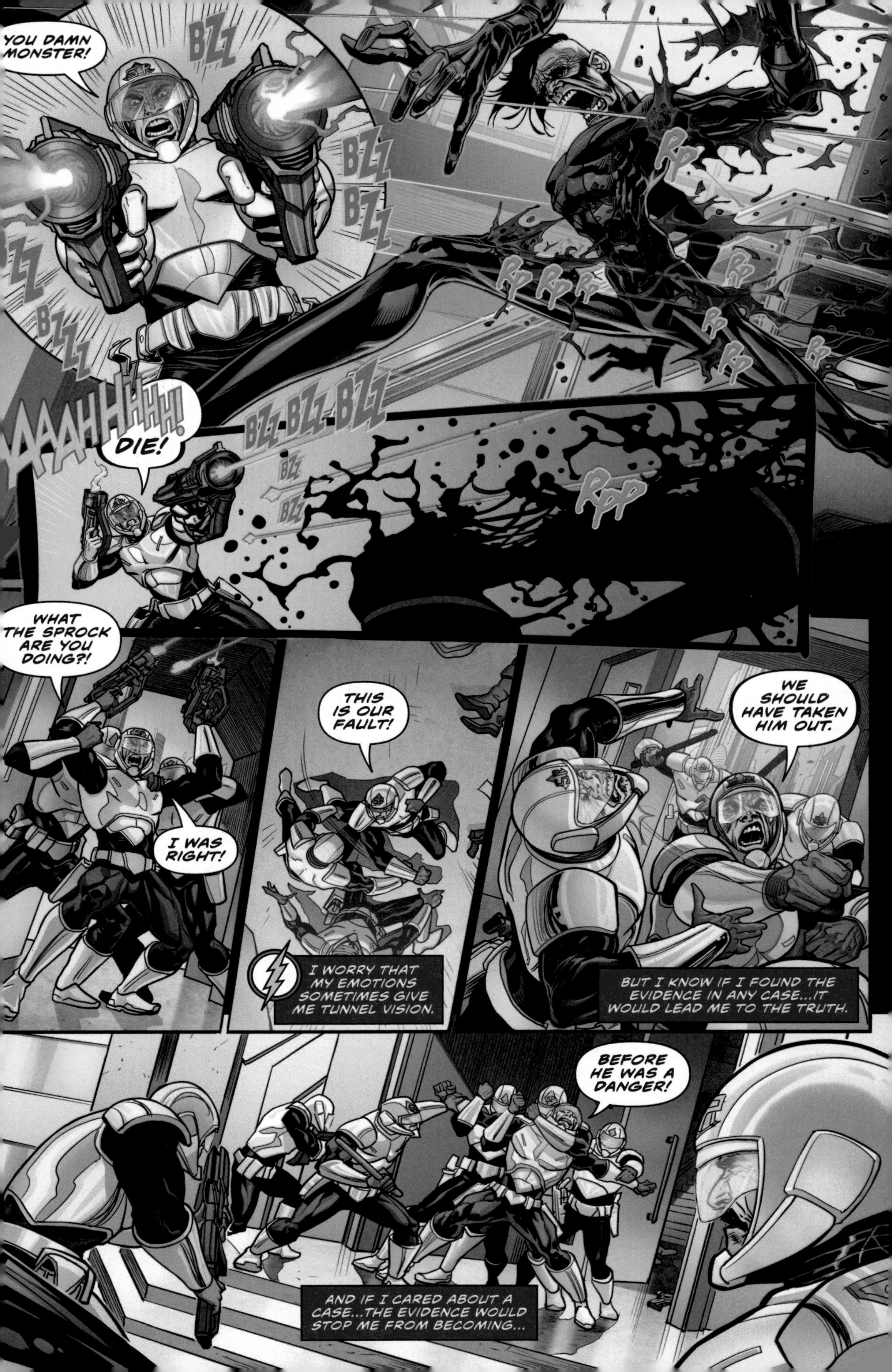

YOU DAMN MONSTER!
BZZ
BZZ
BZZ
BZZ
BZZ
RP
RP RP RP
RP
RP
RP
RP
AAAHHHHH!
DIE!
BZZ-BZZ-BZZ
BZZ
BZZ
RPP
WHAT THE SPROCK ARE YOU DOING?!
I WAS RIGHT!
THIS IS OUR FAULT!
I WORRY THAT MY EMOTIONS SOMETIMES GIVE ME TUNNEL VISION.
WE SHOULD HAVE TAKEN HIM OUT.
BUT I KNOW IF I FOUND THE EVIDENCE IN ANY CASE...IT WOULD LEAD ME TO THE TRUTH.
BEFORE HE WAS A DANGER!
AND IF I CARED ABOUT A CASE...THE EVIDENCE WOULD STOP ME FROM BECOMING...

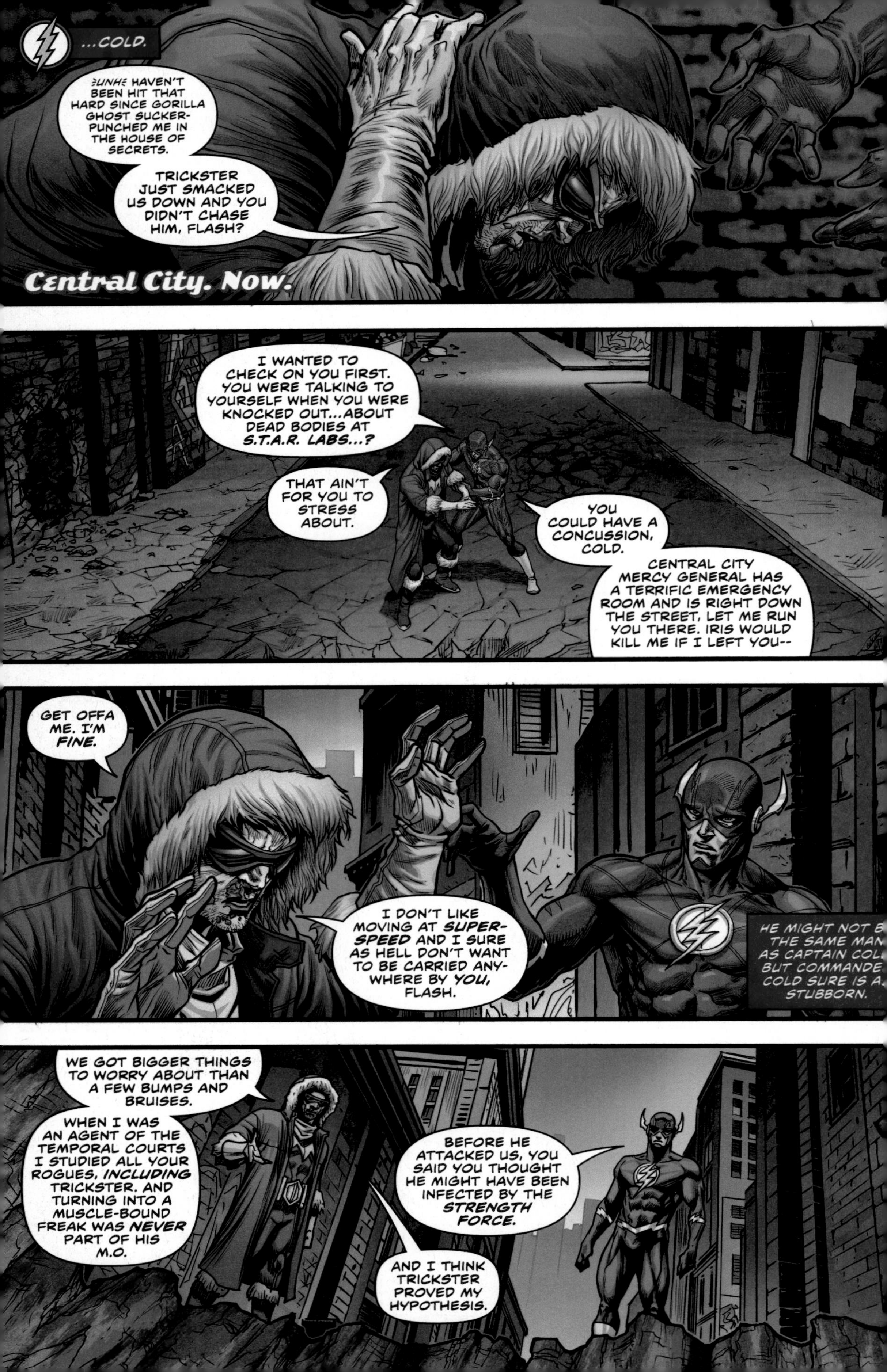
...COLD.
UNHH HAVEN'T BEEN HIT THAT HARD SINCE GORILLA GHOST SUCKER-PUNCHED ME IN THE HOUSE OF SECRETS.
TRICKSTER JUST SMACKED US DOWN AND YOU DIDN'T CHASE HIM, FLASH?
Central City. Now.
I WANTED TO CHECK ON YOU FIRST. YOU WERE TALKING TO YOURSELF WHEN YOU WERE KNOCKED OUT...ABOUT DEAD BODIES AT S.T.A.R. LABS...?
THAT AIN'T FOR YOU TO STRESS ABOUT.
YOU COULD HAVE A CONCUSSION, COLD.
CENTRAL CITY MERCY GENERAL HAS A TERRIFIC EMERGENCY ROOM AND IS RIGHT DOWN THE STREET, LET ME RUN YOU THERE. IRIS WOULD KILL ME IF I LEFT YOU--
GET OFFA ME. I'M FINE.
I DON'T LIKE MOVING AT SUPER-SPEED AND I SURE AS HELL DON'T WANT TO BE CARRIED ANYWHERE BY YOU, FLASH.
HE MIGHT NOT B THE SAME MAN AS CAPTAIN COL BUT COMMANDE COLD SURE IS A STUBBORN.
WE GOT BIGGER THINGS TO WORRY ABOUT THAN A FEW BUMPS AND BRUISES.
WHEN I WAS AN AGENT OF THE TEMPORAL COURTS I STUDIED ALL YOUR ROGUES, INCLUDING TRICKSTER. AND TURNING INTO A MUSCLE-BOUND FREAK WAS NEVER PART OF HIS M.O.
BEFORE HE ATTACKED US, YOU SAID YOU THOUGHT HE MIGHT HAVE BEEN INFECTED BY THE STRENGTH FORCE.
AND I THINK TRICKSTER PROVED MY HYPOTHESIS.

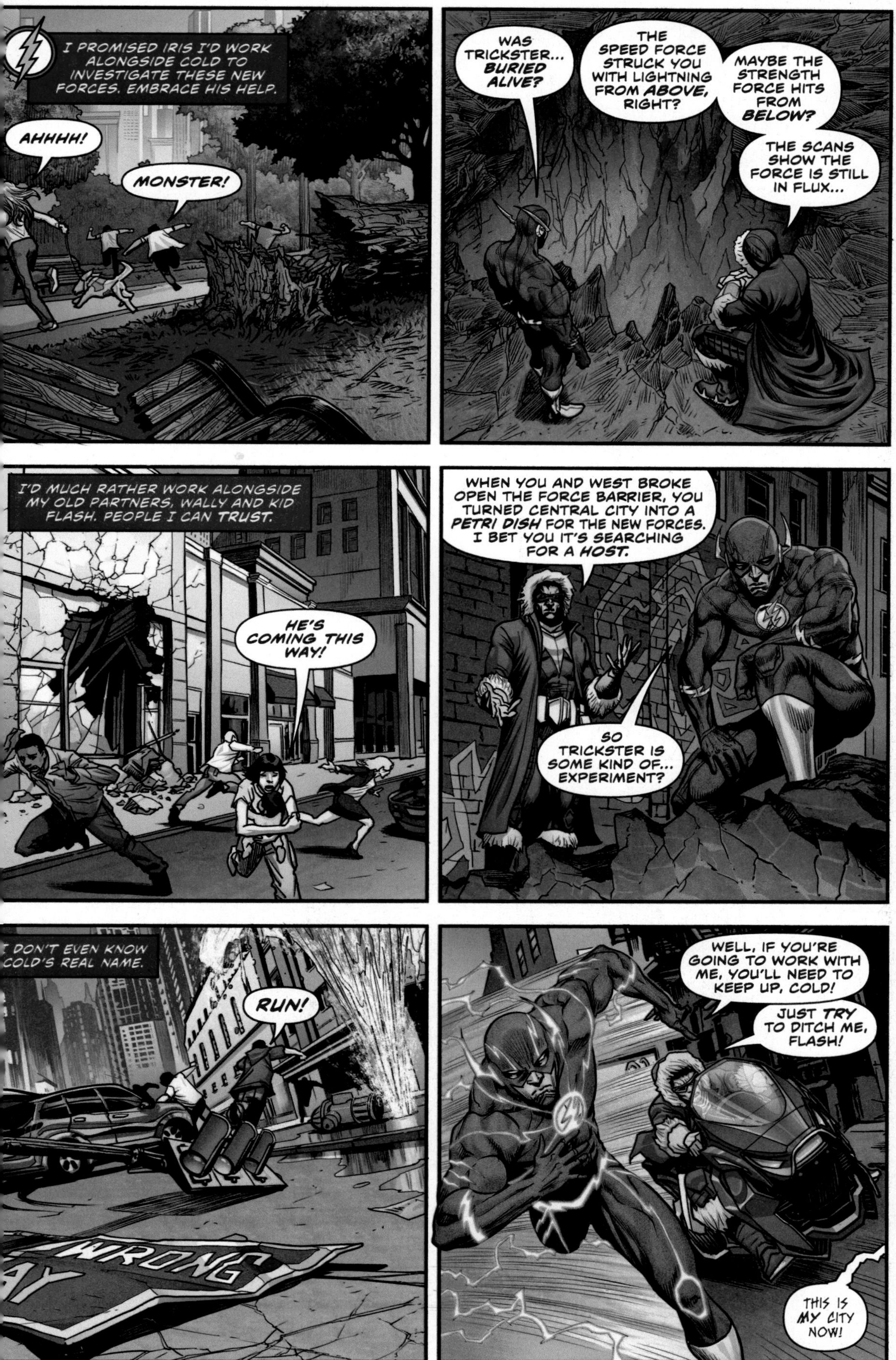
I PROMISED IRIS I'D WORK ALONGSIDE COLD TO INVESTIGATE THESE NEW FORCES. EMBRACE HIS HELP.
AHHHH!
MONSTER!
WAS TRICKSTER... BURIED ALIVE?
THE SPEED FORCE STRUCK YOU WITH LIGHTNING FROM ABOVE, RIGHT?
MAYBE THE STRENGTH FORCE HITS FROM BELOW?
THE SCANS SHOW THE FORCE IS STILL IN FLUX...
I'D MUCH RATHER WORK ALONGSIDE MY OLD PARTNERS, WALLY AND KID FLASH. PEOPLE I CAN TRUST.
HE'S COMING THIS WAY!
WHEN YOU AND WEST BROKE OPEN THE FORCE BARRIER, YOU TURNED CENTRAL CITY INTO A PETRI DISH FOR THE NEW FORCES. I BET YOU IT'S SEARCHING FOR A HOST.
SO TRICKSTER IS SOME KIND OF... EXPERIMENT?
I DON'T EVEN KNOW COLD'S REAL NAME.
RUN!
WRONG
WELL, IF YOU'RE GOING TO WORK WITH ME, YOU'LL NEED TO KEEP UP, COLD!
JUST TRY TO DITCH ME, FLASH!
THIS IS MY CITY NOW!

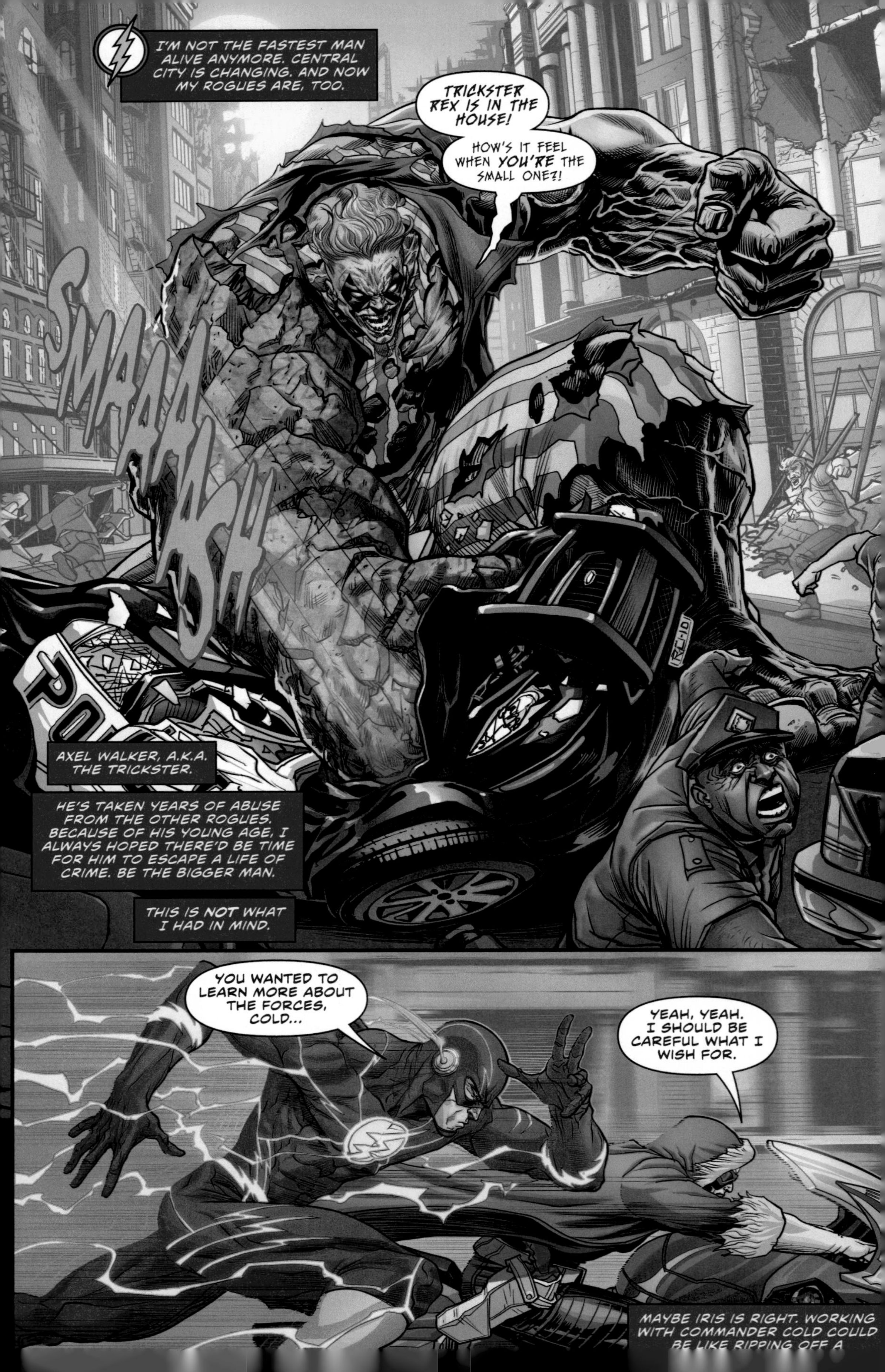
I'M NOT THE FASTEST MAN ALIVE ANYMORE. CENTRAL CITY IS CHANGING. AND NOW MY ROGUES ARE, TOO.
TRICKSTER REX IS IN THE HOUSE!
HOW'S IT FEEL WHEN YOU'RE THE SMALL ONE?!
SMAAASH
AXEL WALKER, A.K.A. THE TRICKSTER.
HE'S TAKEN YEARS OF ABUSE FROM THE OTHER ROGUES. BECAUSE OF HIS YOUNG AGE, I ALWAYS HOPED THERE'D BE TIME FOR HIM TO ESCAPE A LIFE OF CRIME. BE THE BIGGER MAN.
THIS IS NOT WHAT I HAD IN MIND.
YOU WANTED TO LEARN MORE ABOUT THE FORCES, COLD...
YEAH, YEAH. I SHOULD BE CAREFUL WHAT I WISH FOR.
MAYBE IRIS IS RIGHT. WORKING WITH COMMANDER COLD COULD BE LIKE RIPPING OFF A

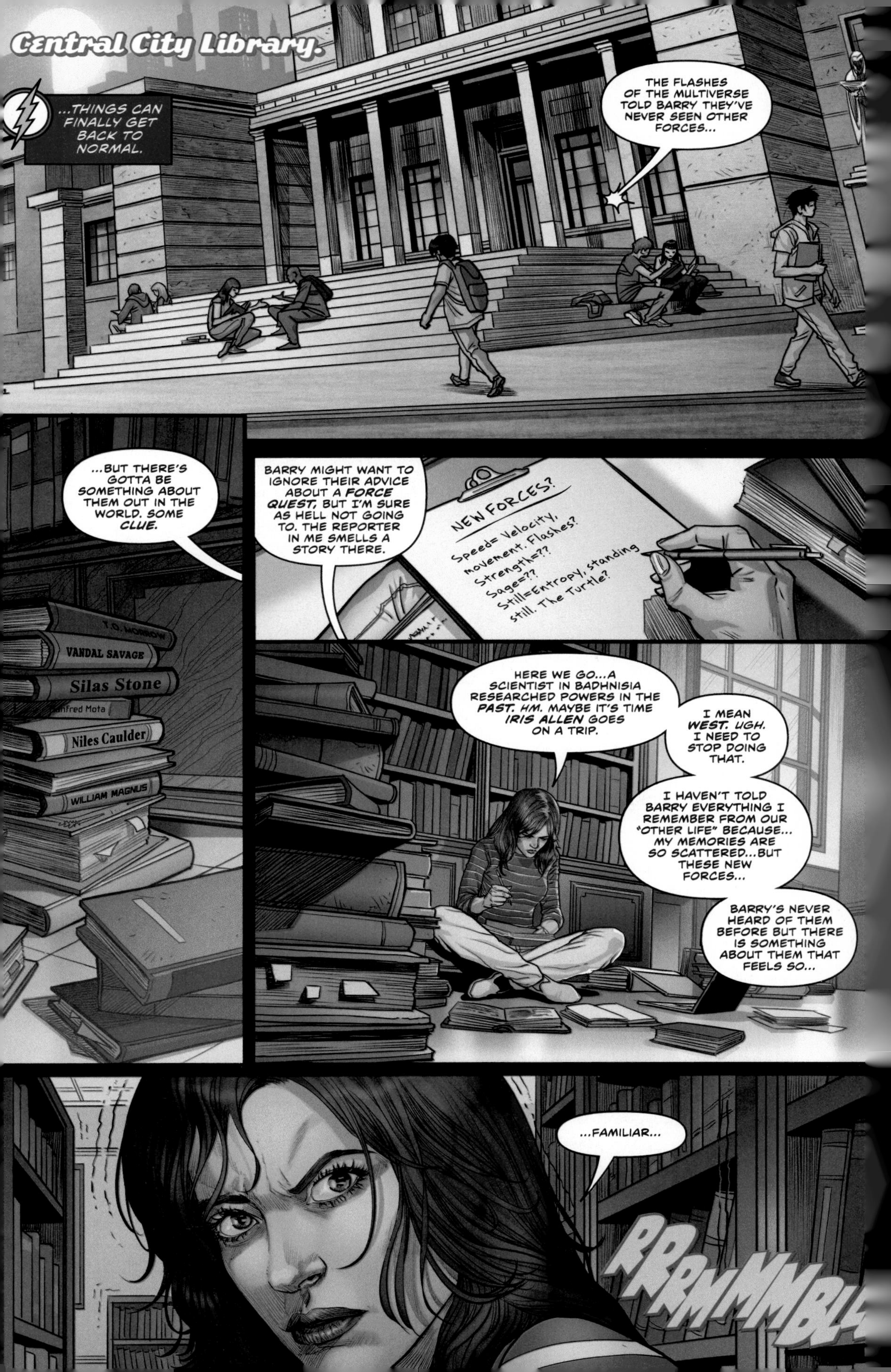

Central City Library.
...THINGS CAN FINALLY GET BACK TO NORMAL.
THE FLASHES OF THE MULTIVERSE TOLD BARRY THEY'VE NEVER SEEN OTHER FORCES...
...BUT THERE'S GOTTA BE SOMETHING ABOUT THEM OUT IN THE WORLD. SOME CLUE.
BARRY MIGHT WANT TO IGNORE THEIR ADVICE ABOUT A FORCE QUEST, BUT I'M SURE AS HELL NOT GOING TO. THE REPORTER IN ME SMELLS A STORY THERE.
NEW FORCES?
Speed= Velocity, movement. Flashes?
Strength=??
Sage=??
Still=Entropy, standing still. The Turtle?
T.O. MORROW
VANDAL SAVAGE
Silas Stone
Niles Caulder
WILLIAM MAGNUS
HERE WE GO...A SCIENTIST IN BADHNISIA RESEARCHED POWERS IN THE PAST. HM. MAYBE IT'S TIME IRIS ALLEN GOES ON A TRIP.
I MEAN WEST. UGH. I NEED TO STOP DOING THAT.
I HAVEN'T TOLD BARRY EVERYTHING I REMEMBER FROM OUR "OTHER LIFE" BECAUSE... MY MEMORIES ARE SO SCATTERED...BUT THESE NEW FORCES...
BARRY'S NEVER HEARD OF THEM BEFORE BUT THERE IS SOMETHING ABOUT THEM THAT FEELS SO...
...FAMILIAR...
RRRMMMMBL

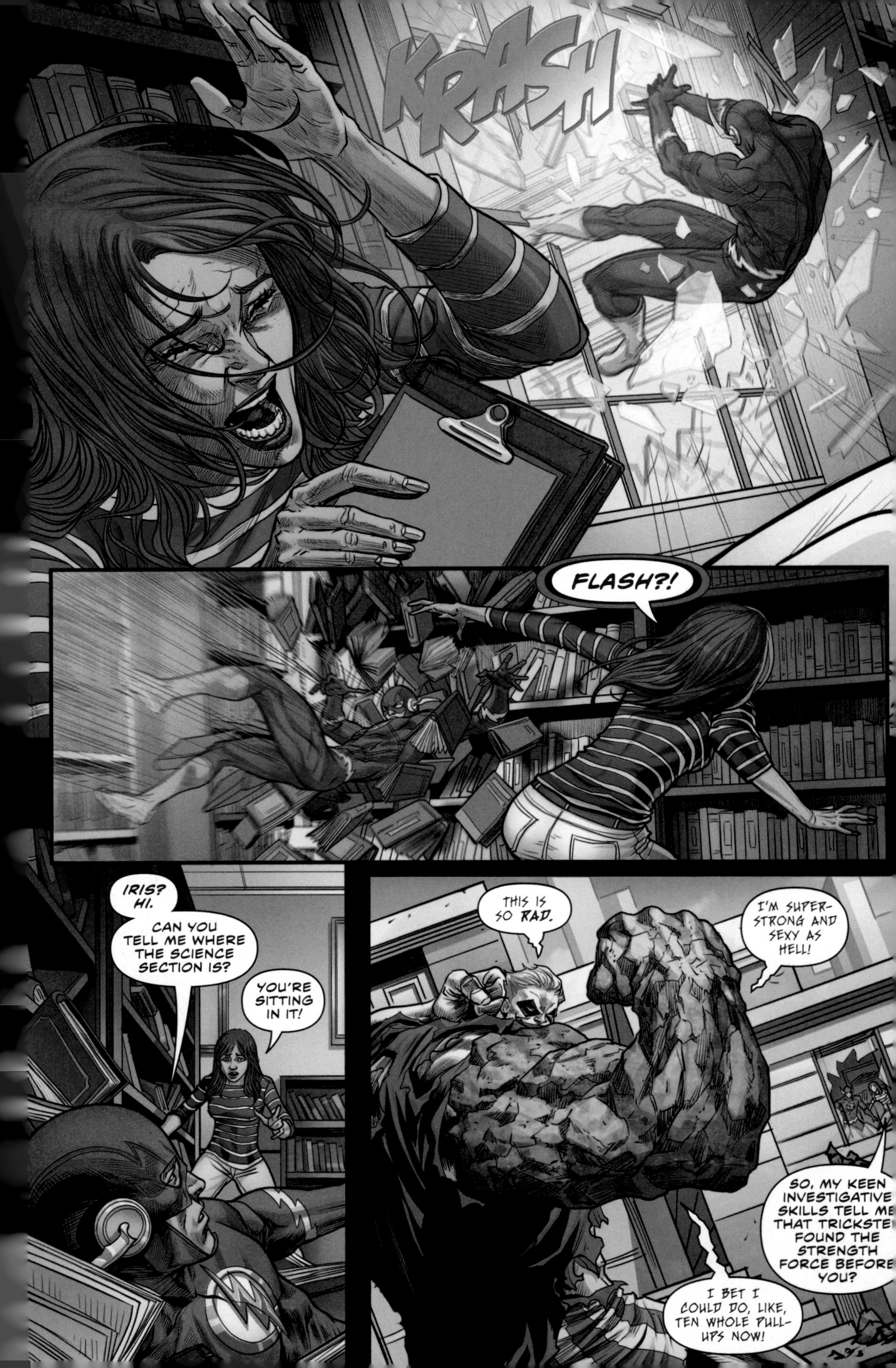
KRASH
FLASH?!
IRIS? HI.
CAN YOU TELL ME WHERE THE SCIENCE SECTION IS?
YOU'RE SITTING IN IT!
THIS IS SO RAD.
I'M SUPER-STRONG AND SEXY AS HELL!
SO, MY KEEN INVESTIGATIVE SKILLS TELL ME THAT TRICKSTER FOUND THE STRENGTH FORCE BEFORE YOU?
I BET I COULD DO, LIKE, TEN WHOLE PULL-UPS NOW!

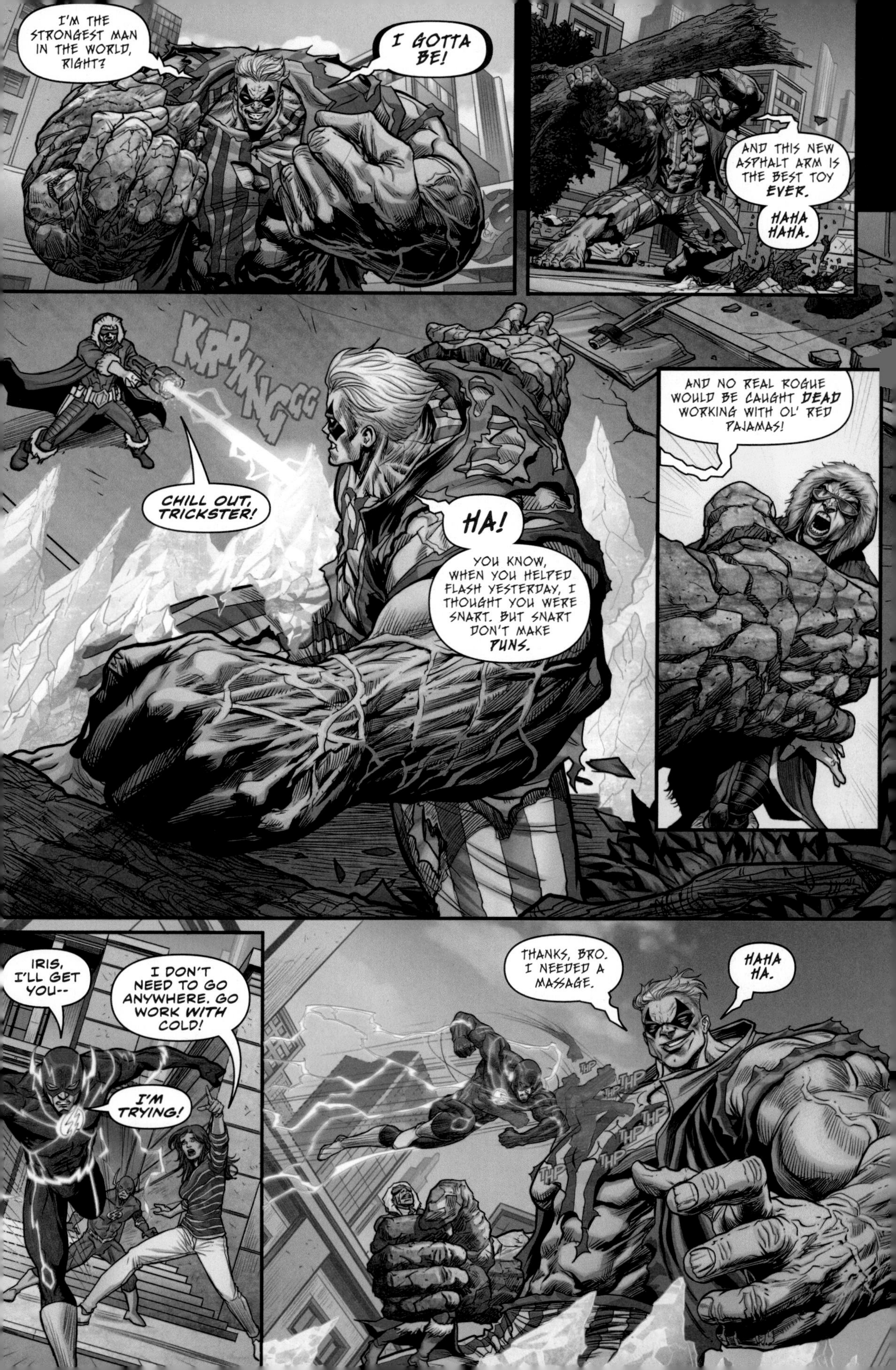
I'M THE STRONGEST MAN IN THE WORLD, RIGHT?
I GOTTA BE!
AND THIS NEW ASPHALT ARM IS THE BEST TOY EVER.
HAHA HAHA.
KRRNNGGG
CHILL OUT, TRICKSTER!
HA!
YOU KNOW, WHEN YOU HELPED FLASH YESTERDAY, I THOUGHT YOU WERE SNART. BUT SNART DON'T MAKE PUNS.
AND NO REAL ROGUE WOULD BE CAUGHT DEAD WORKING WITH OL' RED PAJAMAS!
IRIS, I'LL GET YOU--
I DON'T NEED TO GO ANYWHERE. GO WORK WITH COLD!
I'M TRYING!
THANKS, BRO. I NEEDED A MASSAGE.
HAHA HA.
THP THP THP THP THP THP THP

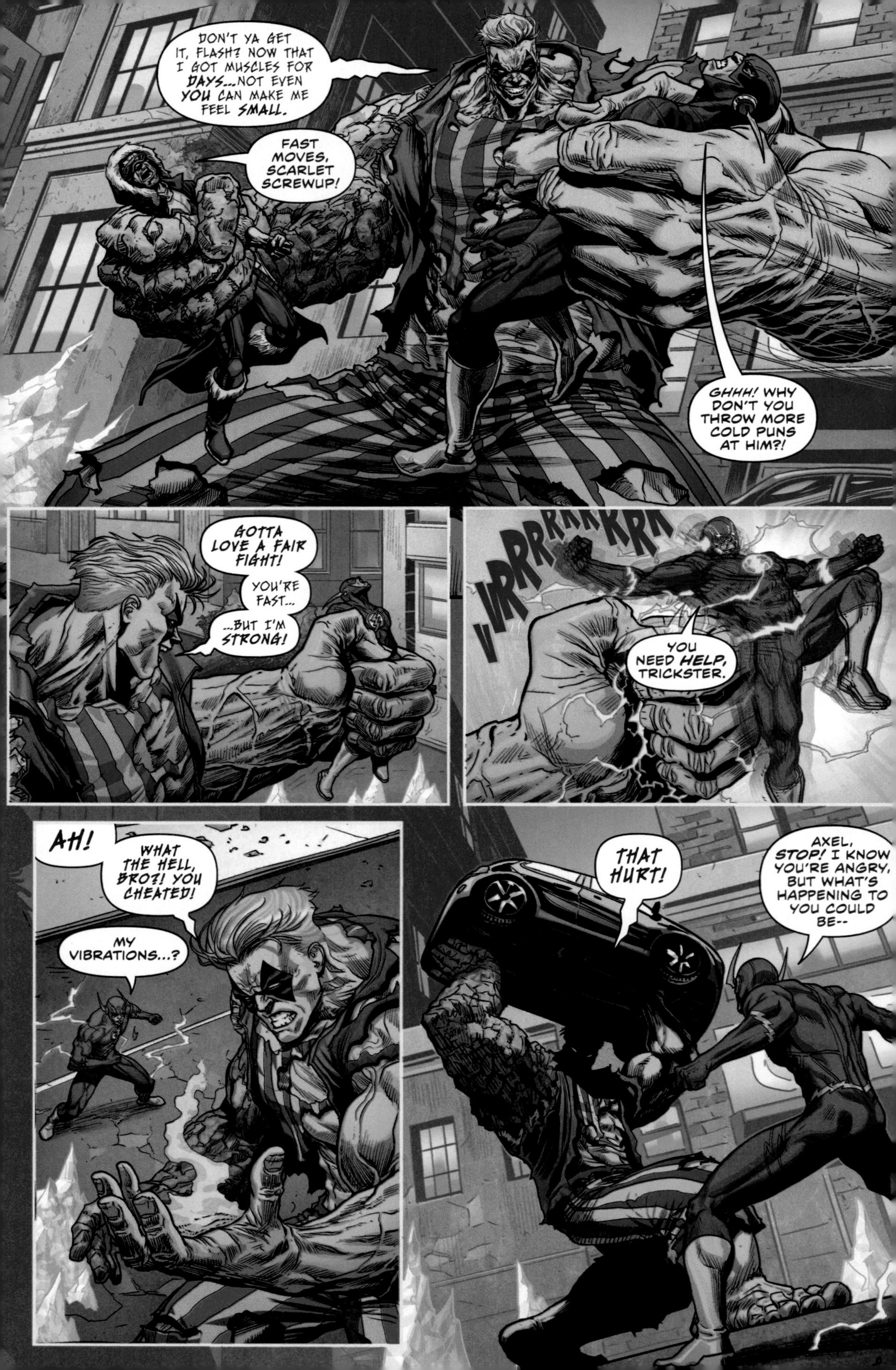
DON'T YA GET IT, FLASH? NOW THAT I GOT MUSCLES FOR DAYS...NOT EVEN YOU CAN MAKE ME FEEL SMALL.
FAST MOVES, SCARLET SCREWUP!
GHHH! WHY DON'T YOU THROW MORE COLD PUNS AT HIM?!
GOTTA LOVE A FAIR FIGHT!
YOU'RE FAST...
...BUT I'M STRONG!
VRRRRRRRRR
YOU NEED HELP, TRICKSTER.
AH!
WHAT THE HELL, BRO?! YOU CHEATED!
MY VIBRATIONS...?
THAT HURT!
AXEL, STOP! I KNOW YOU'RE ANGRY, BUT WHAT'S HAPPENING TO YOU COULD BE--

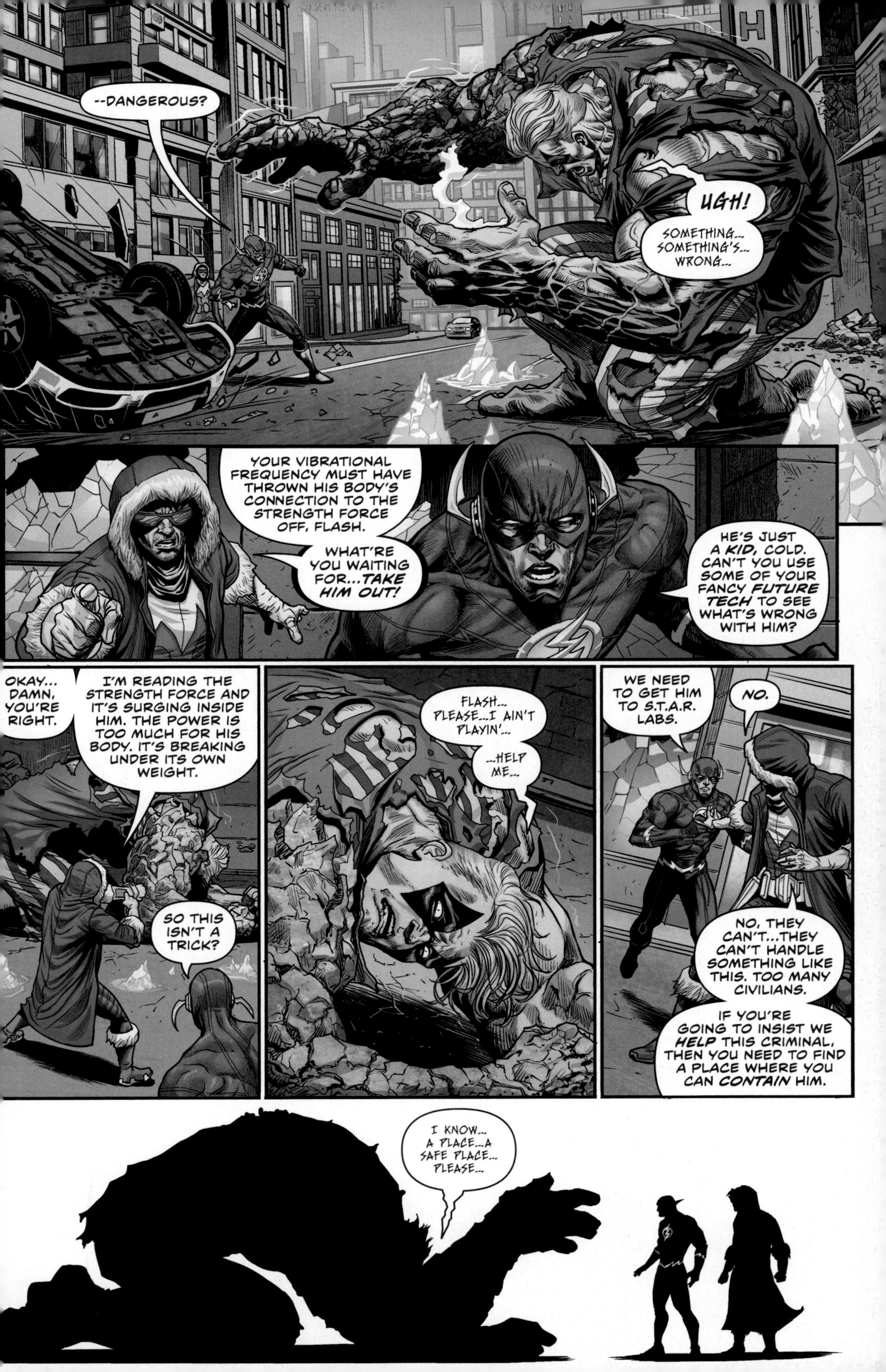
--DANGEROUS?
UGH!
SOMETHING... SOMETHING'S... WRONG...
YOUR VIBRATIONAL FREQUENCY MUST HAVE THROWN HIS BODY'S CONNECTION TO THE STRENGTH FORCE OFF, FLASH.
WHAT'RE YOU WAITING FOR...TAKE HIM OUT!
HE'S JUST A KID, COLD. CAN'T YOU USE SOME OF YOUR FANCY FUTURE TECH TO SEE WHAT'S WRONG WITH HIM?
OKAY... DAMN, YOU'RE RIGHT.
I'M READING THE STRENGTH FORCE AND IT'S SURGING INSIDE HIM. THE POWER IS TOO MUCH FOR HIS BODY. IT'S BREAKING UNDER ITS OWN WEIGHT.
SO THIS ISN'T A TRICK?
FLASH... PLEASE...I AIN'T PLAYIN'...
...HELP ME...
WE NEED TO GET HIM TO S.T.A.R. LABS.
NO.
NO, THEY CAN'T...THEY CAN'T HANDLE SOMETHING LIKE THIS. TOO MANY CIVILIANS.
IF YOU'RE GOING TO INSIST WE HELP THIS CRIMINAL, THEN YOU NEED TO FIND A PLACE WHERE YOU CAN CONTAIN HIM.
I KNOW... A PLACE...A SAFE PLACE... PLEASE...

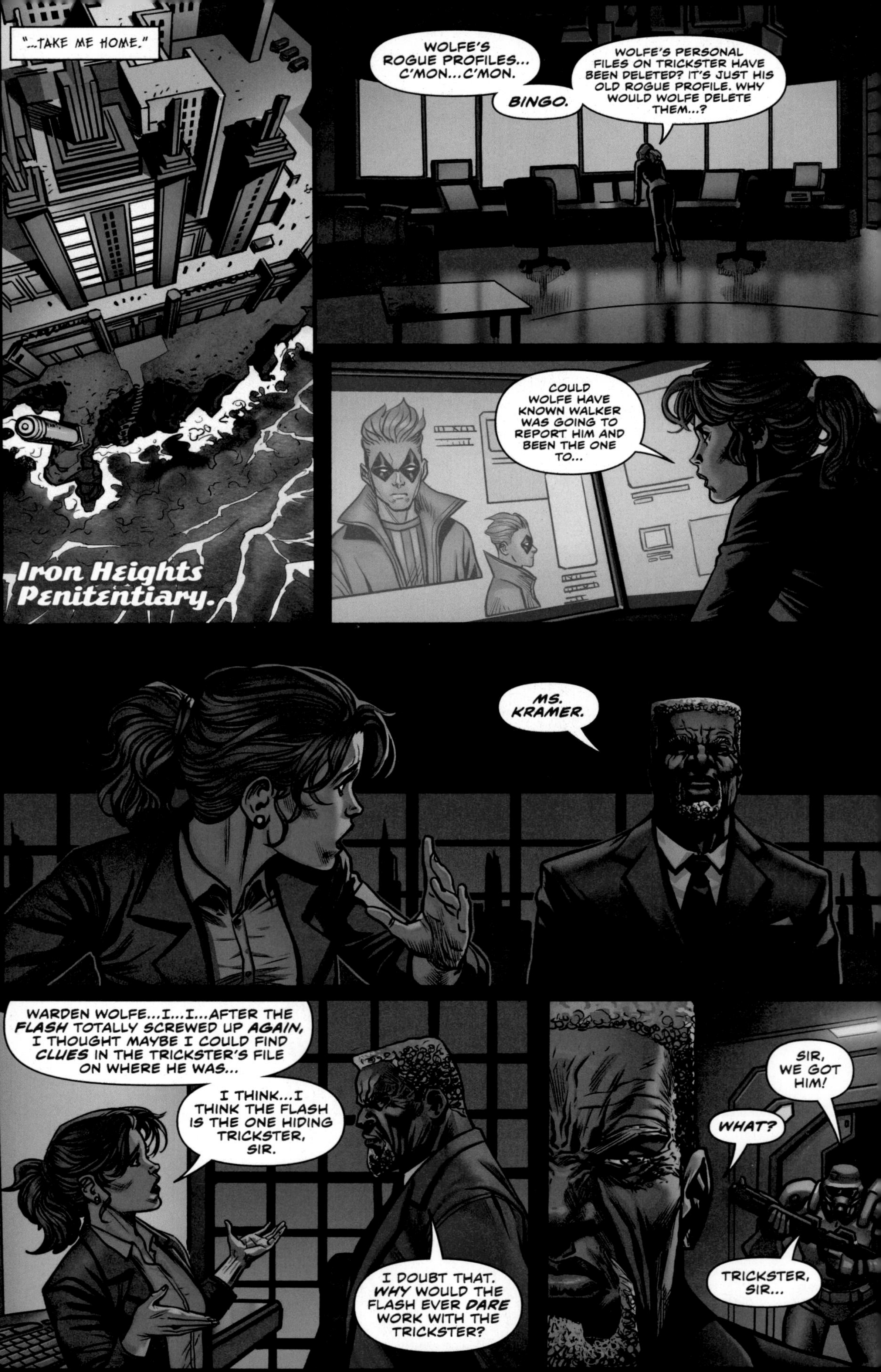
"...TAKE ME HOME."
Iron Heights Penitentiary.
WOLFE'S ROGUE PROFILES... C'MON...C'MON.
BINGO.
WOLFE'S PERSONAL FILES ON TRICKSTER HAVE BEEN DELETED? IT'S JUST HIS OLD ROGUE PROFILE. WHY WOULD WOLFE DELETE THEM...?
COULD WOLFE HAVE KNOWN WALKER WAS GOING TO REPORT HIM AND BEEN THE ONE TO...
MS. KRAMER.
WARDEN WOLFE...I...I...AFTER THE FLASH TOTALLY SCREWED UP AGAIN, I THOUGHT MAYBE I COULD FIND CLUES IN THE TRICKSTER'S FILE ON WHERE HE WAS...
I THINK...I THINK THE FLASH IS THE ONE HIDING TRICKSTER, SIR.
I DOUBT THAT. WHY WOULD THE FLASH EVER DARE WORK WITH THE TRICKSTER?
SIR, WE GOT HIM!
WHAT?
TRICKSTER, SIR...

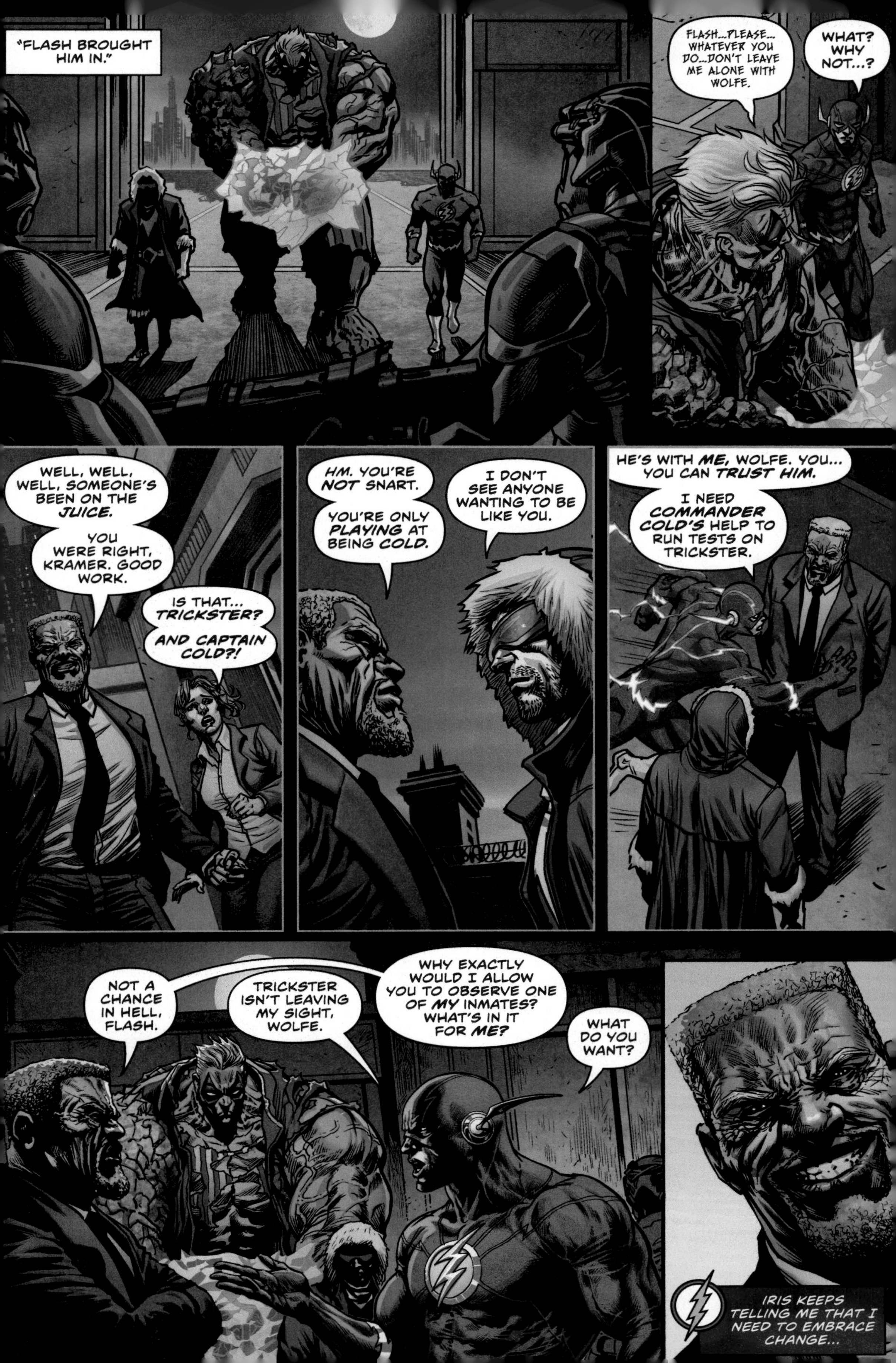
"FLASH BROUGHT HIM IN."
FLASH...PLEASE... WHATEVER YOU DO...DON'T LEAVE ME ALONE WITH WOLFE.
WHAT? WHY NOT...?
WELL, WELL, WELL, SOMEONE'S BEEN ON THE JUICE.
YOU WERE RIGHT, KRAMER. GOOD WORK.
IS THAT... TRICKSTER?
AND CAPTAIN COLD?!
HM. YOU'RE NOT SNART.
YOU'RE ONLY PLAYING AT BEING COLD.
I DON'T SEE ANYONE WANTING TO BE LIKE YOU.
HE'S WITH ME, WOLFE. YOU... YOU CAN TRUST HIM.
I NEED COMMANDER COLD'S HELP TO RUN TESTS ON TRICKSTER.
NOT A CHANCE IN HELL, FLASH.
TRICKSTER ISN'T LEAVING MY SIGHT, WOLFE.
WHY EXACTLY WOULD I ALLOW YOU TO OBSERVE ONE OF MY INMATES? WHAT'S IN IT FOR ME?
WHAT DO YOU WANT?
IRIS KEEPS TELLING ME THAT I NEED TO EMBRACE CHANGE...

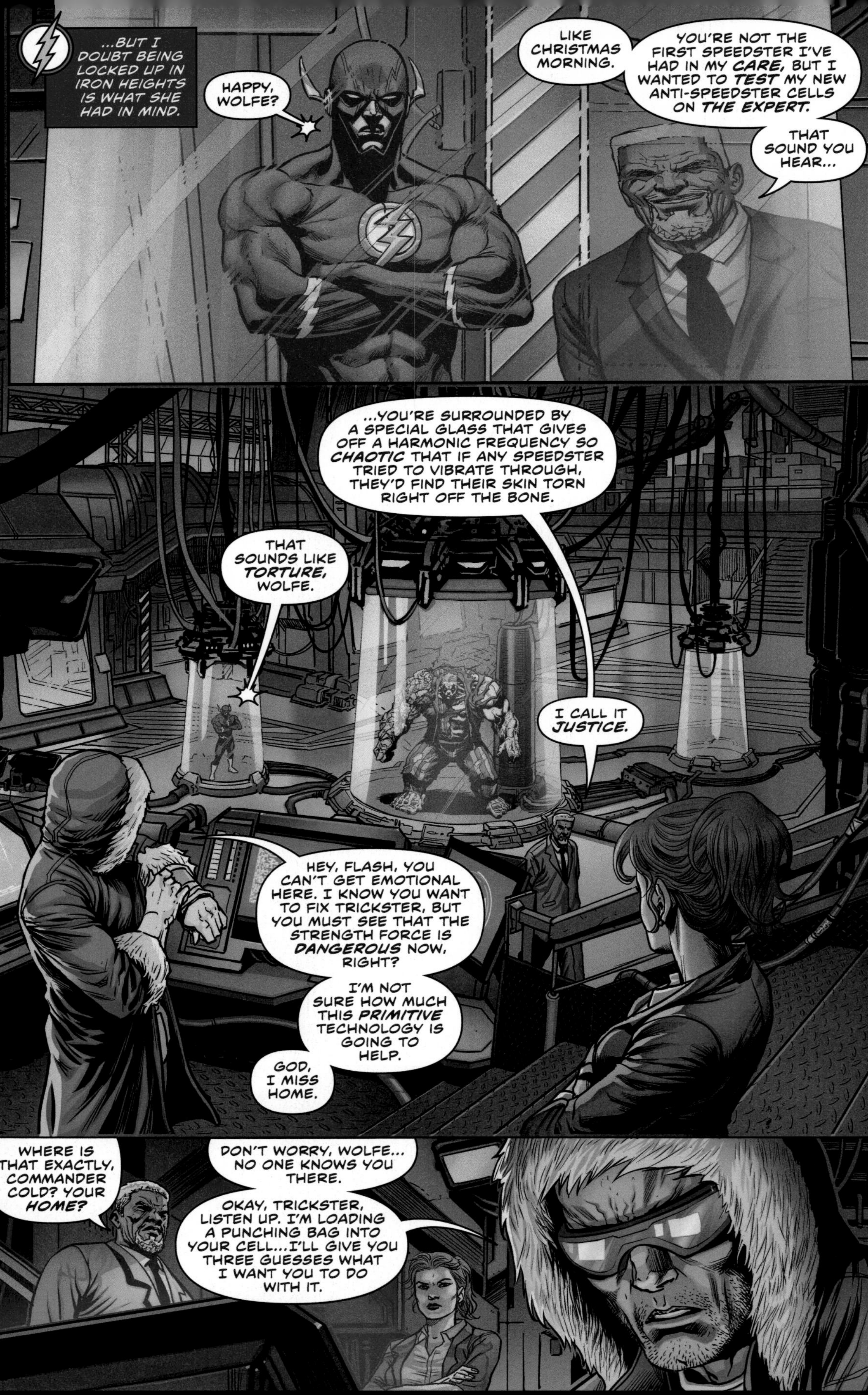
...BUT I DOUBT BEING LOCKED UP IN IRON HEIGHTS IS WHAT SHE HAD IN MIND.
HAPPY, WOLFE?
LIKE CHRISTMAS MORNING.
YOU'RE NOT THE FIRST SPEEDSTER I'VE HAD IN MY CARE, BUT I WANTED TO TEST MY NEW ANTI-SPEEDSTER CELLS ON THE EXPERT.
THAT SOUND YOU HEAR...
...YOU'RE SURROUNDED BY A SPECIAL GLASS THAT GIVES OFF A HARMONIC FREQUENCY SO CHAOTIC THAT IF ANY SPEEDSTER TRIED TO VIBRATE THROUGH, THEY'D FIND THEIR SKIN TORN RIGHT OFF THE BONE.
THAT SOUNDS LIKE TORTURE, WOLFE.
I CALL IT JUSTICE.
HEY, FLASH, YOU CAN'T GET EMOTIONAL HERE. I KNOW YOU WANT TO FIX TRICKSTER, BUT YOU MUST SEE THAT THE STRENGTH FORCE IS DANGEROUS NOW, RIGHT?
I'M NOT SURE HOW MUCH THIS PRIMITIVE TECHNOLOGY IS GOING TO HELP.
GOD, I MISS HOME.
WHERE IS THAT EXACTLY, COMMANDER COLD? YOUR HOME?
DON'T WORRY, WOLFE... NO ONE KNOWS YOU THERE.
OKAY, TRICKSTER, LISTEN UP. I'M LOADING A PUNCHING BAG INTO YOUR CELL...I'LL GIVE YOU THREE GUESSES WHAT I WANT YOU TO DO WITH IT.

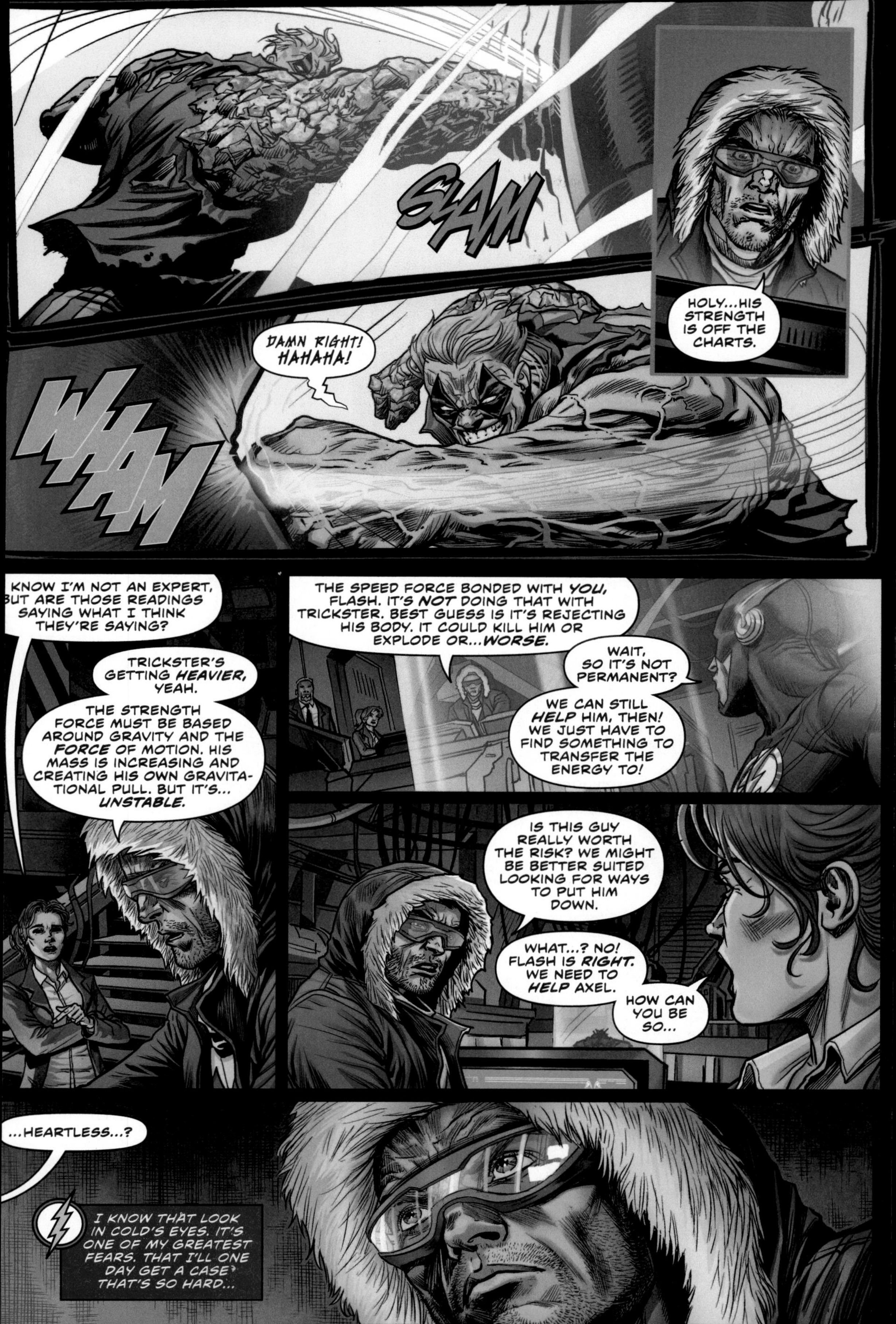
SLAM
HOLY...HIS STRENGTH IS OFF THE CHARTS.
DAMN RIGHT! HAHAHA!
WHAM
KNOW I'M NOT AN EXPERT, BUT ARE THOSE READINGS SAYING WHAT I THINK THEY'RE SAYING?
TRICKSTER'S GETTING HEAVIER, YEAH.
THE STRENGTH FORCE MUST BE BASED AROUND GRAVITY AND THE FORCE OF MOTION. HIS MASS IS INCREASING AND CREATING HIS OWN GRAVITATIONAL PULL. BUT IT'S... UNSTABLE.
THE SPEED FORCE BONDED WITH YOU, FLASH. IT'S NOT DOING THAT WITH TRICKSTER. BEST GUESS IS IT'S REJECTING HIS BODY. IT COULD KILL HIM OR EXPLODE OR...WORSE.
WAIT, SO IT'S NOT PERMANENT?
WE CAN STILL HELP HIM, THEN! WE JUST HAVE TO FIND SOMETHING TO TRANSFER THE ENERGY TO!
IS THIS GUY REALLY WORTH THE RISK? WE MIGHT BE BETTER SUITED LOOKING FOR WAYS TO PUT HIM DOWN.
WHAT...? NO! FLASH IS RIGHT. WE NEED TO HELP AXEL.
HOW CAN YOU BE SO...
...HEARTLESS...?
I KNOW THAT LOOK IN COLD'S EYES. IT'S ONE OF MY GREATEST FEARS. THAT I'LL ONE DAY GET A CASE THAT'S SO HARD...

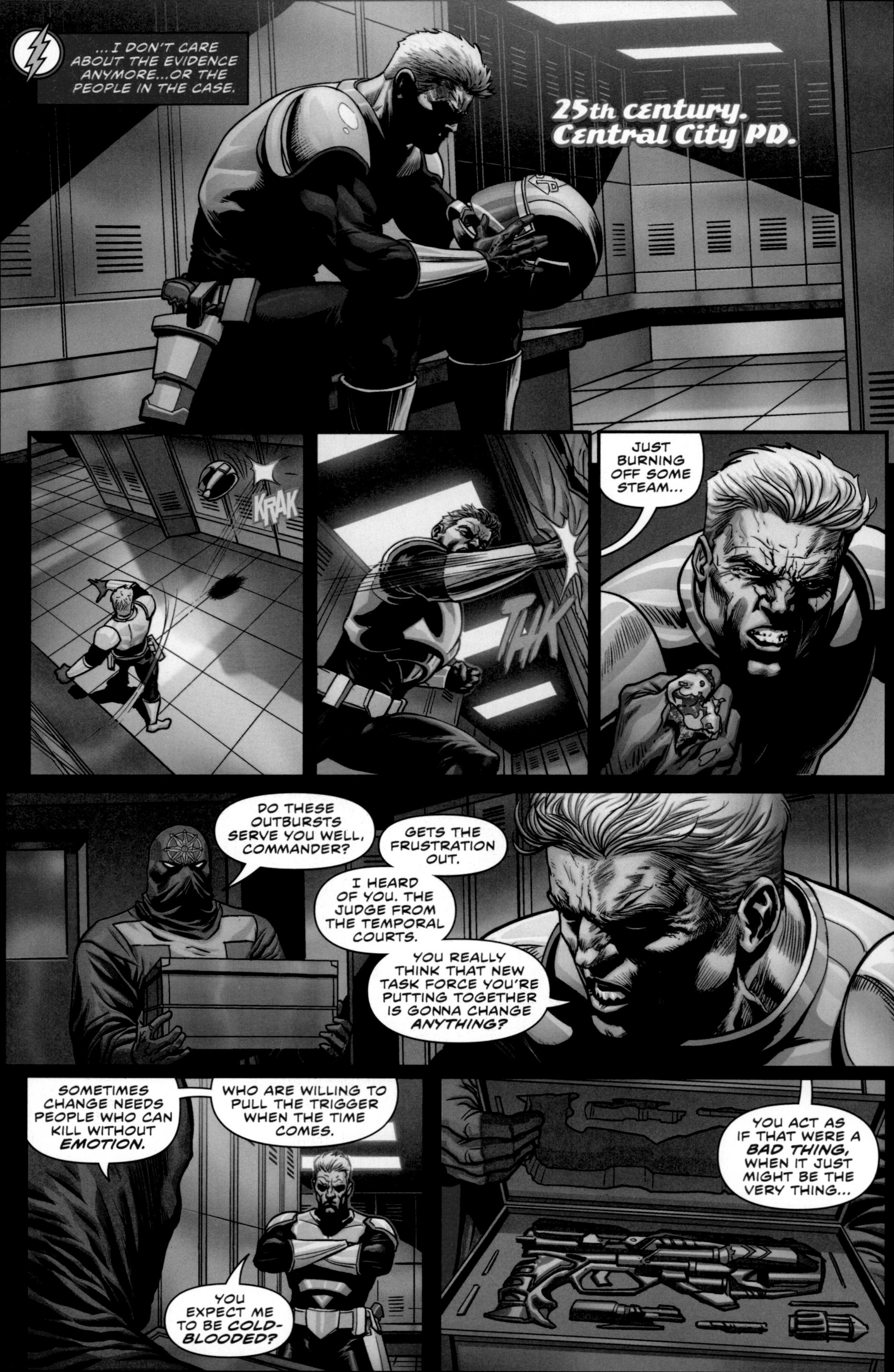
...I DON'T CARE ABOUT THE EVIDENCE ANYMORE...OR THE PEOPLE IN THE CASE.
25th century. Central City PD.
KRAK
THAK
JUST BURNING OFF SOME STEAM...
DO THESE OUTBURSTS SERVE YOU WELL, COMMANDER?
GETS THE FRUSTRATION OUT.
I HEARD OF YOU. THE JUDGE FROM THE TEMPORAL COURTS.
YOU REALLY THINK THAT NEW TASK FORCE YOU'RE PUTTING TOGETHER IS GONNA CHANGE *ANYTHING?*
SOMETIMES CHANGE NEEDS PEOPLE WHO CAN KILL WITHOUT *EMOTION.*
WHO ARE WILLING TO PULL THE TRIGGER WHEN THE TIME COMES.
YOU EXPECT ME TO BE *COLD-BLOODED?*
YOU ACT AS IF THAT WERE A *BAD THING,* WHEN IT JUST MIGHT BE THE VERY THING...

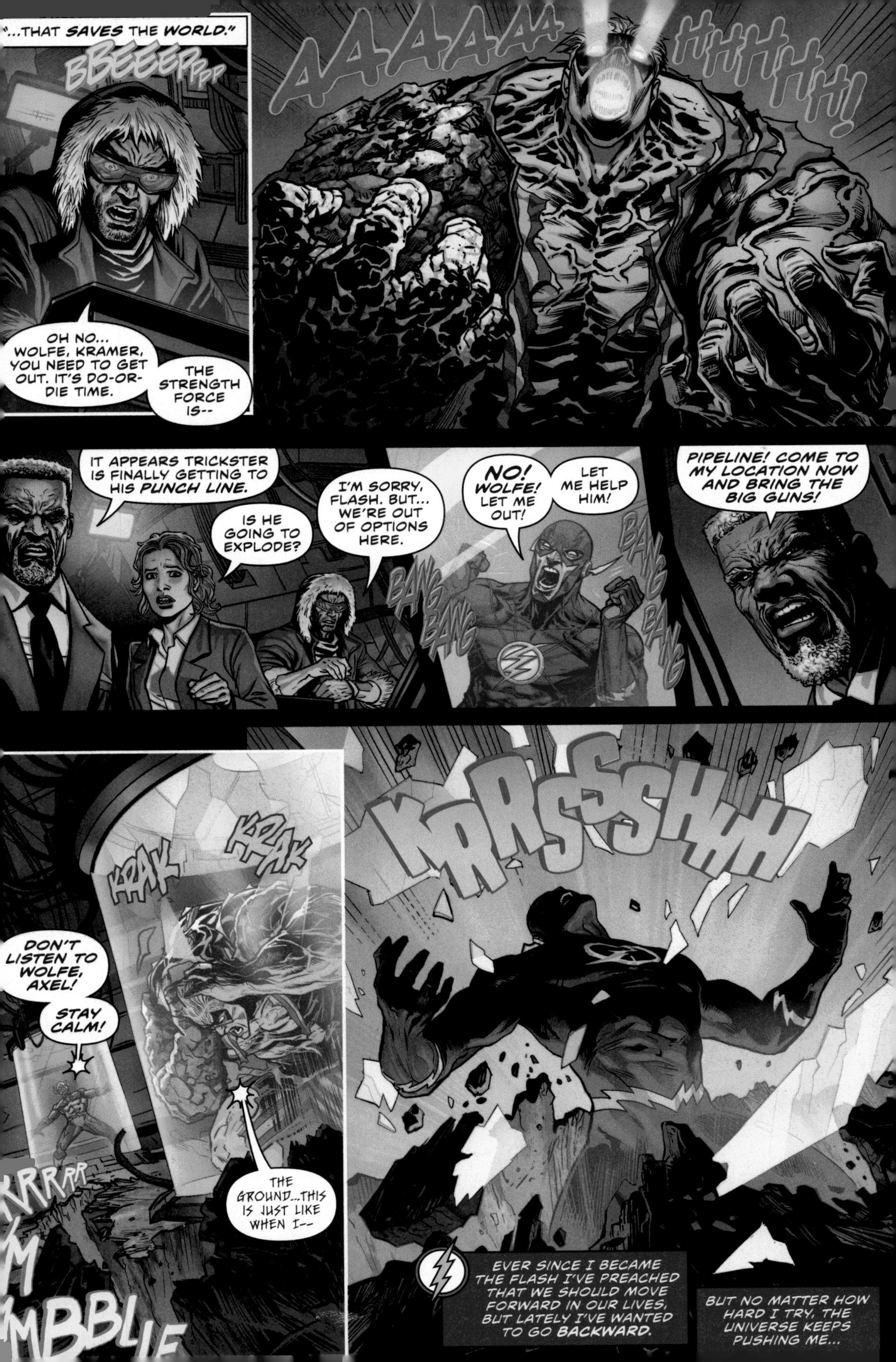
"...THAT SAVES THE WORLD."
BBEEEEPPPP
OH NO... WOLFE, KRAMER, YOU NEED TO GET OUT. IT'S DO-OR-DIE TIME.
THE STRENGTH FORCE IS--
AAAAAAHHHHHHH!
IT APPEARS TRICKSTER IS FINALLY GETTING TO HIS PUNCH LINE.
IS HE GOING TO EXPLODE?
I'M SORRY, FLASH. BUT... WE'RE OUT OF OPTIONS HERE.
NO! WOLFE! LET ME OUT!
LET ME HELP HIM!
BANG BANG
BANG BANG
PIPELINE! COME TO MY LOCATION NOW AND BRING THE BIG GUNS!
KRAK
KRAK
DON'T LISTEN TO WOLFE, AXEL!
STAY CALM!
THE GROUND...THIS IS JUST LIKE WHEN I--
KRRRRR
KRRSSSHHH
EVER SINCE I BECAME THE FLASH I'VE PREACHED THAT WE SHOULD MOVE FORWARD IN OUR LIVES, BUT LATELY I'VE WANTED TO GO BACKWARD.
BUT NO MATTER HOW HARD I TRY, THE UNIVERSE KEEPS PUSHING ME...

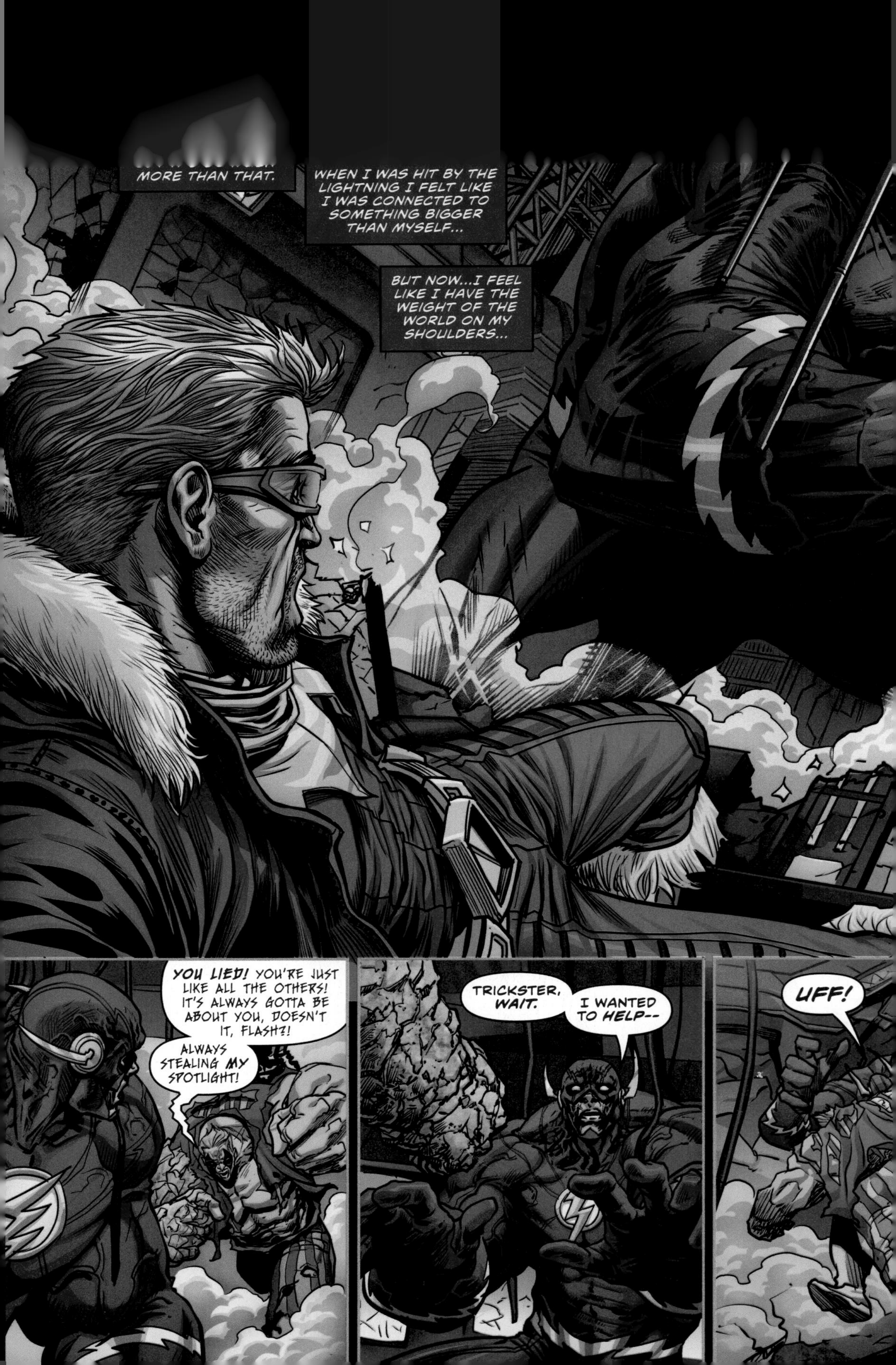

MORE THAN THAT.
WHEN I WAS HIT BY THE LIGHTNING I FELT LIKE I WAS CONNECTED TO SOMETHING BIGGER THAN MYSELF...
BUT NOW...I FEEL LIKE I HAVE THE WEIGHT OF THE WORLD ON MY SHOULDERS...
YOU LIED! YOU'RE JUST LIKE ALL THE OTHERS! IT'S ALWAYS GOTTA BE ABOUT YOU, DOESN'T IT, FLASH?!
ALWAYS STEALING MY SPOTLIGHT!
TRICKSTER, WAIT.
I WANTED TO HELP--
UFF!

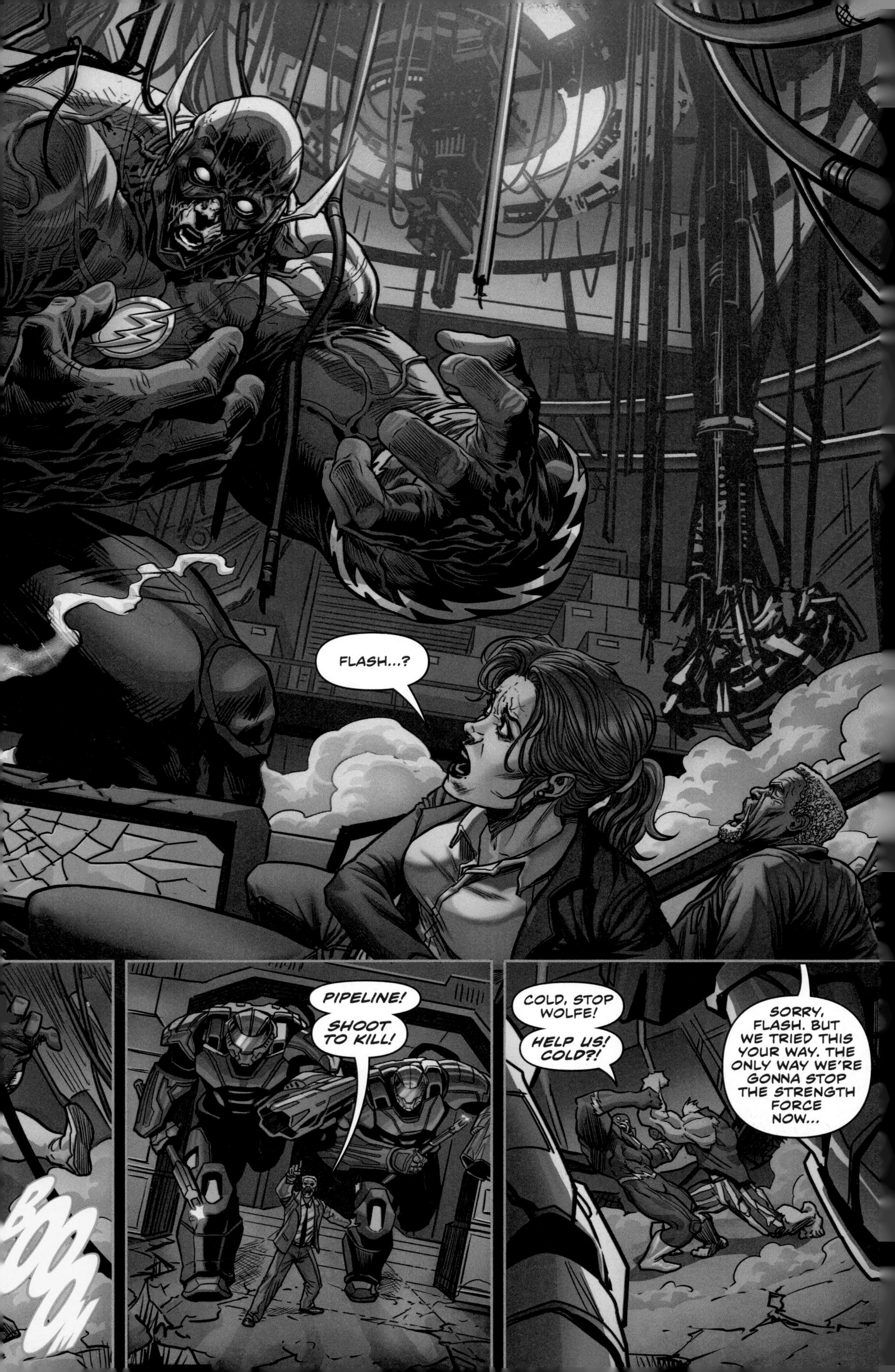
FLASH...?
BOOM
PIPELINE!
SHOOT TO KILL!
COLD, STOP WOLFE!
HELP US! COLD?!
SORRY, FLASH. BUT WE TRIED THIS YOUR WAY. THE ONLY WAY WE'RE GONNA STOP THE STRENGTH FORCE NOW...

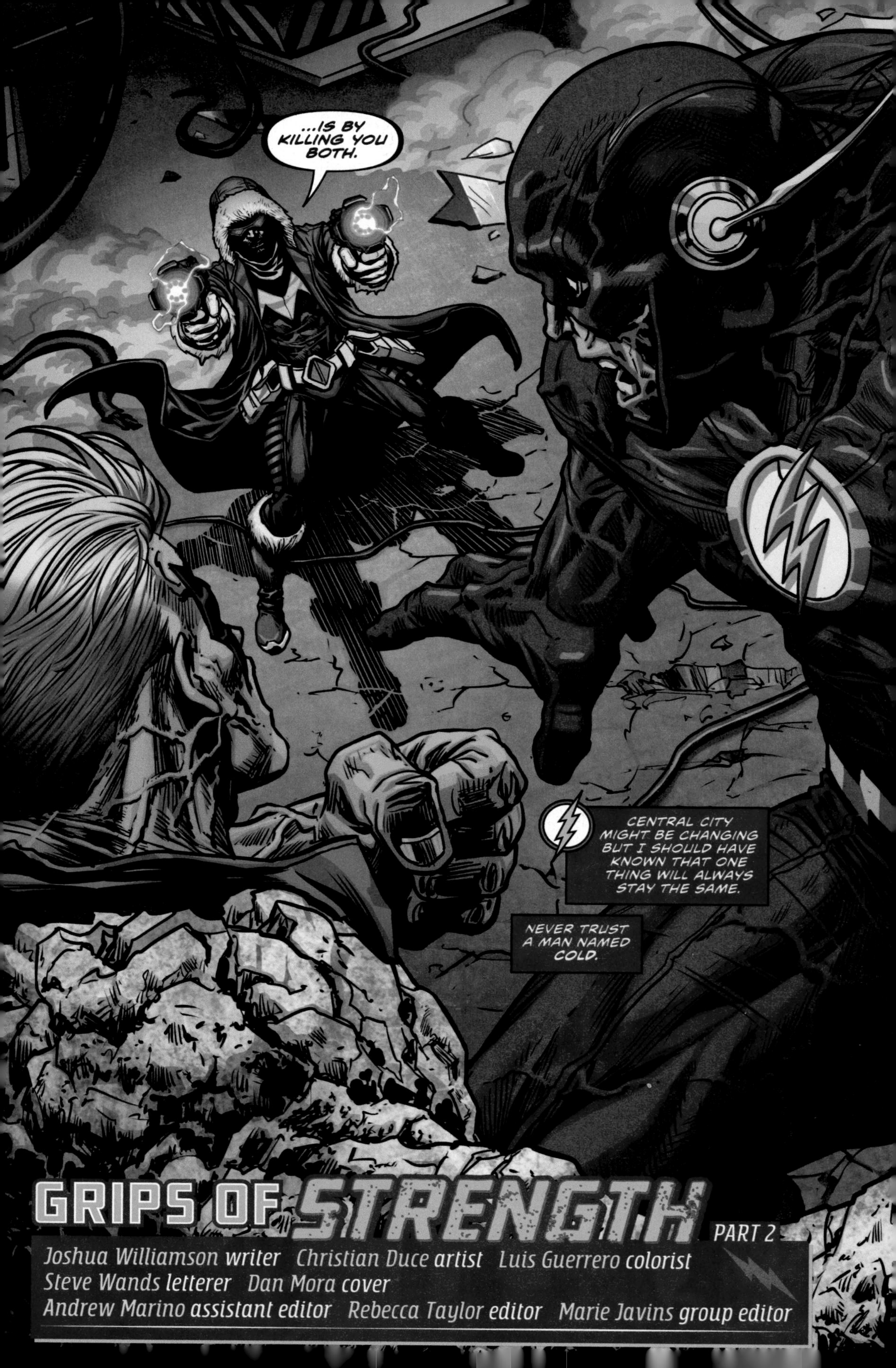
...IS BY KILLING YOU BOTH.
CENTRAL CITY MIGHT BE CHANGING BUT I SHOULD HAVE KNOWN THAT ONE THING WILL ALWAYS STAY THE SAME.
NEVER TRUST A MAN NAMED COLD.
GRIPS OF STRENGTH PART 2
Joshua Williamson writer Christian Duce artist Luis Guerrero colorist
Steve Wands letterer Dan Mora cover
Andrew Marino assistant editor Rebecca Taylor editor Marie Javins group editor

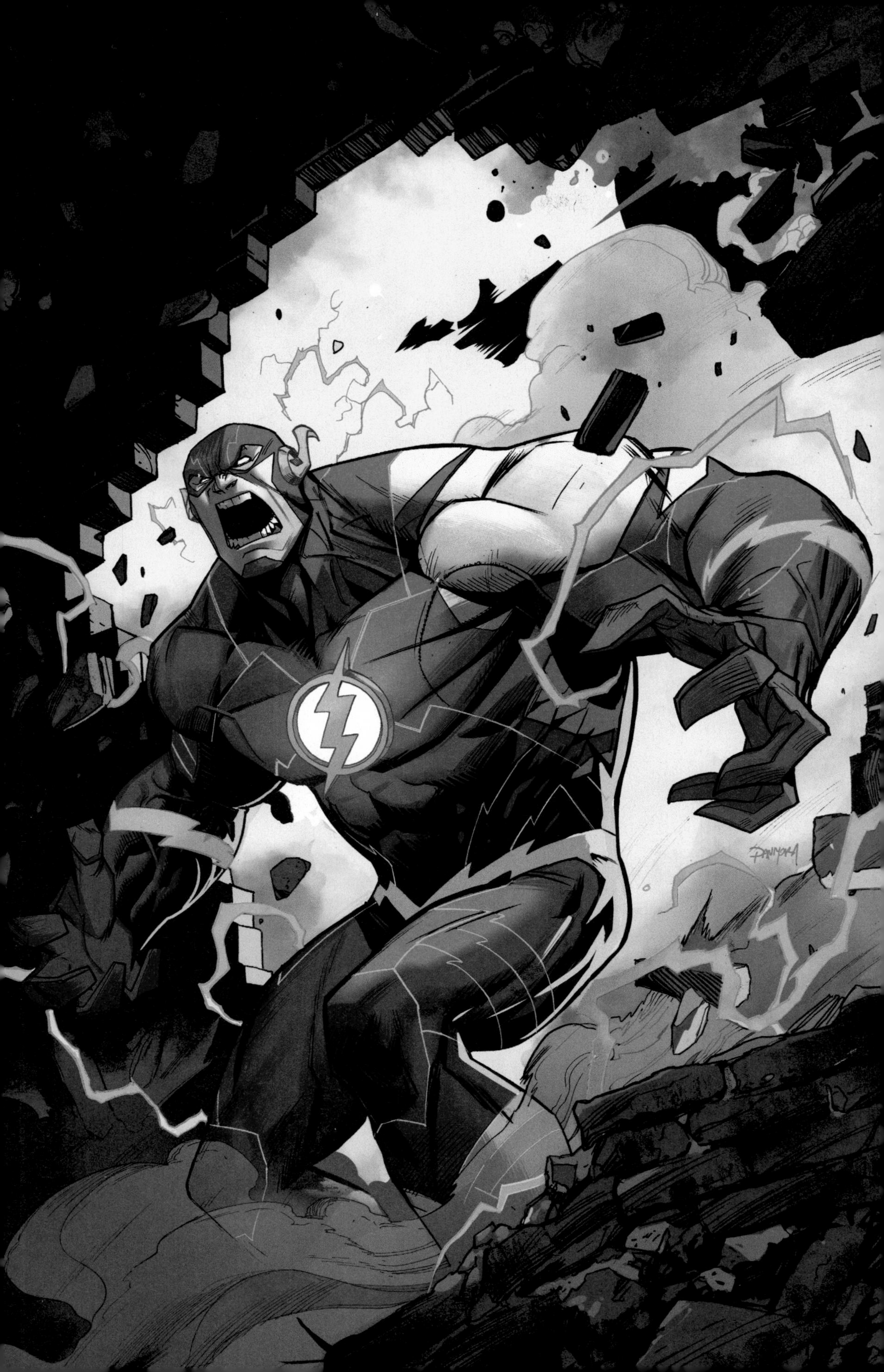

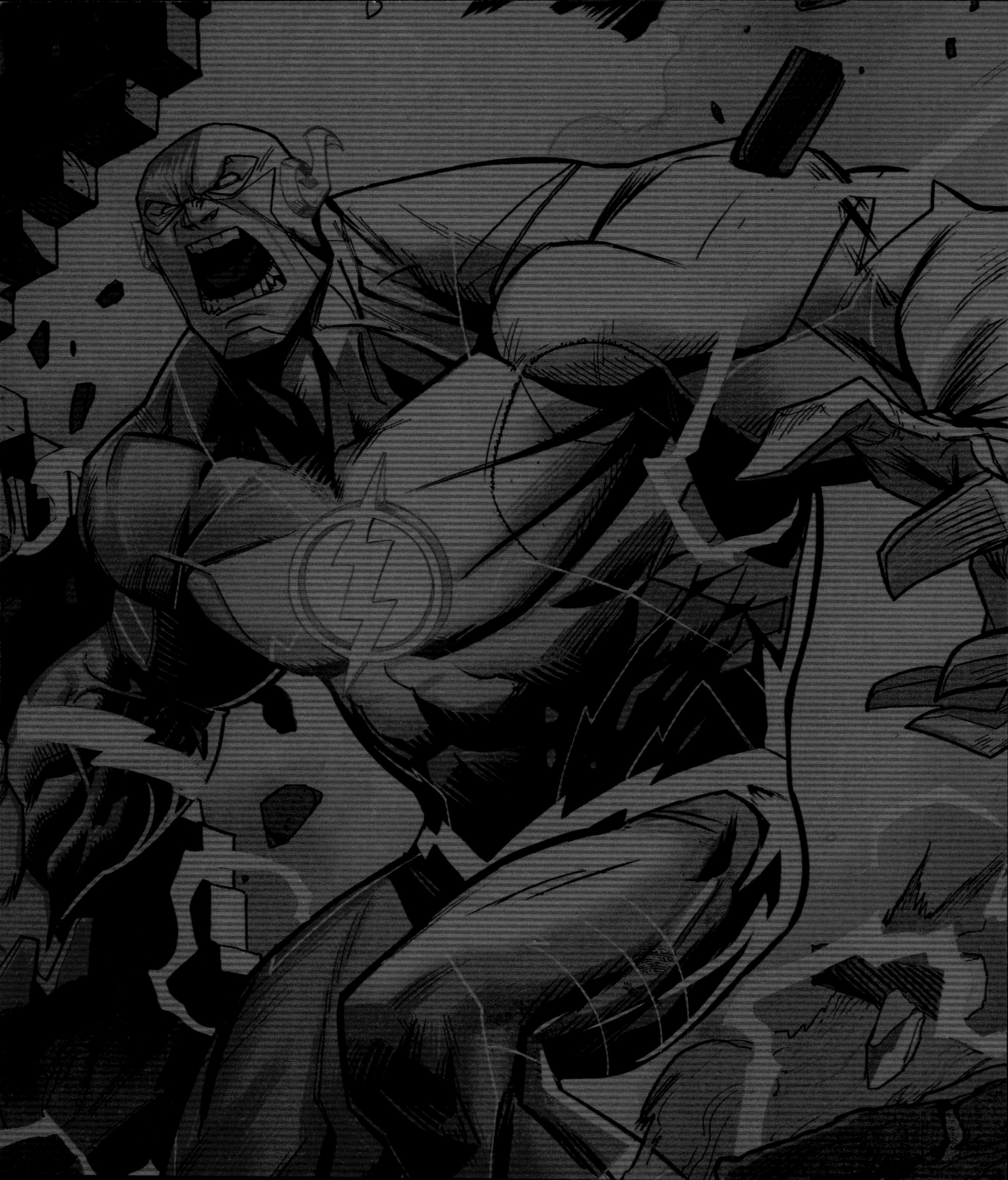

THE FLASH
#54

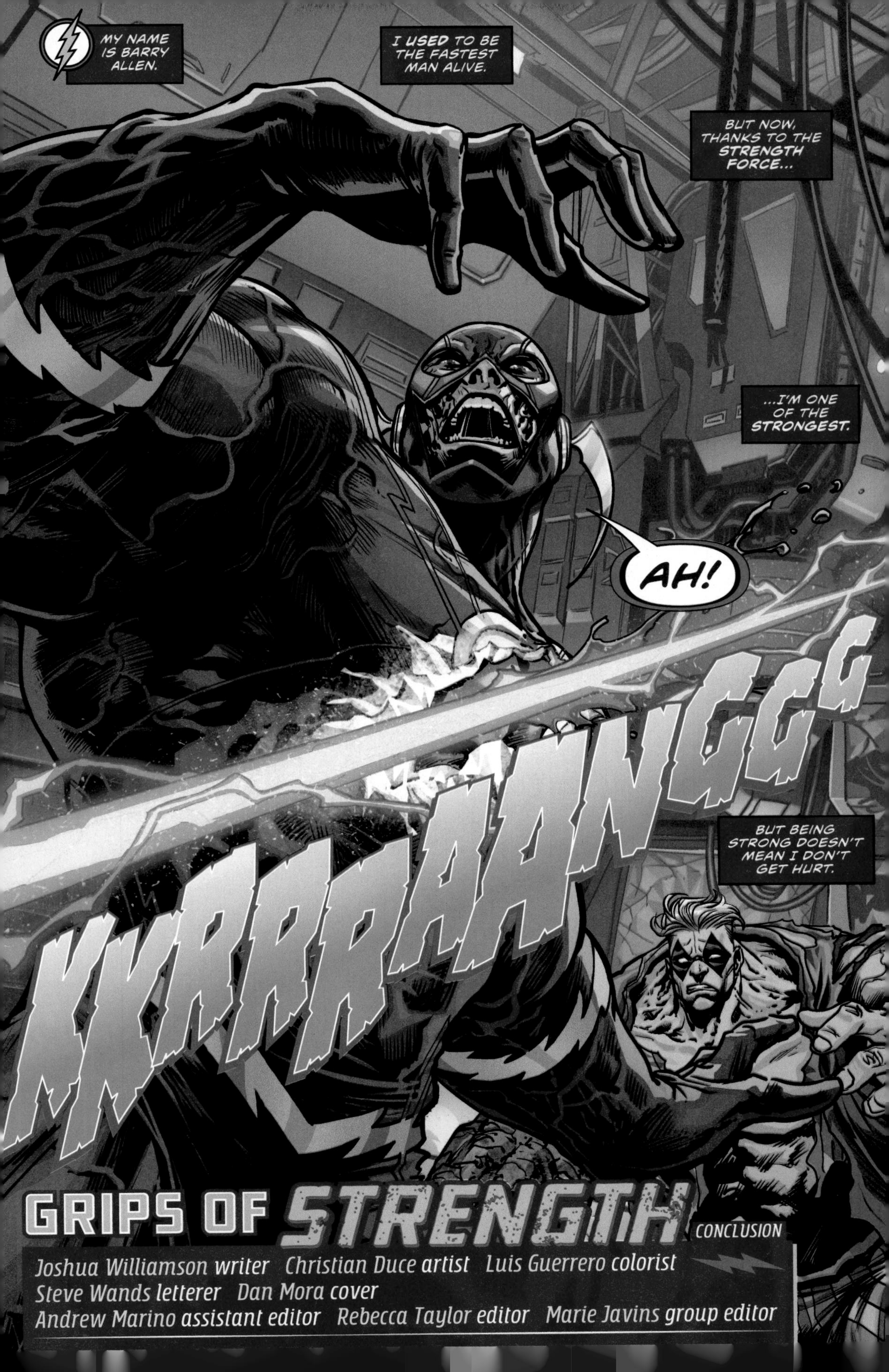
MY NAME IS BARRY ALLEN.
I USED TO BE THE FASTEST MAN ALIVE.
BUT NOW, THANKS TO THE STRENGTH FORCE...
...I'M ONE OF THE STRONGEST.
AH!
KKRRRAANGGG
BUT BEING STRONG DOESN'T MEAN I DON'T GET HURT.

GRIPS OF STRENGTH CONCLUSION

Joshua Williamson writer *Christian Duce* artist *Luis Guerrero* colorist
Steve Wands letterer *Dan Mora* cover
Andrew Marino assistant editor *Rebecca Taylor* editor *Marie Javins* group editor

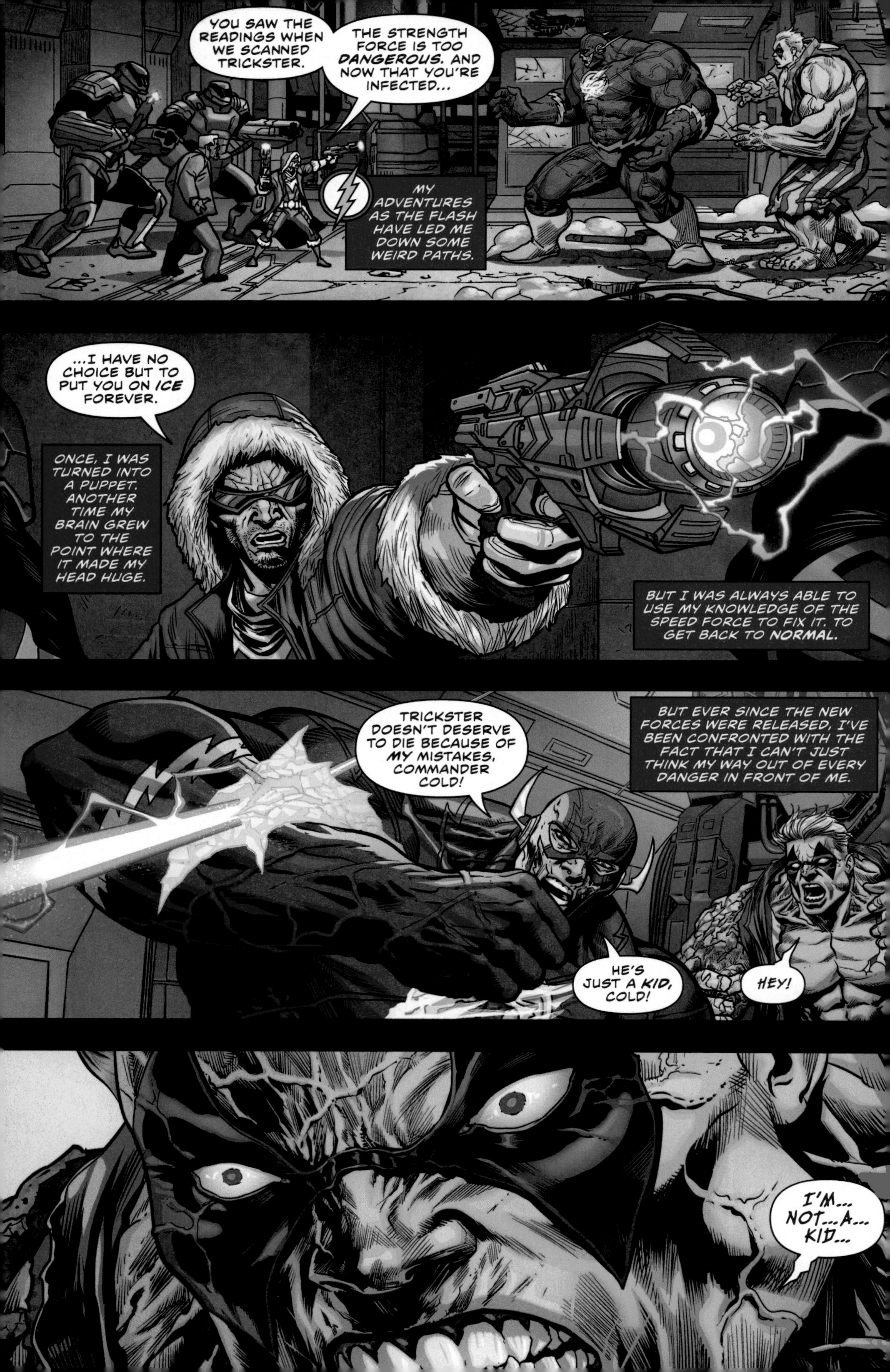
YOU SAW THE READINGS WHEN WE SCANNED TRICKSTER.
THE STRENGTH FORCE IS TOO DANGEROUS. AND NOW THAT YOU'RE INFECTED...
MY ADVENTURES AS THE FLASH HAVE LED ME DOWN SOME WEIRD PATHS.
...I HAVE NO CHOICE BUT TO PUT YOU ON ICE FOREVER.
ONCE, I WAS TURNED INTO A PUPPET. ANOTHER TIME MY BRAIN GREW TO THE POINT WHERE IT MADE MY HEAD HUGE.
BUT I WAS ALWAYS ABLE TO USE MY KNOWLEDGE OF THE SPEED FORCE TO FIX IT. TO GET BACK TO NORMAL.
TRICKSTER DOESN'T DESERVE TO DIE BECAUSE OF MY MISTAKES, COMMANDER COLD!
BUT EVER SINCE THE NEW FORCES WERE RELEASED, I'VE BEEN CONFRONTED WITH THE FACT THAT I CAN'T JUST THINK MY WAY OUT OF EVERY DANGER IN FRONT OF ME.
HE'S JUST A KID, COLD!
HEY!
I'M... NOT...A... KID...

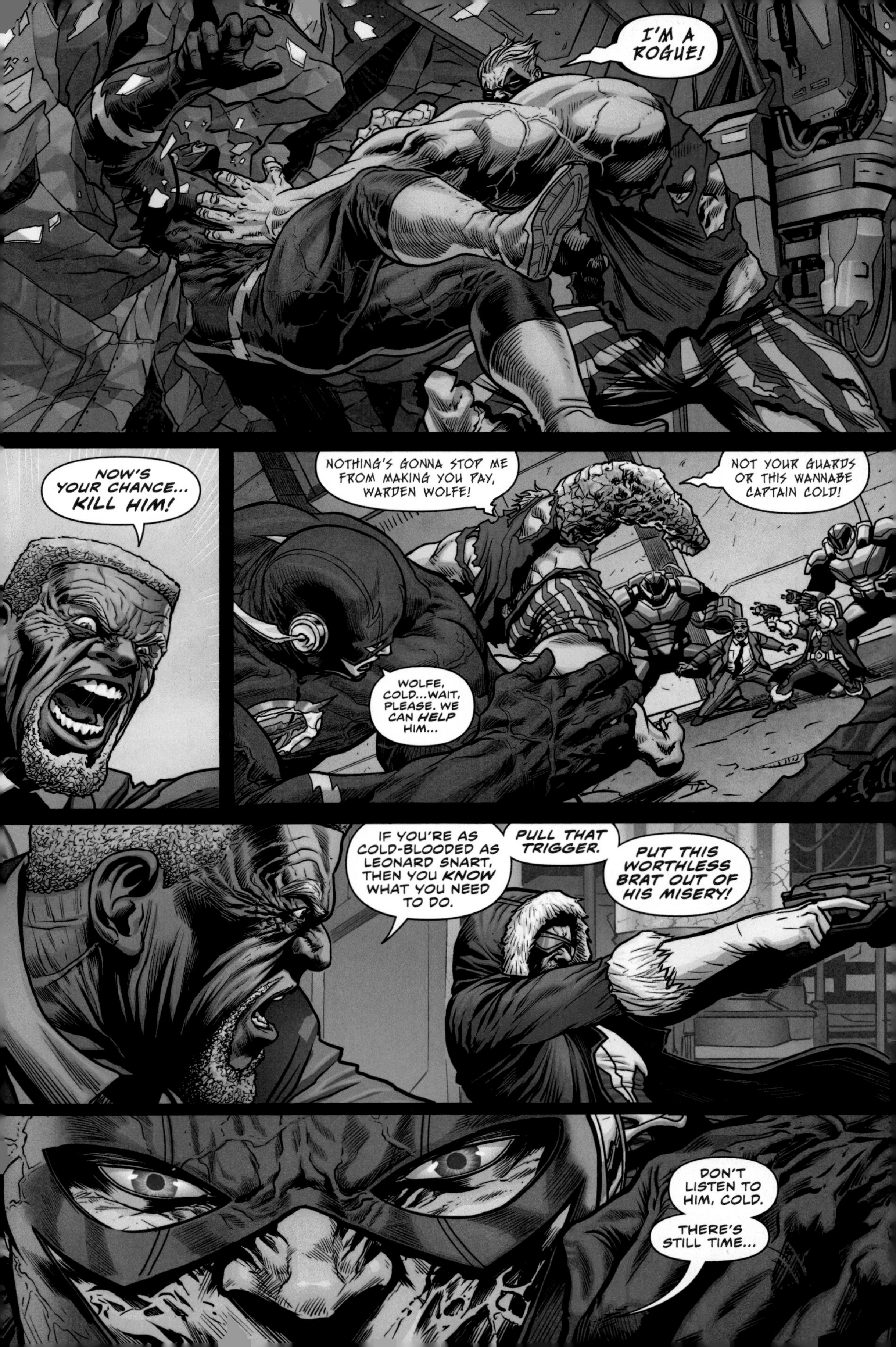
I'M A ROGUE!
NOW'S YOUR CHANCE... KILL HIM!
NOTHING'S GONNA STOP ME FROM MAKING YOU PAY, WARDEN WOLFE!
NOT YOUR GUARDS OR THIS WANNABE CAPTAIN COLD!
WOLFE, COLD...WAIT, PLEASE. WE CAN HELP HIM...
IF YOU'RE AS COLD-BLOODED AS LEONARD SNART, THEN YOU KNOW WHAT YOU NEED TO DO.
PULL THAT TRIGGER.
PUT THIS WORTHLESS BRAT OUT OF HIS MISERY!
DON'T LISTEN TO HIM, COLD.
THERE'S STILL TIME...

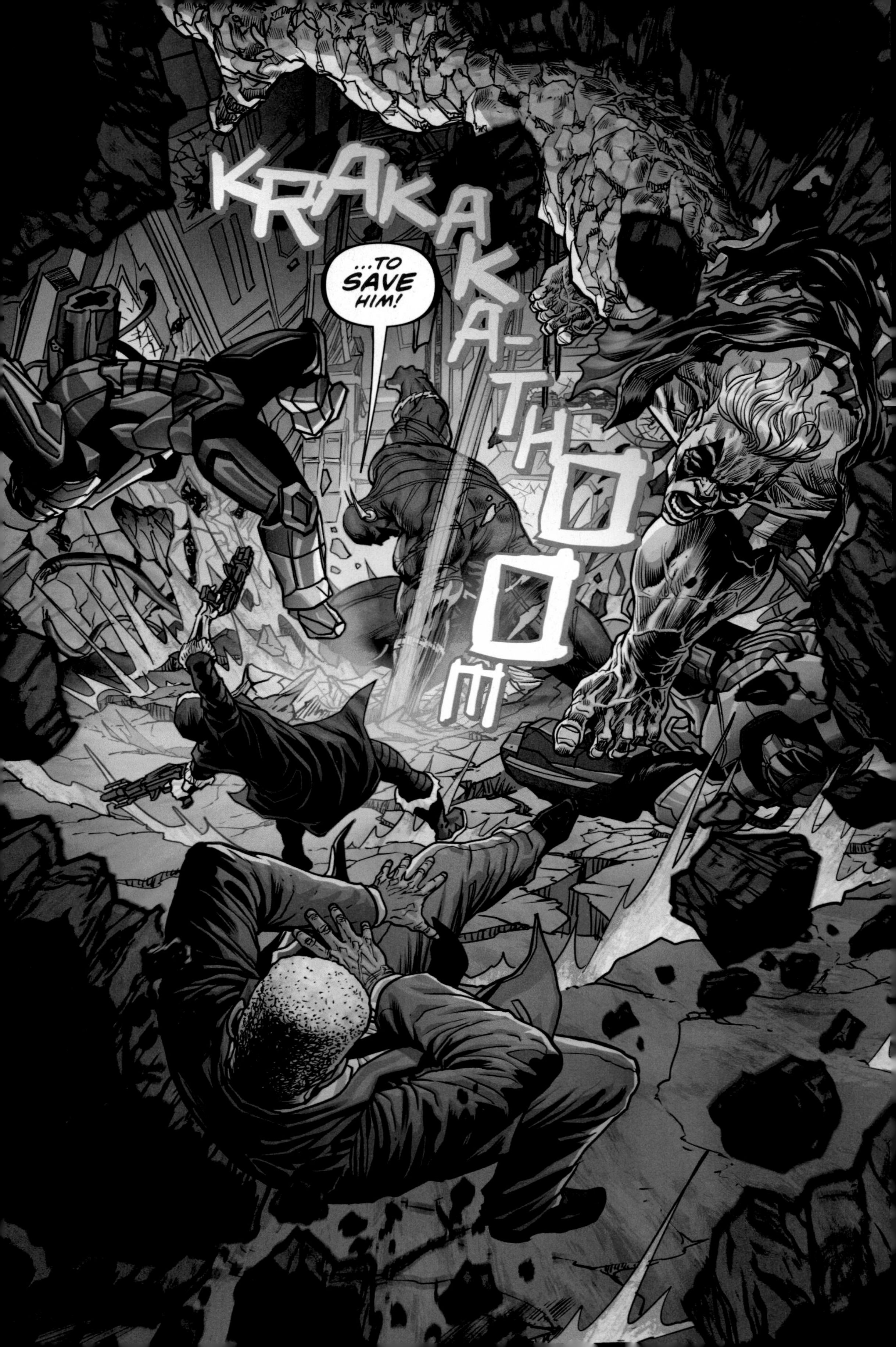
KRAKA-KA-THOOOM
...TO SAVE HIM!

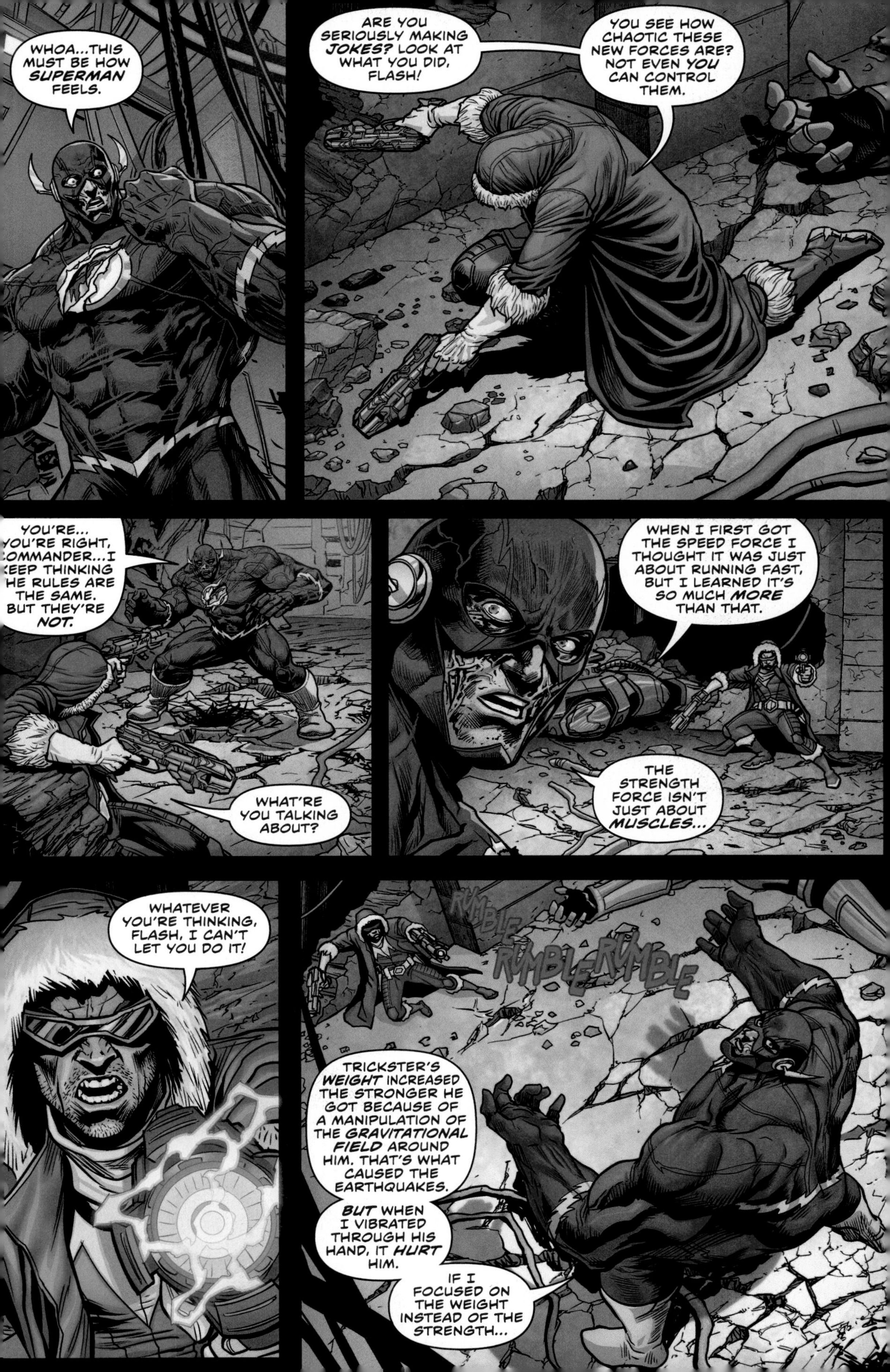
WHOA...THIS MUST BE HOW *SUPERMAN* FEELS.
ARE YOU SERIOUSLY MAKING *JOKES?* LOOK AT WHAT YOU DID, FLASH!
YOU SEE HOW CHAOTIC THESE NEW FORCES ARE? NOT EVEN *YOU* CAN CONTROL THEM.
YOU'RE... YOU'RE RIGHT, COMMANDER...I KEEP THINKING THE RULES ARE THE SAME. BUT THEY'RE *NOT.*
WHAT'RE YOU TALKING ABOUT?
WHEN I FIRST GOT THE SPEED FORCE I THOUGHT IT WAS JUST ABOUT RUNNING FAST, BUT I LEARNED IT'S SO MUCH *MORE* THAN THAT.
THE STRENGTH FORCE ISN'T JUST ABOUT *MUSCLES...*
WHATEVER YOU'RE THINKING, FLASH, I CAN'T LET YOU DO IT!
RUMBLE RUMBLE RUMBLE
TRICKSTER'S *WEIGHT* INCREASED THE STRONGER HE GOT BECAUSE OF A MANIPULATION OF THE *GRAVITATIONAL FIELD* AROUND HIM. THAT'S WHAT CAUSED THE EARTHQUAKES.
BUT WHEN I VIBRATED THROUGH HIS HAND, IT *HURT* HIM.
IF I FOCUSED ON THE WEIGHT INSTEAD OF THE STRENGTH...

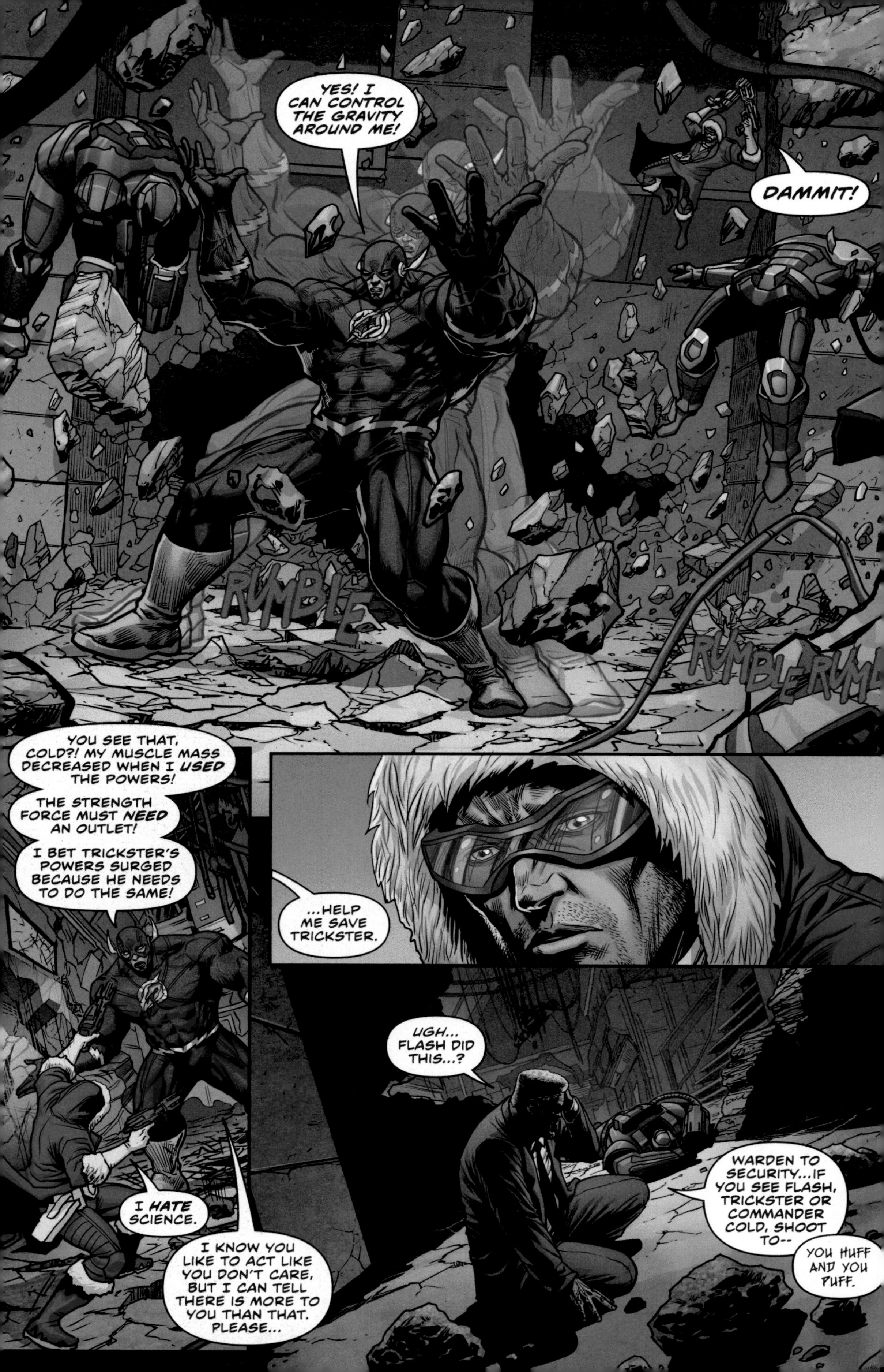
YES! I CAN CONTROL THE GRAVITY AROUND ME!
DAMMIT!
RUMBLE
RUMBLE RUMBLE
YOU SEE THAT, COLD?! MY MUSCLE MASS DECREASED WHEN I USED THE POWERS!
THE STRENGTH FORCE MUST NEED AN OUTLET!
I BET TRICKSTER'S POWERS SURGED BECAUSE HE NEEDS TO DO THE SAME!
...HELP ME SAVE TRICKSTER.
I HATE SCIENCE.
I KNOW YOU LIKE TO ACT LIKE YOU DON'T CARE, BUT I CAN TELL THERE IS MORE TO YOU THAN THAT. PLEASE...
UGH... FLASH DID THIS...?
WARDEN TO SECURITY...IF YOU SEE FLASH, TRICKSTER OR COMMANDER COLD, SHOOT TO--
YOU HUFF AND YOU PUFF.

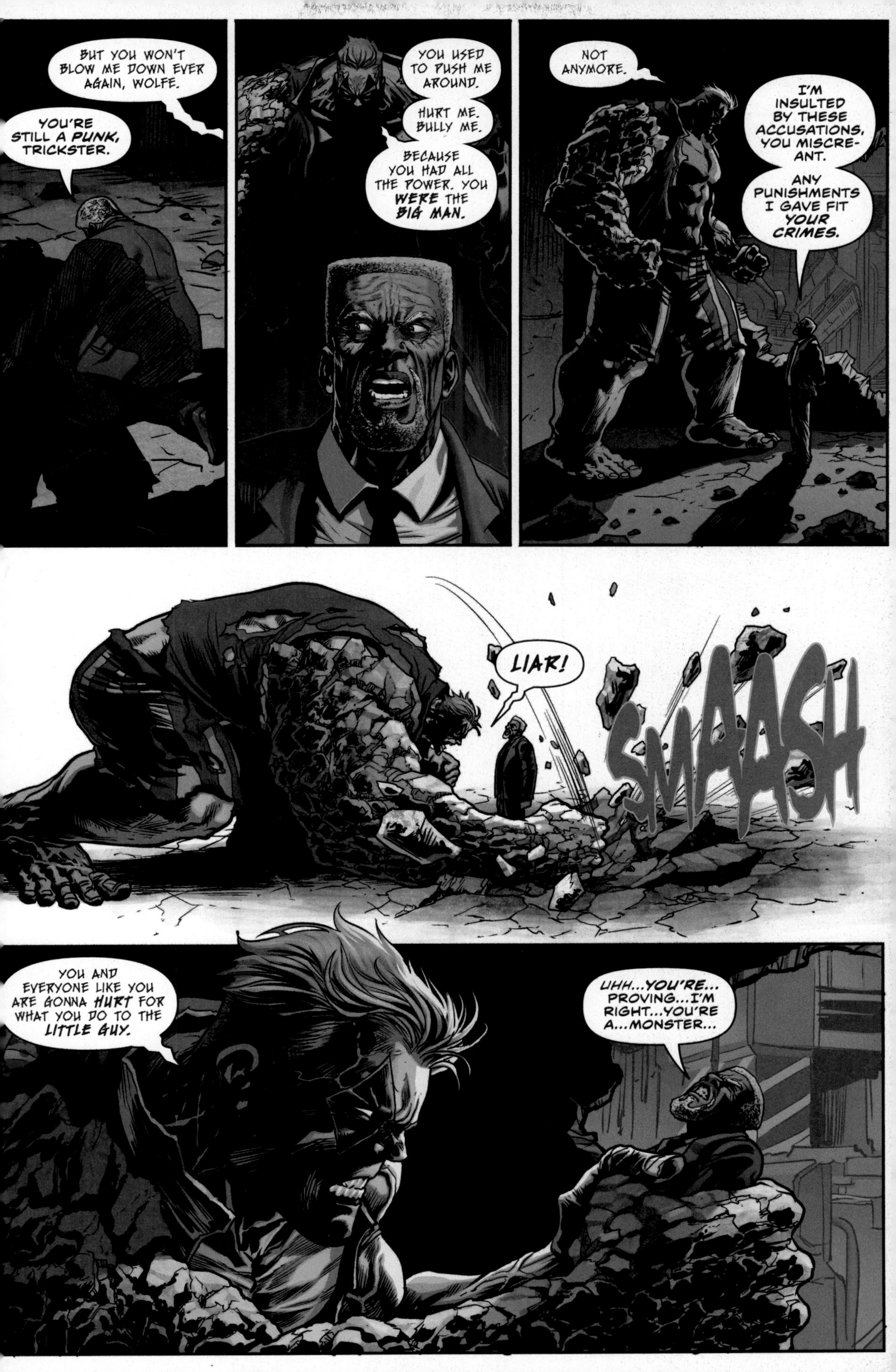
BUT YOU WON'T BLOW ME DOWN EVER AGAIN, WOLFE.
YOU'RE STILL A PUNK, TRICKSTER.
YOU USED TO PUSH ME AROUND.
HURT ME. BULLY ME.
BECAUSE YOU HAD ALL THE POWER. YOU WERE THE BIG MAN.
NOT ANYMORE.
I'M INSULTED BY THESE ACCUSATIONS, YOU MISCRE-ANT.
ANY PUNISHMENTS I GAVE FIT YOUR CRIMES.
LIAR!
SMAASH
YOU AND EVERYONE LIKE YOU ARE GONNA HURT FOR WHAT YOU DO TO THE LITTLE GUY.
UHH...YOU'RE... PROVING...I'M RIGHT...YOU'RE A...MONSTER...

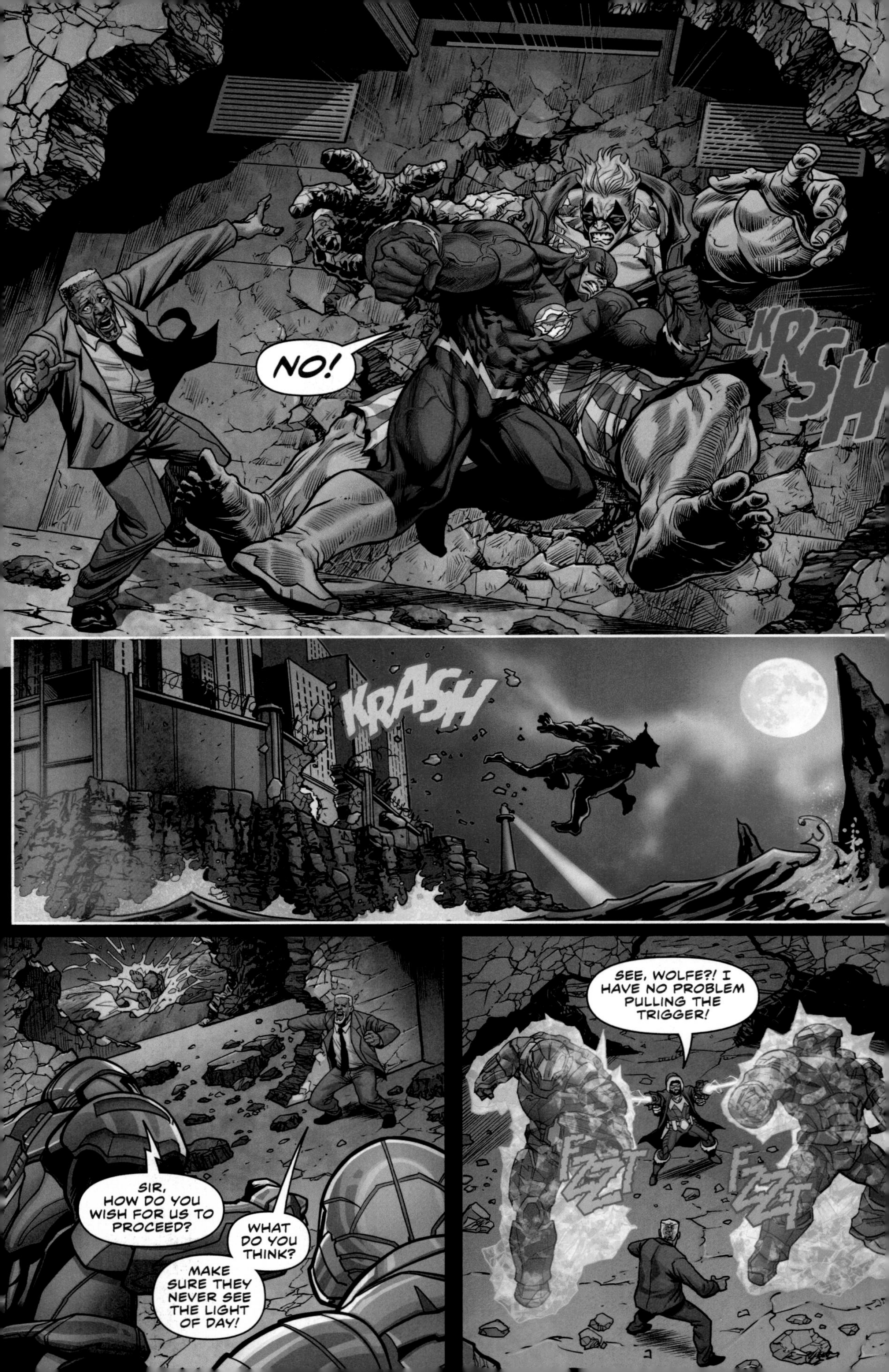
NO!
KRSH
KRASH
SIR, HOW DO YOU WISH FOR US TO PROCEED?
WHAT DO YOU THINK?
MAKE SURE THEY NEVER SEE THE LIGHT OF DAY!
SEE, WOLFE?! I HAVE NO PROBLEM PULLING THE TRIGGER!
FZZT
FZZT

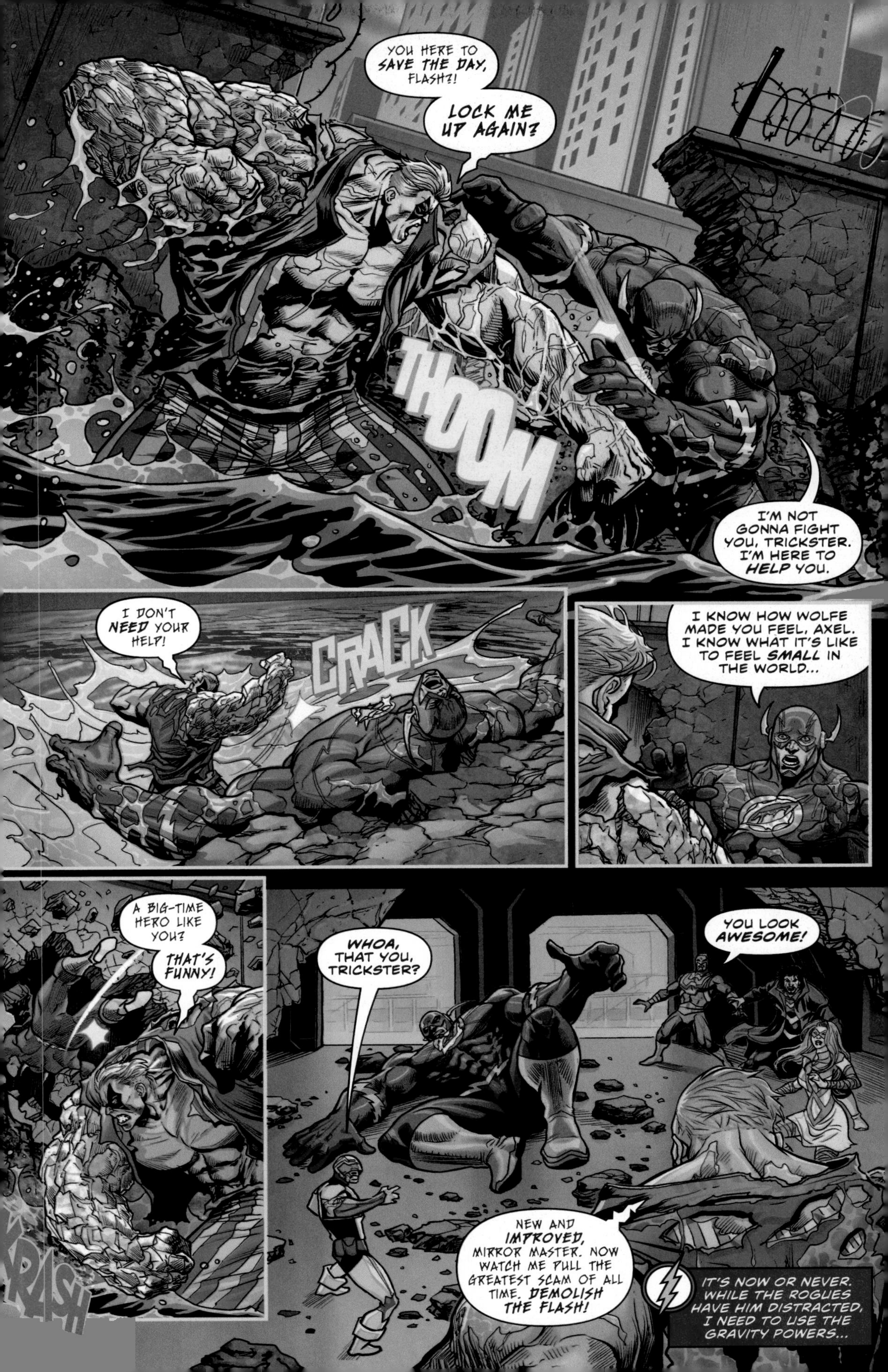

YOU HERE TO SAVE THE DAY, FLASH?!
LOCK ME UP AGAIN?
THOOM
I'M NOT GONNA FIGHT YOU, TRICKSTER. I'M HERE TO HELP YOU.
I DON'T NEED YOUR HELP!
CRACK
I KNOW HOW WOLFE MADE YOU FEEL, AXEL. I KNOW WHAT IT'S LIKE TO FEEL SMALL IN THE WORLD...
A BIG-TIME HERO LIKE YOU?
THAT'S FUNNY!
WHOA, THAT YOU, TRICKSTER?
YOU LOOK AWESOME!
NEW AND IMPROVED, MIRROR MASTER. NOW WATCH ME PULL THE GREATEST SCAM OF ALL TIME. DEMOLISH THE FLASH!
IT'S NOW OR NEVER. WHILE THE ROGUES HAVE HIM DISTRACTED, I NEED TO USE THE GRAVITY POWERS...

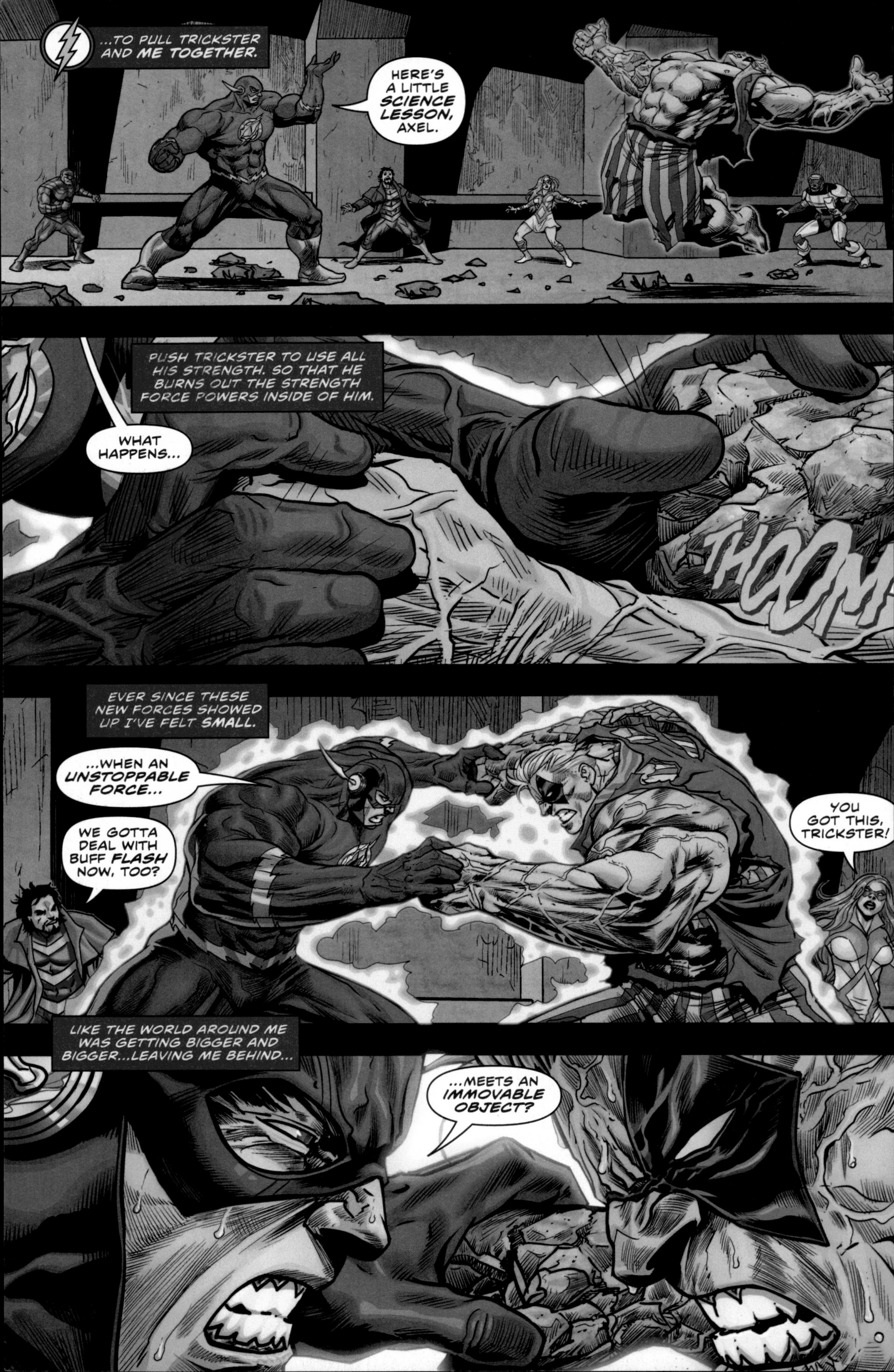
...TO PULL TRICKSTER AND ME TOGETHER.
HERE'S A LITTLE SCIENCE LESSON, AXEL.
PUSH TRICKSTER TO USE ALL HIS STRENGTH. SO THAT HE BURNS OUT THE STRENGTH FORCE POWERS INSIDE OF HIM.
WHAT HAPPENS...
THOOM
EVER SINCE THESE NEW FORCES SHOWED UP I'VE FELT SMALL.
...WHEN AN UNSTOPPABLE FORCE...
WE GOTTA DEAL WITH BUFF FLASH NOW, TOO?
YOU GOT THIS, TRICKSTER!
LIKE THE WORLD AROUND ME WAS GETTING BIGGER AND BIGGER...LEAVING ME BEHIND...
...MEETS AN IMMOVABLE OBJECT?

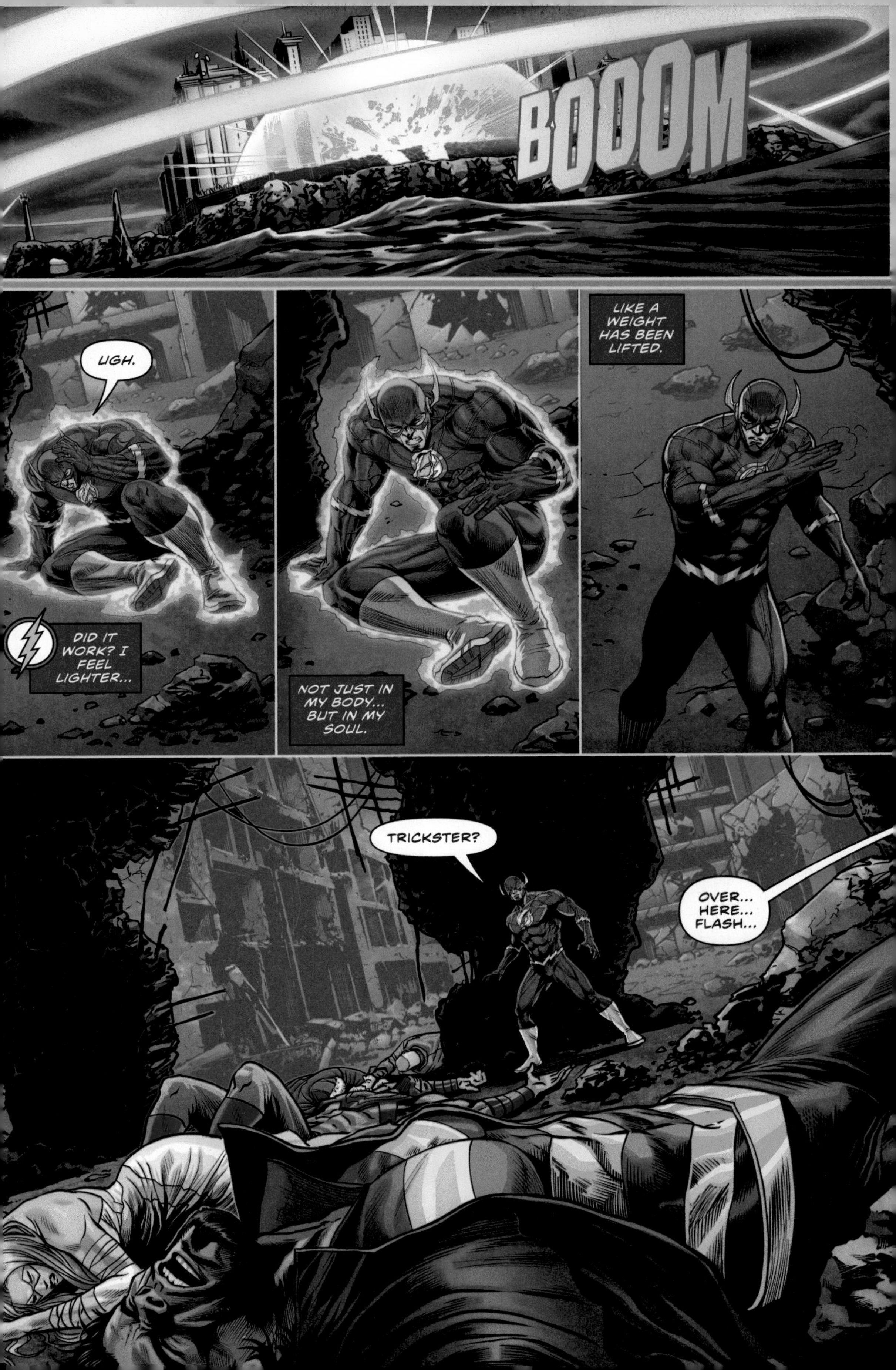
BOOOM
UGH.
DID IT WORK? I FEEL LIGHTER...
NOT JUST IN MY BODY... BUT IN MY SOUL.
LIKE A WEIGHT HAS BEEN LIFTED.
TRICKSTER?
OVER... HERE... FLASH...

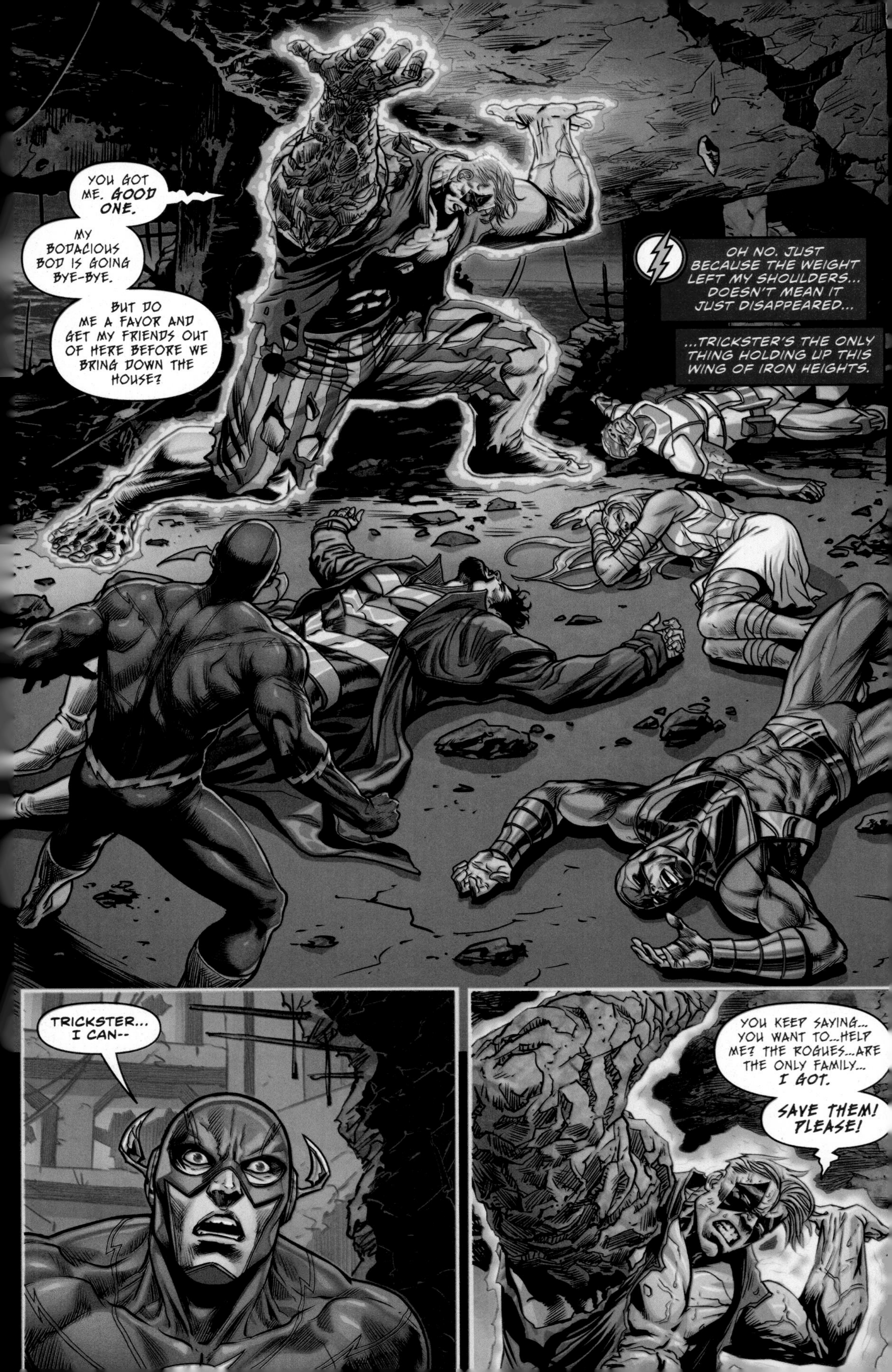
YOU GOT ME. GOOD ONE.
MY BODACIOUS BOD IS GOING BYE-BYE.
BUT DO ME A FAVOR AND GET MY FRIENDS OUT OF HERE BEFORE WE BRING DOWN THE HOUSE?
OH NO. JUST BECAUSE THE WEIGHT LEFT MY SHOULDERS... DOESN'T MEAN IT JUST DISAPPEARED...
...TRICKSTER'S THE ONLY THING HOLDING UP THIS WING OF IRON HEIGHTS.
TRICKSTER... I CAN--
YOU KEEP SAYING... YOU WANT TO...HELP ME? THE ROGUES...ARE THE ONLY FAMILY... I GOT.
SAVE THEM! PLEASE!

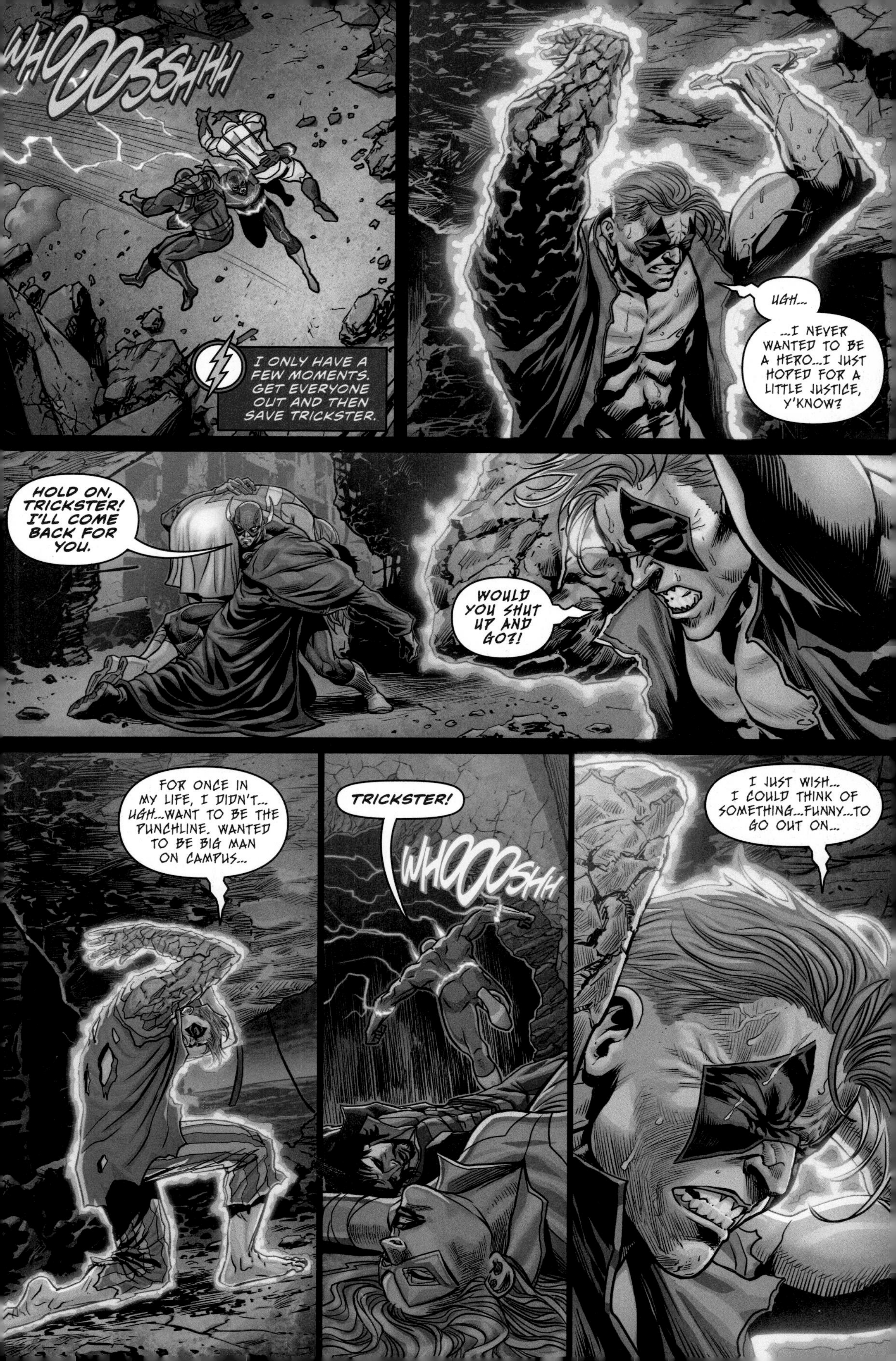
WHOOOOSSHHH
I ONLY HAVE A FEW MOMENTS. GET EVERYONE OUT AND THEN SAVE TRICKSTER.
UGH...
...I NEVER WANTED TO BE A HERO...I JUST HOPED FOR A LITTLE JUSTICE, Y'KNOW?
HOLD ON, TRICKSTER! I'LL COME BACK FOR YOU.
WOULD YOU SHUT UP AND GO?!
FOR ONCE IN MY LIFE, I DIDN'T... UGH...WANT TO BE THE PUNCHLINE. WANTED TO BE BIG MAN ON CAMPUS...
TRICKSTER!
WHOOOSHH
I JUST WISH... I COULD THINK OF SOMETHING...FUNNY...TO GO OUT ON...

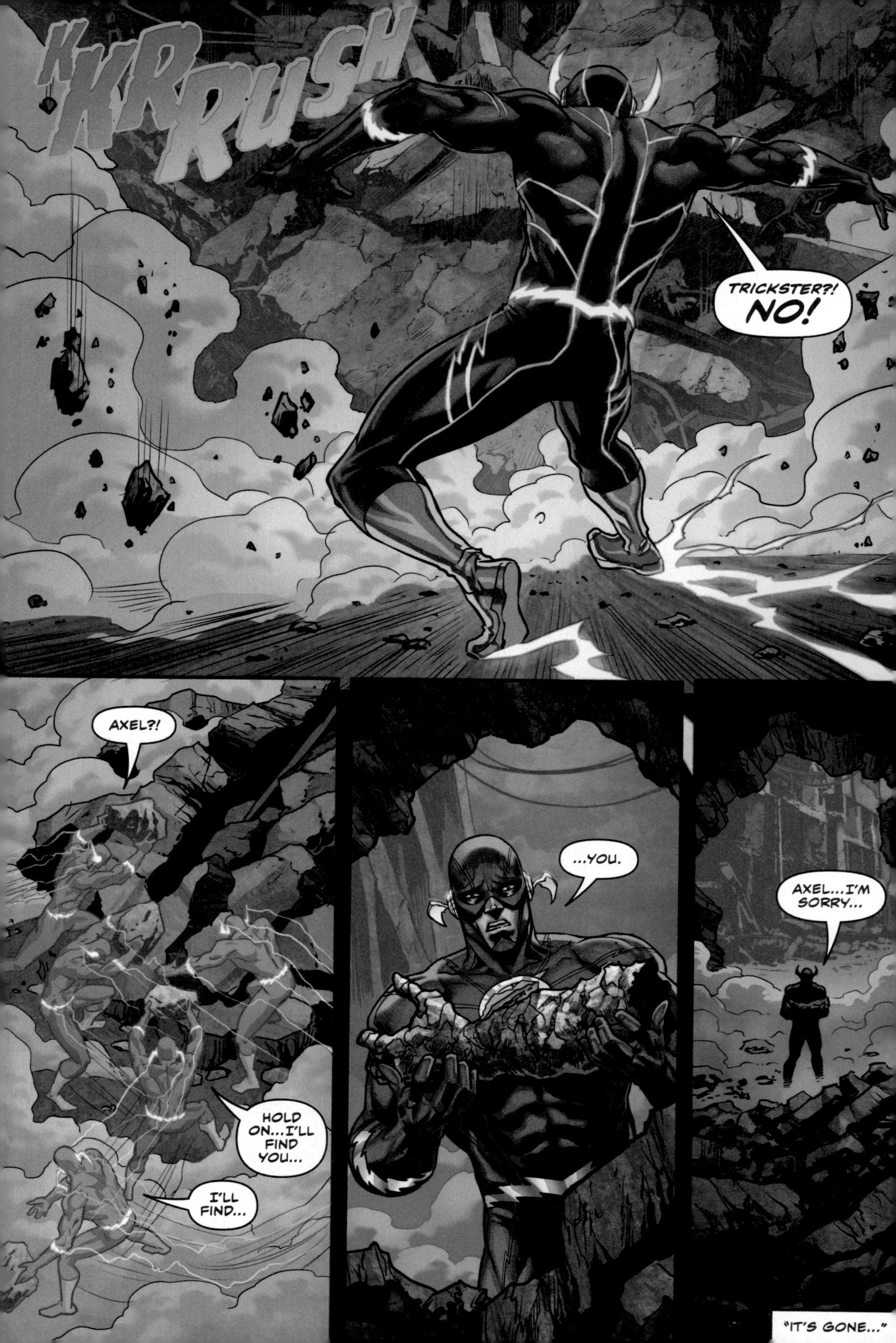
KKRRUSH
TRICKSTER?! NO!
AXEL?!
HOLD ON...I'LL FIND YOU...
I'LL FIND...
...YOU.
AXEL...I'M SORRY...
"IT'S GONE..."

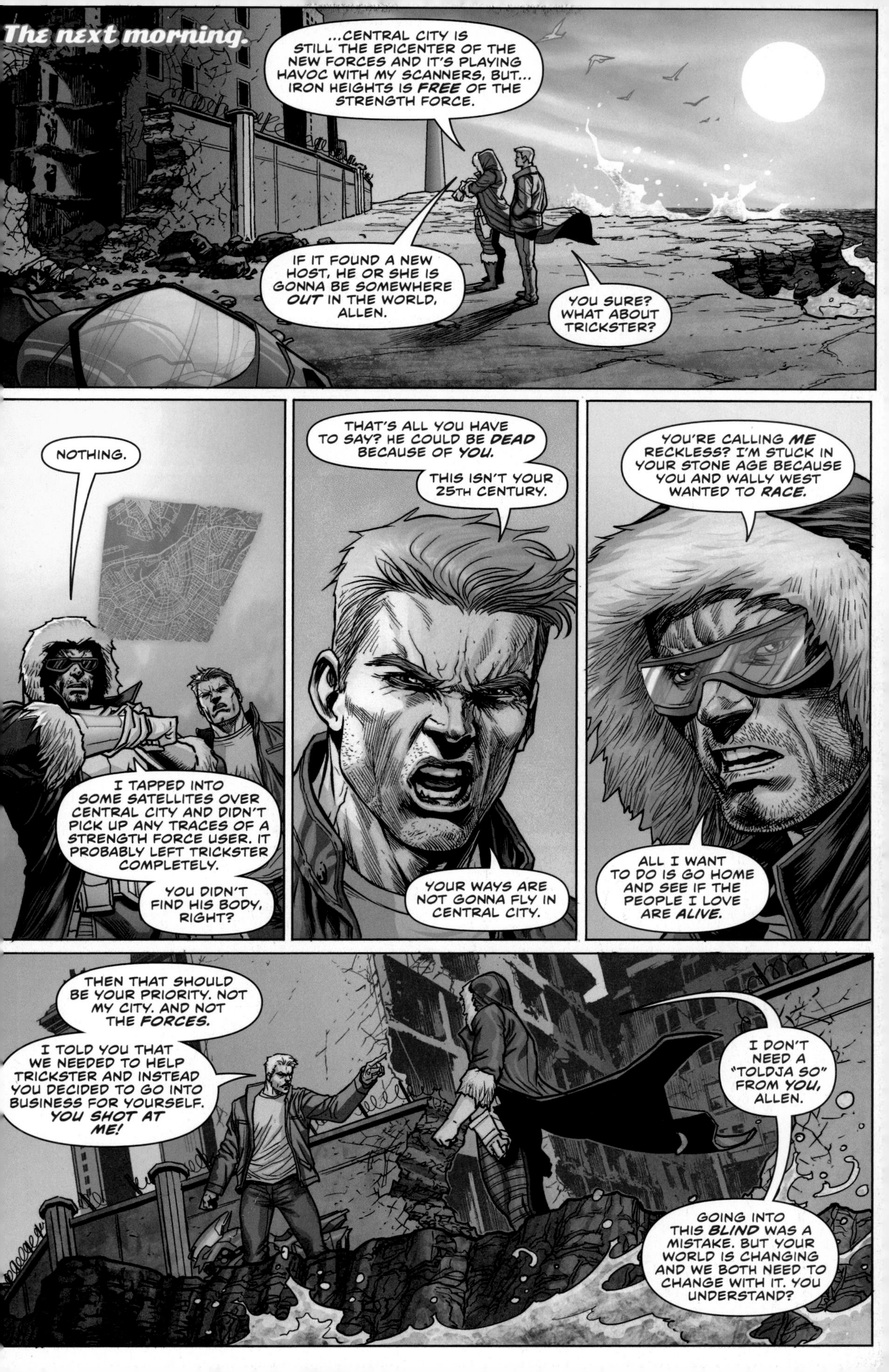

The next morning.
...CENTRAL CITY IS STILL THE EPICENTER OF THE NEW FORCES AND IT'S PLAYING HAVOC WITH MY SCANNERS, BUT... IRON HEIGHTS IS FREE OF THE STRENGTH FORCE.
IF IT FOUND A NEW HOST, HE OR SHE IS GONNA BE SOMEWHERE OUT IN THE WORLD, ALLEN.
YOU SURE? WHAT ABOUT TRICKSTER?
NOTHING.
I TAPPED INTO SOME SATELLITES OVER CENTRAL CITY AND DIDN'T PICK UP ANY TRACES OF A STRENGTH FORCE USER. IT PROBABLY LEFT TRICKSTER COMPLETELY.
YOU DIDN'T FIND HIS BODY, RIGHT?
THAT'S ALL YOU HAVE TO SAY? HE COULD BE DEAD BECAUSE OF YOU.
THIS ISN'T YOUR 25TH CENTURY.
YOUR WAYS ARE NOT GONNA FLY IN CENTRAL CITY.
YOU'RE CALLING ME RECKLESS? I'M STUCK IN YOUR STONE AGE BECAUSE YOU AND WALLY WEST WANTED TO RACE.
ALL I WANT TO DO IS GO HOME AND SEE IF THE PEOPLE I LOVE ARE ALIVE.
THEN THAT SHOULD BE YOUR PRIORITY. NOT MY CITY. AND NOT THE FORCES.
I TOLD YOU THAT WE NEEDED TO HELP TRICKSTER AND INSTEAD YOU DECIDED TO GO INTO BUSINESS FOR YOURSELF. YOU SHOT AT ME!
I DON'T NEED A "TOLDJA SO" FROM YOU, ALLEN.
GOING INTO THIS BLIND WAS A MISTAKE. BUT YOUR WORLD IS CHANGING AND WE BOTH NEED TO CHANGE WITH IT. YOU UNDERSTAND?

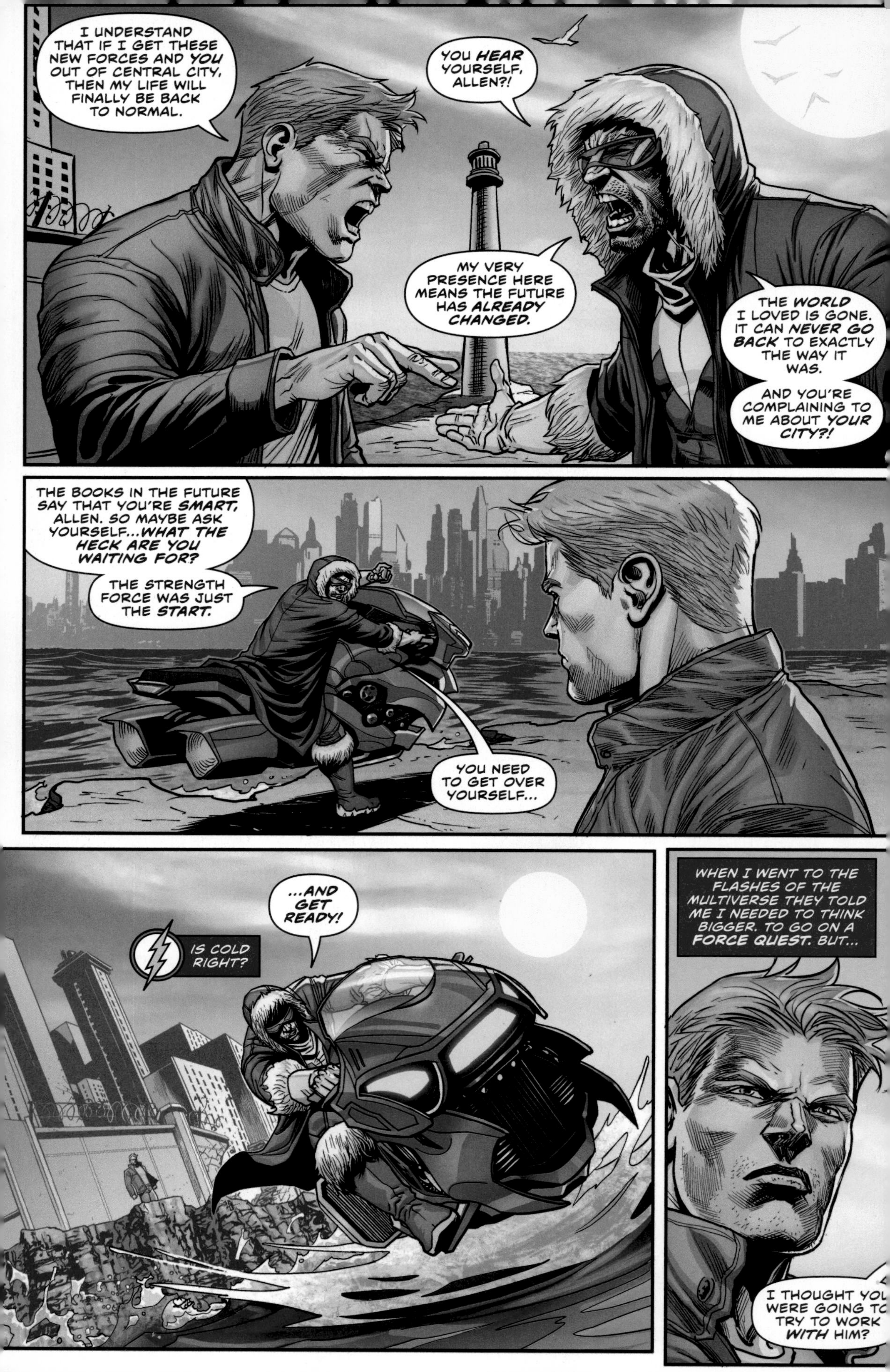
I UNDERSTAND THAT IF I GET THESE NEW FORCES AND YOU OUT OF CENTRAL CITY, THEN MY LIFE WILL FINALLY BE BACK TO NORMAL.
YOU HEAR YOURSELF, ALLEN?!
MY VERY PRESENCE HERE MEANS THE FUTURE HAS ALREADY CHANGED.
THE WORLD I LOVED IS GONE. IT CAN NEVER GO BACK TO EXACTLY THE WAY IT WAS.
AND YOU'RE COMPLAINING TO ME ABOUT YOUR CITY?!
THE BOOKS IN THE FUTURE SAY THAT YOU'RE SMART, ALLEN. SO MAYBE ASK YOURSELF...WHAT THE HECK ARE YOU WAITING FOR?
THE STRENGTH FORCE WAS JUST THE START.
YOU NEED TO GET OVER YOURSELF...
...AND GET READY!
IS COLD RIGHT?
WHEN I WENT TO THE FLASHES OF THE MULTIVERSE THEY TOLD ME I NEEDED TO THINK BIGGER. TO GO ON A FORCE QUEST. BUT...
I THOUGHT YOU WERE GOING TO TRY TO WORK WITH HIM?

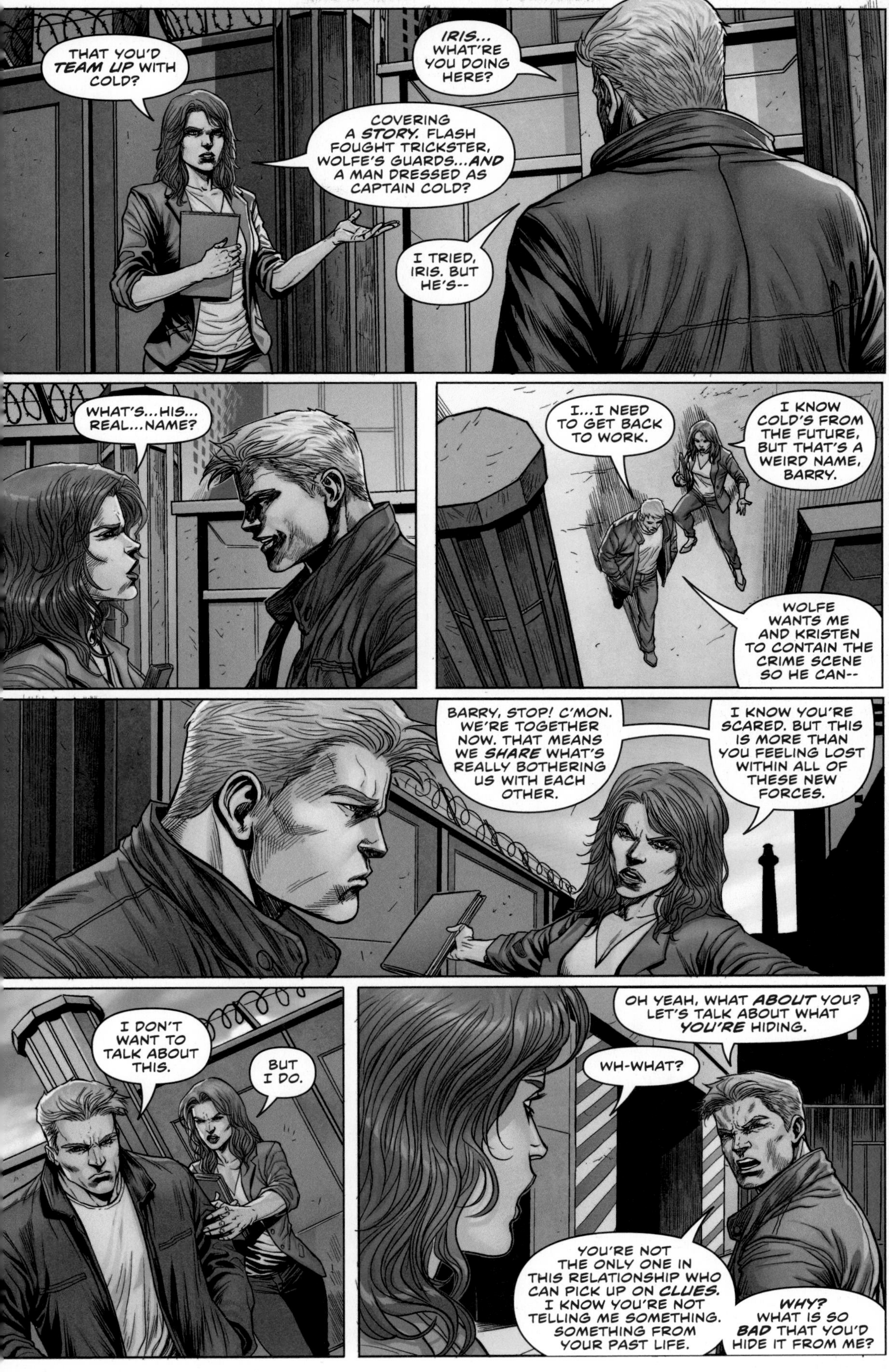
THAT YOU'D *TEAM UP* WITH COLD?
IRIS... WHAT'RE YOU DOING HERE?
COVERING A *STORY.* FLASH FOUGHT TRICKSTER, WOLFE'S GUARDS...*AND* A MAN DRESSED AS CAPTAIN COLD?
I TRIED, IRIS. BUT HE'S--
WHAT'S...HIS... REAL...NAME?
I...I NEED TO GET BACK TO WORK.
I KNOW COLD'S FROM THE FUTURE, BUT THAT'S A WEIRD NAME, BARRY.
WOLFE WANTS ME AND KRISTEN TO CONTAIN THE CRIME SCENE SO HE CAN--
BARRY, STOP! C'MON. WE'RE TOGETHER NOW. THAT MEANS WE *SHARE* WHAT'S REALLY BOTHERING US WITH EACH OTHER.
I KNOW YOU'RE SCARED. BUT THIS IS MORE THAN YOU FEELING LOST WITHIN ALL OF THESE NEW FORCES.
I DON'T WANT TO TALK ABOUT THIS.
BUT I DO.
OH YEAH, WHAT *ABOUT* YOU? LET'S TALK ABOUT WHAT *YOU'RE* HIDING.
WH-WHAT?
YOU'RE NOT THE ONLY ONE IN THIS RELATIONSHIP WHO CAN PICK UP ON *CLUES.* I KNOW YOU'RE NOT TELLING ME SOMETHING. SOMETHING FROM YOUR PAST LIFE.
WHY? WHAT IS SO *BAD* THAT YOU'D HIDE IT FROM ME?

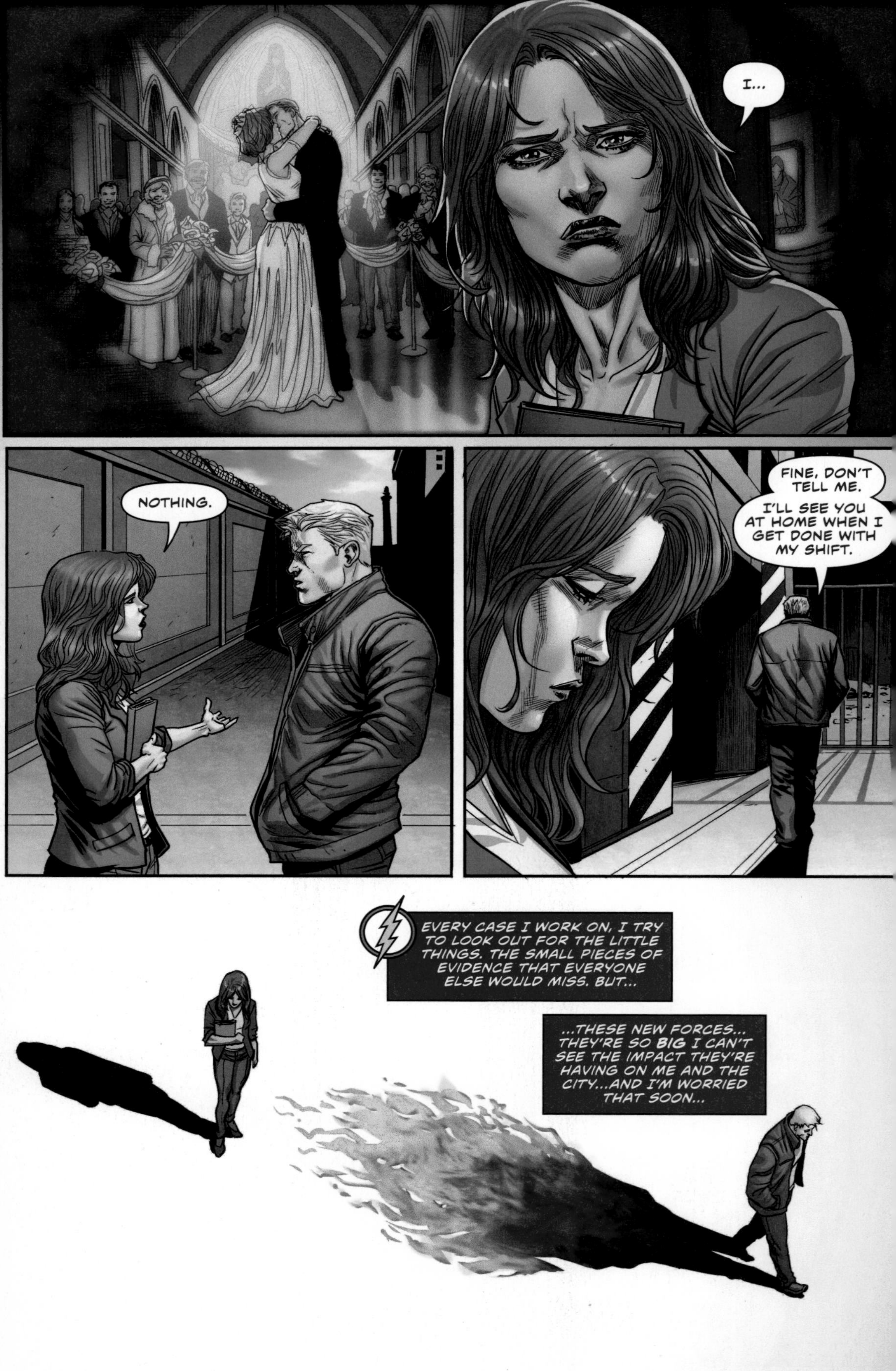
I...
NOTHING.
FINE, DON'T TELL ME.
I'LL SEE YOU AT HOME WHEN I GET DONE WITH MY SHIFT.
EVERY CASE I WORK ON, I TRY TO LOOK OUT FOR THE LITTLE THINGS. THE SMALL PIECES OF EVIDENCE THAT EVERYONE ELSE WOULD MISS. BUT...
...THESE NEW FORCES... THEY'RE SO BIG I CAN'T SEE THE IMPACT THEY'RE HAVING ON ME AND THE CITY...AND I'M WORRIED THAT SOON...

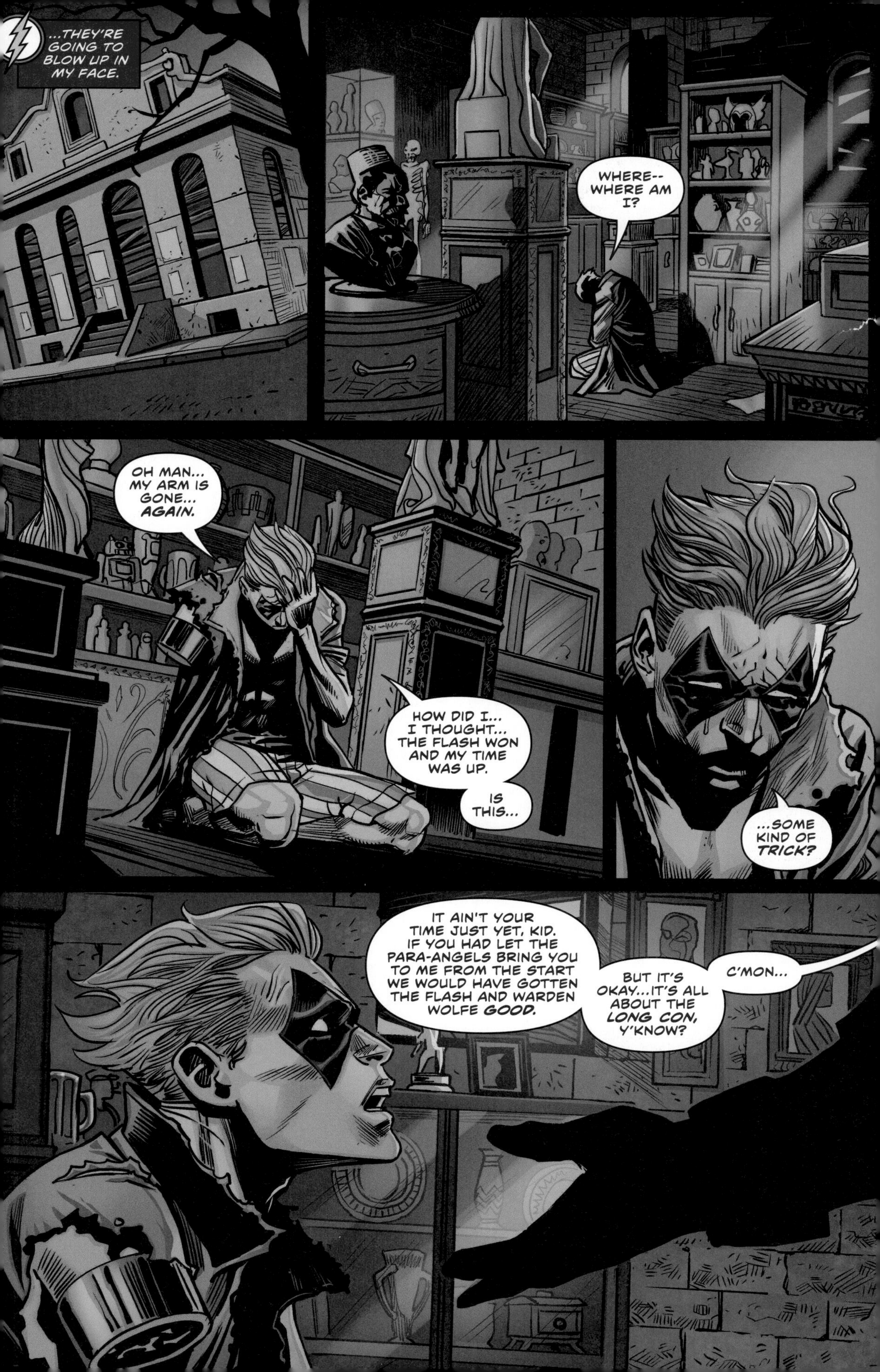
...THEY'RE GOING TO BLOW UP IN MY FACE.
WHERE-- WHERE AM I?
OH MAN... MY ARM IS GONE... AGAIN.
HOW DID I... I THOUGHT... THE FLASH WON AND MY TIME WAS UP.
IS THIS...
...SOME KIND OF TRICK?
IT AIN'T YOUR TIME JUST YET, KID. IF YOU HAD LET THE PARA-ANGELS BRING YOU TO ME FROM THE START WE WOULD HAVE GOTTEN THE FLASH AND WARDEN WOLFE GOOD.
BUT IT'S OKAY...IT'S ALL ABOUT THE LONG CON, Y'KNOW?
C'MON...

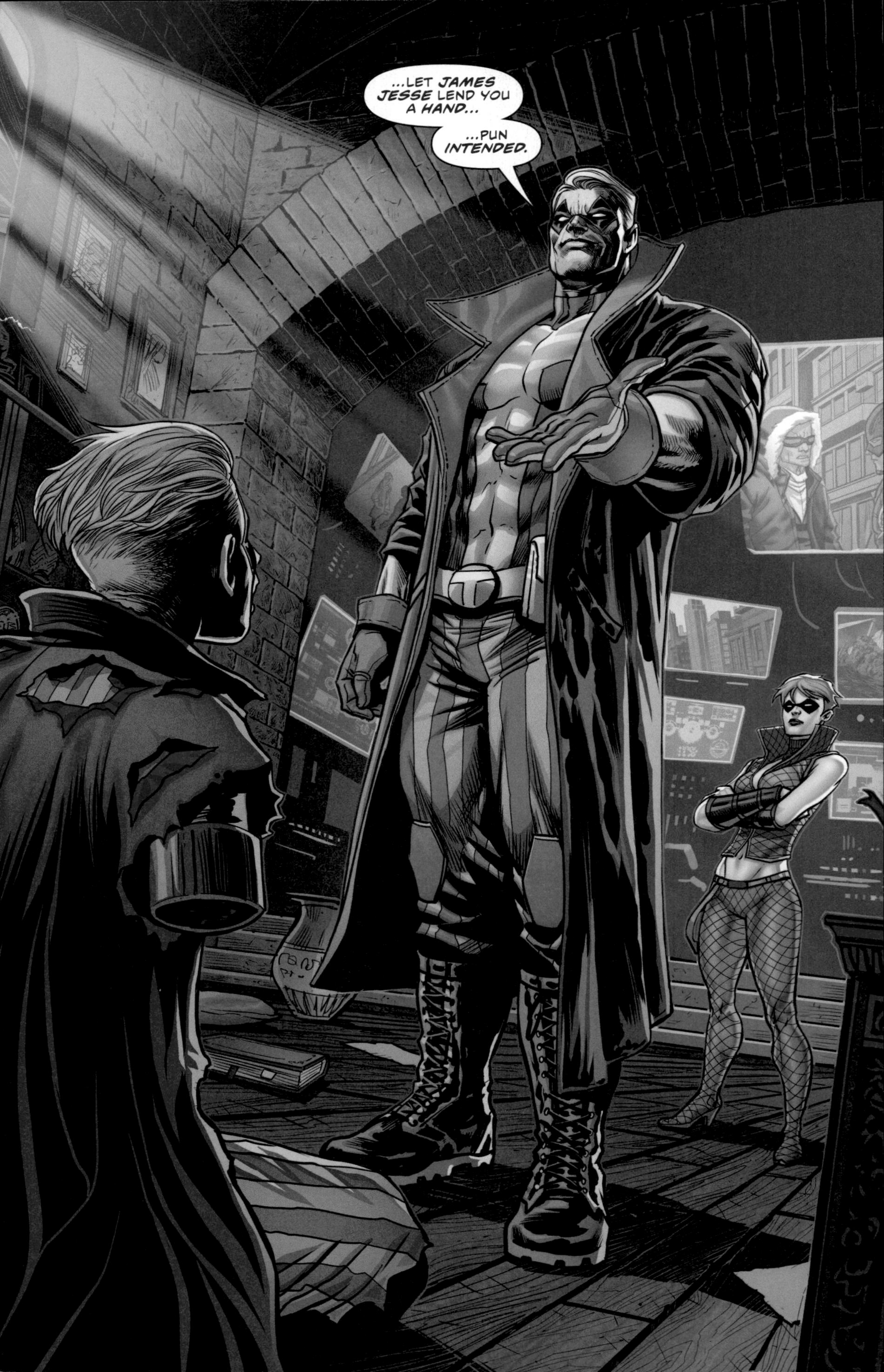
...LET JAMES JESSE LEND YOU A HAND...
...PUN INTENDED.

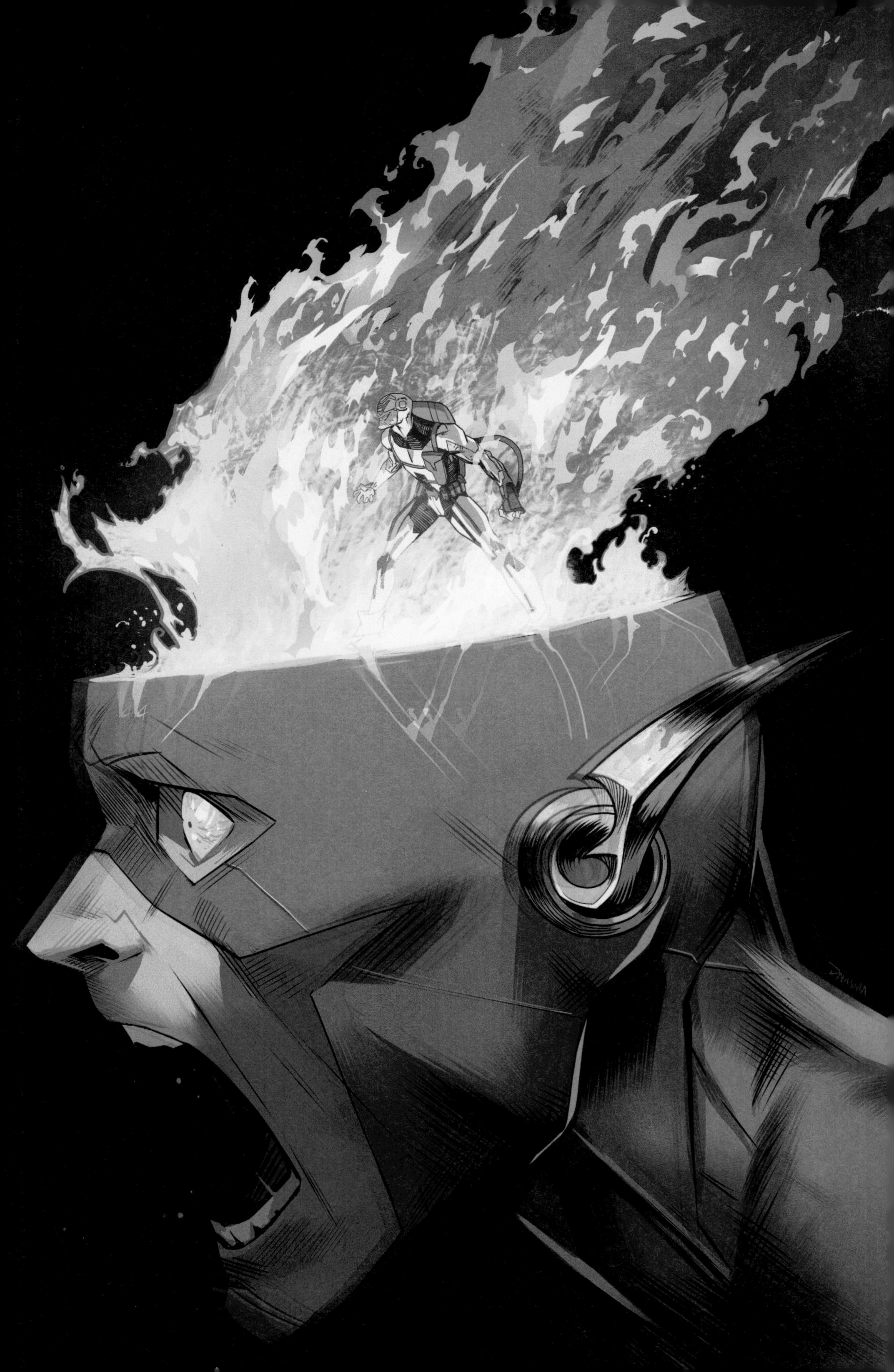

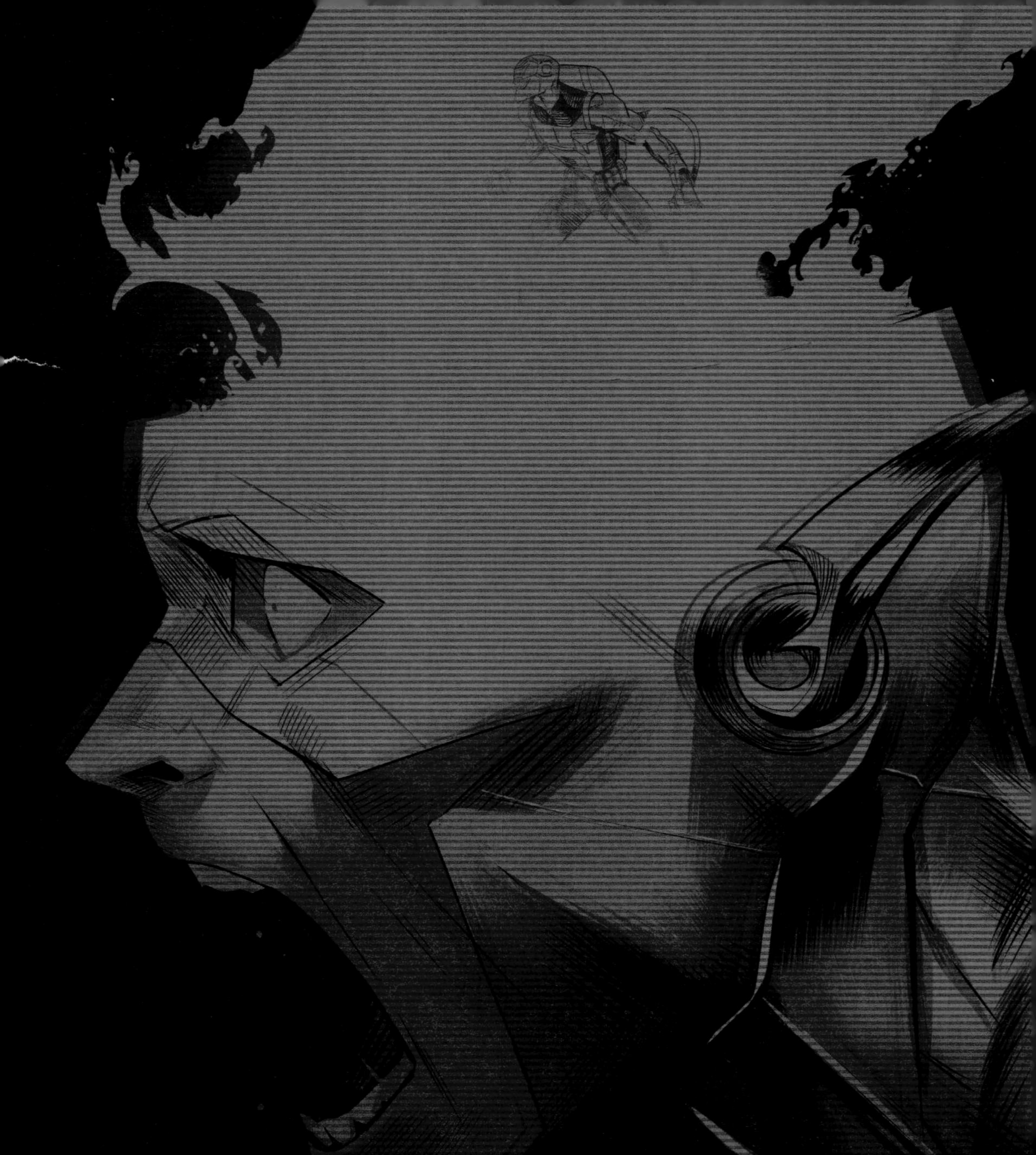

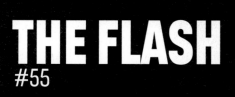

THE FLASH
#55

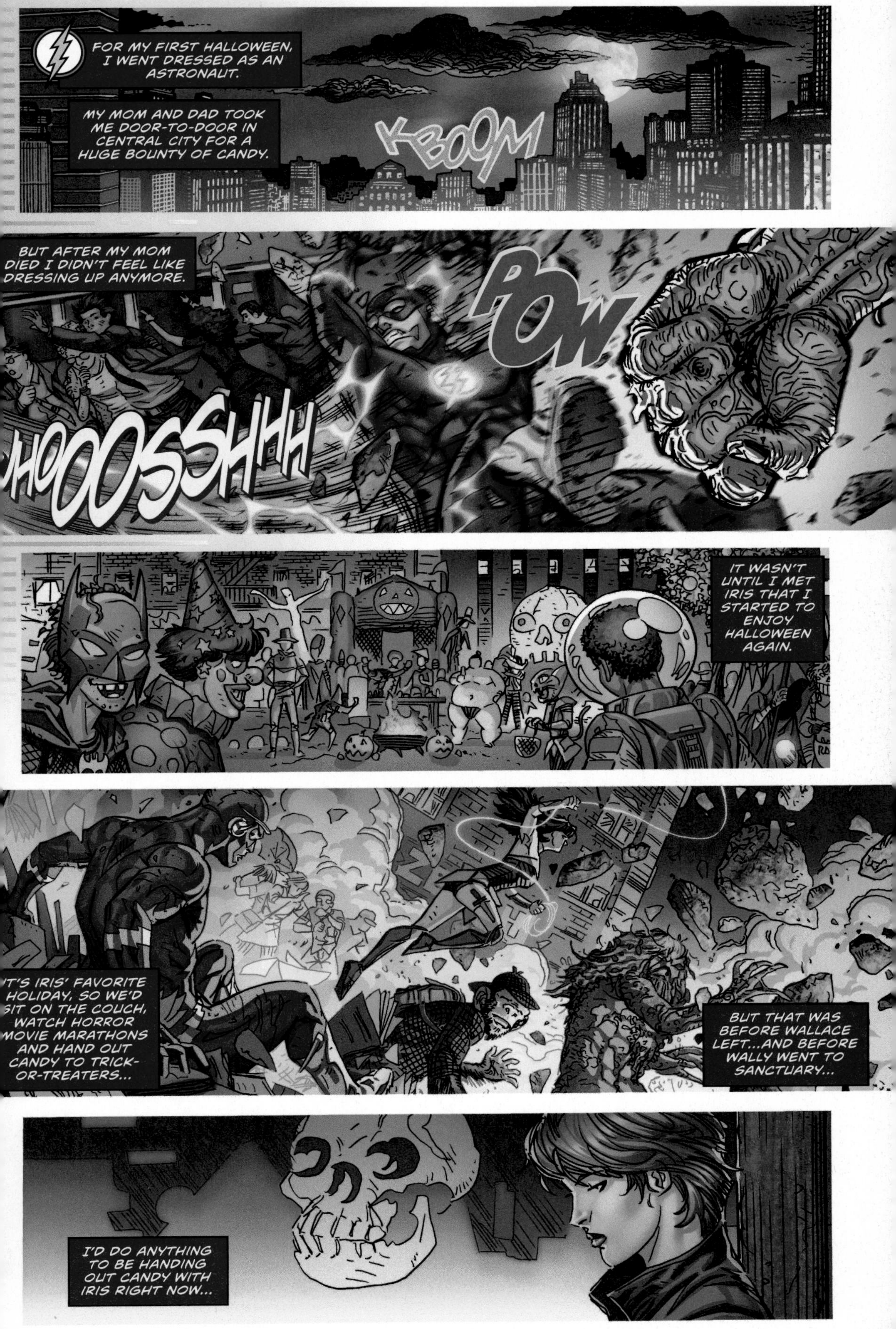
FOR MY FIRST HALLOWEEN, I WENT DRESSED AS AN ASTRONAUT.
MY MOM AND DAD TOOK ME DOOR-TO-DOOR IN CENTRAL CITY FOR A HUGE BOUNTY OF CANDY.
K-BOOM
BUT AFTER MY MOM DIED I DIDN'T FEEL LIKE DRESSING UP ANYMORE.
POW
HOOOSSHHH
IT WASN'T UNTIL I MET IRIS THAT I STARTED TO ENJOY HALLOWEEN AGAIN.
IT'S IRIS' FAVORITE HOLIDAY, SO WE'D SIT ON THE COUCH, WATCH HORROR MOVIE MARATHONS AND HAND OUT CANDY TO TRICK-OR-TREATERS...
BUT THAT WAS BEFORE WALLACE LEFT...AND BEFORE WALLY WENT TO SANCTUARY...
I'D DO ANYTHING TO BE HANDING OUT CANDY WITH IRIS RIGHT NOW...

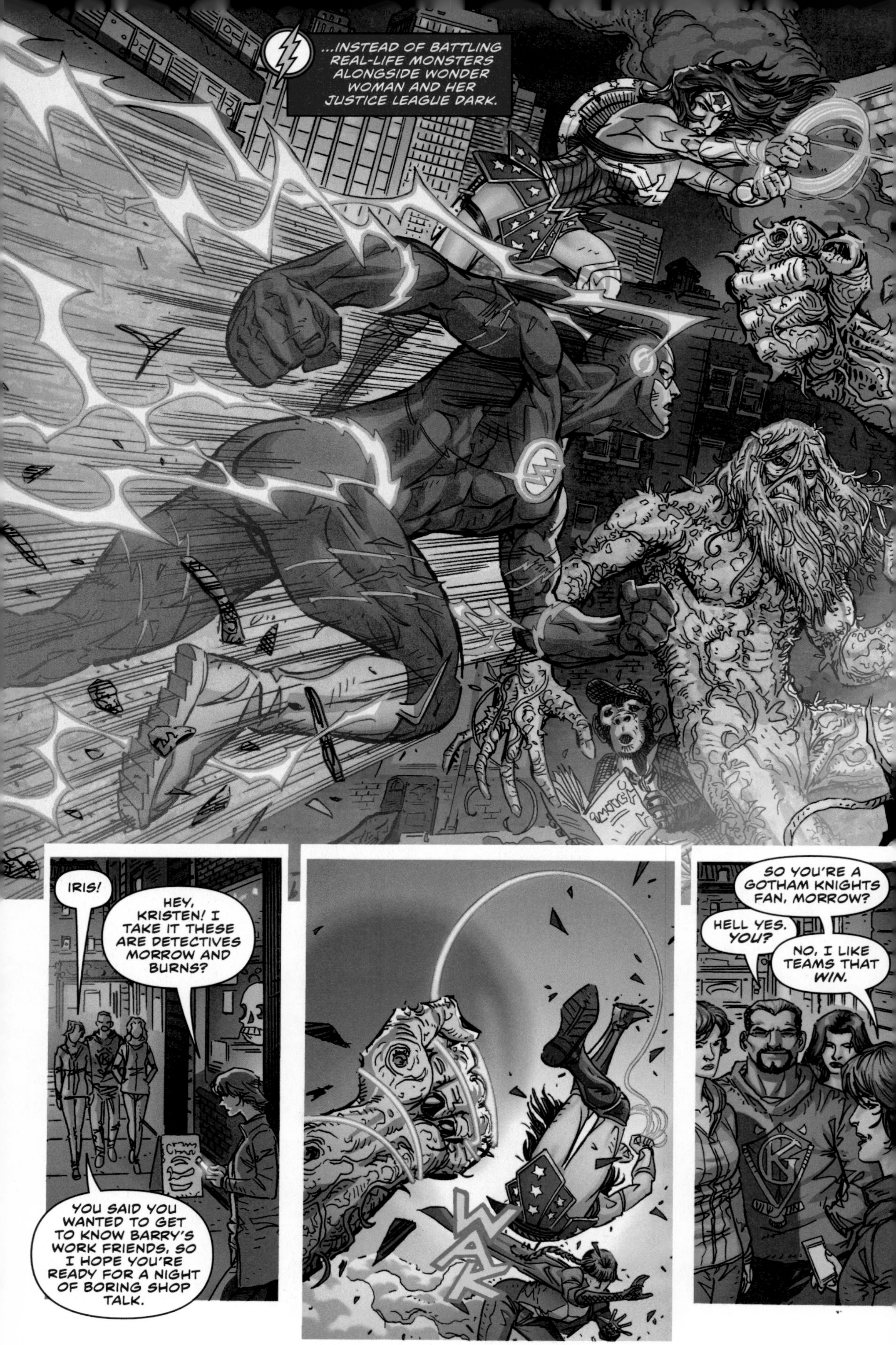
...INSTEAD OF BATTLING REAL-LIFE MONSTERS ALONGSIDE WONDER WOMAN AND HER JUSTICE LEAGUE DARK.
IRIS!
HEY, KRISTEN! I TAKE IT THESE ARE DETECTIVES MORROW AND BURNS?
YOU SAID YOU WANTED TO GET TO KNOW BARRY'S WORK FRIENDS, SO I HOPE YOU'RE READY FOR A NIGHT OF BORING SHOP TALK.
WAK
SO YOU'RE A GOTHAM KNIGHTS FAN, MORROW?
HELL YES. *YOU?*
NO, I LIKE TEAMS THAT *WIN.*

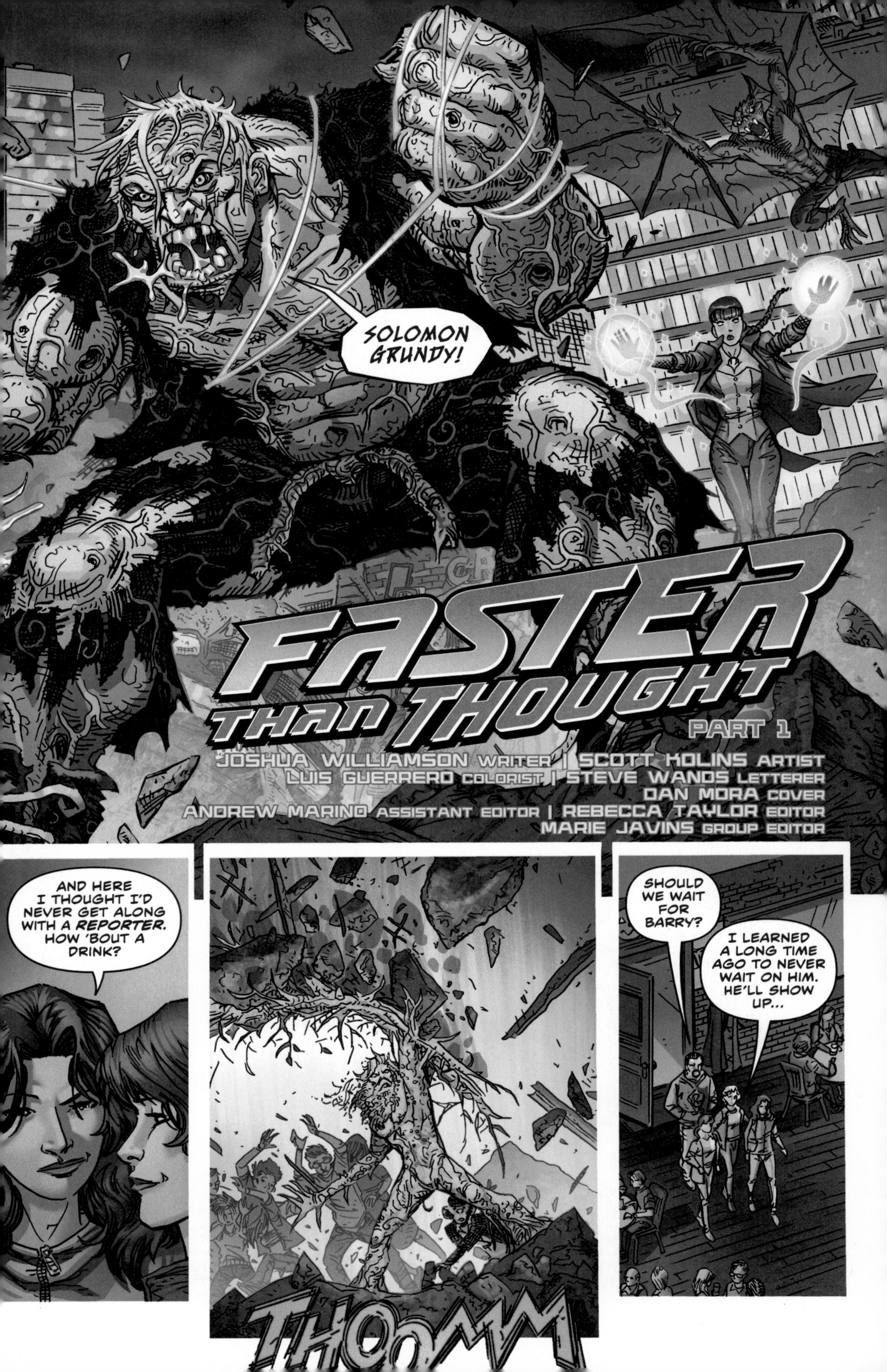
SOLOMON GRUNDY!
FASTER THAN THOUGHT
PART 1
JOSHUA WILLIAMSON WRITER | SCOTT KOLINS ARTIST
LUIS GUERRERO COLORIST | STEVE WANDS LETTERER
DAN MORA COVER
ANDREW MARINO ASSISTANT EDITOR | REBECCA TAYLOR EDITOR
MARIE JAVINS GROUP EDITOR
AND HERE I THOUGHT I'D NEVER GET ALONG WITH A *REPORTER*. HOW 'BOUT A DRINK?
THOOMM
SHOULD WE WAIT FOR BARRY?
I LEARNED A LONG TIME AGO TO NEVER WAIT ON HIM. HE'LL SHOW UP...

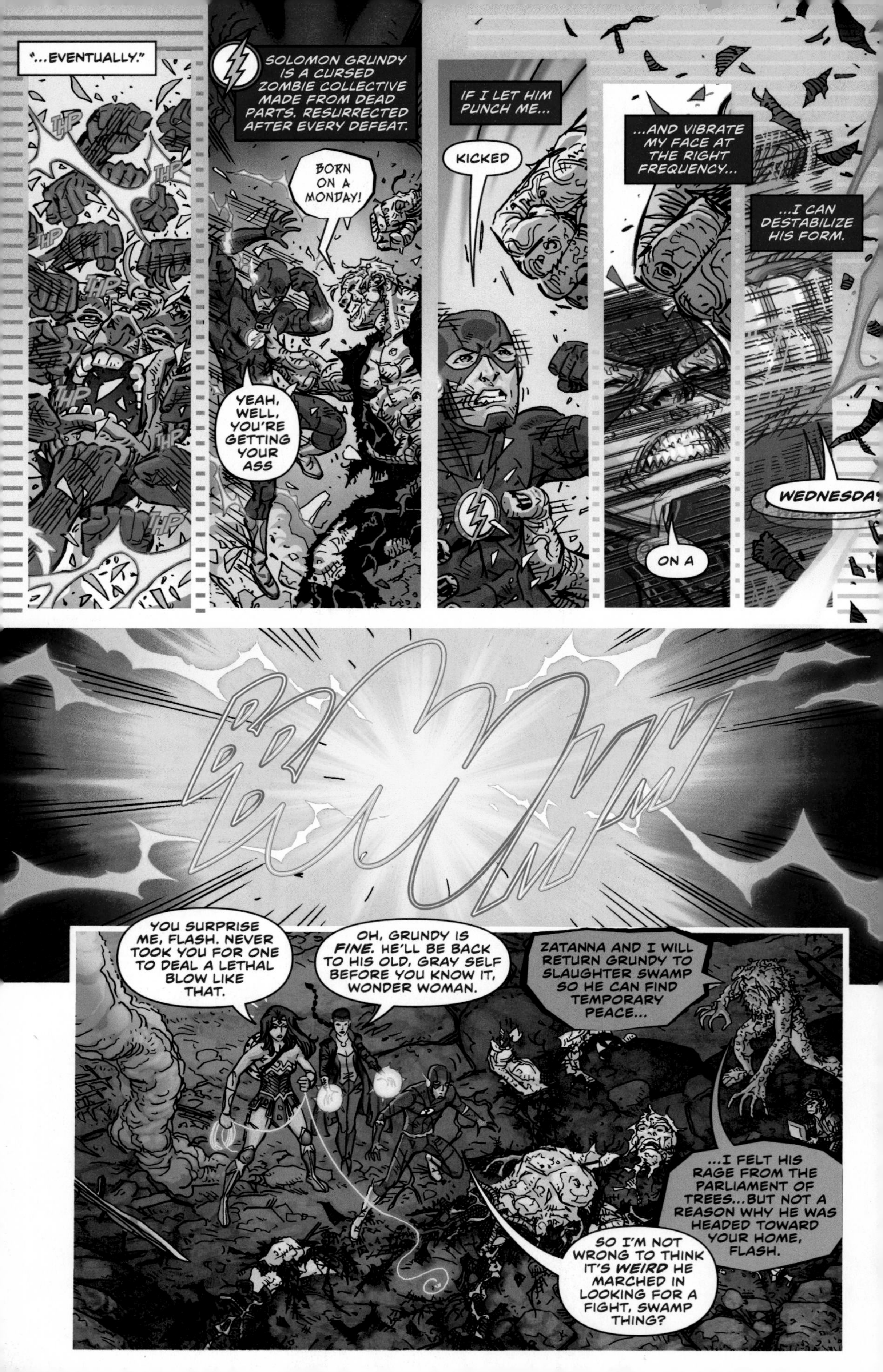
"...EVENTUALLY."
THP
THP
THP
THP
THP
THP
THP
SOLOMON GRUNDY IS A CURSED ZOMBIE COLLECTIVE MADE FROM DEAD PARTS. RESURRECTED AFTER EVERY DEFEAT.
BORN ON A MONDAY!
YEAH, WELL, YOU'RE GETTING YOUR ASS
IF I LET HIM PUNCH ME...
KICKED
...AND VIBRATE MY FACE AT THE RIGHT FREQUENCY...
ON A
...I CAN DESTABILIZE HIS FORM.
WEDNESDA
YOU SURPRISE ME, FLASH. NEVER TOOK YOU FOR ONE TO DEAL A LETHAL BLOW LIKE THAT.
OH, GRUNDY IS FINE. HE'LL BE BACK TO HIS OLD, GRAY SELF BEFORE YOU KNOW IT, WONDER WOMAN.
ZATANNA AND I WILL RETURN GRUNDY TO SLAUGHTER SWAMP SO HE CAN FIND TEMPORARY PEACE...
...I FELT HIS RAGE FROM THE PARLIAMENT OF TREES...BUT NOT A REASON WHY HE WAS HEADED TOWARD YOUR HOME, FLASH.
SO I'M NOT WRONG TO THINK IT'S WEIRD HE MARCHED IN LOOKING FOR A FIGHT, SWAMP THING?

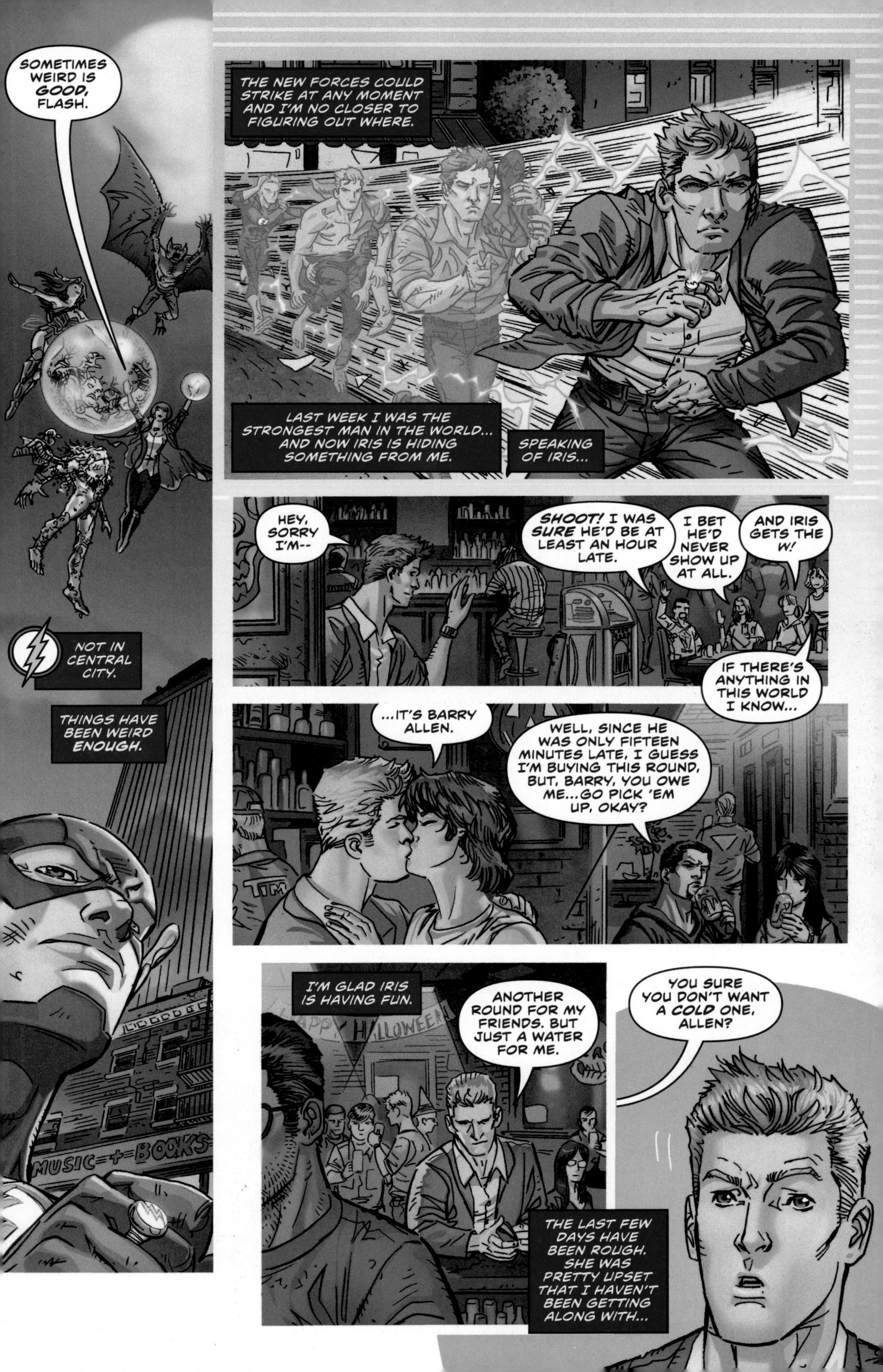

SOMETIMES WEIRD IS GOOD, FLASH.
NOT IN CENTRAL CITY.
THINGS HAVE BEEN WEIRD ENOUGH.
MUSIC + BOOKS
THE NEW FORCES COULD STRIKE AT ANY MOMENT AND I'M NO CLOSER TO FIGURING OUT WHERE.
LAST WEEK I WAS THE STRONGEST MAN IN THE WORLD... AND NOW IRIS IS HIDING SOMETHING FROM ME.
SPEAKING OF IRIS...
HEY, SORRY I'M--
SHOOT! I WAS SURE HE'D BE AT LEAST AN HOUR LATE.
I BET HE'D NEVER SHOW UP AT ALL.
AND IRIS GETS THE W!
IF THERE'S ANYTHING IN THIS WORLD I KNOW...
...IT'S BARRY ALLEN.
WELL, SINCE HE WAS ONLY FIFTEEN MINUTES LATE, I GUESS I'M BUYING THIS ROUND, BUT, BARRY, YOU OWE ME...GO PICK 'EM UP, OKAY?
I'M GLAD IRIS IS HAVING FUN.
HAPPY HALLOWEEN
ANOTHER ROUND FOR MY FRIENDS. BUT JUST A WATER FOR ME.
THE LAST FEW DAYS HAVE BEEN ROUGH. SHE WAS PRETTY UPSET THAT I HAVEN'T BEEN GETTING ALONG WITH...
YOU SURE YOU DON'T WANT A COLD ONE, ALLEN?

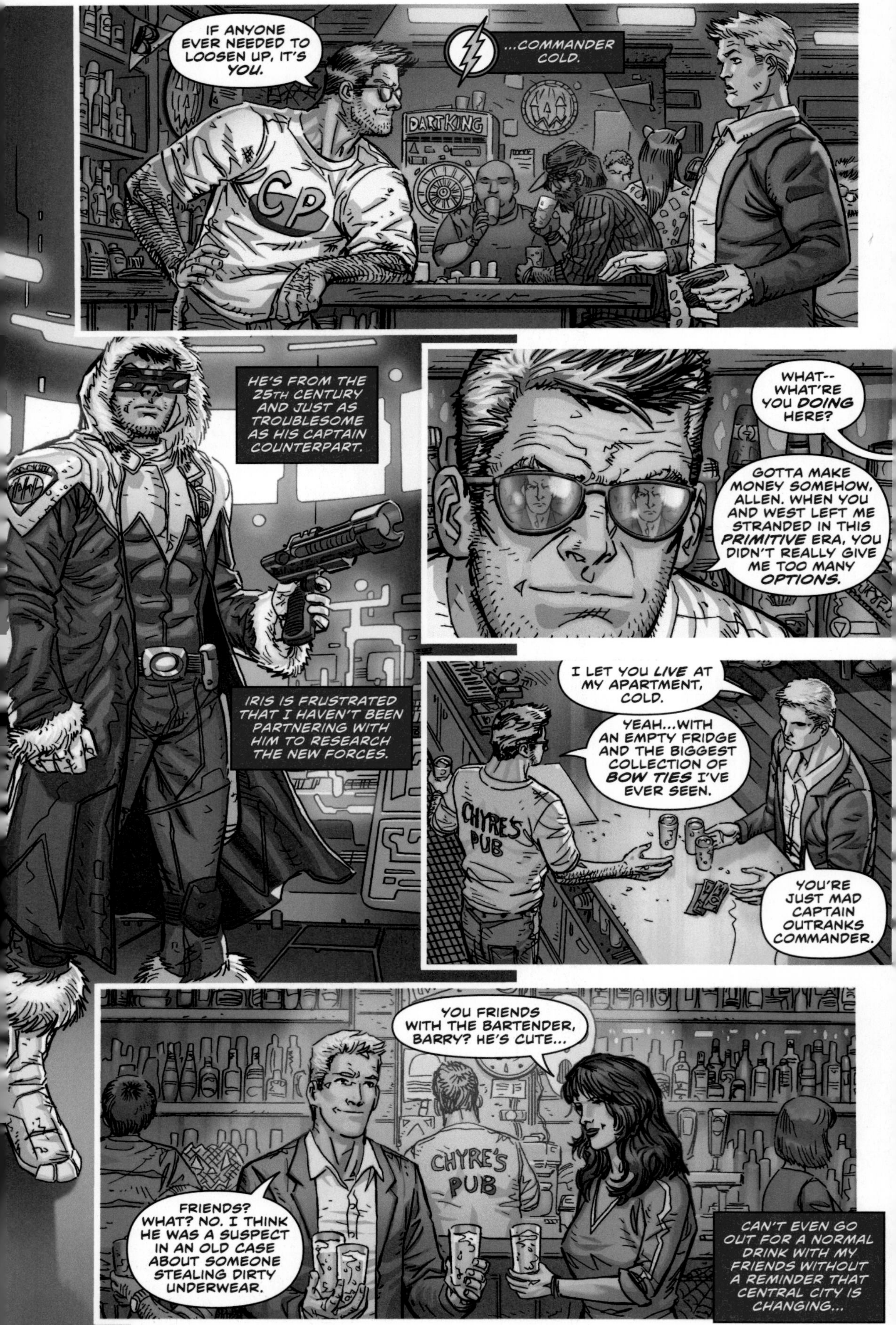
IF ANYONE EVER NEEDED TO LOOSEN UP, IT'S YOU.
...COMMANDER COLD.
DART KING
HE'S FROM THE 25TH CENTURY AND JUST AS TROUBLESOME AS HIS CAPTAIN COUNTERPART.
IRIS IS FRUSTRATED THAT I HAVEN'T BEEN PARTNERING WITH HIM TO RESEARCH THE NEW FORCES.
WHAT-- WHAT'RE YOU DOING HERE?
GOTTA MAKE MONEY SOMEHOW, ALLEN. WHEN YOU AND WEST LEFT ME STRANDED IN THIS PRIMITIVE ERA, YOU DIDN'T REALLY GIVE ME TOO MANY OPTIONS.
I LET YOU LIVE AT MY APARTMENT, COLD.
YEAH...WITH AN EMPTY FRIDGE AND THE BIGGEST COLLECTION OF BOW TIES I'VE EVER SEEN.
CHYRE'S PUB
YOU'RE JUST MAD CAPTAIN OUTRANKS COMMANDER.
YOU FRIENDS WITH THE BARTENDER, BARRY? HE'S CUTE...
CHYRE'S PUB
FRIENDS? WHAT? NO. I THINK HE WAS A SUSPECT IN AN OLD CASE ABOUT SOMEONE STEALING DIRTY UNDERWEAR.
CAN'T EVEN GO OUT FOR A NORMAL DRINK WITH MY FRIENDS WITHOUT A REMINDER THAT CENTRAL CITY IS CHANGING...

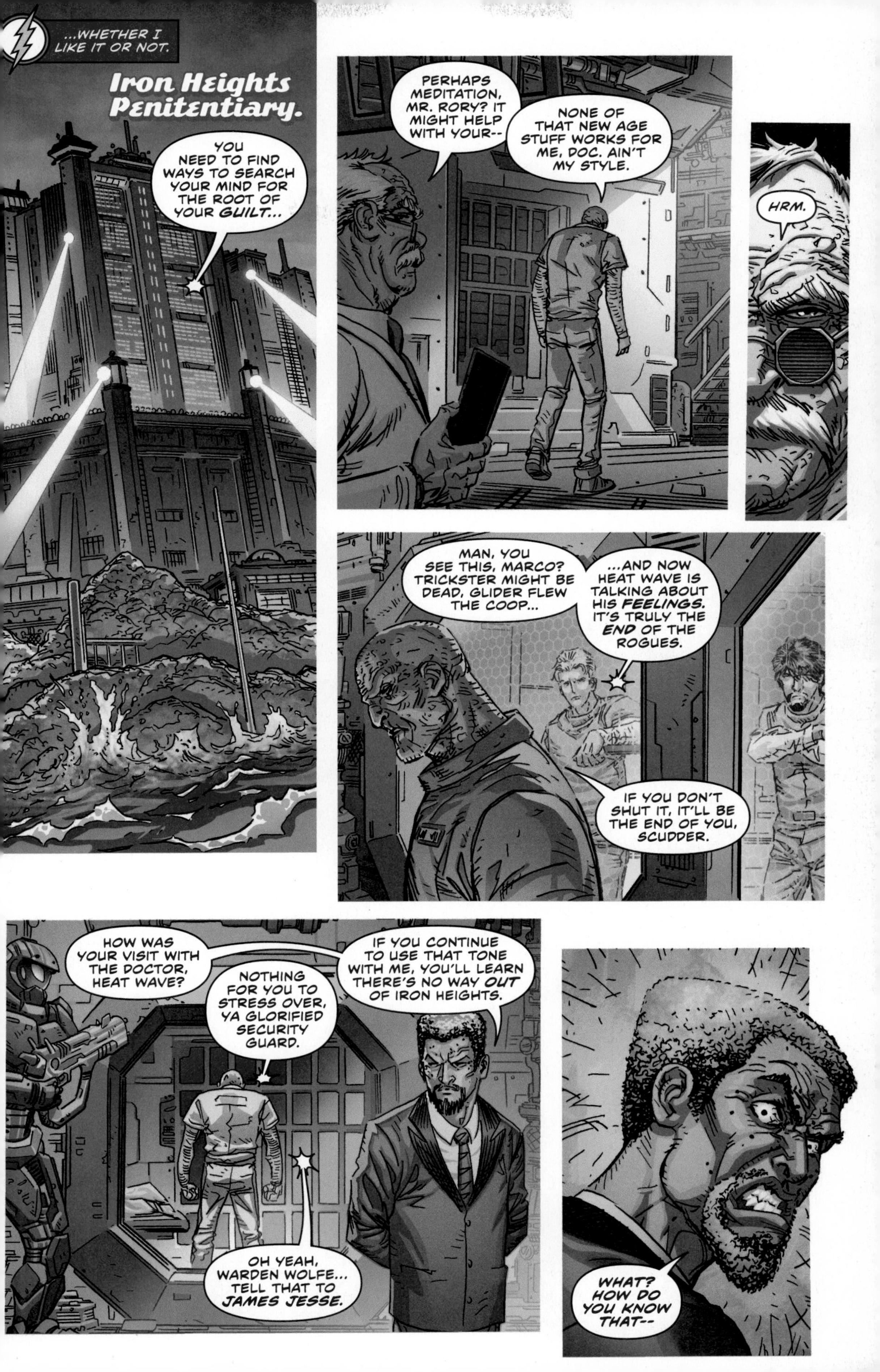
...WHETHER I LIKE IT OR NOT.
Iron Heights Penitentiary.
YOU NEED TO FIND WAYS TO SEARCH YOUR MIND FOR THE ROOT OF YOUR GUILT...
PERHAPS MEDITATION, MR. RORY? IT MIGHT HELP WITH YOUR--
NONE OF THAT NEW AGE STUFF WORKS FOR ME, DOC. AIN'T MY STYLE.
HRM.
MAN, YOU SEE THIS, MARCO? TRICKSTER MIGHT BE DEAD, GLIDER FLEW THE COOP...
...AND NOW HEAT WAVE IS TALKING ABOUT HIS FEELINGS. IT'S TRULY THE END OF THE ROGUES.
IF YOU DON'T SHUT IT, IT'LL BE THE END OF YOU, SCUDDER.
HOW WAS YOUR VISIT WITH THE DOCTOR, HEAT WAVE?
NOTHING FOR YOU TO STRESS OVER, YA GLORIFIED SECURITY GUARD.
IF YOU CONTINUE TO USE THAT TONE WITH ME, YOU'LL LEARN THERE'S NO WAY OUT OF IRON HEIGHTS.
OH YEAH, WARDEN WOLFE... TELL THAT TO JAMES JESSE.
WHAT? HOW DO YOU KNOW THAT--

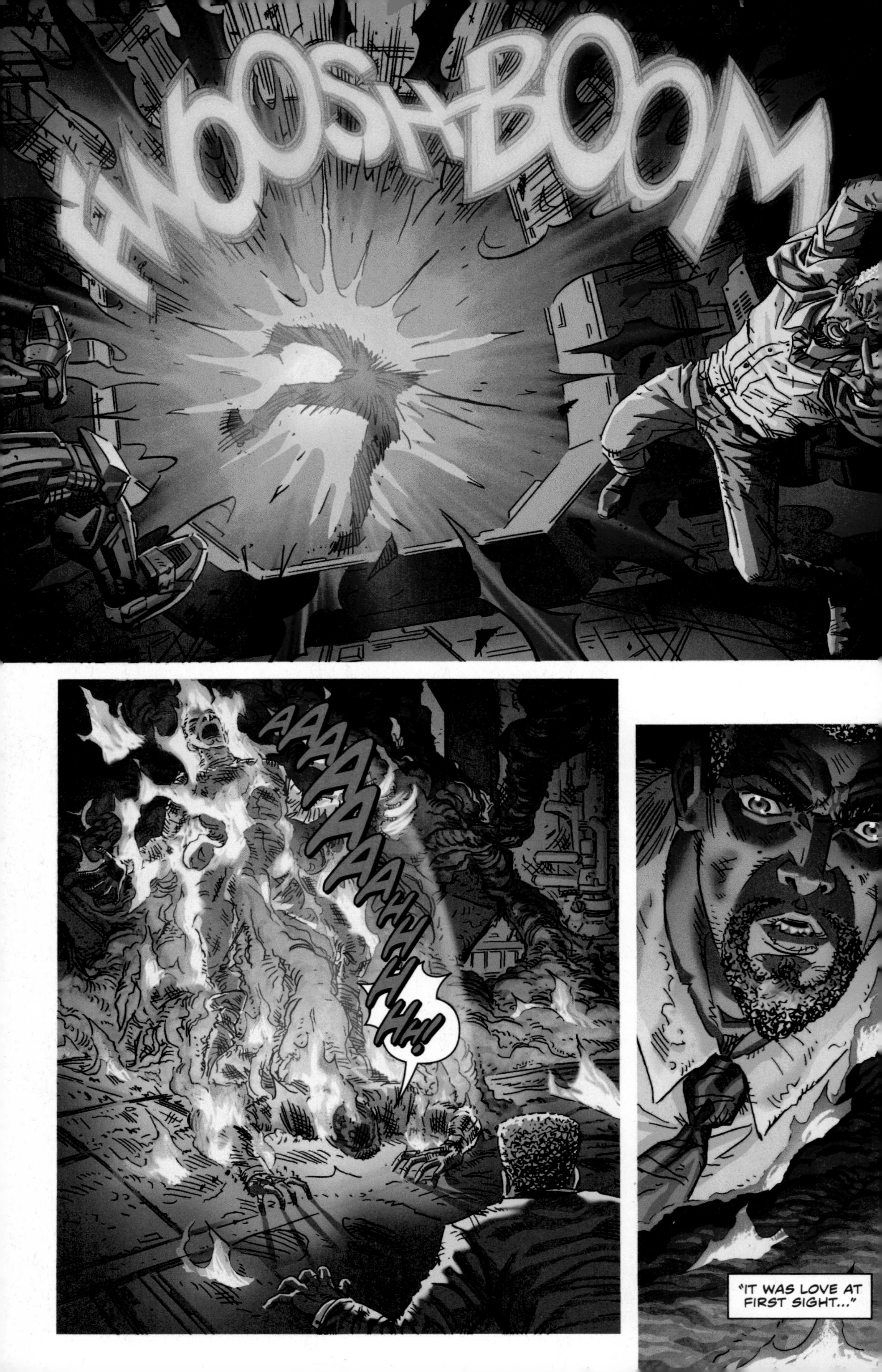
WHOOSH-BOOM
AAAAAAAAHHHHH!
"IT WAS LOVE AT FIRST SIGHT..."

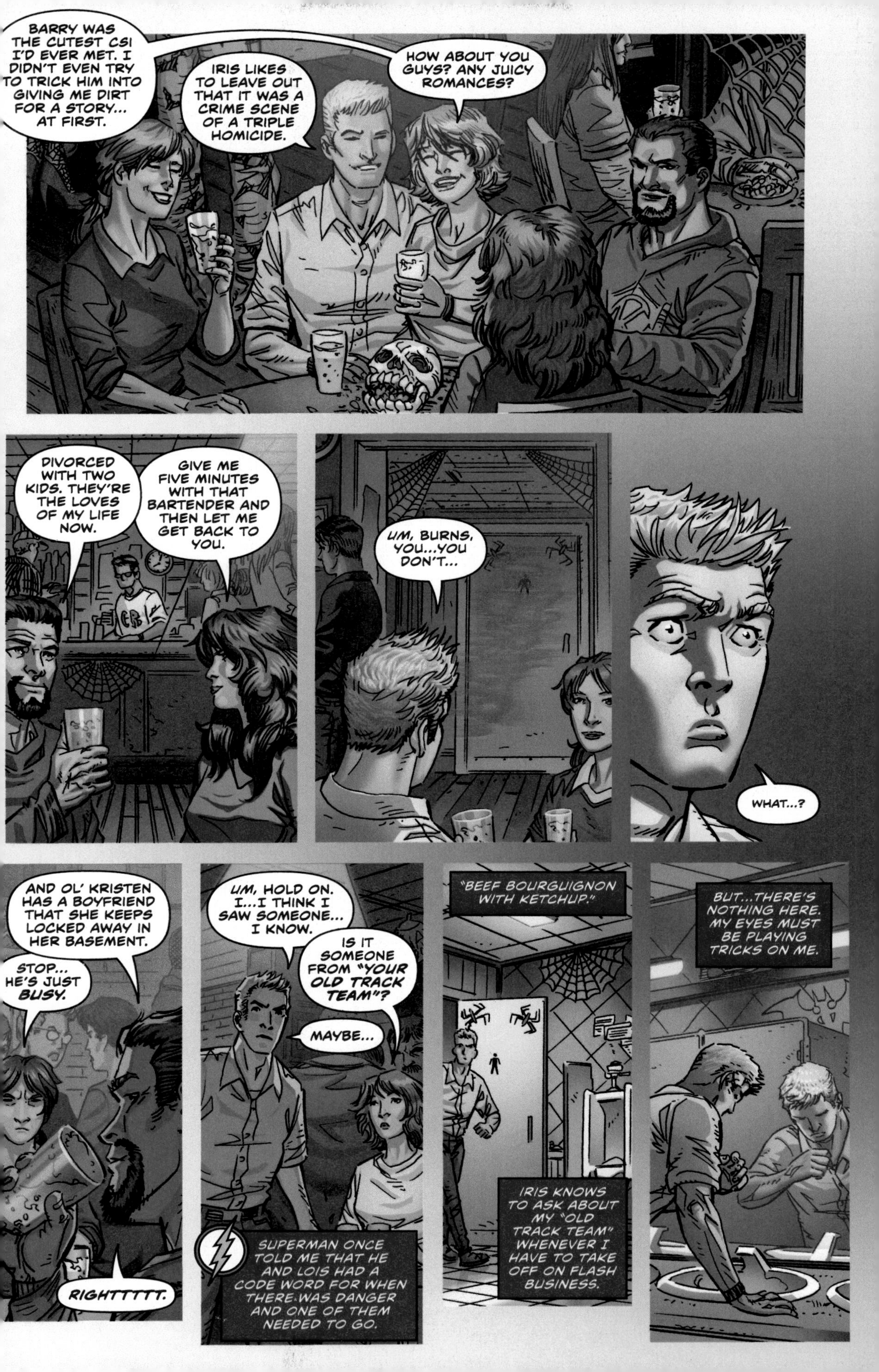
BARRY WAS THE CUTEST CSI I'D EVER MET. I DIDN'T EVEN TRY TO TRICK HIM INTO GIVING ME DIRT FOR A STORY... AT FIRST.
IRIS LIKES TO LEAVE OUT THAT IT WAS A CRIME SCENE OF A TRIPLE HOMICIDE.
HOW ABOUT YOU GUYS? ANY JUICY ROMANCES?
DIVORCED WITH TWO KIDS. THEY'RE THE LOVES OF MY LIFE NOW.
GIVE ME FIVE MINUTES WITH THAT BARTENDER AND THEN LET ME GET BACK TO YOU.
UM, BURNS, YOU...YOU DON'T...
WHAT...?
AND OL' KRISTEN HAS A BOYFRIEND THAT SHE KEEPS LOCKED AWAY IN HER BASEMENT.
STOP... HE'S JUST BUSY.
RIGHTTTTTT.
UM, HOLD ON. I...I THINK I SAW SOMEONE... I KNOW.
IS IT SOMEONE FROM "YOUR OLD TRACK TEAM"?
MAYBE...
SUPERMAN ONCE TOLD ME THAT HE AND LOIS HAD A CODE WORD FOR WHEN THERE WAS DANGER AND ONE OF THEM NEEDED TO GO.
"BEEF BOURGUIGNON WITH KETCHUP."
IRIS KNOWS TO ASK ABOUT MY "OLD TRACK TEAM" WHENEVER I HAVE TO TAKE OFF ON FLASH BUSINESS.
BUT...THERE'S NOTHING HERE. MY EYES MUST BE PLAYING TRICKS ON ME.

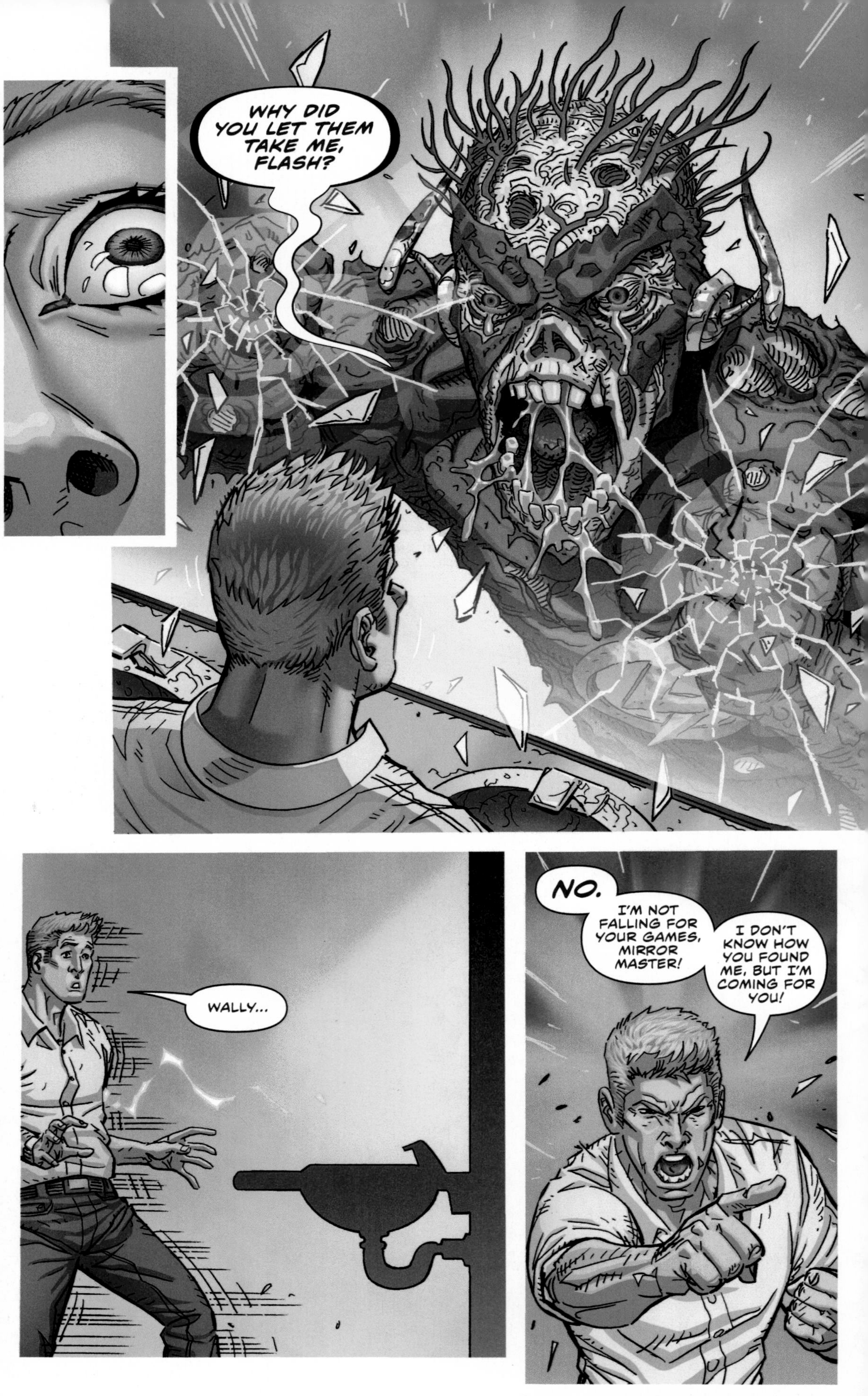
WHY DID YOU LET THEM TAKE ME, FLASH?
WALLY...
NO.
I'M NOT FALLING FOR YOUR GAMES, MIRROR MASTER!
I DON'T KNOW HOW YOU FOUND ME, BUT I'M COMING FOR YOU!

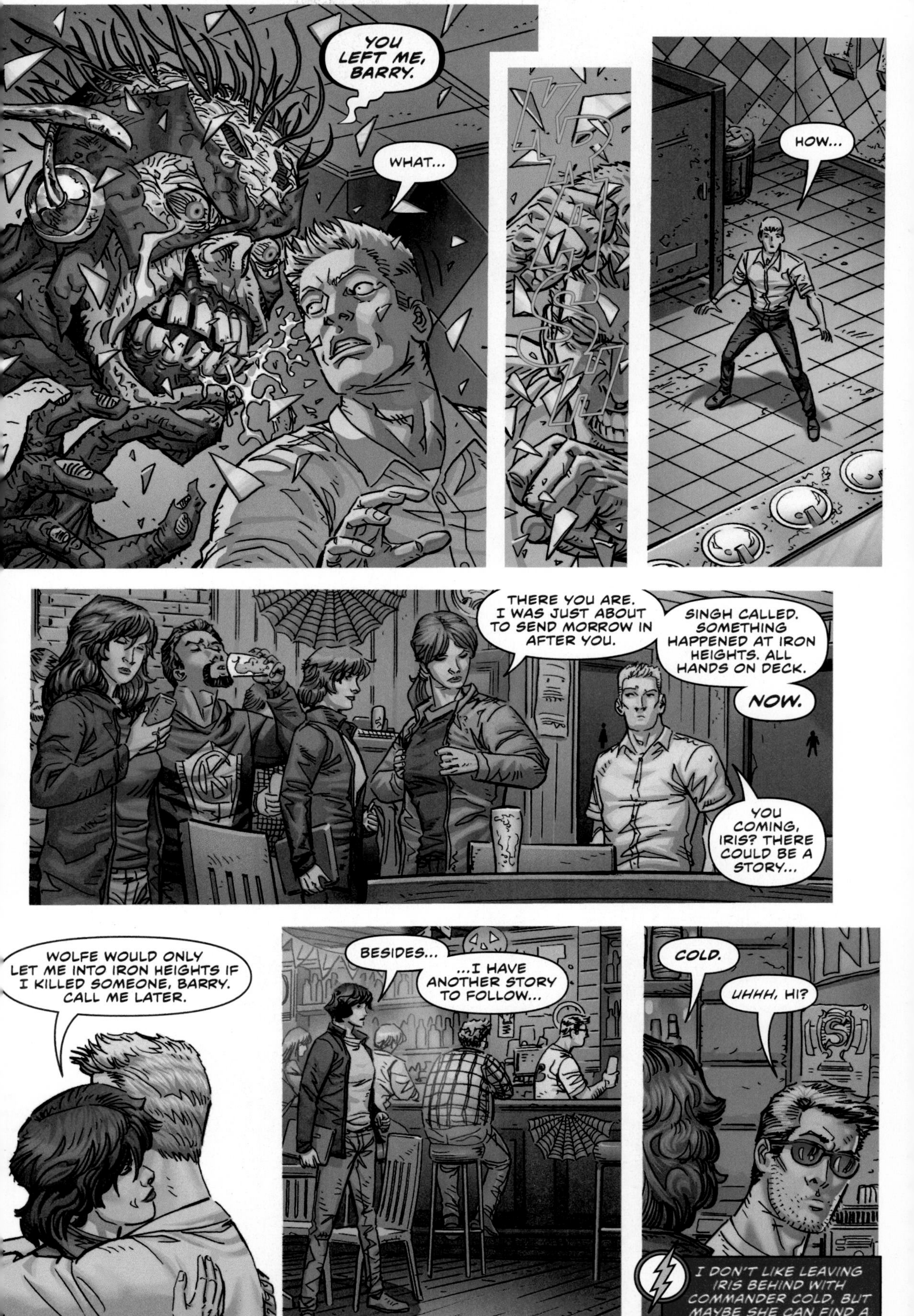
YOU LEFT ME, BARRY.
WHAT...
KRSSH
HOW...
THERE YOU ARE. I WAS JUST ABOUT TO SEND MORROW IN AFTER YOU.
SINGH CALLED. SOMETHING HAPPENED AT IRON HEIGHTS. ALL HANDS ON DECK.
NOW.
YOU COMING, IRIS? THERE COULD BE A STORY...
WOLFE WOULD ONLY LET ME INTO IRON HEIGHTS IF I KILLED SOMEONE, BARRY. CALL ME LATER.
BESIDES...
...I HAVE ANOTHER STORY TO FOLLOW...
COLD.
UHHH, HI?
I DON'T LIKE LEAVING IRIS BEHIND WITH COMMANDER COLD, BUT MAYBE SHE CAN FIND A WAY TO GET HIM TO OPEN UP ABOUT WHAT HE REALLY KNOWS...

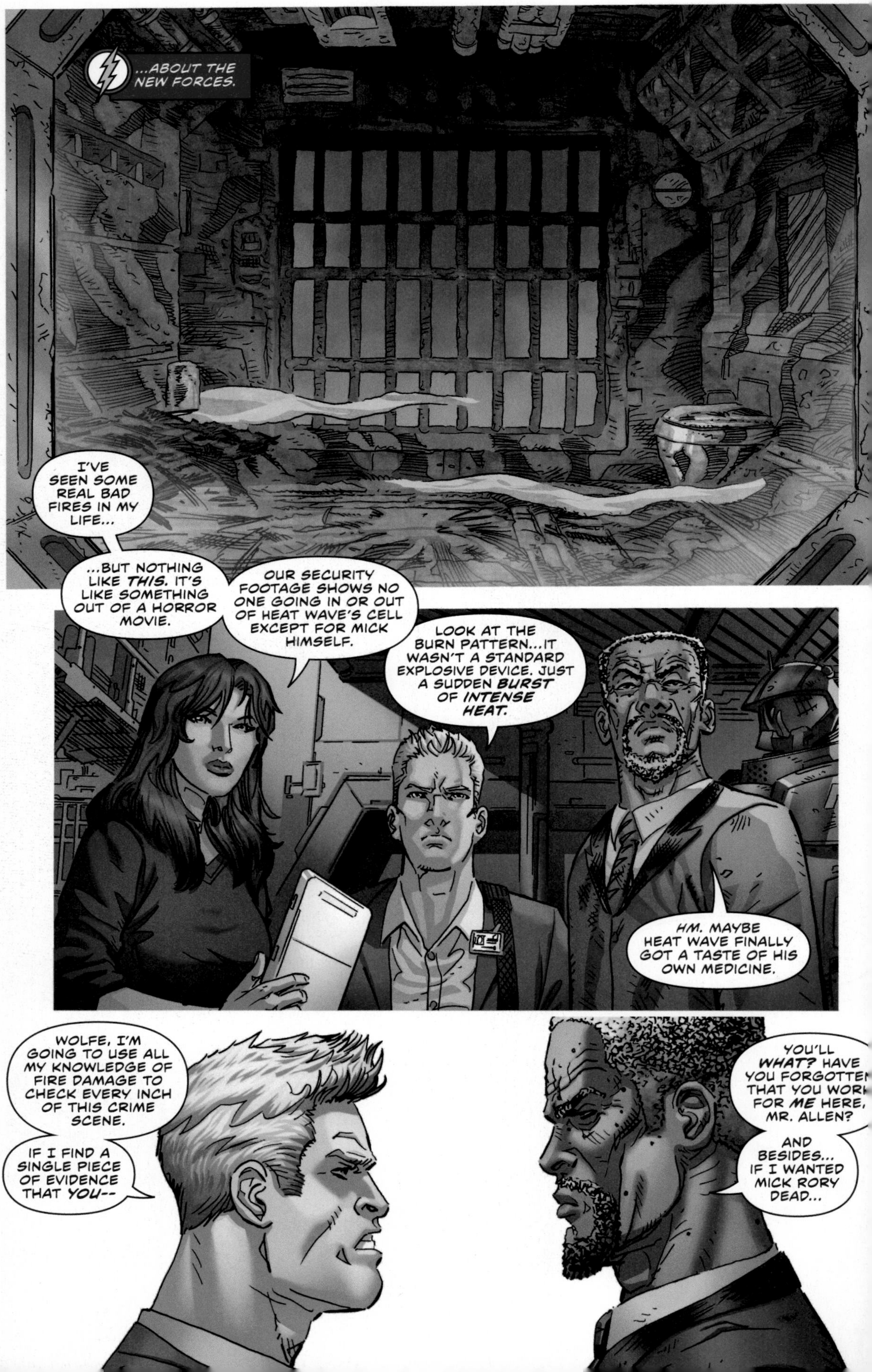
...ABOUT THE NEW FORCES.
I'VE SEEN SOME REAL BAD FIRES IN MY LIFE...
...BUT NOTHING LIKE THIS. IT'S LIKE SOMETHING OUT OF A HORROR MOVIE.
OUR SECURITY FOOTAGE SHOWS NO ONE GOING IN OR OUT OF HEAT WAVE'S CELL EXCEPT FOR MICK HIMSELF.
LOOK AT THE BURN PATTERN...IT WASN'T A STANDARD EXPLOSIVE DEVICE. JUST A SUDDEN BURST OF INTENSE HEAT.
HM. MAYBE HEAT WAVE FINALLY GOT A TASTE OF HIS OWN MEDICINE.
WOLFE, I'M GOING TO USE ALL MY KNOWLEDGE OF FIRE DAMAGE TO CHECK EVERY INCH OF THIS CRIME SCENE.
IF I FIND A SINGLE PIECE OF EVIDENCE THAT YOU--
YOU'LL WHAT? HAVE YOU FORGOTTEN THAT YOU WORK FOR ME HERE, MR. ALLEN?
AND BESIDES... IF I WANTED MICK RORY DEAD...

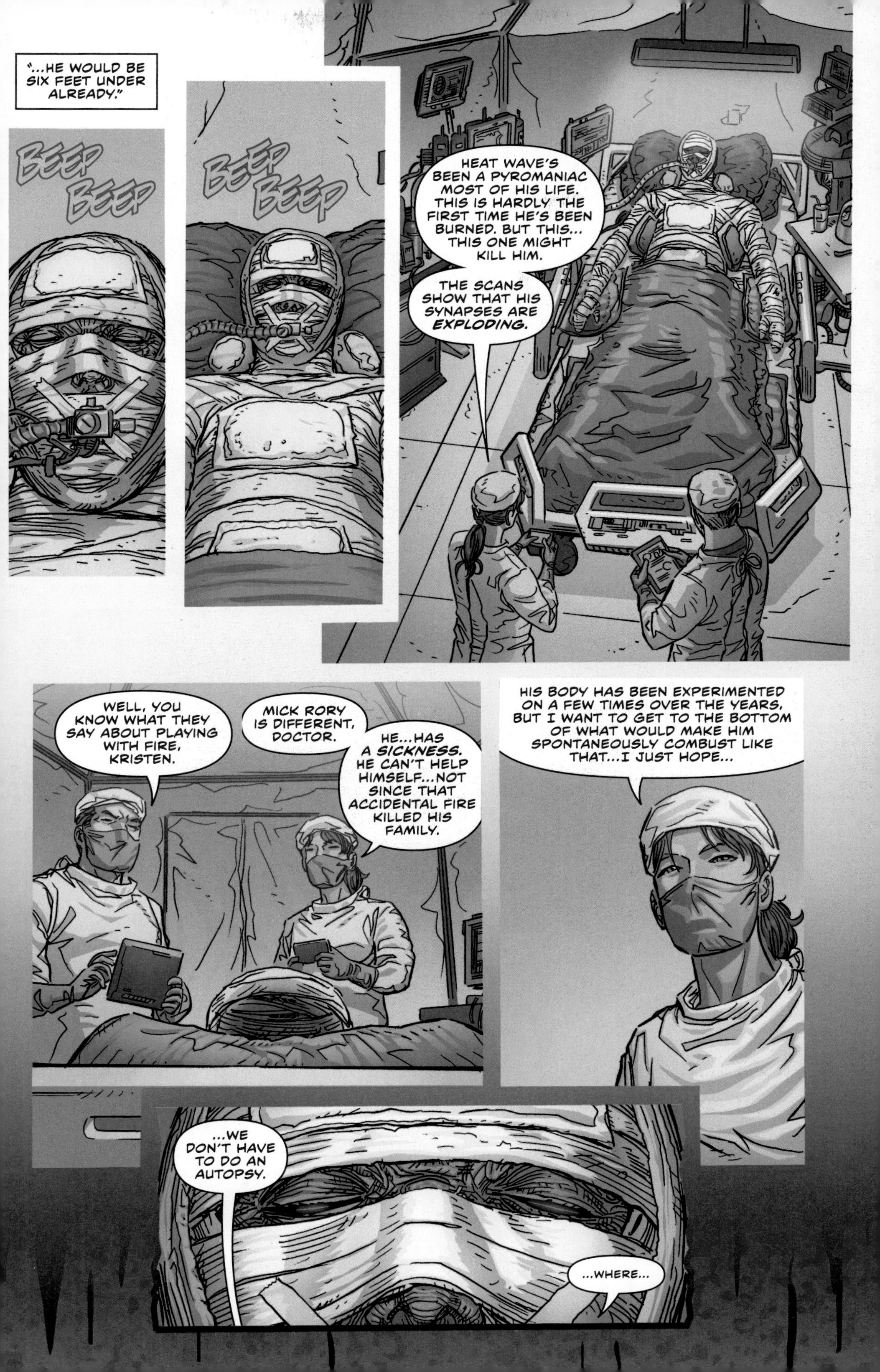
"...HE WOULD BE SIX FEET UNDER ALREADY."
BEEP BEEP
BEEP BEEP
HEAT WAVE'S BEEN A PYROMANIAC MOST OF HIS LIFE. THIS IS HARDLY THE FIRST TIME HE'S BEEN BURNED. BUT THIS... THIS ONE MIGHT KILL HIM.
THE SCANS SHOW THAT HIS SYNAPSES ARE EXPLODING.
WELL, YOU KNOW WHAT THEY SAY ABOUT PLAYING WITH FIRE, KRISTEN.
MICK RORY IS DIFFERENT, DOCTOR.
HE...HAS A SICKNESS. HE CAN'T HELP HIMSELF...NOT SINCE THAT ACCIDENTAL FIRE KILLED HIS FAMILY.
HIS BODY HAS BEEN EXPERIMENTED ON A FEW TIMES OVER THE YEARS, BUT I WANT TO GET TO THE BOTTOM OF WHAT WOULD MAKE HIM SPONTANEOUSLY COMBUST LIKE THAT...I JUST HOPE...
...WE DON'T HAVE TO DO AN AUTOPSY.
...WHERE...

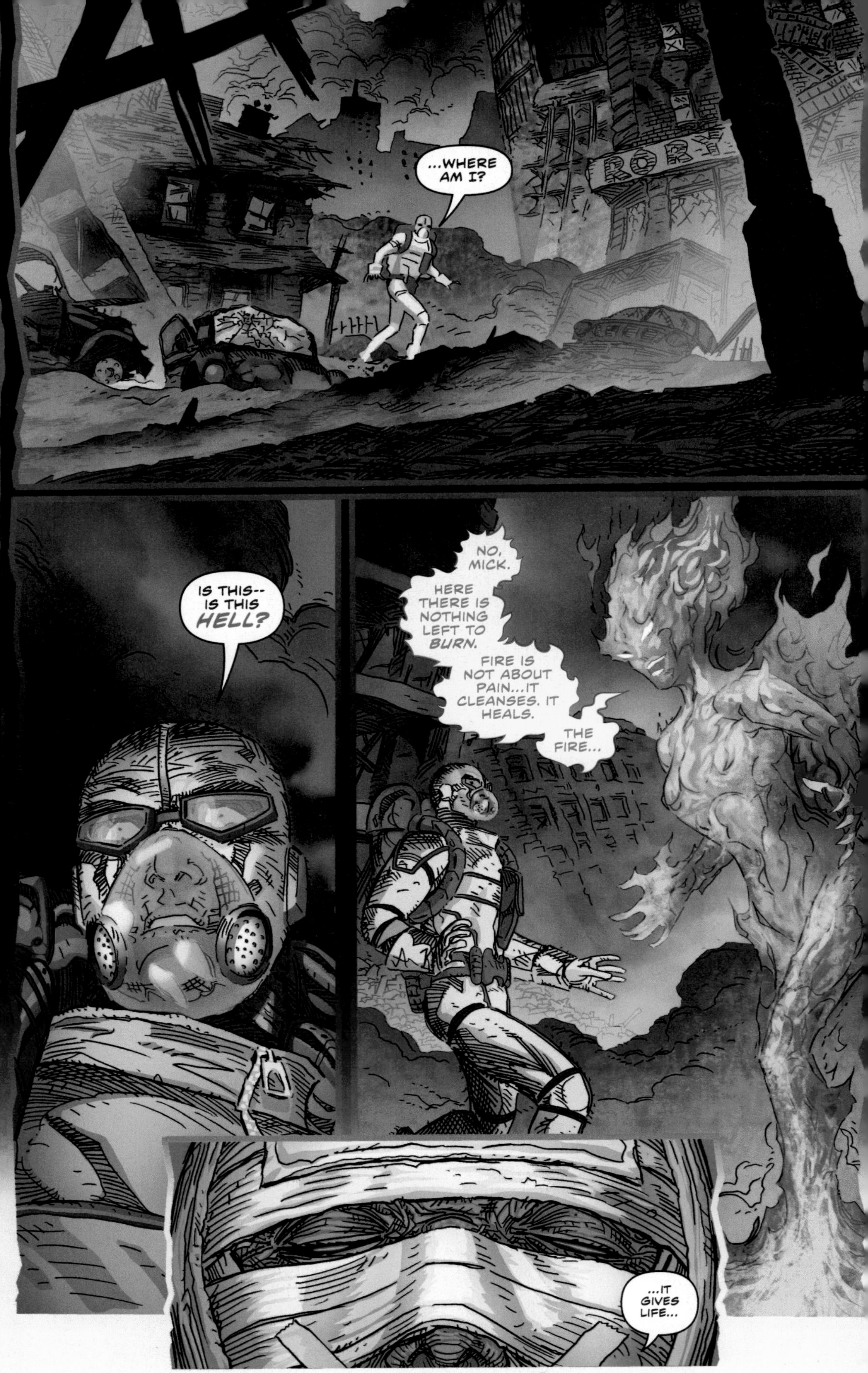
...WHERE AM I?
IS THIS-- IS THIS HELL?
NO, MICK.
HERE THERE IS NOTHING LEFT TO BURN.
FIRE IS NOT ABOUT PAIN...IT CLEANSES. IT HEALS.
THE FIRE...
...IT GIVES LIFE...

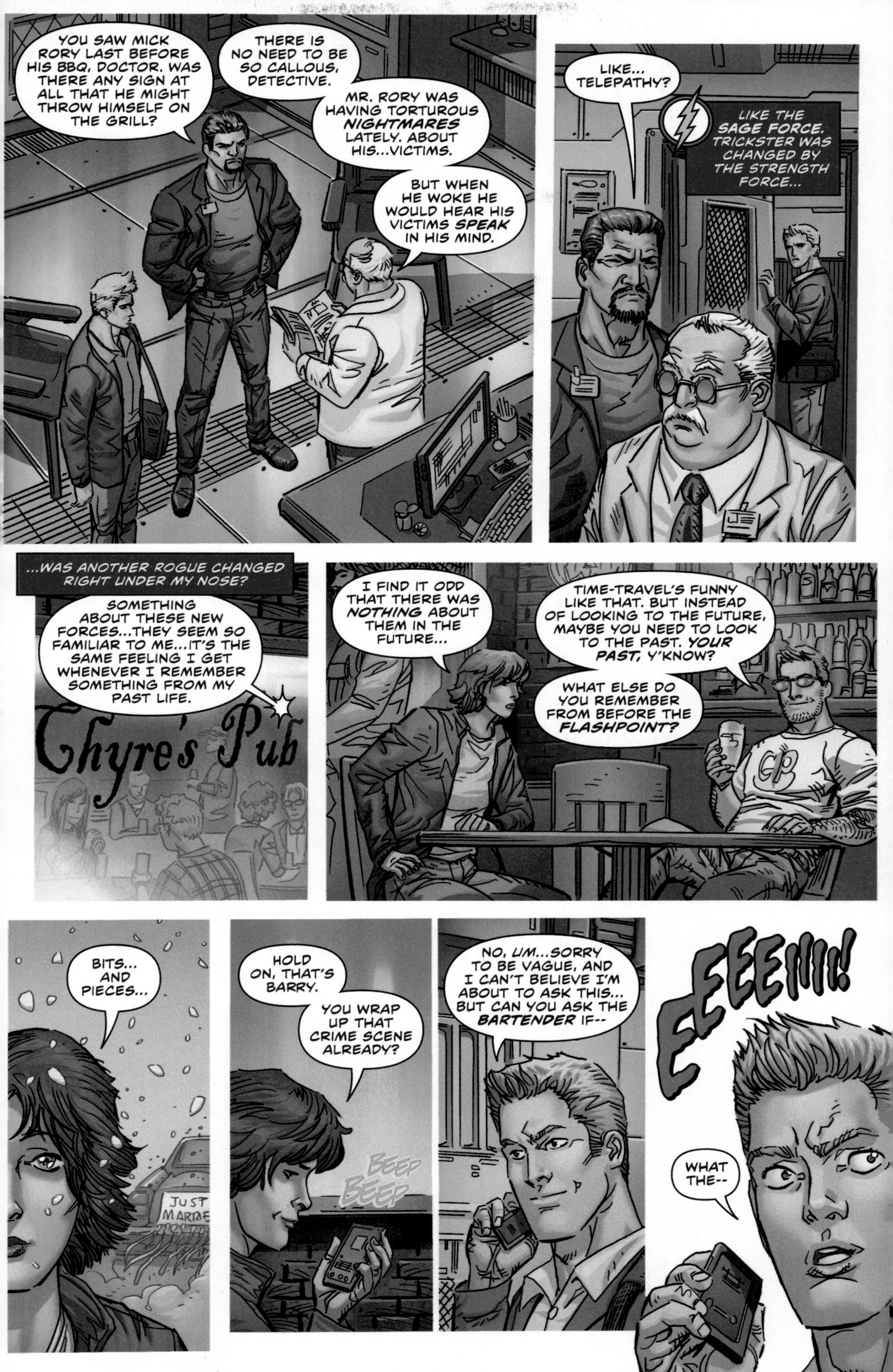
YOU SAW MICK RORY LAST BEFORE HIS BBQ, DOCTOR. WAS THERE ANY SIGN AT ALL THAT HE MIGHT THROW HIMSELF ON THE GRILL?
THERE IS NO NEED TO BE SO CALLOUS, DETECTIVE.
MR. RORY WAS HAVING TORTUROUS NIGHTMARES LATELY. ABOUT HIS...VICTIMS.
BUT WHEN HE WOKE HE WOULD HEAR HIS VICTIMS SPEAK IN HIS MIND.
LIKE... TELEPATHY?
LIKE THE SAGE FORCE. TRICKSTER WAS CHANGED BY THE STRENGTH FORCE...
...WAS ANOTHER ROGUE CHANGED RIGHT UNDER MY NOSE?
SOMETHING ABOUT THESE NEW FORCES...THEY SEEM SO FAMILIAR TO ME...IT'S THE SAME FEELING I GET WHENEVER I REMEMBER SOMETHING FROM MY PAST LIFE.
Chyre's Pub
I FIND IT ODD THAT THERE WAS NOTHING ABOUT THEM IN THE FUTURE...
TIME-TRAVEL'S FUNNY LIKE THAT. BUT INSTEAD OF LOOKING TO THE FUTURE, MAYBE YOU NEED TO LOOK TO THE PAST. YOUR PAST, Y'KNOW?
WHAT ELSE DO YOU REMEMBER FROM BEFORE THE FLASHPOINT?
BITS... AND PIECES...
JUST MARRIE
HOLD ON, THAT'S BARRY.
YOU WRAP UP THAT CRIME SCENE ALREADY?
BEEP BEEP
NO, UM...SORRY TO BE VAGUE, AND I CAN'T BELIEVE I'M ABOUT TO ASK THIS... BUT CAN YOU ASK THE BARTENDER IF--
EEEEIIIII!
WHAT THE--

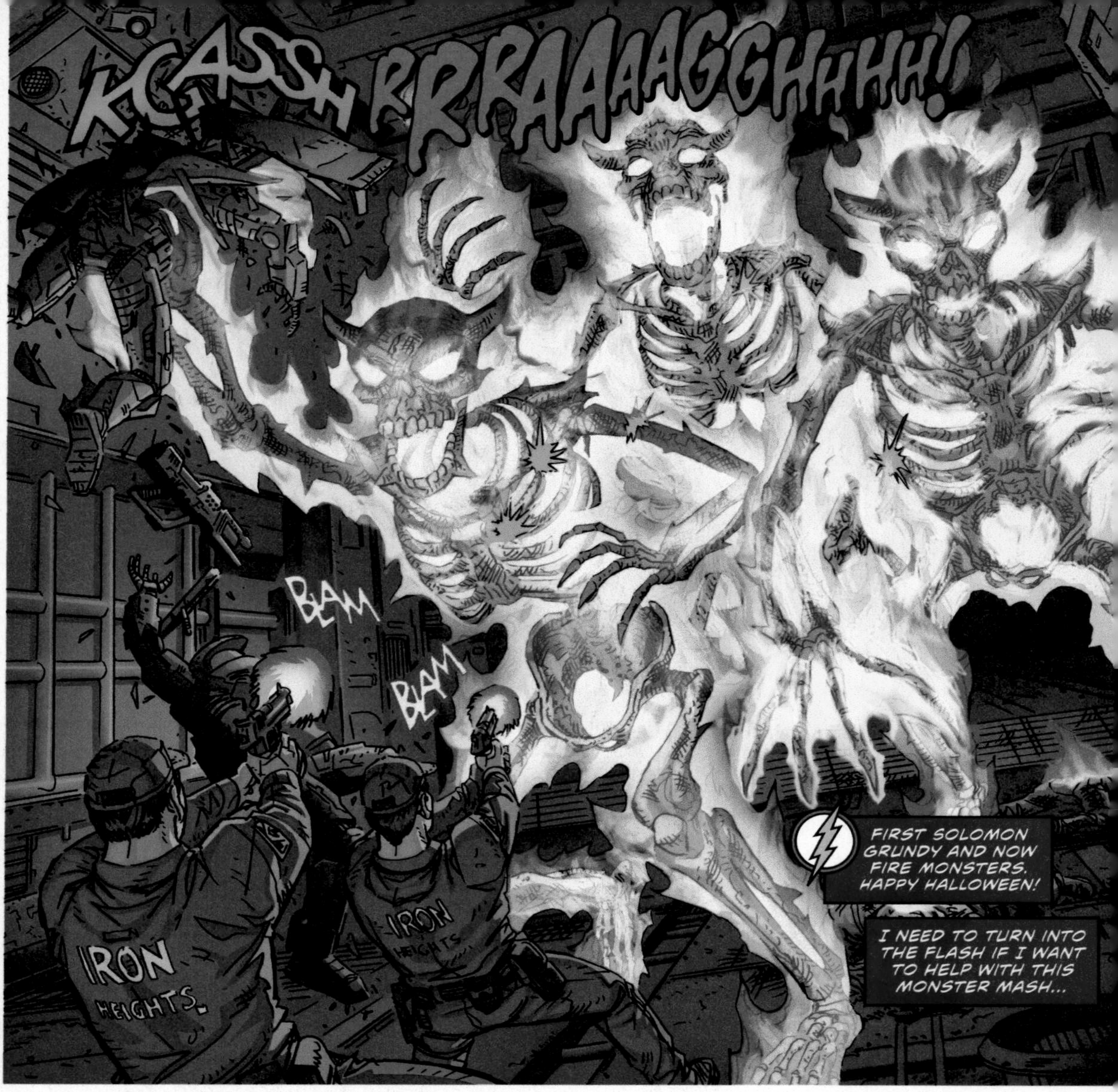
KCASSH
RRRAAAAGGHHHH!
BLAM
BLAM
IRON HEIGHTS
IRON HEIGHTS
FIRST SOLOMON GRUNDY AND NOW FIRE MONSTERS. HAPPY HALLOWEEN!
I NEED TO TURN INTO THE FLASH IF I WANT TO HELP WITH THIS MONSTER MASH...

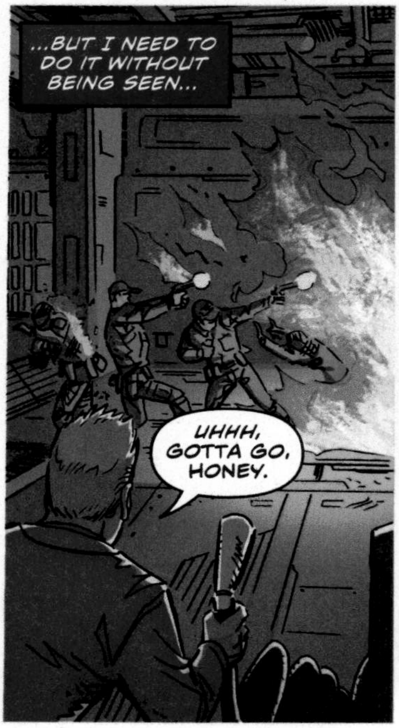
...BUT I NEED TO DO IT WITHOUT BEING SEEN...
UHHH, GOTTA GO, HONEY.

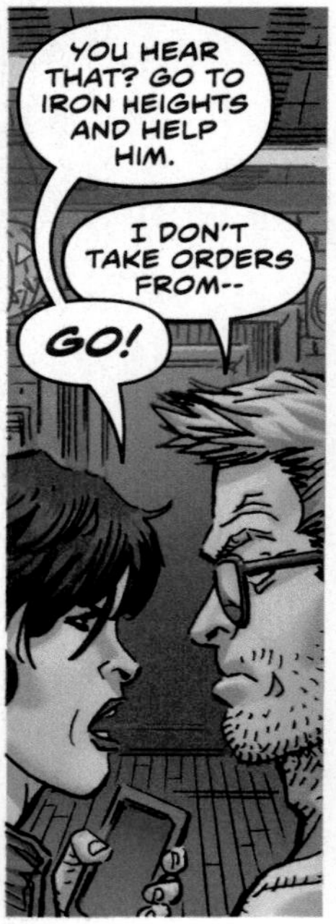
YOU HEAR THAT? GO TO IRON HEIGHTS AND HELP HIM.
I DON'T TAKE ORDERS FROM--
GO!

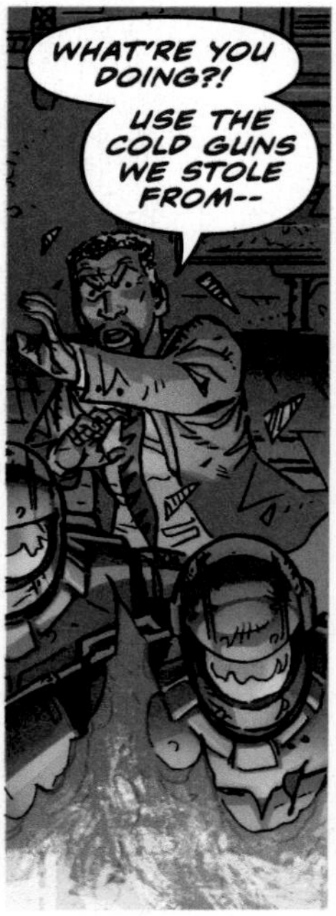
WHAT'RE YOU DOING?!
USE THE COLD GUNS WE STOLE FROM--

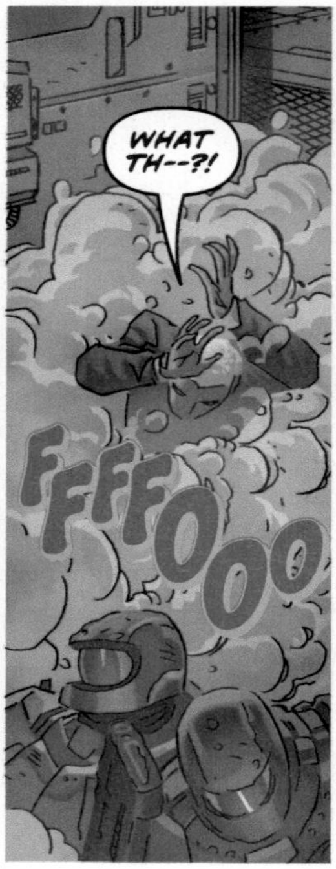
WHAT TH--?!
FFFFOOOO

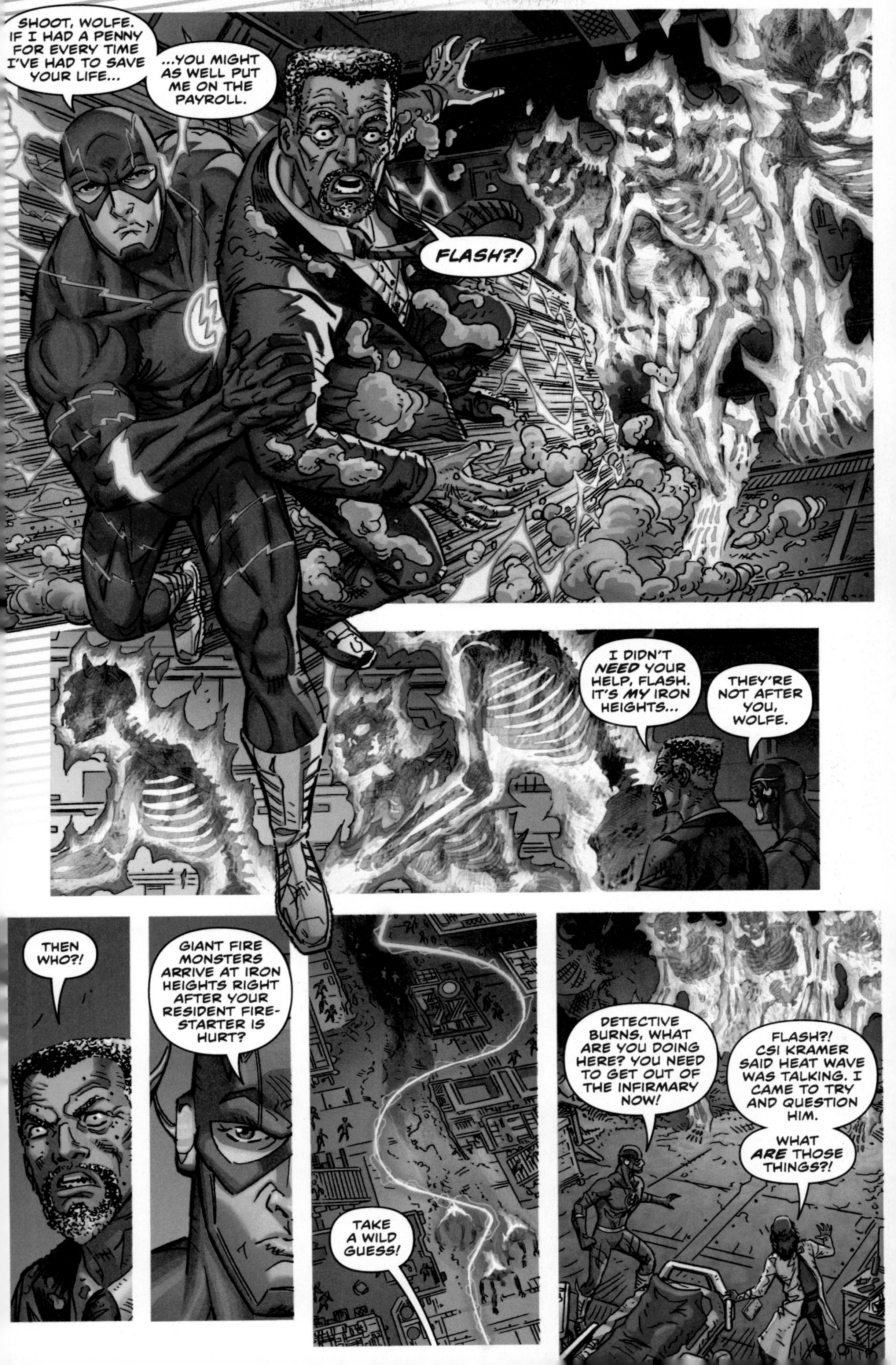
SHOOT, WOLFE. IF I HAD A PENNY FOR EVERY TIME I'VE HAD TO SAVE YOUR LIFE...
...YOU MIGHT AS WELL PUT ME ON THE PAYROLL.
FLASH?!
I DIDN'T NEED YOUR HELP, FLASH. IT'S MY IRON HEIGHTS...
THEY'RE NOT AFTER YOU, WOLFE.
THEN WHO?!
GIANT FIRE MONSTERS ARRIVE AT IRON HEIGHTS RIGHT AFTER YOUR RESIDENT FIRE-STARTER IS HURT?
TAKE A WILD GUESS!
DETECTIVE BURNS, WHAT ARE YOU DOING HERE? YOU NEED TO GET OUT OF THE INFIRMARY NOW!
FLASH?! CSI KRAMER SAID HEAT WAVE WAS TALKING. I CAME TO TRY AND QUESTION HIM.
WHAT ARE THOSE THINGS?!

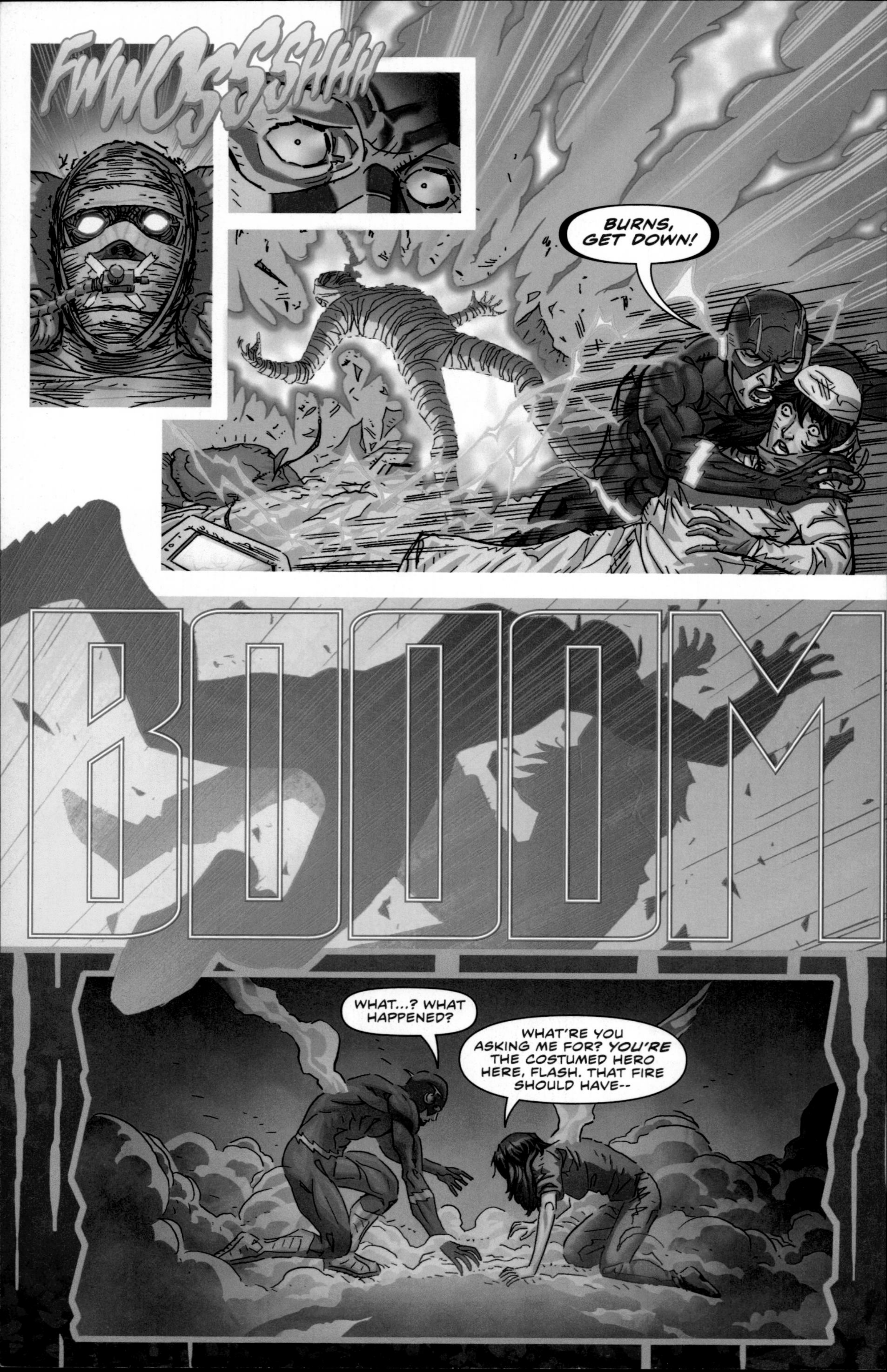
FWWOSSSHHH
BURNS, GET DOWN!
BOOM
WHAT...? WHAT HAPPENED?
WHAT'RE YOU ASKING ME FOR? *YOU'RE* THE COSTUMED HERO HERE, FLASH. THAT FIRE SHOULD HAVE--

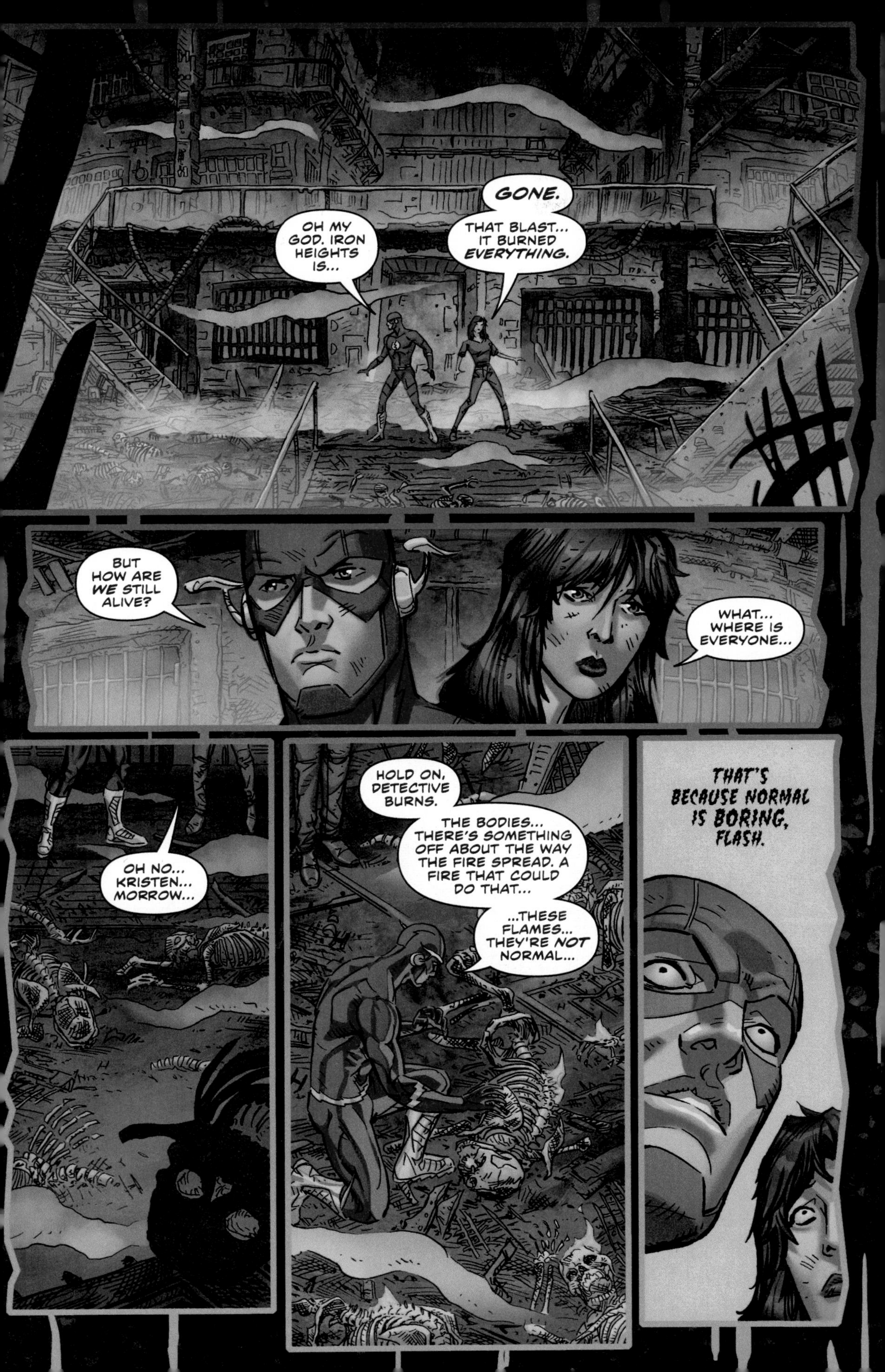
OH MY GOD. IRON HEIGHTS IS...
GONE.
THAT BLAST... IT BURNED EVERYTHING.
BUT HOW ARE WE STILL ALIVE?
WHAT... WHERE IS EVERYONE...
OH NO... KRISTEN... MORROW...
HOLD ON, DETECTIVE BURNS.
THE BODIES... THERE'S SOMETHING OFF ABOUT THE WAY THE FIRE SPREAD. A FIRE THAT COULD DO THAT...
...THESE FLAMES... THEY'RE NOT NORMAL...
THAT'S BECAUSE NORMAL IS BORING, FLASH.

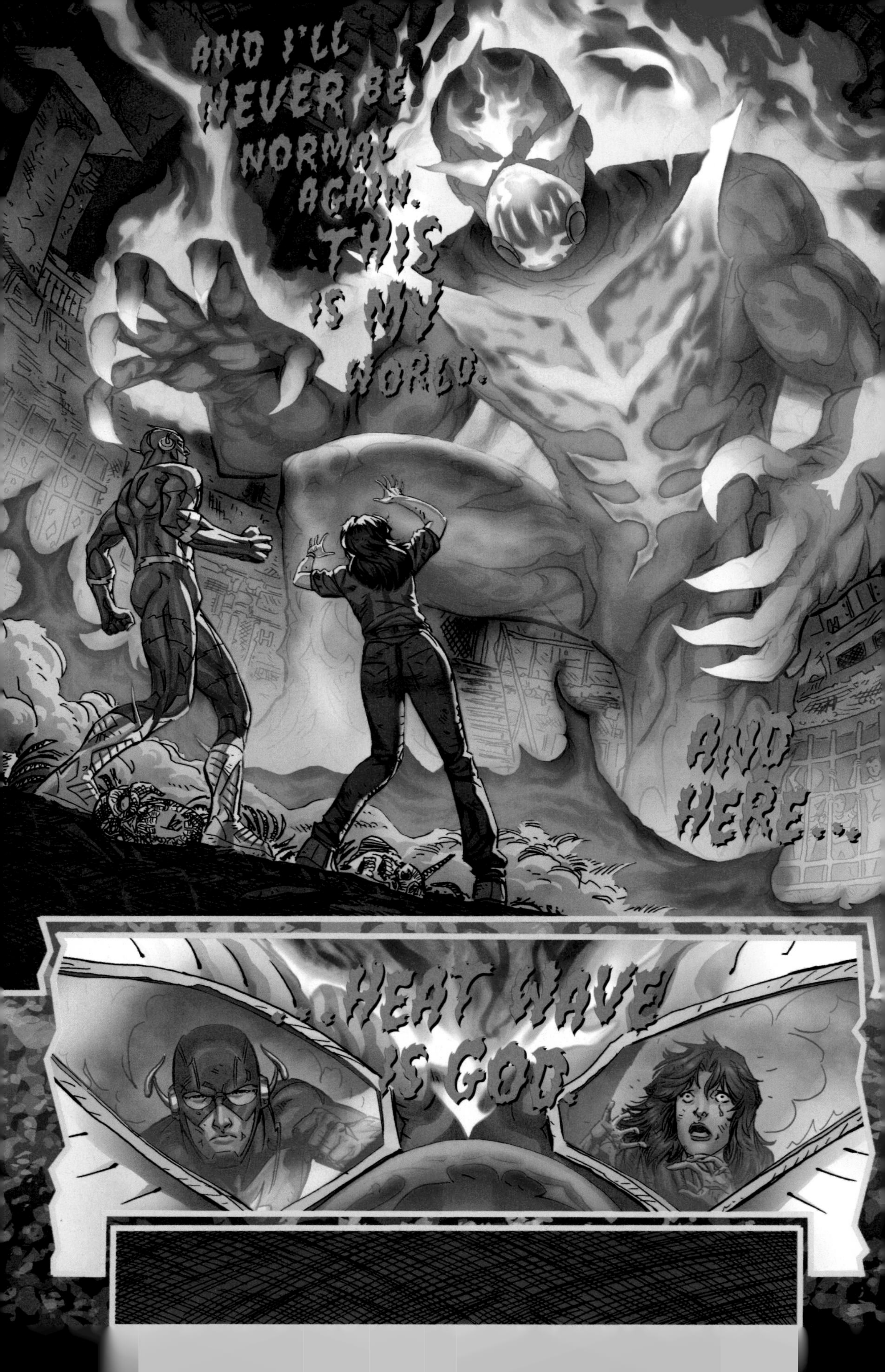
AND I'LL NEVER BE NORMAL AGAIN.
THIS IS MY WORLD.
AND HERE...
...HEAT WAVE IS GOD.

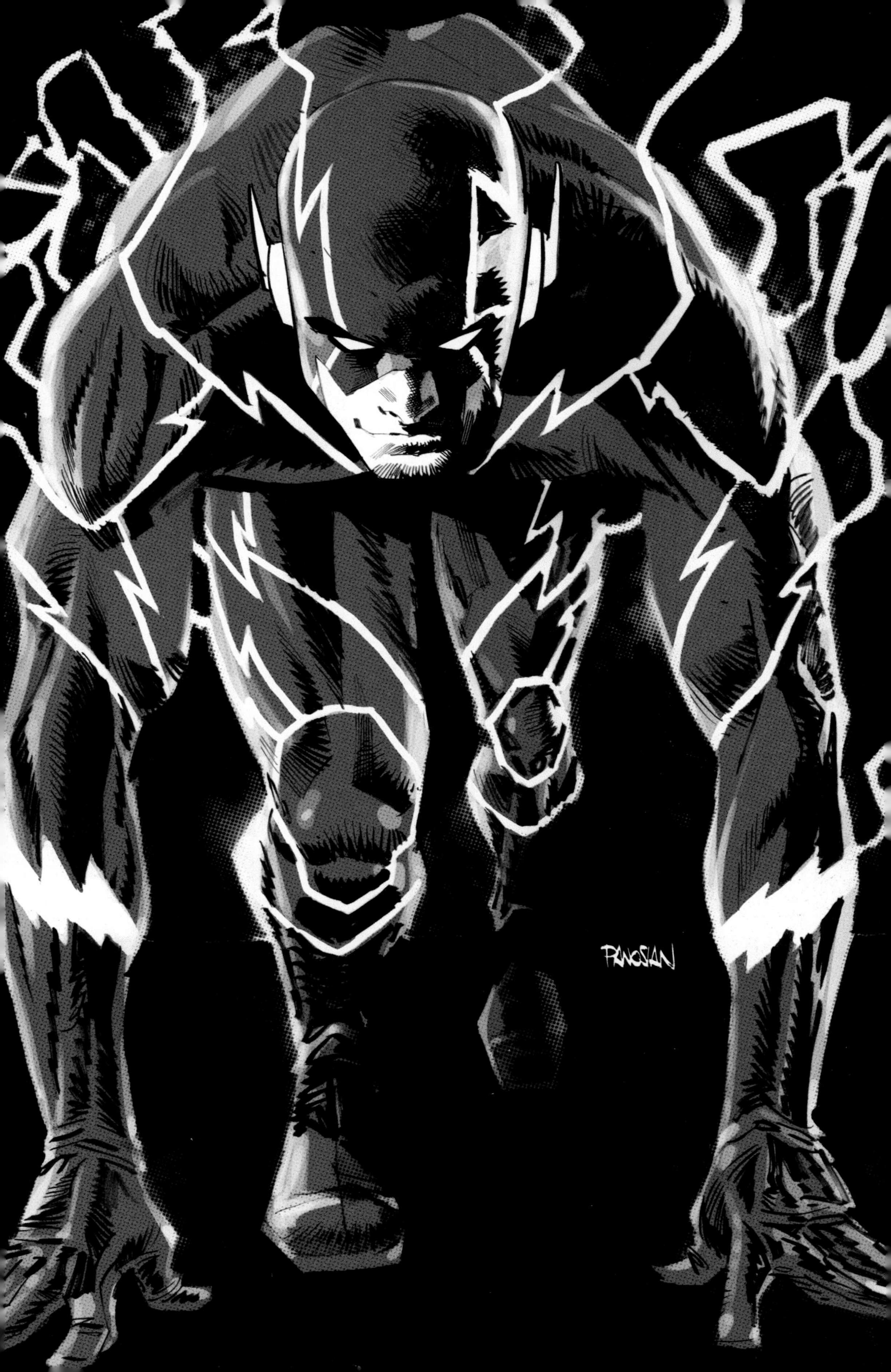
PANOSIAN

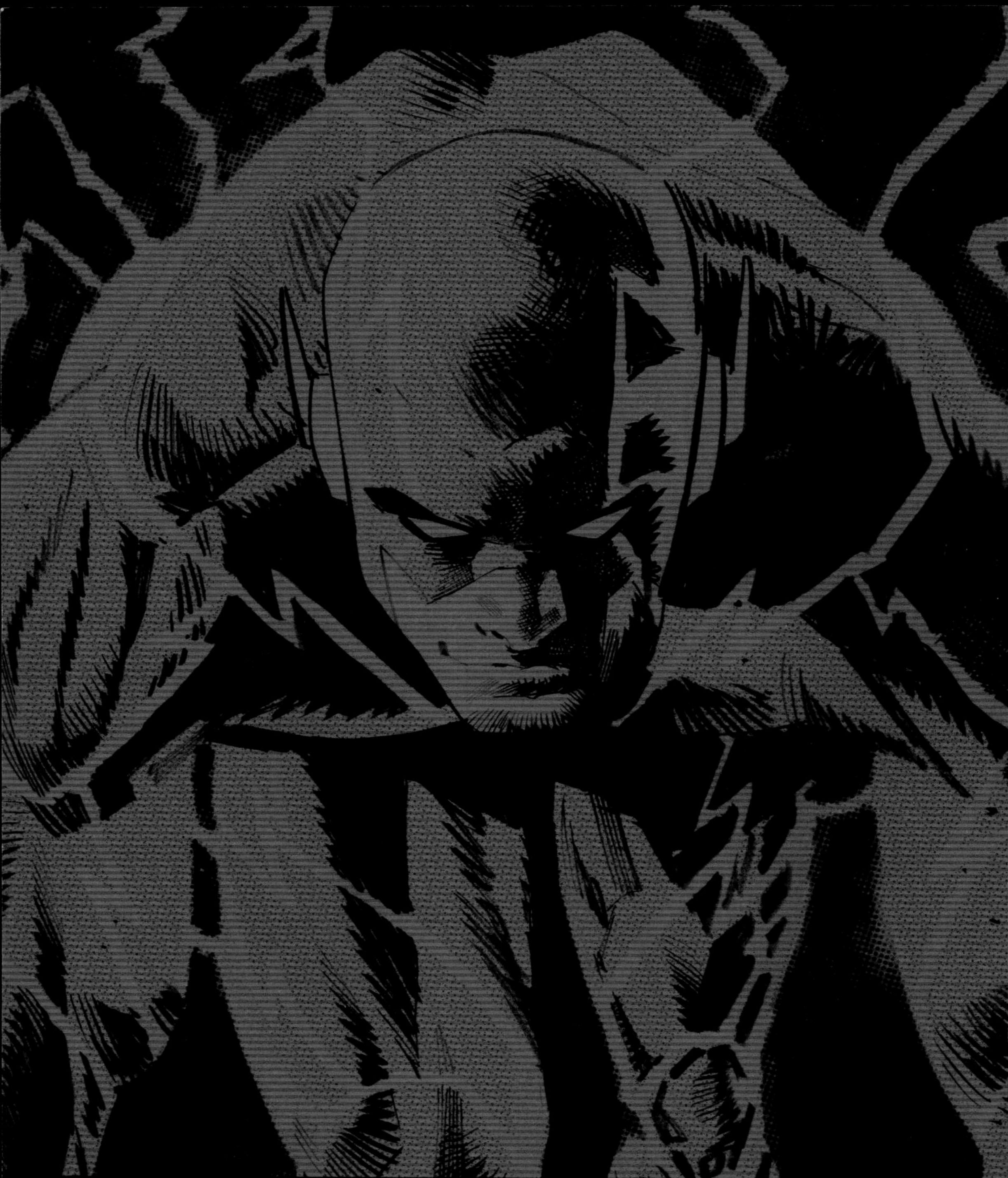

THE FLASH
#56

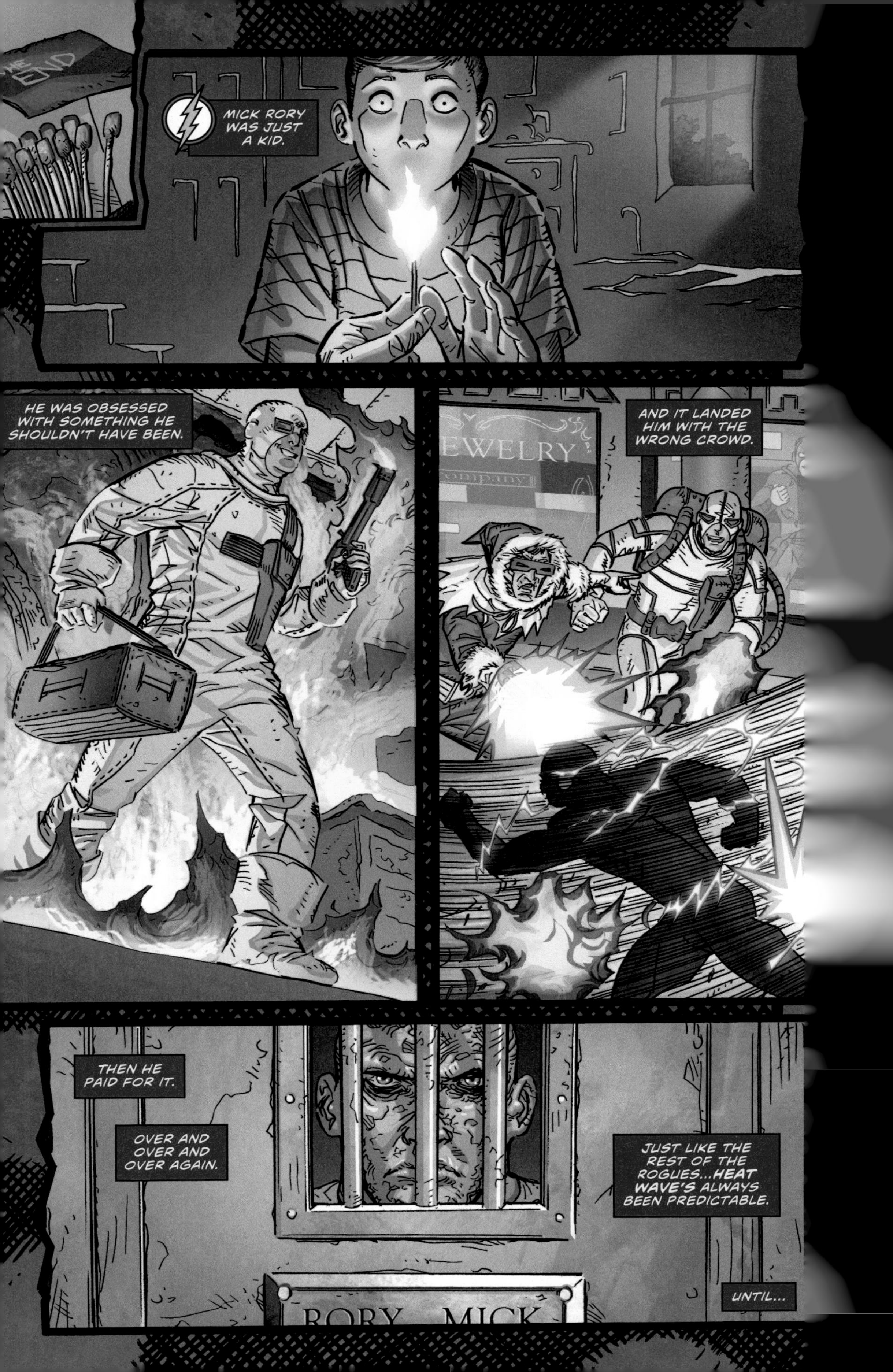
THE END
MICK RORY WAS JUST A KID.
HE WAS OBSESSED WITH SOMETHING HE SHOULDN'T HAVE BEEN.
AND IT LANDED HIM WITH THE WRONG CROWD.
EWELRY
Company
THEN HE PAID FOR IT.
OVER AND OVER AND OVER AGAIN.
JUST LIKE THE REST OF THE ROGUES...HEAT WAVE'S ALWAYS BEEN PREDICTABLE.
UNTIL...
RORY MICK

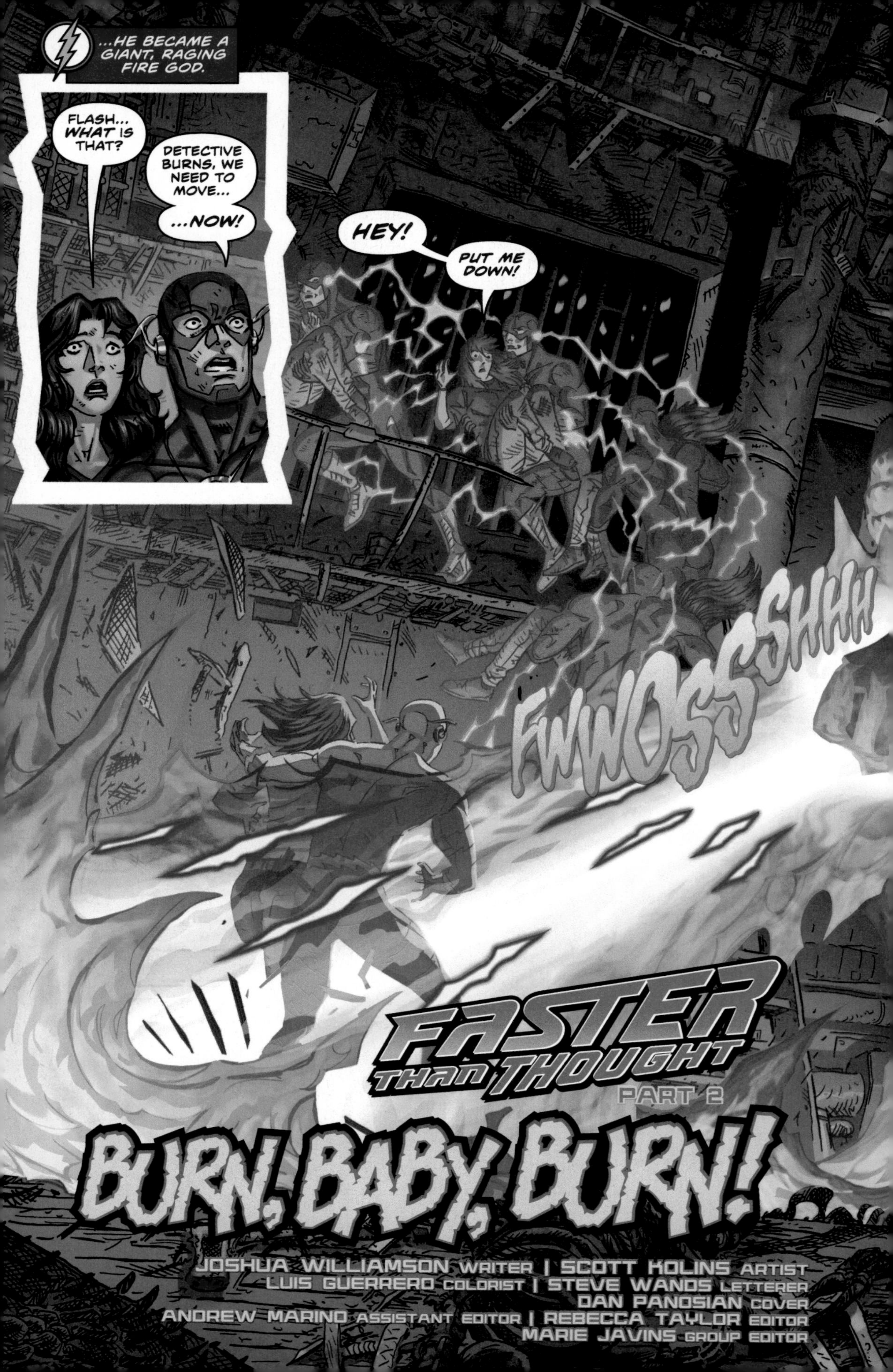

...HE BECAME A GIANT, RAGING FIRE GOD.
FLASH... WHAT IS THAT?
DETECTIVE BURNS, WE NEED TO MOVE...
...NOW!
HEY!
PUT ME DOWN!
FWWOSSSHHH
FASTER THAN THOUGHT
PART 2
BURN, BABY, BURN!
JOSHUA WILLIAMSON WRITER | SCOTT KOLINS ARTIST
LUIS GUERRERO COLORIST | STEVE WANDS LETTERER
DAN PANOSIAN COVER
ANDREW MARINO ASSISTANT EDITOR | REBECCA TAYLOR EDITOR
MARIE JAVINS GROUP EDITOR

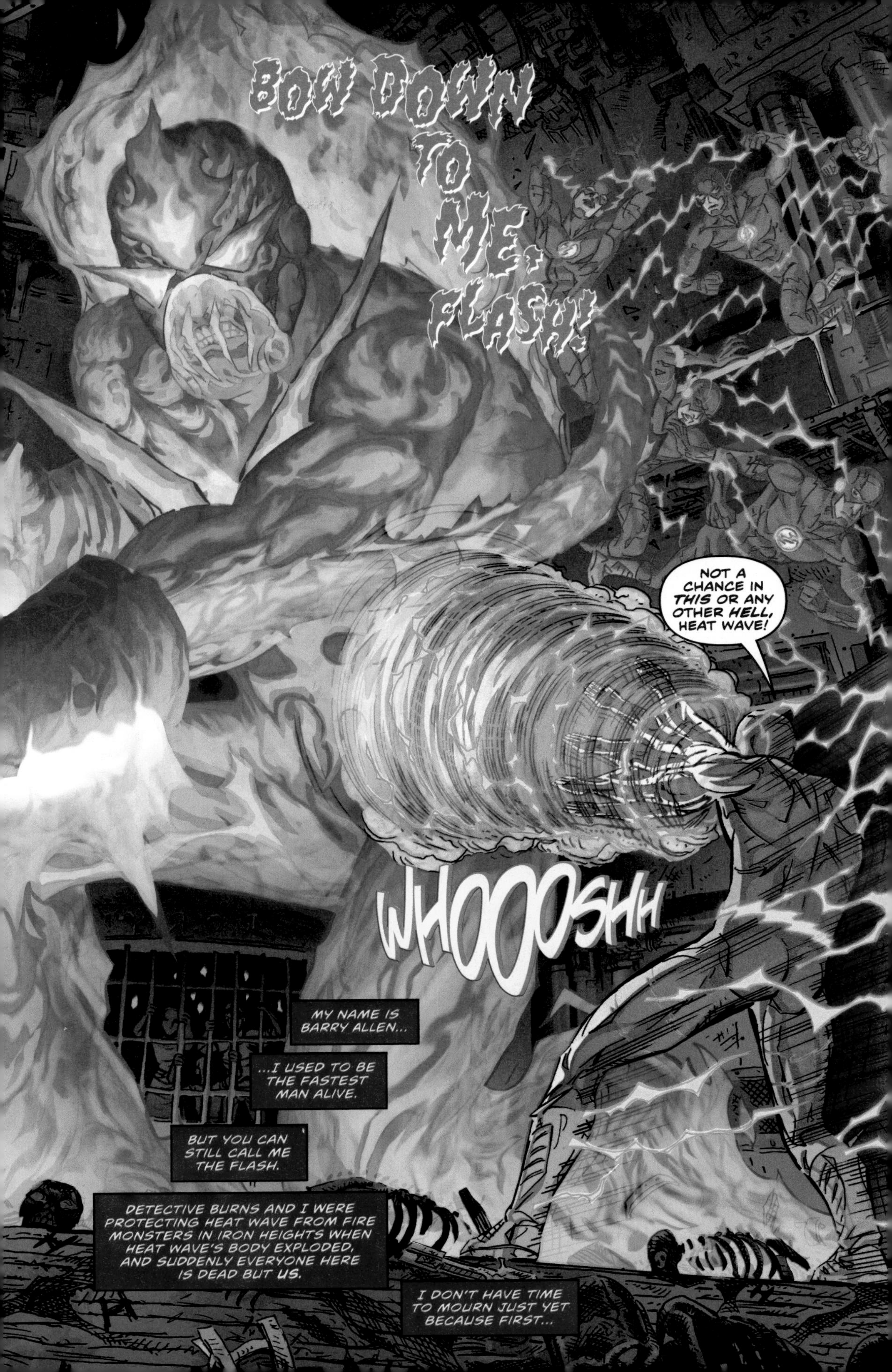
BOW DOWN TO ME, FLASH!
NOT A CHANCE IN THIS OR ANY OTHER HELL, HEAT WAVE!
WHOOOOSHH
MY NAME IS BARRY ALLEN...
...I USED TO BE THE FASTEST MAN ALIVE.
BUT YOU CAN STILL CALL ME THE FLASH.
DETECTIVE BURNS AND I WERE PROTECTING HEAT WAVE FROM FIRE MONSTERS IN IRON HEIGHTS WHEN HEAT WAVE'S BODY EXPLODED, AND SUDDENLY EVERYONE HERE IS DEAD BUT US.
I DON'T HAVE TIME TO MOURN JUST YET BECAUSE FIRST...

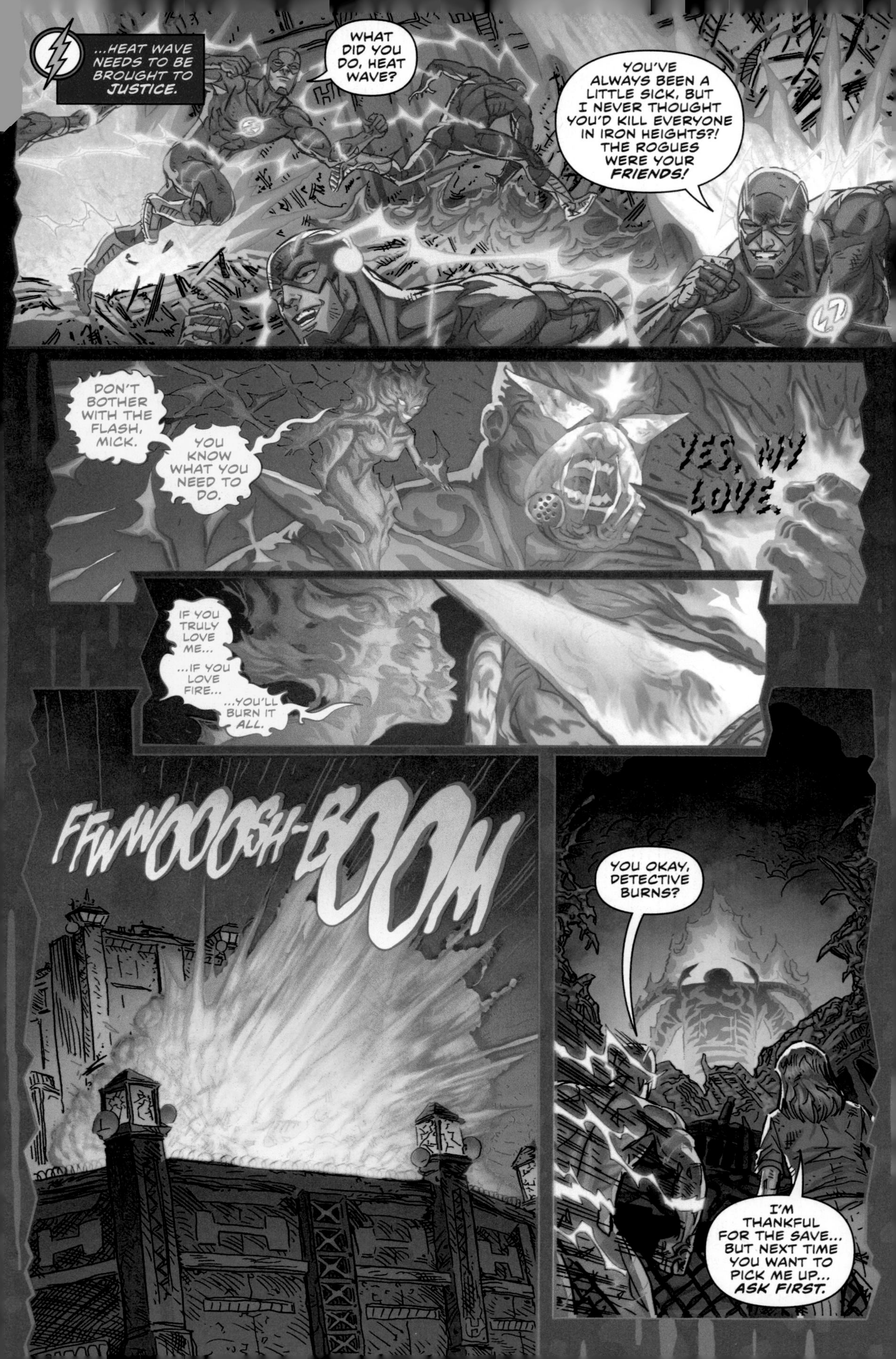
...HEAT WAVE NEEDS TO BE BROUGHT TO JUSTICE.
WHAT DID YOU DO, HEAT WAVE?
YOU'VE ALWAYS BEEN A LITTLE SICK, BUT I NEVER THOUGHT YOU'D KILL EVERYONE IN IRON HEIGHTS?! THE ROGUES WERE YOUR FRIENDS!
DON'T BOTHER WITH THE FLASH, MICK.
YOU KNOW WHAT YOU NEED TO DO.
YES, MY LOVE.
IF YOU TRULY LOVE ME...
...IF YOU LOVE FIRE...
...YOU'LL BURN IT ALL.
FFWWOOOOSH-BOOM
YOU OKAY, DETECTIVE BURNS?
I'M THANKFUL FOR THE SAVE... BUT NEXT TIME YOU WANT TO PICK ME UP... ASK FIRST.

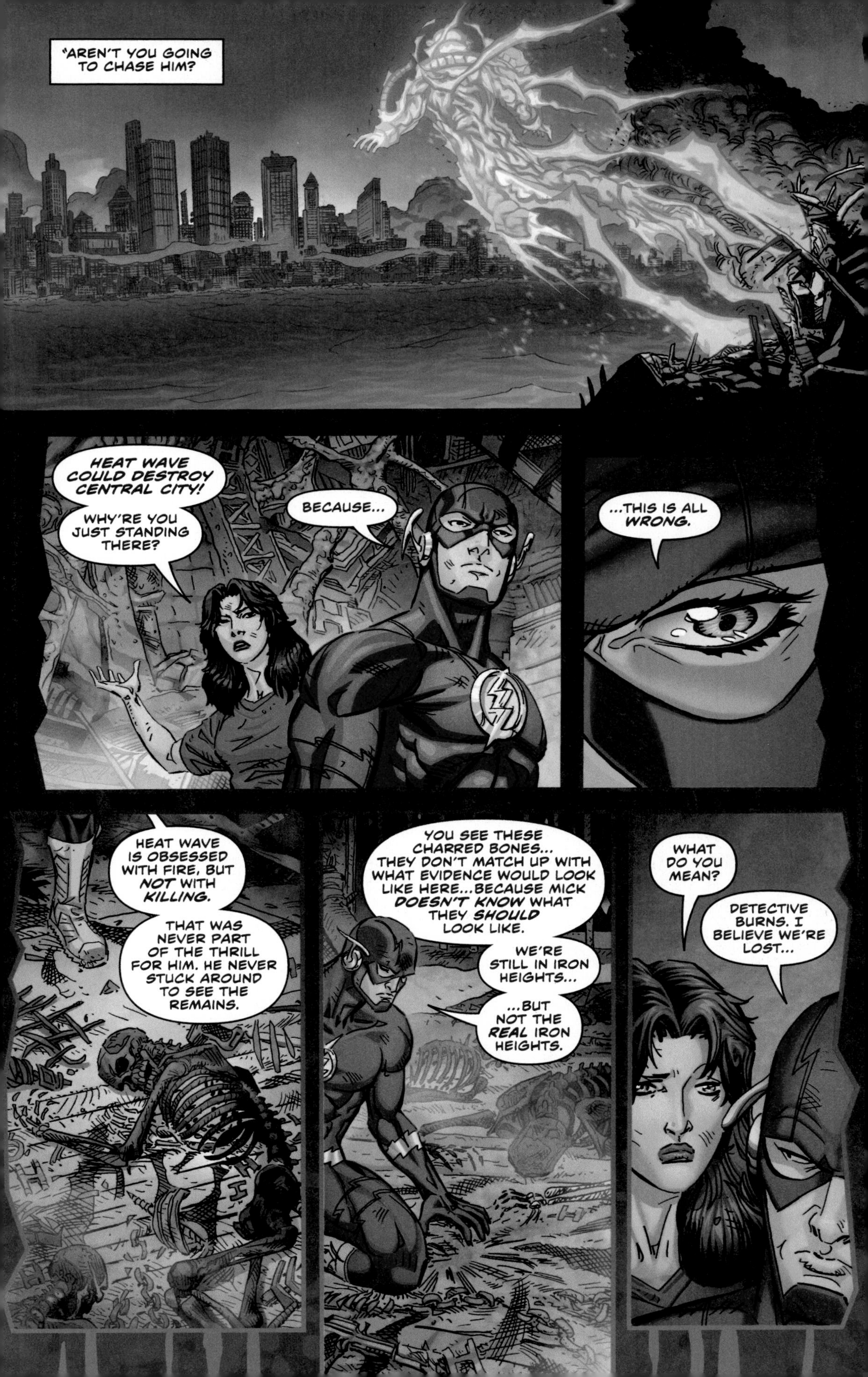
"AREN'T YOU GOING TO CHASE HIM?
HEAT WAVE COULD DESTROY CENTRAL CITY!
WHY'RE YOU JUST STANDING THERE?
BECAUSE...
...THIS IS ALL WRONG.
HEAT WAVE IS OBSESSED WITH FIRE, BUT NOT WITH KILLING.
THAT WAS NEVER PART OF THE THRILL FOR HIM. HE NEVER STUCK AROUND TO SEE THE REMAINS.
YOU SEE THESE CHARRED BONES... THEY DON'T MATCH UP WITH WHAT EVIDENCE WOULD LOOK LIKE HERE...BECAUSE MICK DOESN'T KNOW WHAT THEY SHOULD LOOK LIKE.
WE'RE STILL IN IRON HEIGHTS...
...BUT NOT THE REAL IRON HEIGHTS.
WHAT DO YOU MEAN?
DETECTIVE BURNS. I BELIEVE WE'RE LOST...

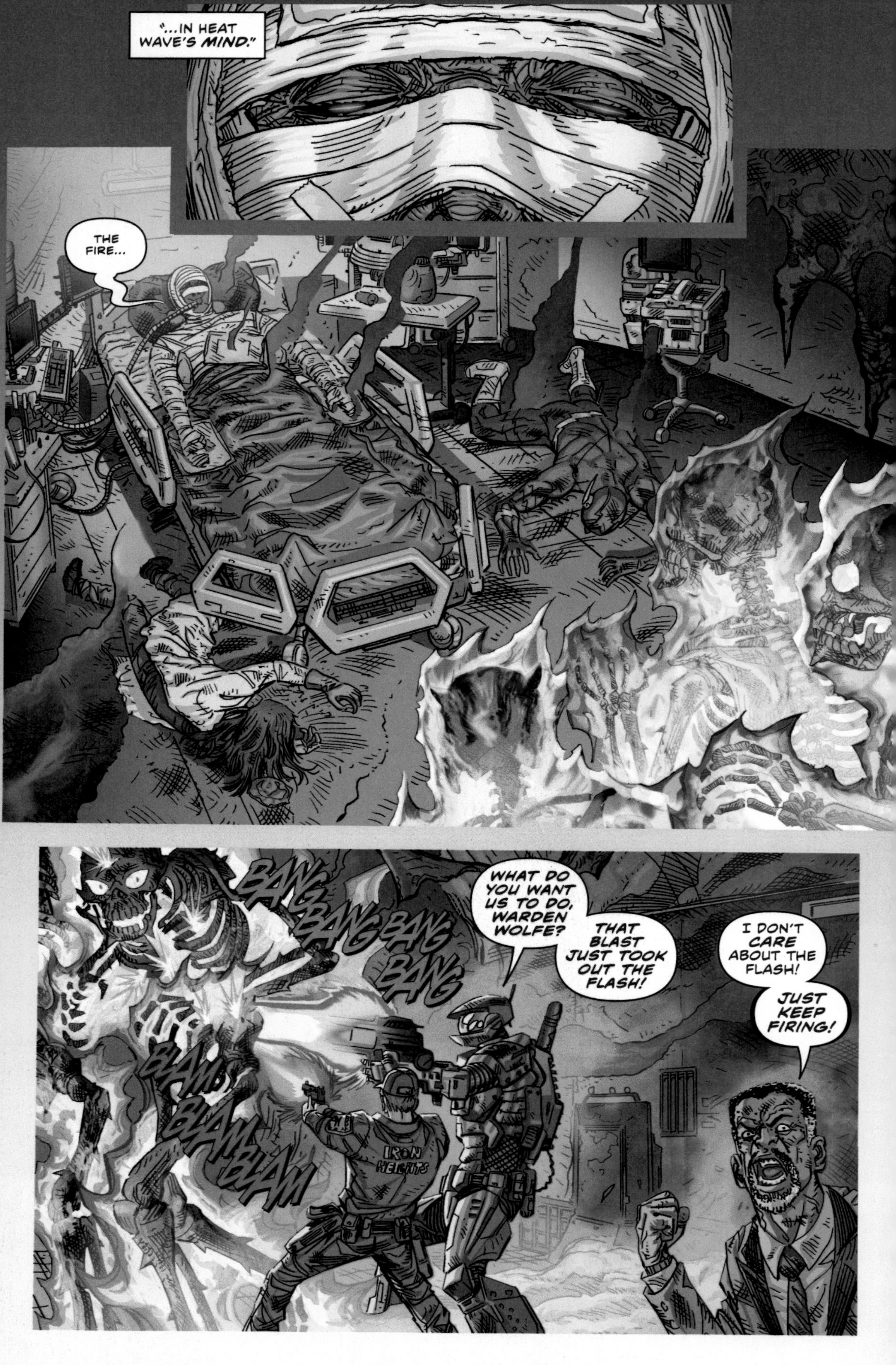
"...IN HEAT WAVE'S MIND."
THE FIRE...
BANG BANG BANG BANG
BLAM BLAM BLAM BLAM
WHAT DO YOU WANT US TO DO, WARDEN WOLFE?
THAT BLAST JUST TOOK OUT THE FLASH!
I DON'T CARE ABOUT THE FLASH!
JUST KEEP FIRING!
IRON HEIGHTS

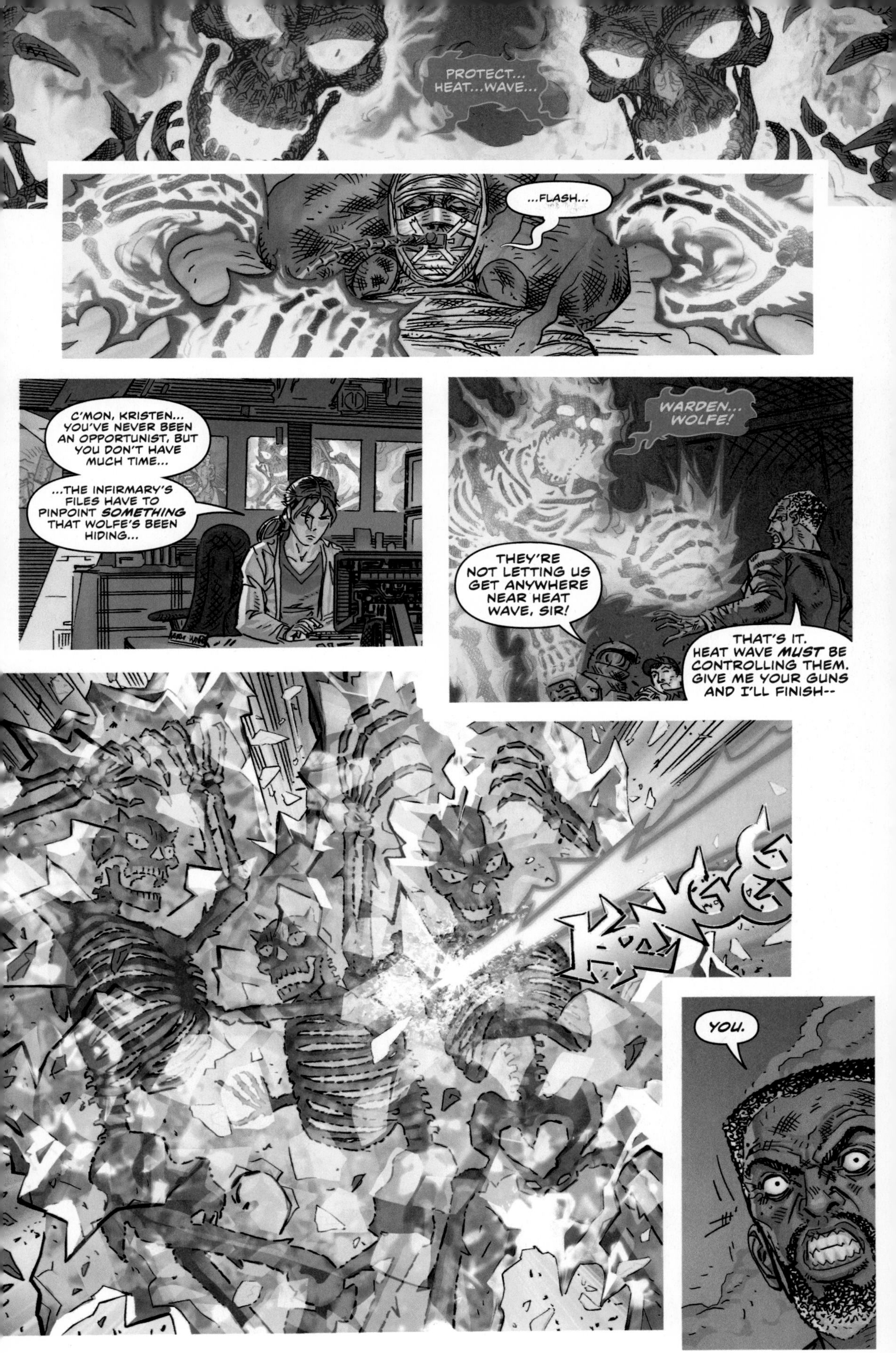
PROTECT... HEAT...WAVE...
...FLASH...
C'MON, KRISTEN... YOU'VE NEVER BEEN AN OPPORTUNIST, BUT YOU DON'T HAVE MUCH TIME...
...THE INFIRMARY'S FILES HAVE TO PINPOINT *SOMETHING* THAT WOLFE'S BEEN HIDING...
WARDEN... WOLFE!
THEY'RE NOT LETTING US GET ANYWHERE NEAR HEAT WAVE, SIR!
THAT'S IT. HEAT WAVE *MUST* BE CONTROLLING THEM. GIVE ME YOUR GUNS AND I'LL FINISH--
YOU.

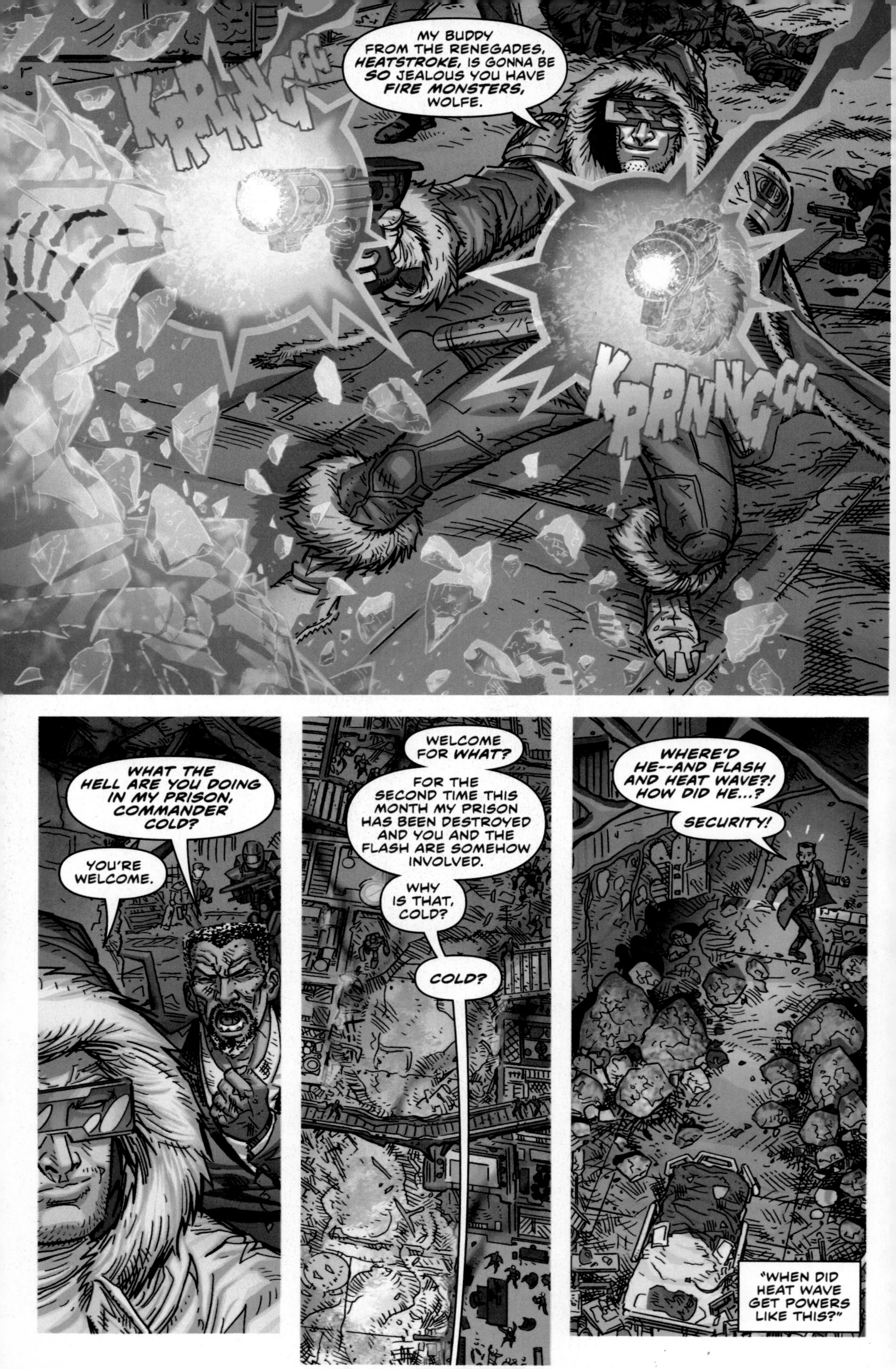
KRRNNGGG
MY BUDDY FROM THE RENEGADES, HEATSTROKE, IS GONNA BE SO JEALOUS YOU HAVE FIRE MONSTERS, WOLFE.
KRRNNGGG
WHAT THE HELL ARE YOU DOING IN MY PRISON, COMMANDER COLD?
YOU'RE WELCOME.
WELCOME FOR WHAT?
FOR THE SECOND TIME THIS MONTH MY PRISON HAS BEEN DESTROYED AND YOU AND THE FLASH ARE SOMEHOW INVOLVED.
WHY IS THAT, COLD?
COLD?
WHERE'D HE--AND FLASH AND HEAT WAVE?! HOW DID HE...?
SECURITY!
"WHEN DID HEAT WAVE GET POWERS LIKE THIS?"

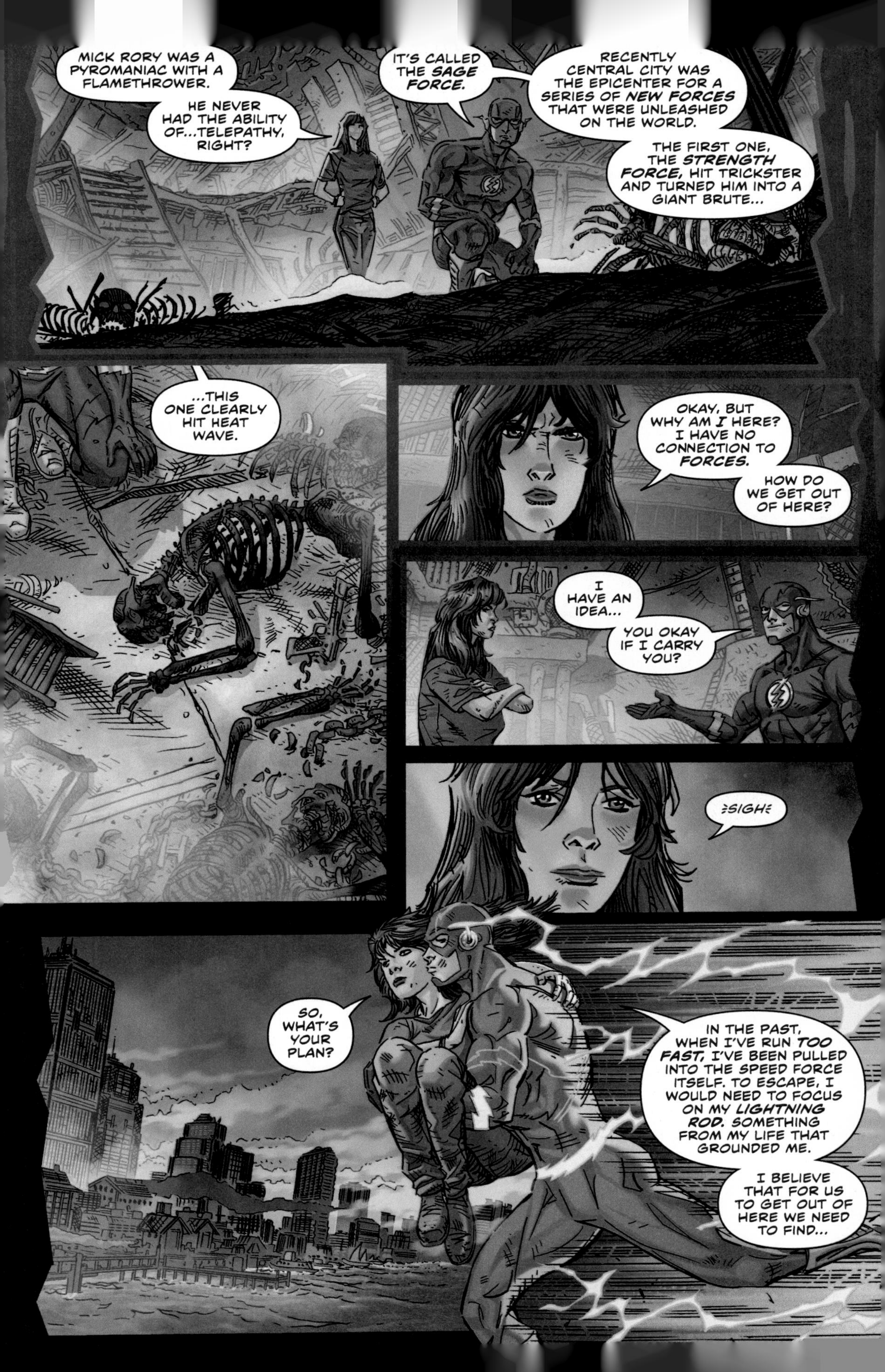
MICK RORY WAS A PYROMANIAC WITH A FLAMETHROWER.
HE NEVER HAD THE ABILITY OF...TELEPATHY, RIGHT?
IT'S CALLED THE *SAGE FORCE.*
RECENTLY CENTRAL CITY WAS THE EPICENTER FOR A SERIES OF *NEW FORCES* THAT WERE UNLEASHED ON THE WORLD.
THE FIRST ONE, THE *STRENGTH FORCE,* HIT TRICKSTER AND TURNED HIM INTO A GIANT BRUTE...
...THIS ONE CLEARLY HIT HEAT WAVE.
OKAY, BUT WHY AM *I* HERE? I HAVE NO CONNECTION TO *FORCES.*
HOW DO WE GET OUT OF HERE?
I HAVE AN IDEA...
YOU OKAY IF I CARRY YOU?
SIGH
SO, WHAT'S YOUR PLAN?
IN THE PAST, WHEN I'VE RUN *TOO FAST,* I'VE BEEN PULLED INTO THE SPEED FORCE ITSELF. TO ESCAPE, I WOULD NEED TO FOCUS ON MY *LIGHTNING ROD.* SOMETHING FROM MY LIFE THAT GROUNDED ME.
I BELIEVE THAT FOR US TO GET OUT OF HERE WE NEED TO FIND...

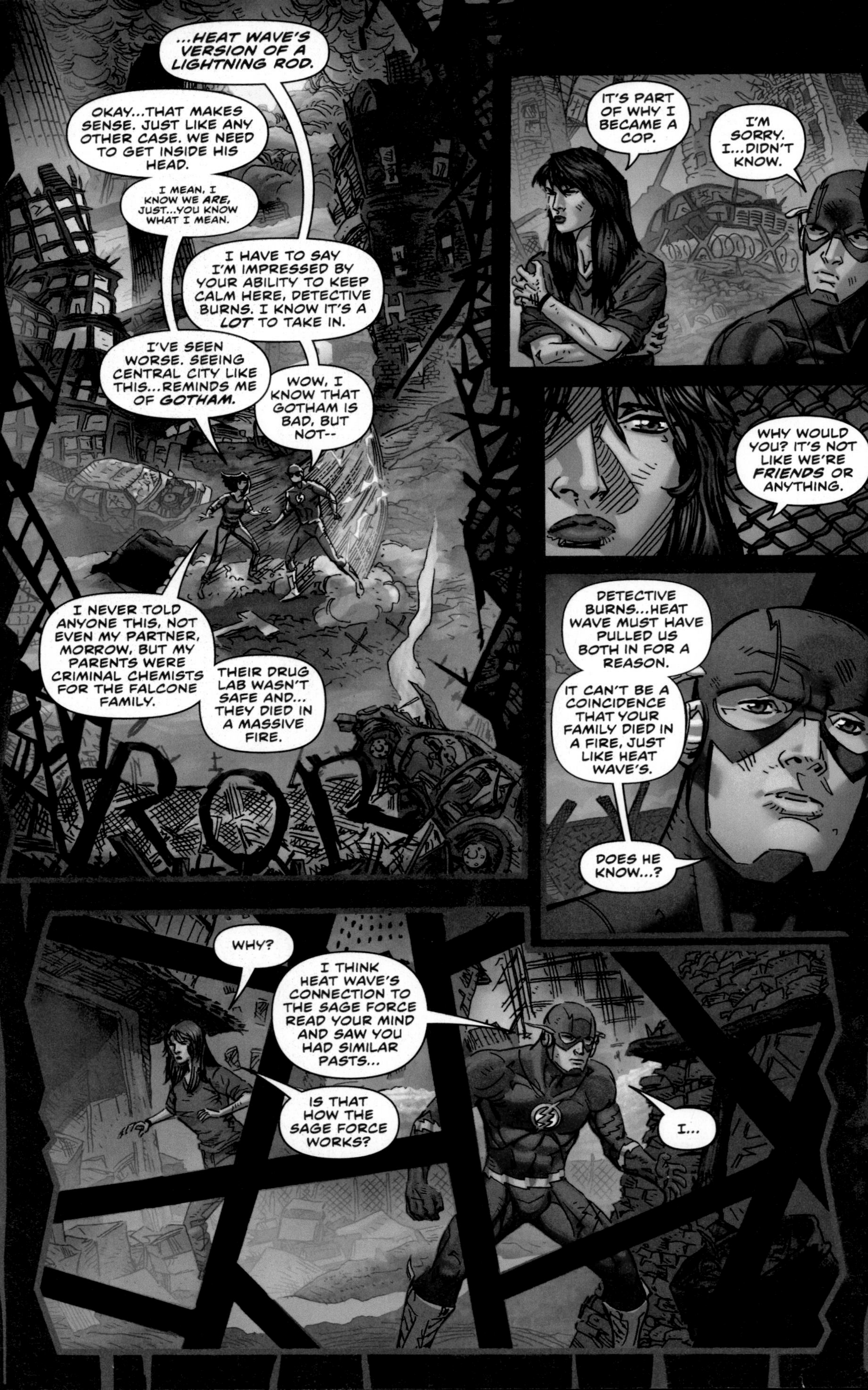
...HEAT WAVE'S VERSION OF A LIGHTNING ROD.
OKAY...THAT MAKES SENSE. JUST LIKE ANY OTHER CASE. WE NEED TO GET INSIDE HIS HEAD.
I MEAN, I KNOW WE ARE, JUST...YOU KNOW WHAT I MEAN.
I HAVE TO SAY I'M IMPRESSED BY YOUR ABILITY TO KEEP CALM HERE, DETECTIVE BURNS. I KNOW IT'S A LOT TO TAKE IN.
I'VE SEEN WORSE. SEEING CENTRAL CITY LIKE THIS...REMINDS ME OF GOTHAM.
WOW, I KNOW THAT GOTHAM IS BAD, BUT NOT--
I NEVER TOLD ANYONE THIS, NOT EVEN MY PARTNER, MORROW, BUT MY PARENTS WERE CRIMINAL CHEMISTS FOR THE FALCONE FAMILY.
THEIR DRUG LAB WASN'T SAFE AND... THEY DIED IN A MASSIVE FIRE.
IT'S PART OF WHY I BECAME A COP.
I'M SORRY. I...DIDN'T KNOW.
WHY WOULD YOU? IT'S NOT LIKE WE'RE FRIENDS OR ANYTHING.
DETECTIVE BURNS...HEAT WAVE MUST HAVE PULLED US BOTH IN FOR A REASON.
IT CAN'T BE A COINCIDENCE THAT YOUR FAMILY DIED IN A FIRE, JUST LIKE HEAT WAVE'S.
DOES HE KNOW...?
WHY?
I THINK HEAT WAVE'S CONNECTION TO THE SAGE FORCE READ YOUR MIND AND SAW YOU HAD SIMILAR PASTS...
IS THAT HOW THE SAGE FORCE WORKS?
I...

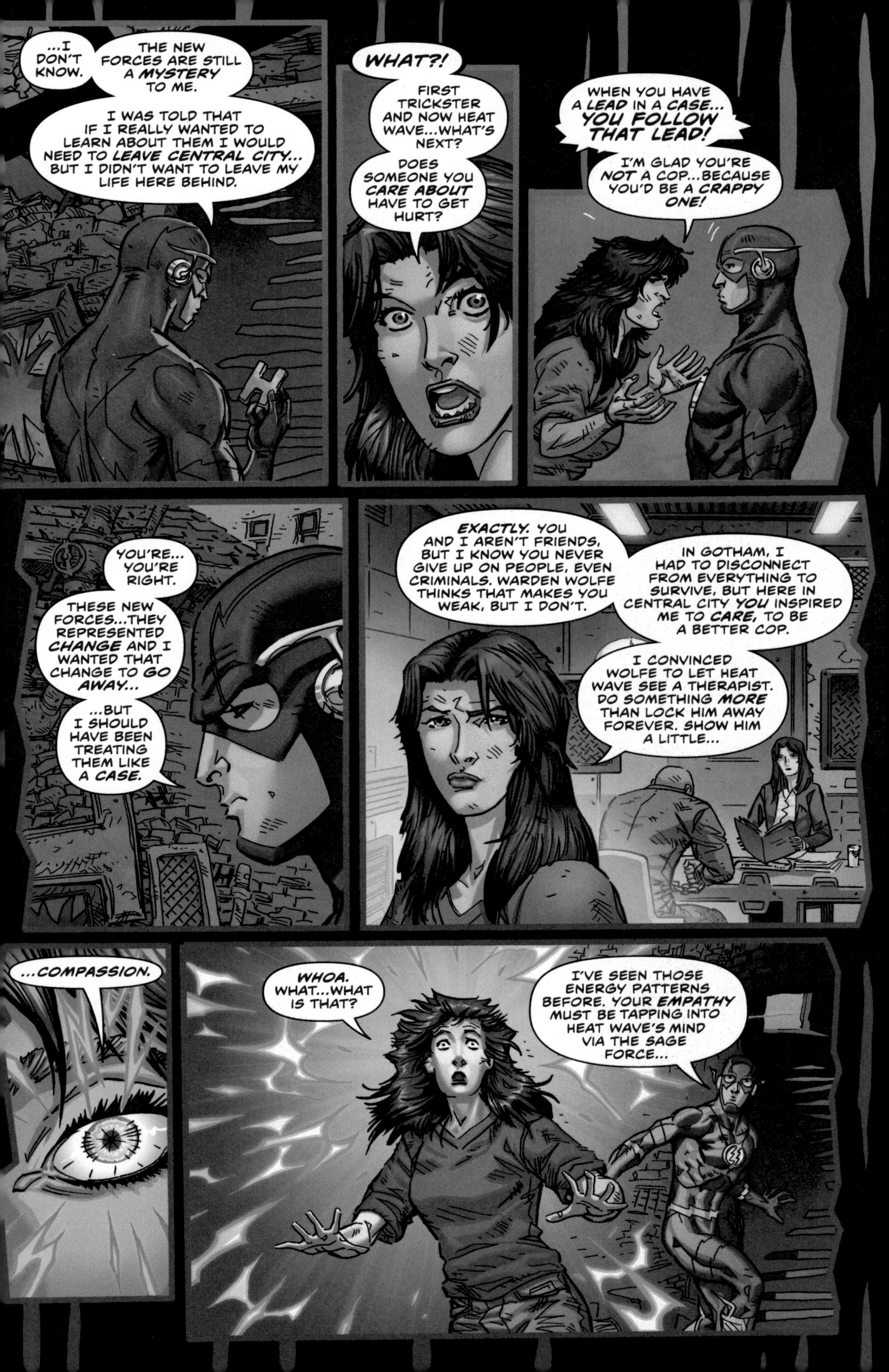
...I DON'T KNOW.
THE NEW FORCES ARE STILL A MYSTERY TO ME.
I WAS TOLD THAT IF I REALLY WANTED TO LEARN ABOUT THEM I WOULD NEED TO LEAVE CENTRAL CITY... BUT I DIDN'T WANT TO LEAVE MY LIFE HERE BEHIND.
WHAT?!
FIRST TRICKSTER AND NOW HEAT WAVE...WHAT'S NEXT?
DOES SOMEONE YOU CARE ABOUT HAVE TO GET HURT?
WHEN YOU HAVE A LEAD IN A CASE... YOU FOLLOW THAT LEAD!
I'M GLAD YOU'RE NOT A COP...BECAUSE YOU'D BE A CRAPPY ONE!
YOU'RE... YOU'RE RIGHT.
THESE NEW FORCES...THEY REPRESENTED CHANGE AND I WANTED THAT CHANGE TO GO AWAY...
...BUT I SHOULD HAVE BEEN TREATING THEM LIKE A CASE.
EXACTLY. YOU AND I AREN'T FRIENDS, BUT I KNOW YOU NEVER GIVE UP ON PEOPLE, EVEN CRIMINALS. WARDEN WOLFE THINKS THAT MAKES YOU WEAK, BUT I DON'T.
IN GOTHAM, I HAD TO DISCONNECT FROM EVERYTHING TO SURVIVE, BUT HERE IN CENTRAL CITY YOU INSPIRED ME TO CARE, TO BE A BETTER COP.
I CONVINCED WOLFE TO LET HEAT WAVE SEE A THERAPIST. DO SOMETHING MORE THAN LOCK HIM AWAY FOREVER. SHOW HIM A LITTLE...
...COMPASSION.
WHOA. WHAT...WHAT IS THAT?
I'VE SEEN THOSE ENERGY PATTERNS BEFORE. YOUR EMPATHY MUST BE TAPPING INTO HEAT WAVE'S MIND VIA THE SAGE FORCE...

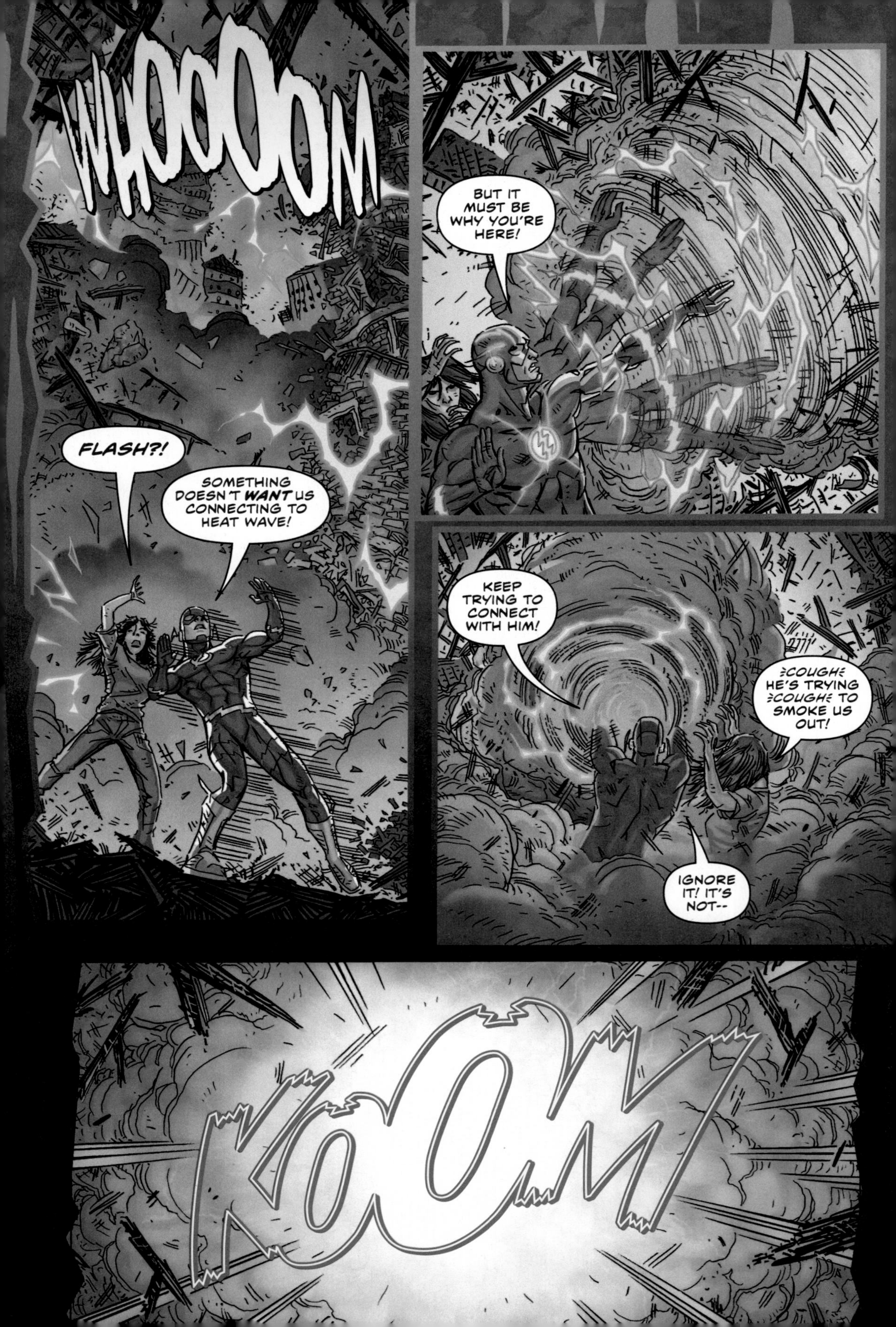
WHOOOOM
FLASH?!
SOMETHING DOESN'T **WANT** US CONNECTING TO HEAT WAVE!
BUT IT MUST BE WHY YOU'RE HERE!
KEEP TRYING TO CONNECT WITH HIM!
≡COUGH≡ HE'S TRYING ≡COUGH≡ TO SMOKE US OUT!
IGNORE IT! IT'S NOT--
KOOM

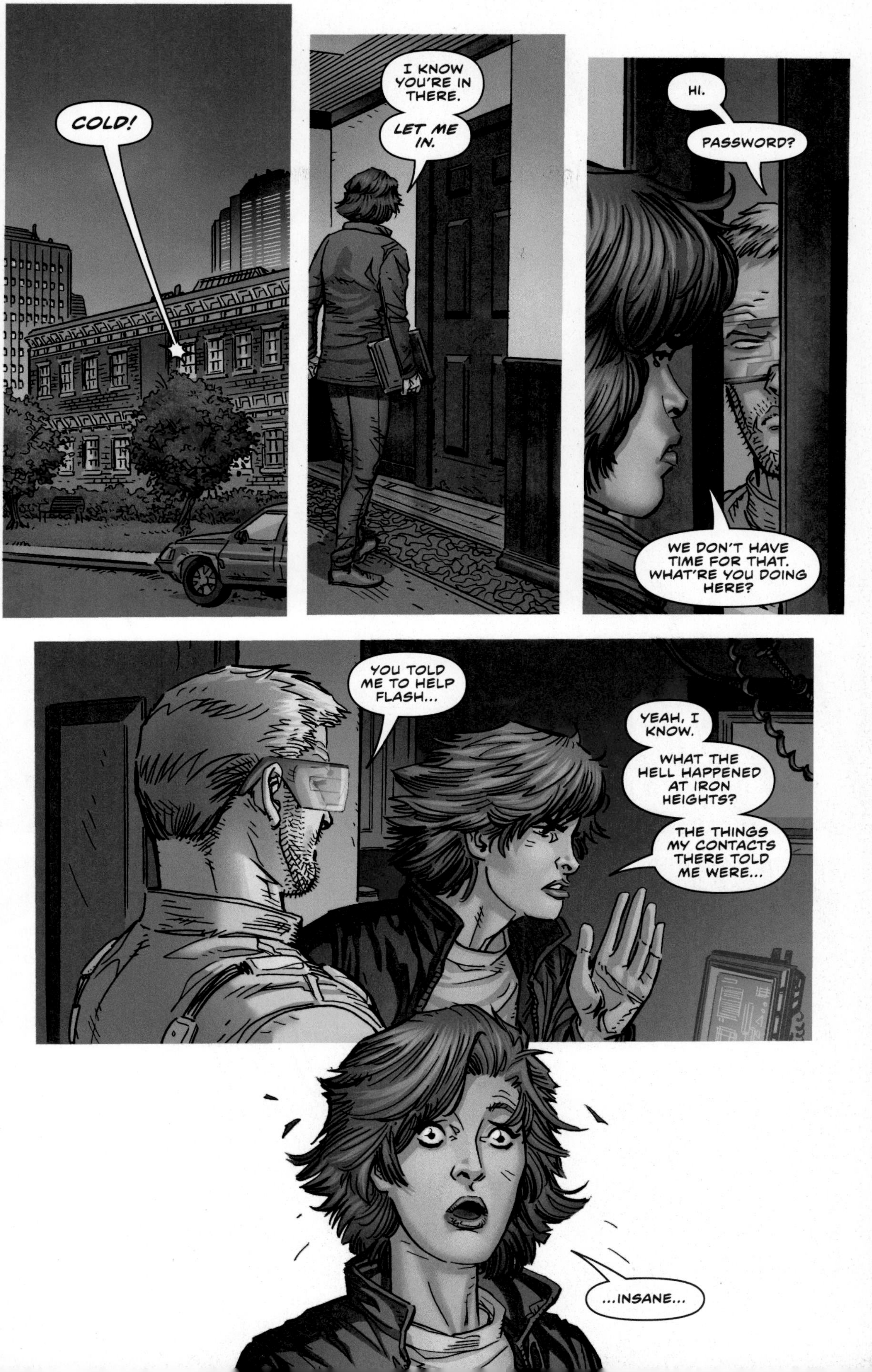
COLD!
I KNOW YOU'RE IN THERE.
LET ME IN.
HI.
PASSWORD?
WE DON'T HAVE TIME FOR THAT. WHAT'RE YOU DOING HERE?
YOU TOLD ME TO HELP FLASH...
YEAH, I KNOW.
WHAT THE HELL HAPPENED AT IRON HEIGHTS?
THE THINGS MY CONTACTS THERE TOLD ME WERE...
...INSANE...

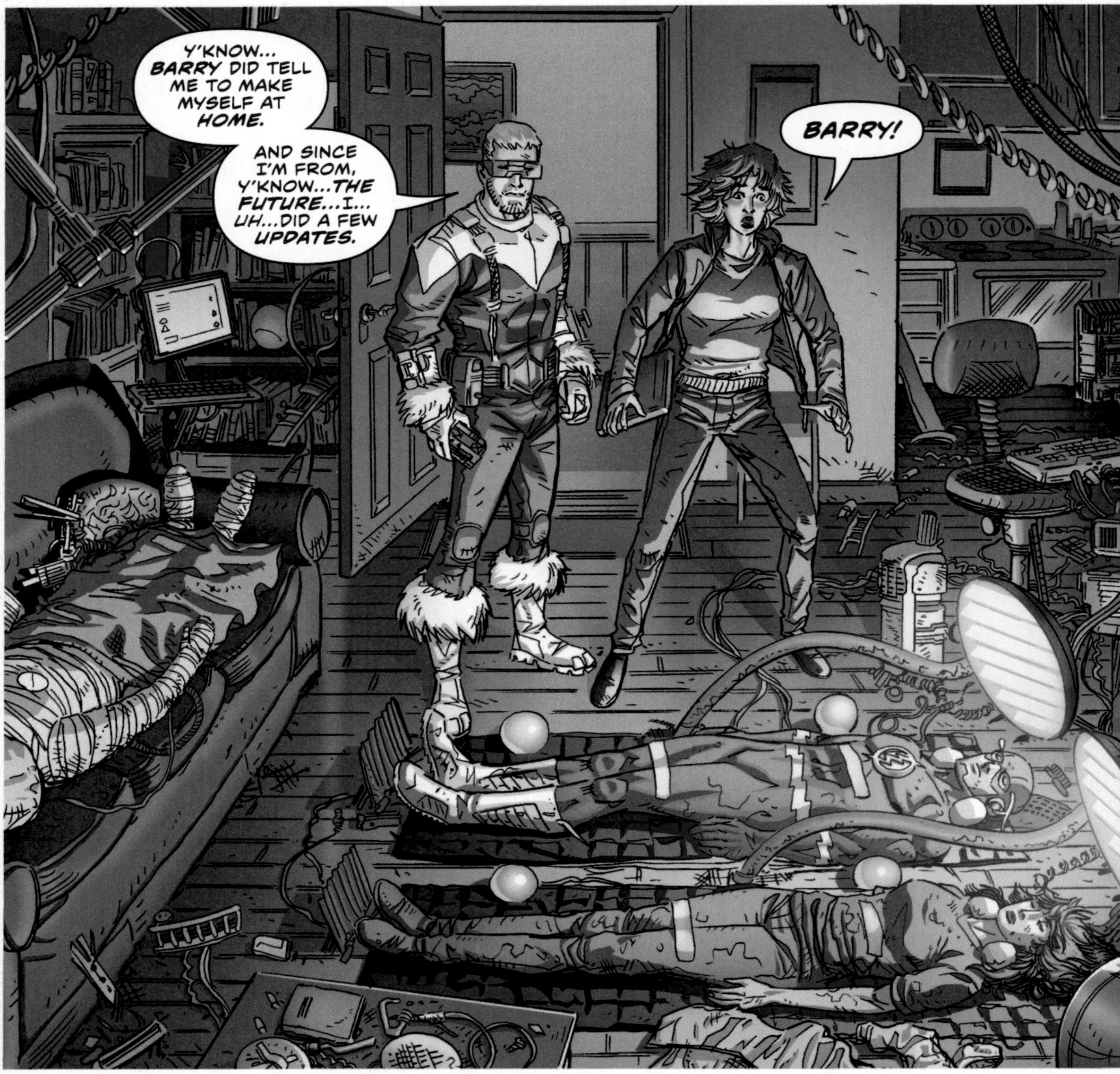
Y'KNOW... BARRY DID TELL ME TO MAKE MYSELF AT HOME.
AND SINCE I'M FROM, Y'KNOW... THE FUTURE... I... UH... DID A FEW UPDATES.
BARRY!

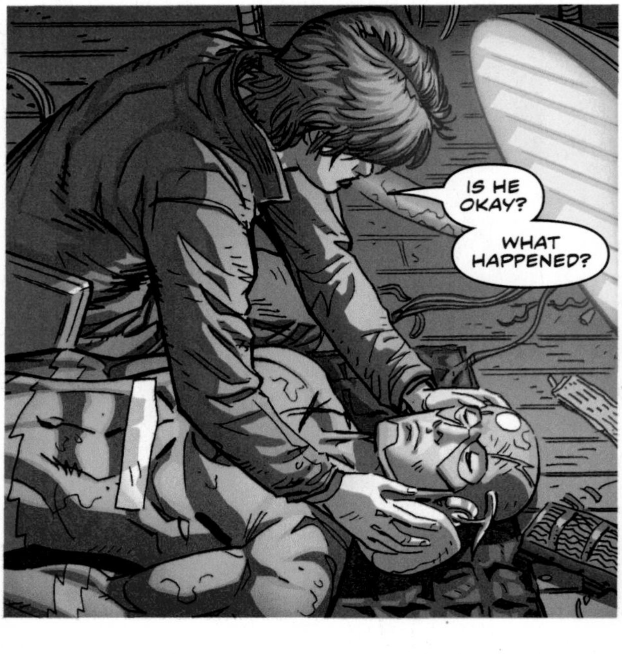
IS HE OKAY?
WHAT HAPPENED?

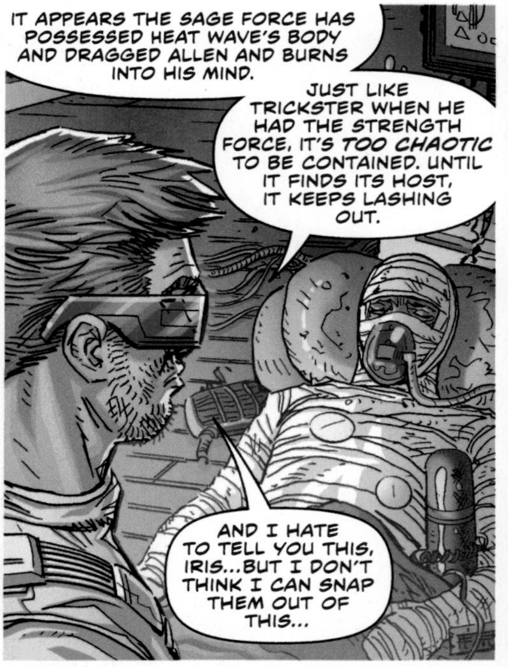
IT APPEARS THE SAGE FORCE HAS POSSESSED HEAT WAVE'S BODY AND DRAGGED ALLEN AND BURNS INTO HIS MIND.
JUST LIKE TRICKSTER WHEN HE HAD THE STRENGTH FORCE, IT'S TOO CHAOTIC TO BE CONTAINED. UNTIL IT FINDS ITS HOST, IT KEEPS LASHING OUT.
AND I HATE TO TELL YOU THIS, IRIS... BUT I DON'T THINK I CAN SNAP THEM OUT OF THIS...

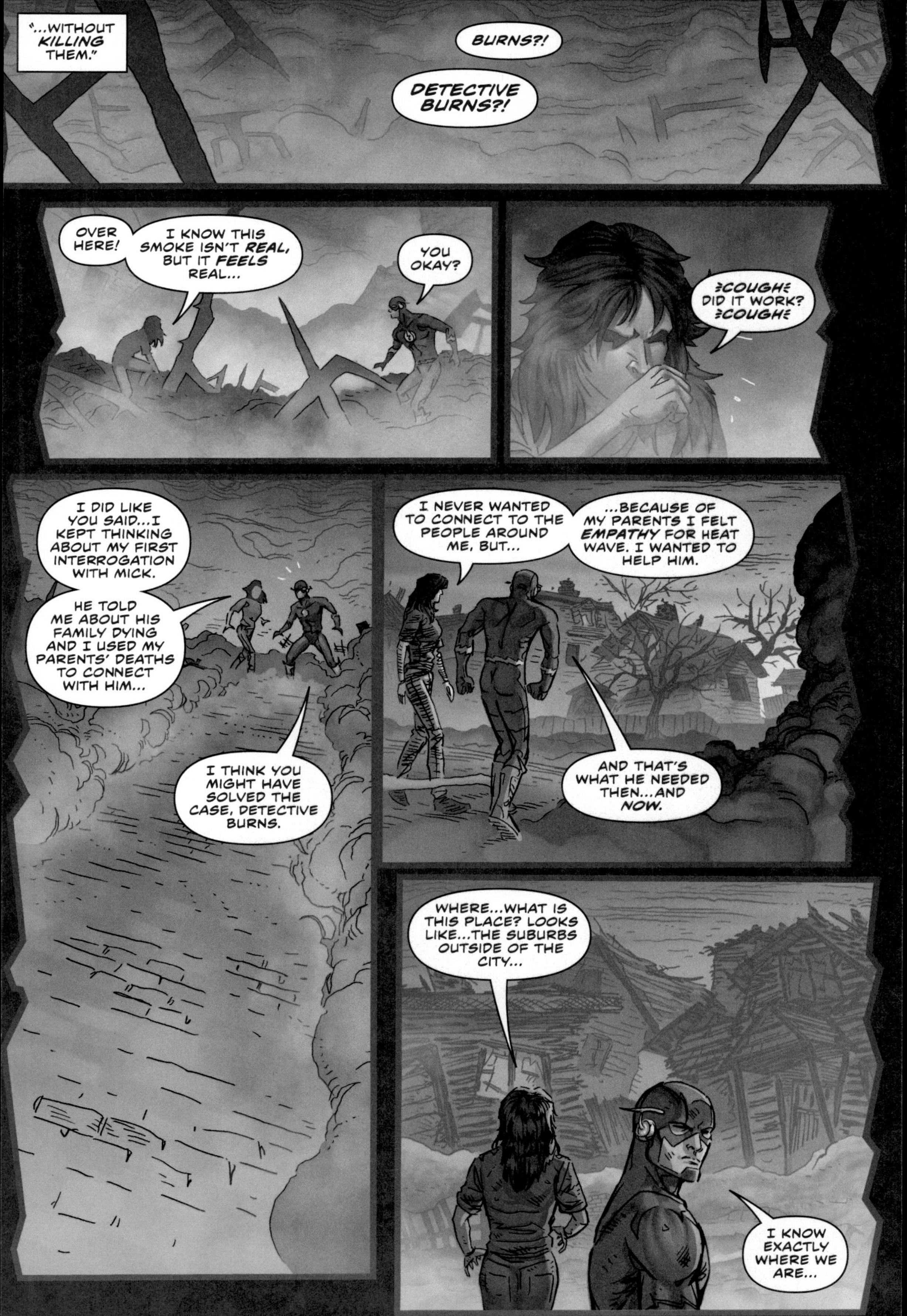
"...WITHOUT KILLING THEM."
BURNS?!
DETECTIVE BURNS?!
OVER HERE!
I KNOW THIS SMOKE ISN'T REAL, BUT IT FEELS REAL...
YOU OKAY?
COUGH DID IT WORK? COUGH
I DID LIKE YOU SAID...I KEPT THINKING ABOUT MY FIRST INTERROGATION WITH MICK.
HE TOLD ME ABOUT HIS FAMILY DYING AND I USED MY PARENTS' DEATHS TO CONNECT WITH HIM...
I THINK YOU MIGHT HAVE SOLVED THE CASE, DETECTIVE BURNS.
I NEVER WANTED TO CONNECT TO THE PEOPLE AROUND ME, BUT...
...BECAUSE OF MY PARENTS I FELT EMPATHY FOR HEAT WAVE. I WANTED TO HELP HIM.
AND THAT'S WHAT HE NEEDED THEN...AND NOW.
WHERE...WHAT IS THIS PLACE? LOOKS LIKE...THE SUBURBS OUTSIDE OF THE CITY...
I KNOW EXACTLY WHERE WE ARE...

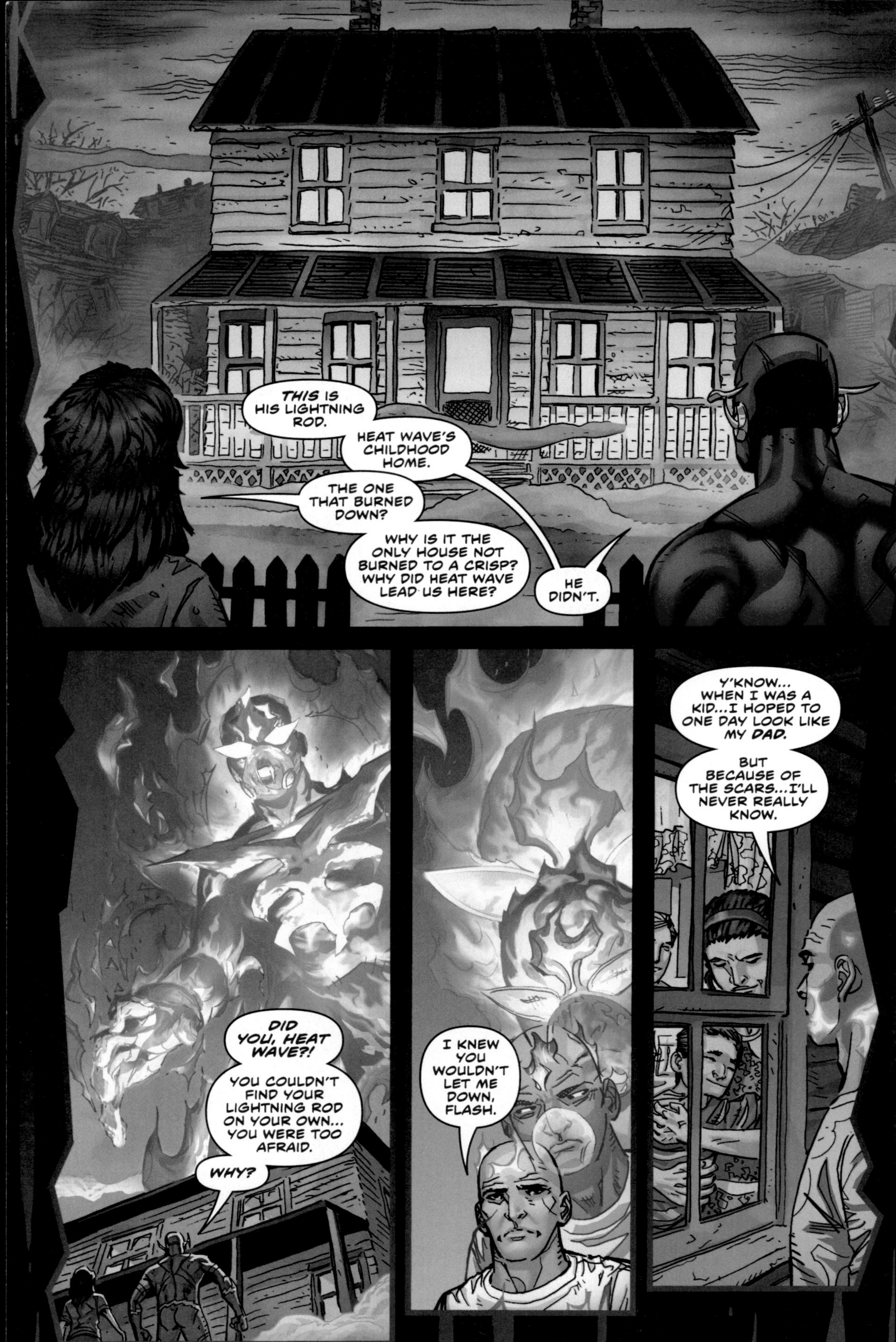

THIS IS HIS LIGHTNING ROD.
HEAT WAVE'S CHILDHOOD HOME.
THE ONE THAT BURNED DOWN?
WHY IS IT THE ONLY HOUSE NOT BURNED TO A CRISP? WHY DID HEAT WAVE LEAD US HERE?
HE DIDN'T.
DID YOU, HEAT WAVE?!
YOU COULDN'T FIND YOUR LIGHTNING ROD ON YOUR OWN... YOU WERE TOO AFRAID.
WHY?
I KNEW YOU WOULDN'T LET ME DOWN, FLASH.
Y'KNOW... WHEN I WAS A KID...I HOPED TO ONE DAY LOOK LIKE MY DAD.
BUT BECAUSE OF THE SCARS...I'LL NEVER REALLY KNOW.

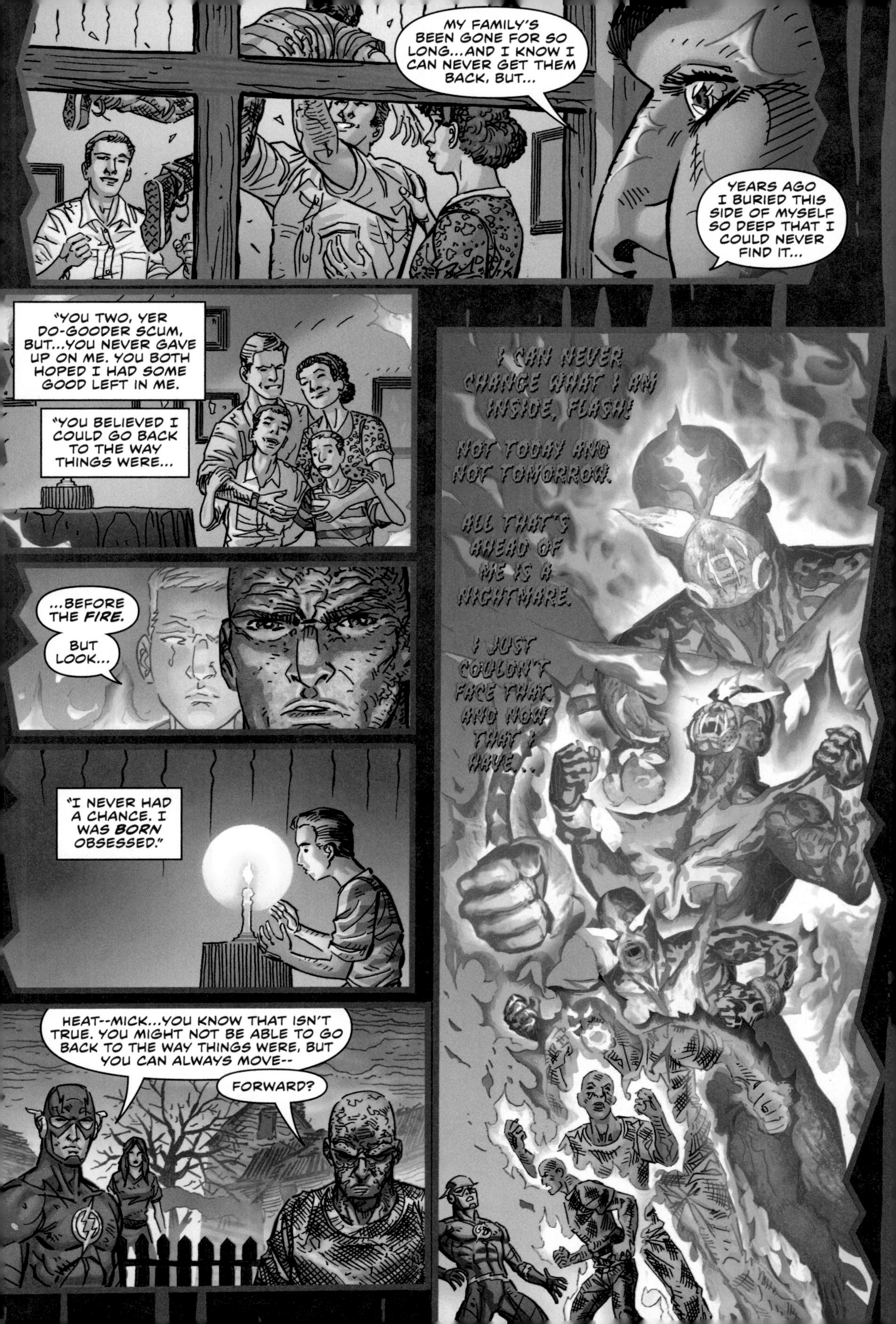
MY FAMILY'S BEEN GONE FOR SO LONG...AND I KNOW I CAN NEVER GET THEM BACK, BUT...
YEARS AGO I BURIED THIS SIDE OF MYSELF SO DEEP THAT I COULD NEVER FIND IT...
"YOU TWO, YER DO-GOODER SCUM, BUT...YOU NEVER GAVE UP ON ME. YOU BOTH HOPED I HAD SOME GOOD LEFT IN ME.
"YOU BELIEVED I COULD GO BACK TO THE WAY THINGS WERE...
...BEFORE THE *FIRE*.
BUT LOOK...
"I NEVER HAD A CHANCE. I WAS *BORN* OBSESSED."
HEAT--MICK...YOU KNOW THAT ISN'T TRUE. YOU MIGHT NOT BE ABLE TO GO BACK TO THE WAY THINGS WERE, BUT YOU CAN ALWAYS MOVE--
FORWARD?
I CAN NEVER CHANGE WHAT I AM INSIDE, FLASH!
NOT TODAY AND NOT TOMORROW.
ALL THAT'S AHEAD OF ME IS A NIGHTMARE.
I JUST COULDN'T FACE THAT AND NOW THAT I HAVE...

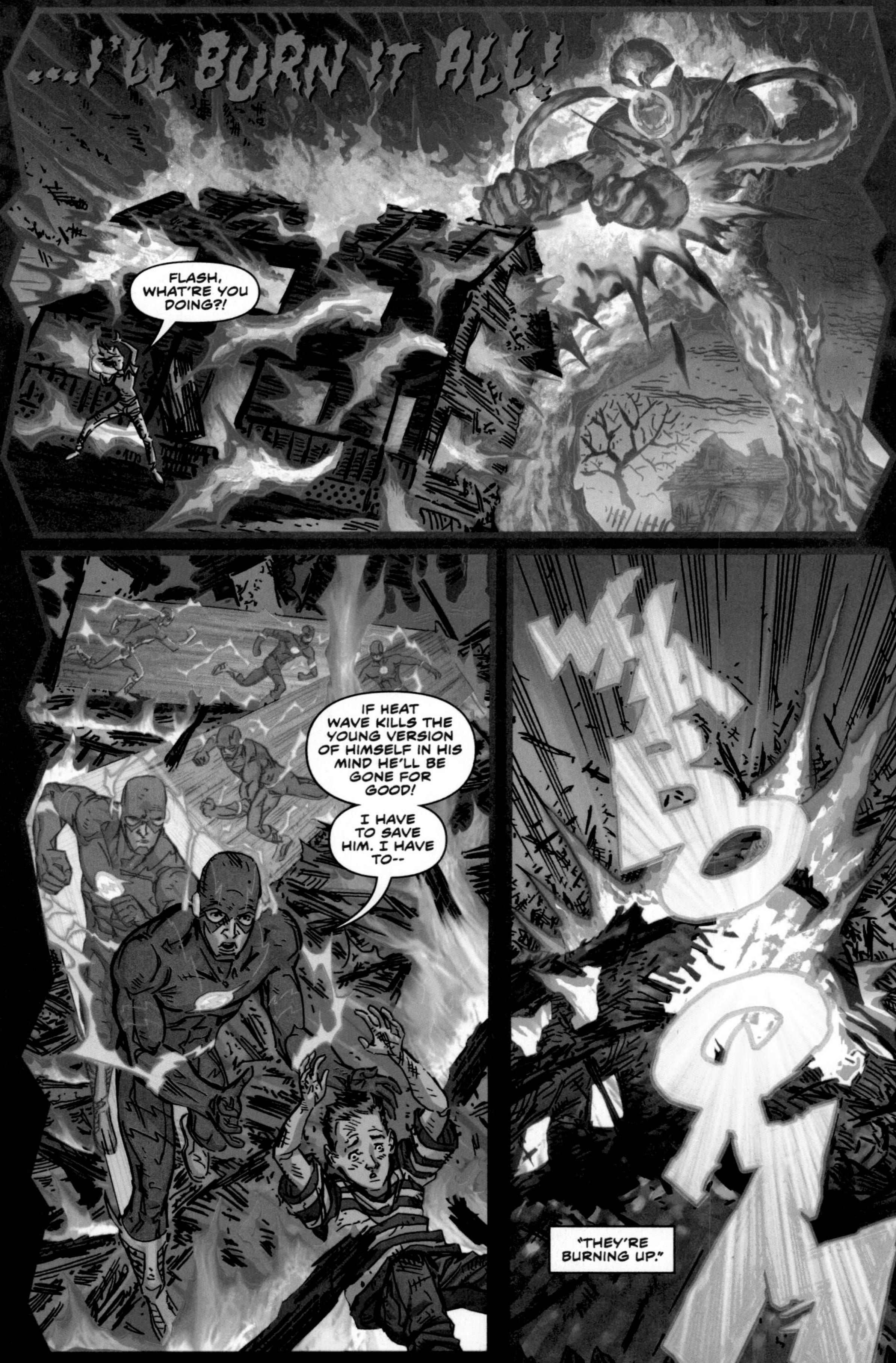
...I'LL BURN IT ALL!
FLASH, WHAT'RE YOU DOING?!
IF HEAT WAVE KILLS THE YOUNG VERSION OF HIMSELF IN HIS MIND HE'LL BE GONE FOR GOOD!
I HAVE TO SAVE HIM. I HAVE TO--
"THEY'RE BURNING UP."

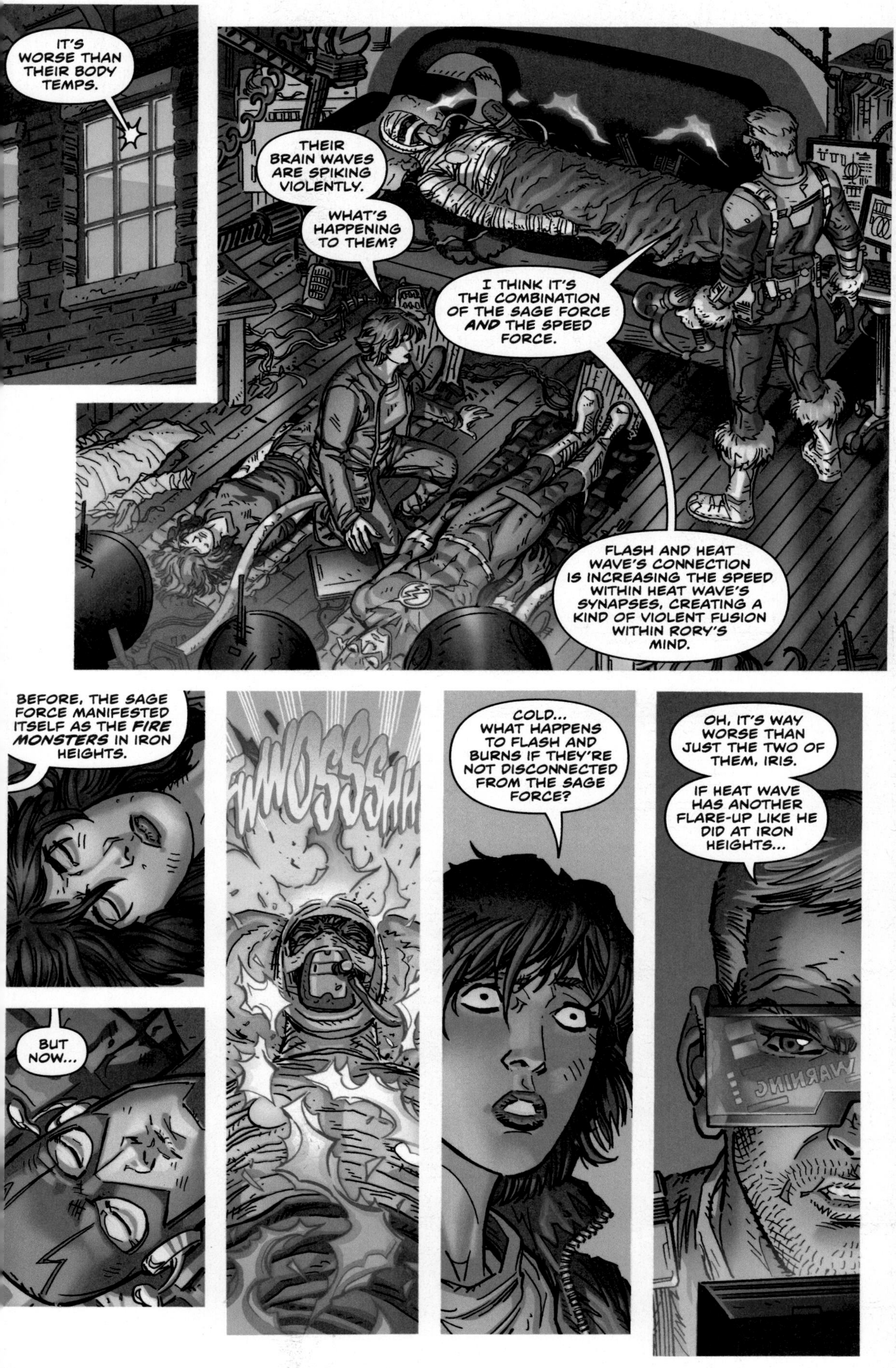
IT'S WORSE THAN THEIR BODY TEMPS.
THEIR BRAIN WAVES ARE SPIKING VIOLENTLY.
WHAT'S HAPPENING TO THEM?
I THINK IT'S THE COMBINATION OF THE SAGE FORCE AND THE SPEED FORCE.
FLASH AND HEAT WAVE'S CONNECTION IS INCREASING THE SPEED WITHIN HEAT WAVE'S SYNAPSES, CREATING A KIND OF VIOLENT FUSION WITHIN RORY'S MIND.
BEFORE, THE SAGE FORCE MANIFESTED ITSELF AS THE FIRE MONSTERS IN IRON HEIGHTS.
BUT NOW...
WHOSSSHH
COLD... WHAT HAPPENS TO FLASH AND BURNS IF THEY'RE NOT DISCONNECTED FROM THE SAGE FORCE?
OH, IT'S WAY WORSE THAN JUST THE TWO OF THEM, IRIS.
IF HEAT WAVE HAS ANOTHER FLARE-UP LIKE HE DID AT IRON HEIGHTS...
WARNING

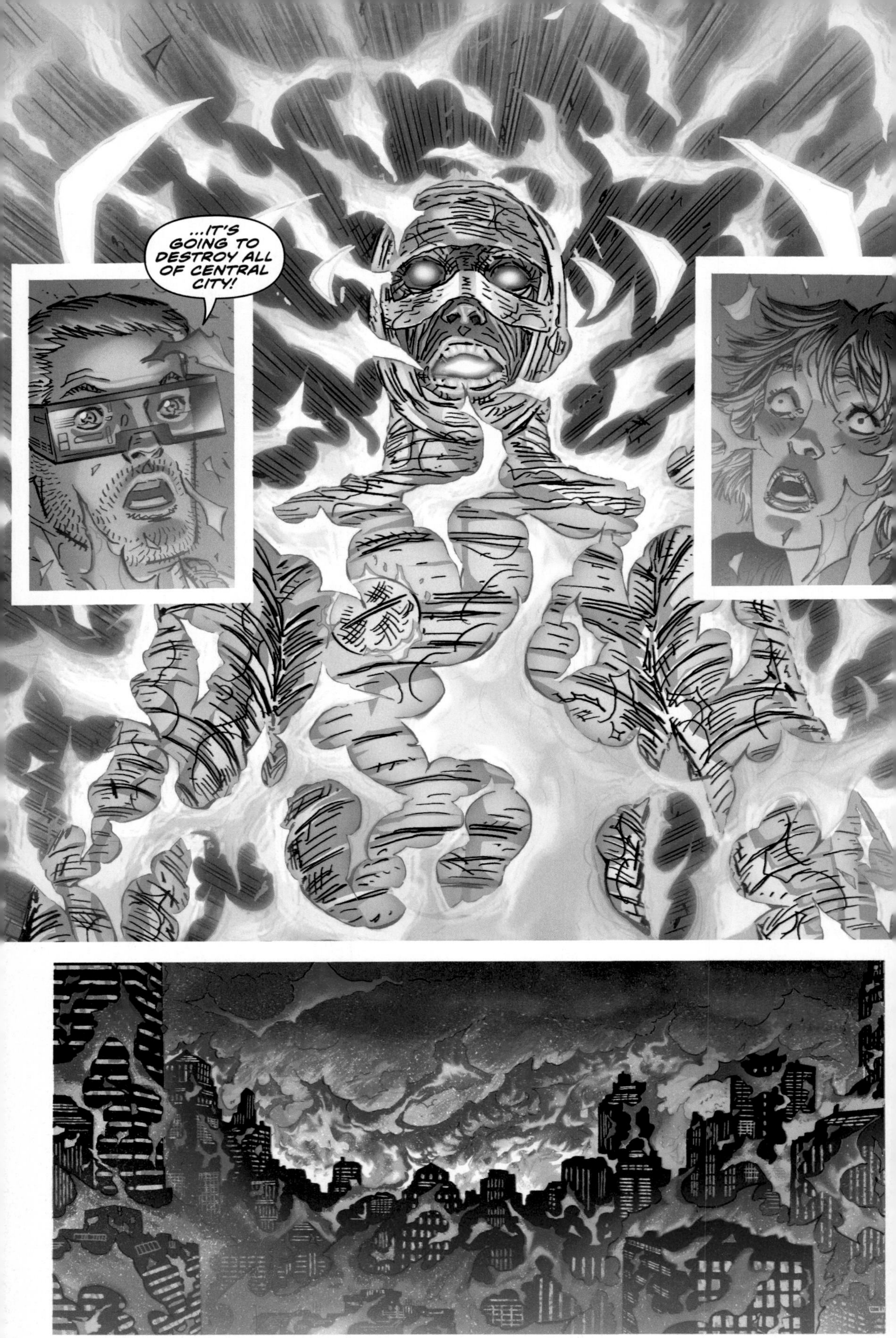
...IT'S GOING TO DESTROY ALL OF CENTRAL CITY!

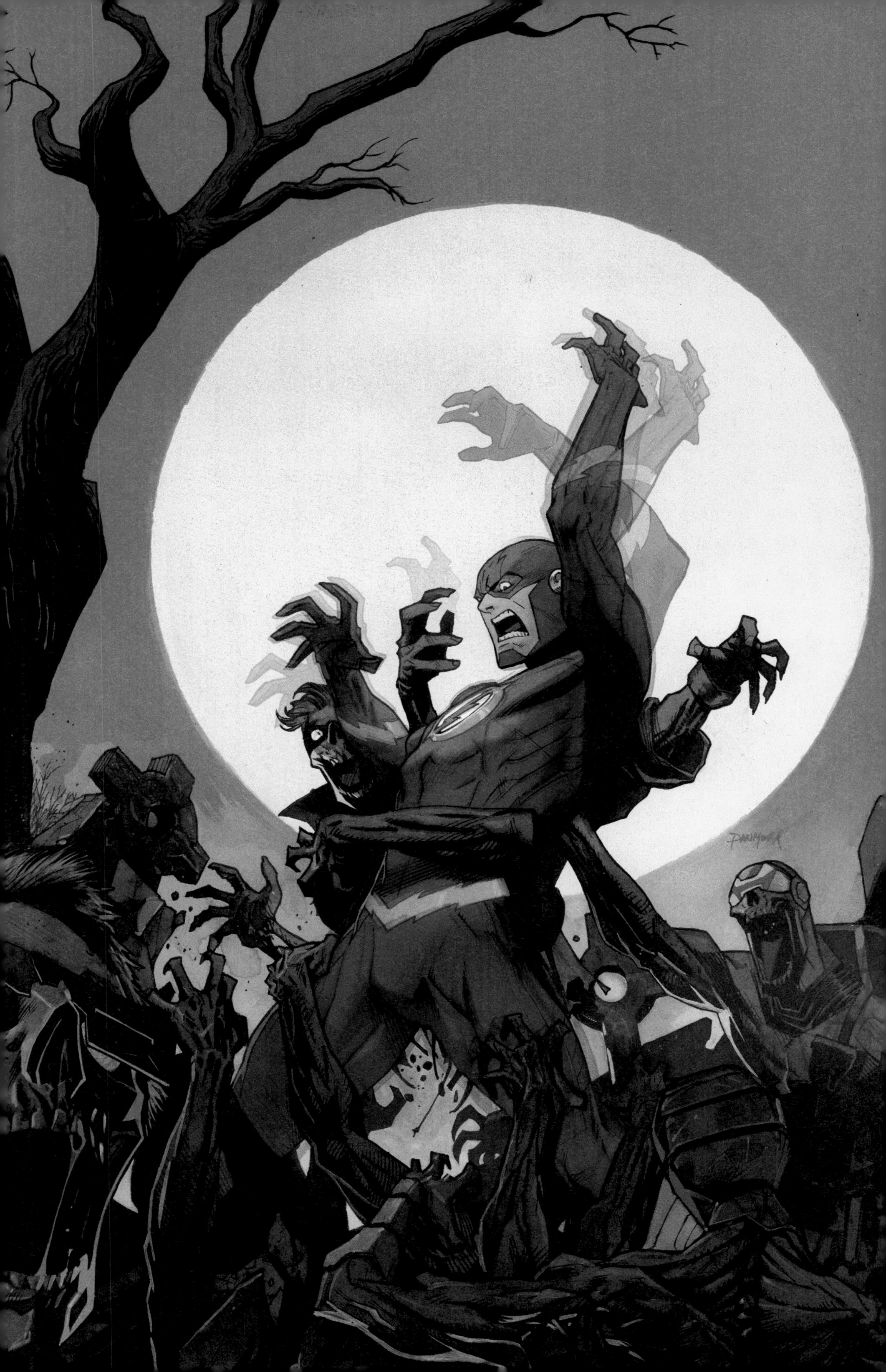

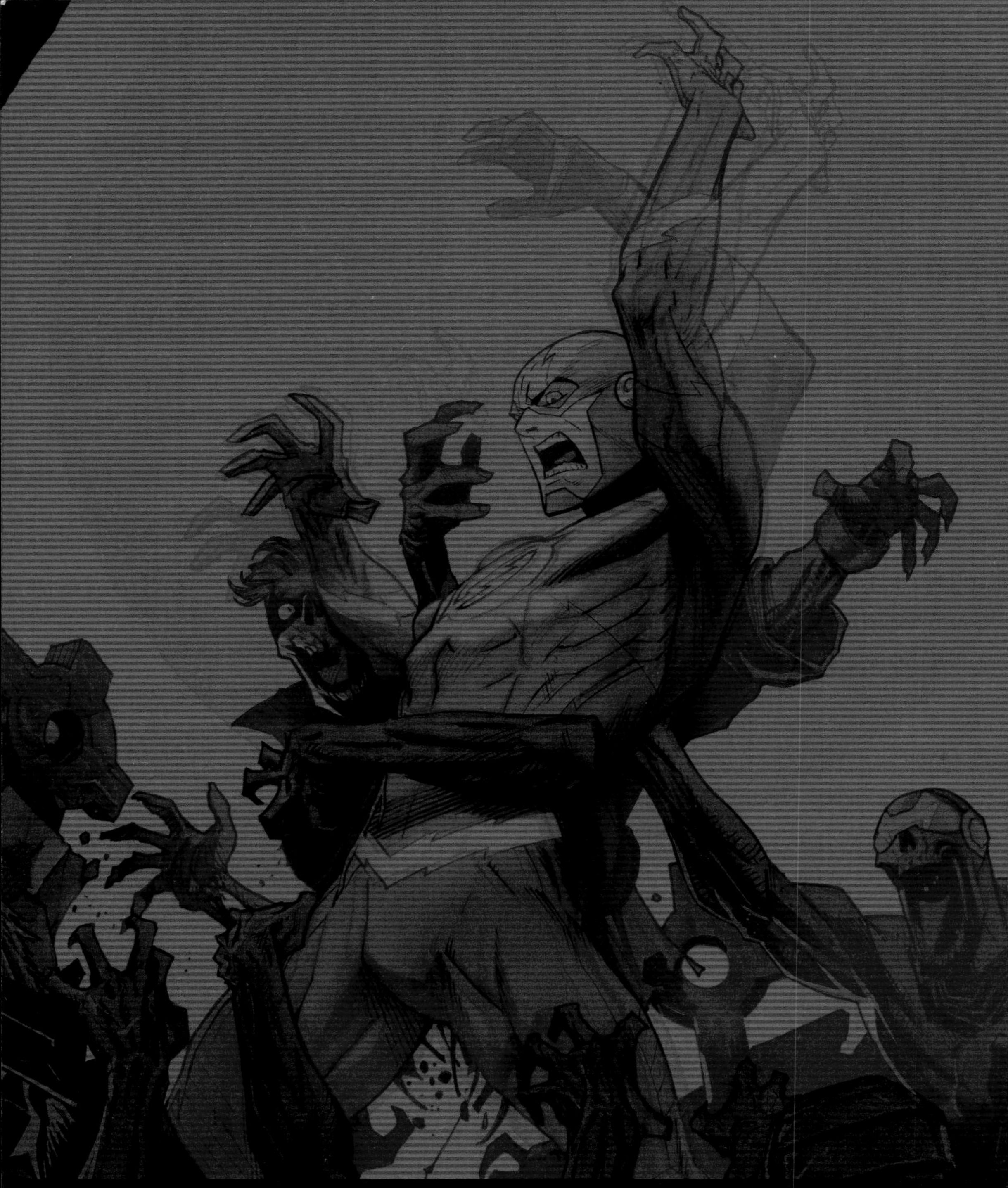

THE FLASH
#57

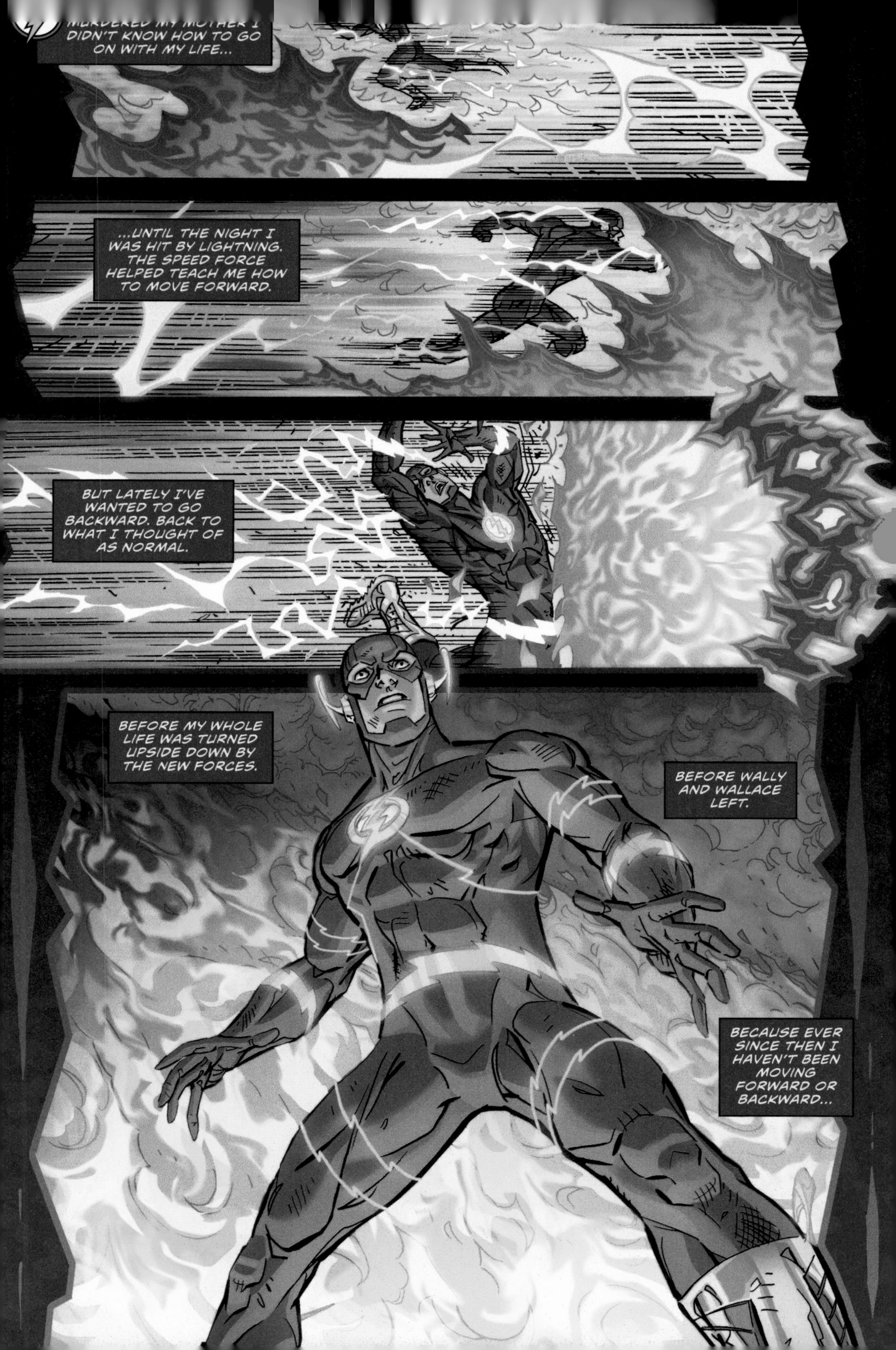
MURDERED MY MOTHER I DIDN'T KNOW HOW TO GO ON WITH MY LIFE...
...UNTIL THE NIGHT I WAS HIT BY LIGHTNING. THE SPEED FORCE HELPED TEACH ME HOW TO MOVE FORWARD.
BUT LATELY I'VE WANTED TO GO BACKWARD. BACK TO WHAT I THOUGHT OF AS NORMAL.
BEFORE MY WHOLE LIFE WAS TURNED UPSIDE DOWN BY THE NEW FORCES.
BEFORE WALLY AND WALLACE LEFT.
BECAUSE EVER SINCE THEN I HAVEN'T BEEN MOVING FORWARD OR BACKWARD...

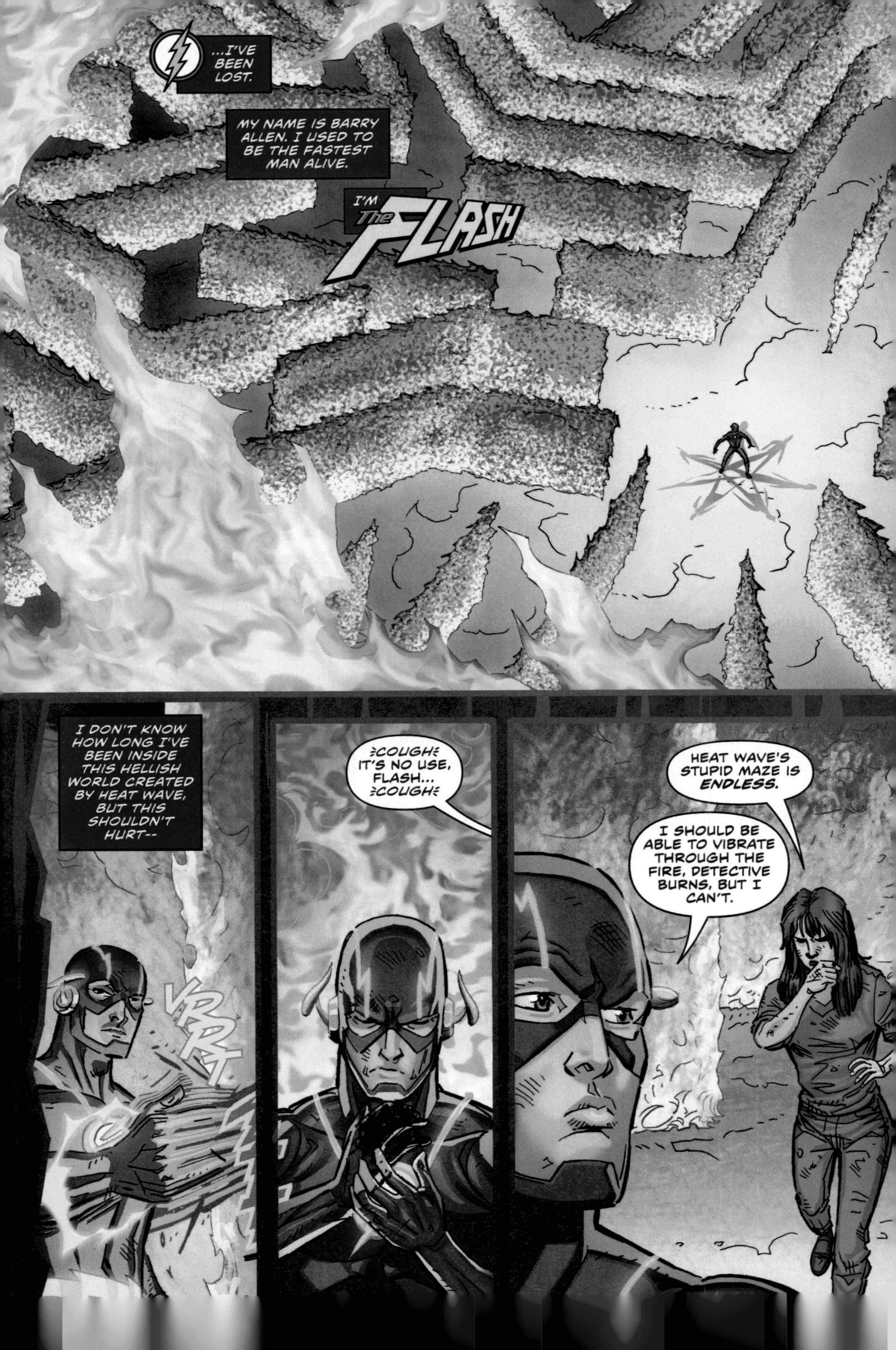
...I'VE BEEN LOST.
MY NAME IS BARRY ALLEN. I USED TO BE THE FASTEST MAN ALIVE.
I'M The FLASH
I DON'T KNOW HOW LONG I'VE BEEN INSIDE THIS HELLISH WORLD CREATED BY HEAT WAVE, BUT THIS SHOULDN'T HURT--
VRRT
COUGH IT'S NO USE, FLASH... COUGH
HEAT WAVE'S STUPID MAZE IS ENDLESS.
I SHOULD BE ABLE TO VIBRATE THROUGH THE FIRE, DETECTIVE BURNS, BUT I CAN'T.

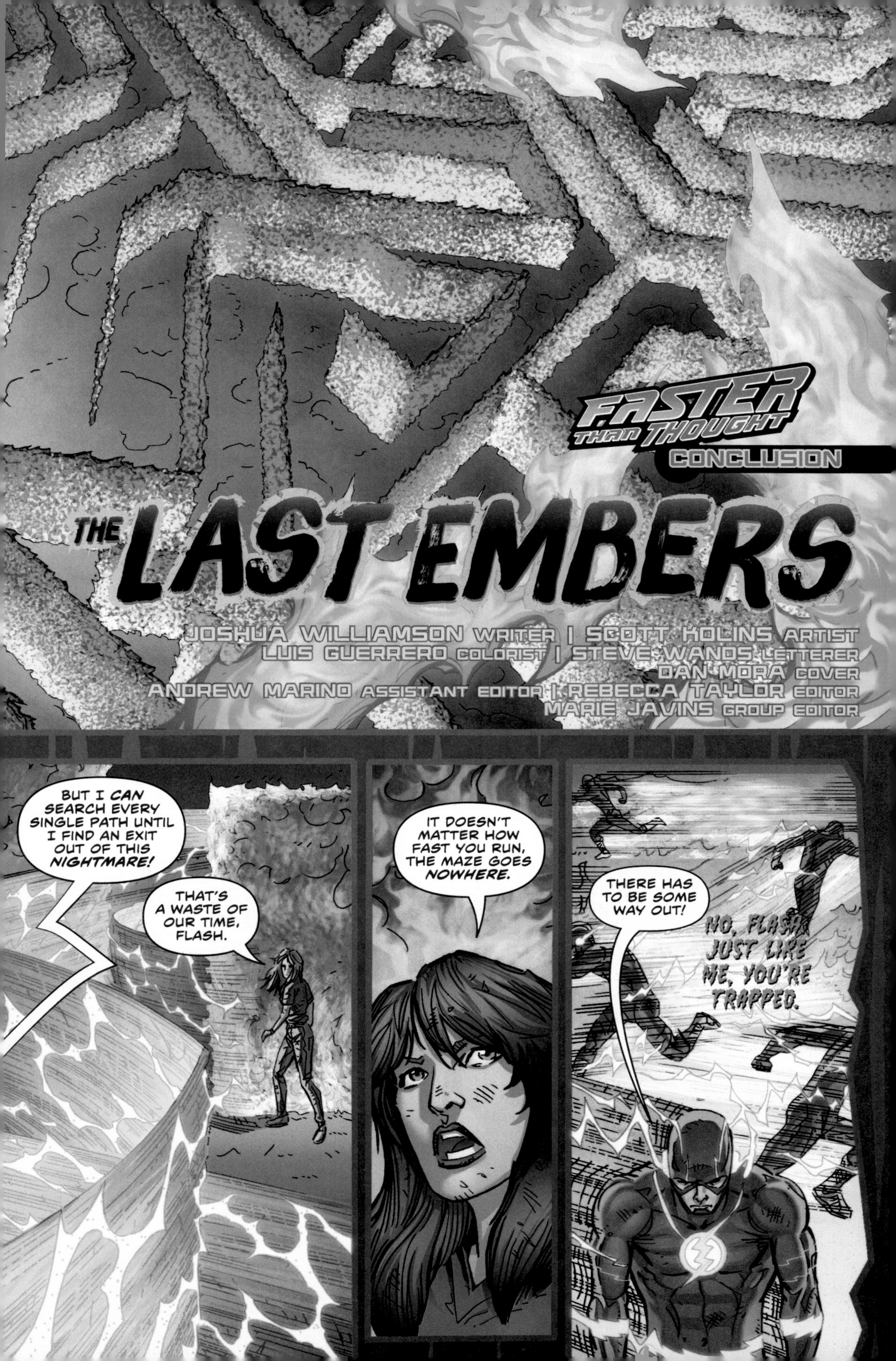
FASTER THAN THOUGHT
CONCLUSION
THE LAST EMBERS
JOSHUA WILLIAMSON WRITER | SCOTT KOLINS ARTIST
LUIS GUERRERO COLORIST | STEVE WANDS LETTERER
DAN MORA COVER
ANDREW MARINO ASSISTANT EDITOR | REBECCA TAYLOR EDITOR
MARIE JAVINS GROUP EDITOR
BUT I CAN SEARCH EVERY SINGLE PATH UNTIL I FIND AN EXIT OUT OF THIS NIGHTMARE!
THAT'S A WASTE OF OUR TIME, FLASH.
IT DOESN'T MATTER HOW FAST YOU RUN, THE MAZE GOES NOWHERE.
THERE HAS TO BE SOME WAY OUT!
NO, FLASH. JUST LIKE ME, YOU'RE TRAPPED.

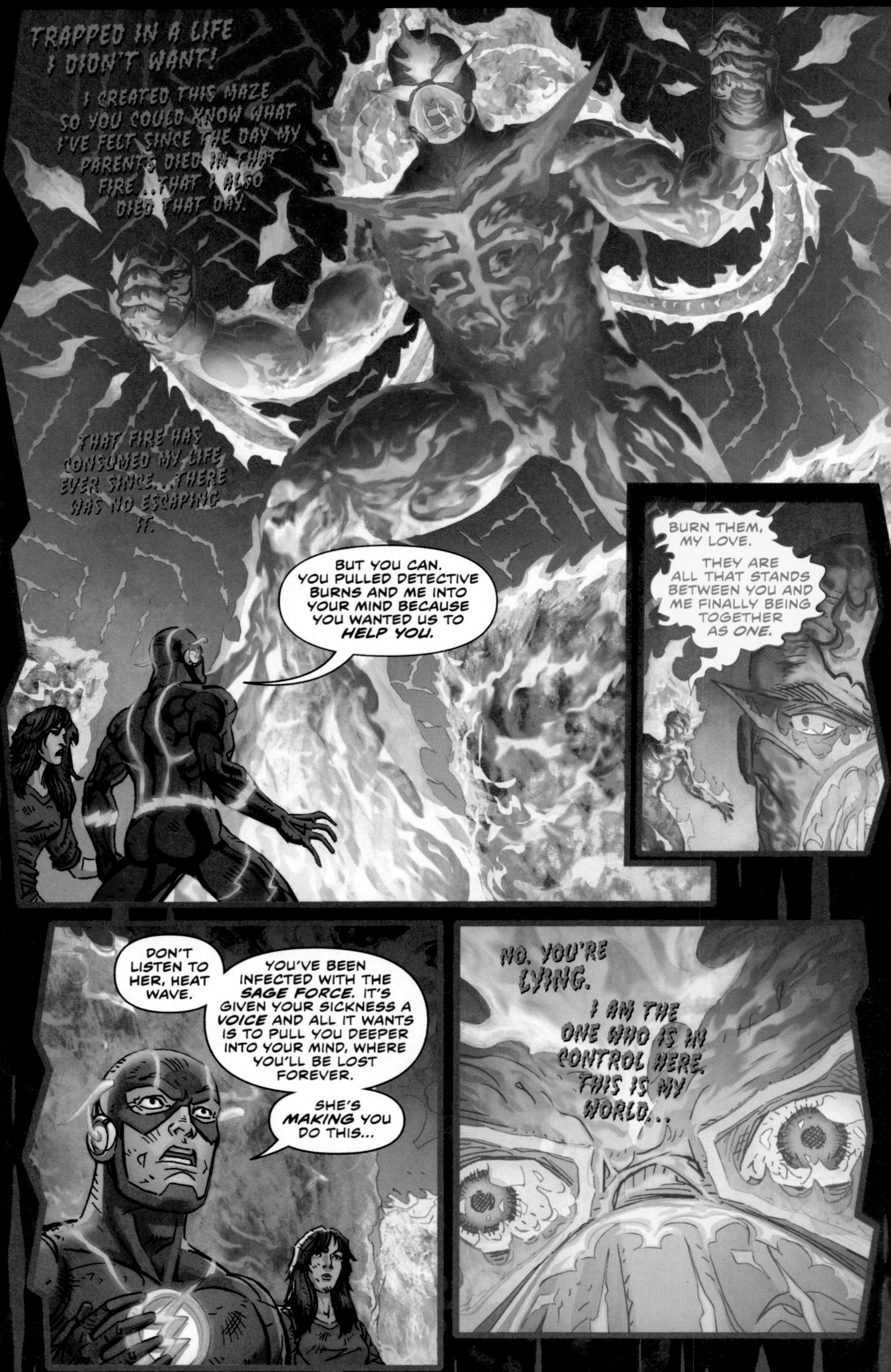
TRAPPED IN A LIFE I DIDN'T WANT!
I CREATED THIS MAZE SO YOU COULD KNOW WHAT I'VE FELT SINCE THE DAY MY PARENTS DIED IN THAT FIRE...THAT I ALSO DIED THAT DAY.
THAT FIRE HAS CONSUMED MY LIFE EVER SINCE...THERE WAS NO ESCAPING IT.
BUT YOU CAN. YOU PULLED DETECTIVE BURNS AND ME INTO YOUR MIND BECAUSE YOU WANTED US TO HELP YOU.
BURN THEM, MY LOVE.
THEY ARE ALL THAT STANDS BETWEEN YOU AND ME FINALLY BEING TOGETHER AS ONE.
DON'T LISTEN TO HER, HEAT WAVE.
YOU'VE BEEN INFECTED WITH THE SAGE FORCE. IT'S GIVEN YOUR SICKNESS A VOICE AND ALL IT WANTS IS TO PULL YOU DEEPER INTO YOUR MIND, WHERE YOU'LL BE LOST FOREVER.
SHE'S MAKING YOU DO THIS...
NO. YOU'RE LYING.
I AM THE ONE WHO IS IN CONTROL HERE. THIS IS MY WORLD...

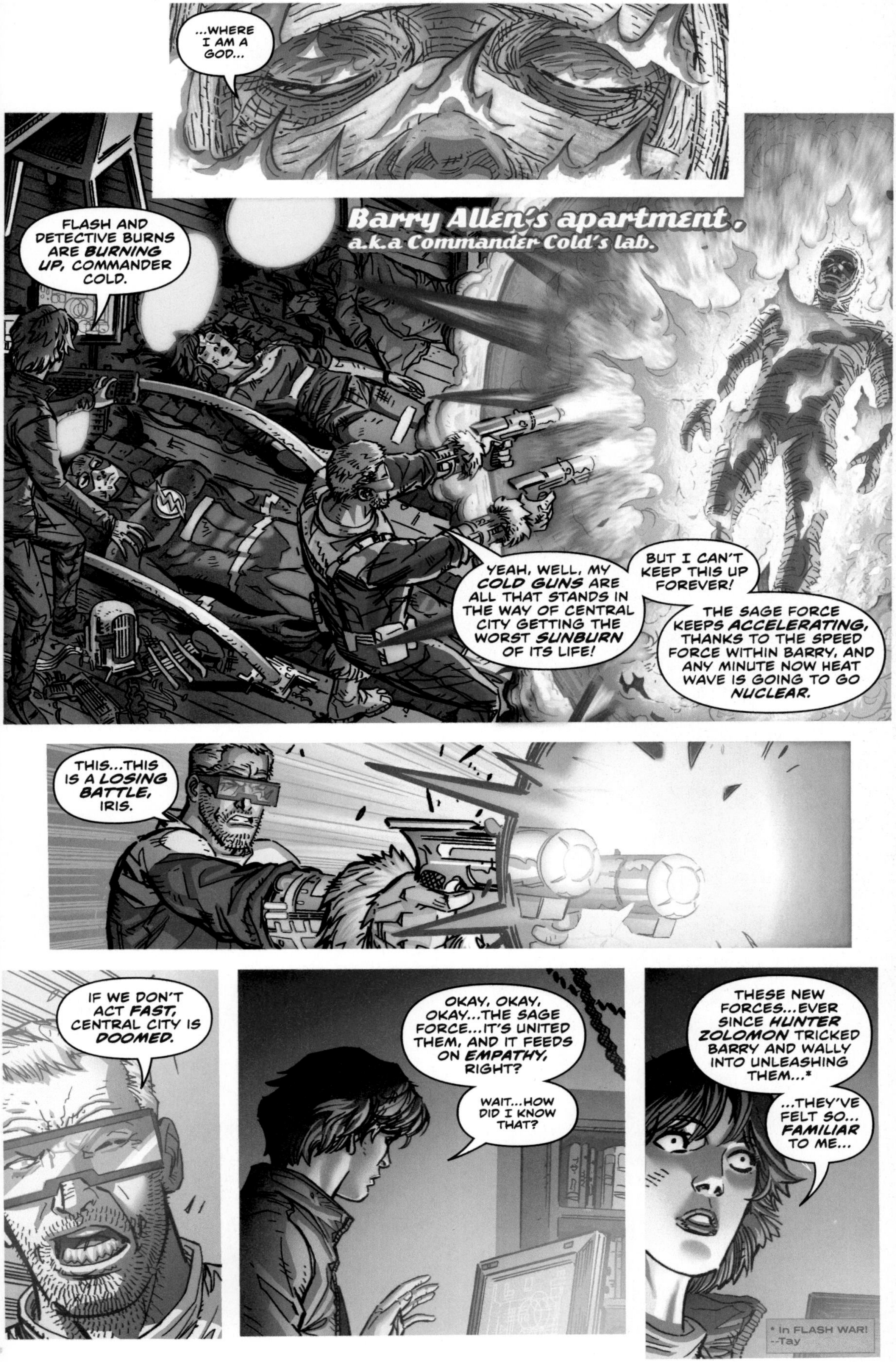
...WHERE I AM A GOD...
Barry Allen's apartment, a.k.a Commander Cold's lab.
FLASH AND DETECTIVE BURNS ARE BURNING UP, COMMANDER COLD.
YEAH, WELL, MY COLD GUNS ARE ALL THAT STANDS IN THE WAY OF CENTRAL CITY GETTING THE WORST SUNBURN OF ITS LIFE!
BUT I CAN'T KEEP THIS UP FOREVER!
THE SAGE FORCE KEEPS ACCELERATING, THANKS TO THE SPEED FORCE WITHIN BARRY, AND ANY MINUTE NOW HEAT WAVE IS GOING TO GO NUCLEAR.
THIS...THIS IS A LOSING BATTLE, IRIS.
IF WE DON'T ACT FAST, CENTRAL CITY IS DOOMED.
OKAY, OKAY, OKAY...THE SAGE FORCE...IT'S UNITED THEM, AND IT FEEDS ON EMPATHY, RIGHT?
WAIT...HOW DID I KNOW THAT?
THESE NEW FORCES...EVER SINCE HUNTER ZOLOMON TRICKED BARRY AND WALLY INTO UNLEASHING THEM...*
...THEY'VE FELT SO... FAMILIAR TO ME...
* In FLASH WAR! --Tay

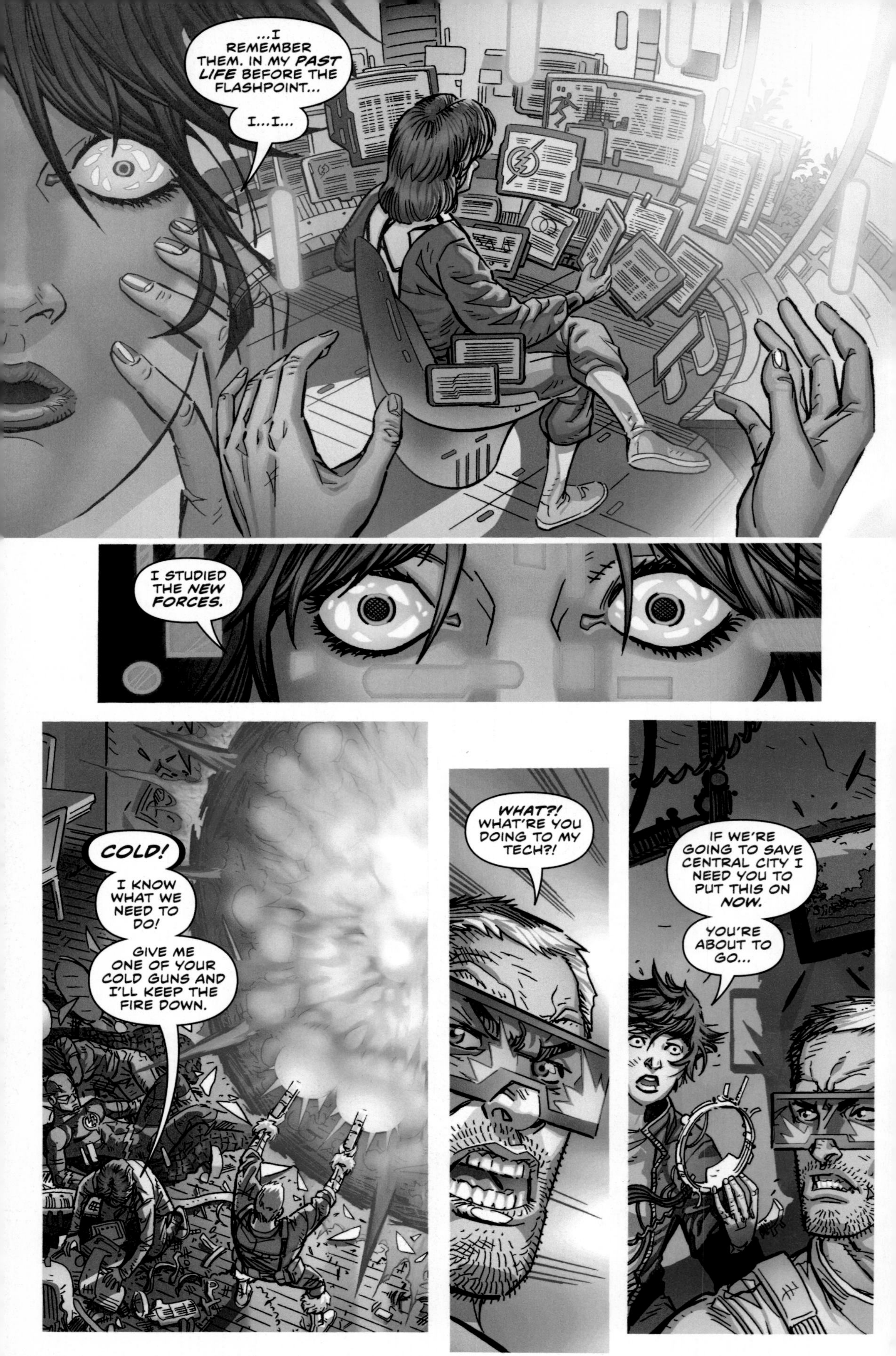
...I REMEMBER THEM. IN MY *PAST LIFE* BEFORE THE FLASHPOINT...
I...I...
I STUDIED THE *NEW FORCES.*
COLD!
I KNOW WHAT WE NEED TO DO!
GIVE ME ONE OF YOUR COLD GUNS AND I'LL KEEP THE FIRE DOWN.
WHAT?! WHAT'RE YOU DOING TO MY TECH?!
IF WE'RE GOING TO SAVE CENTRAL CITY I NEED YOU TO PUT THIS ON *NOW.*
YOU'RE ABOUT TO GO...

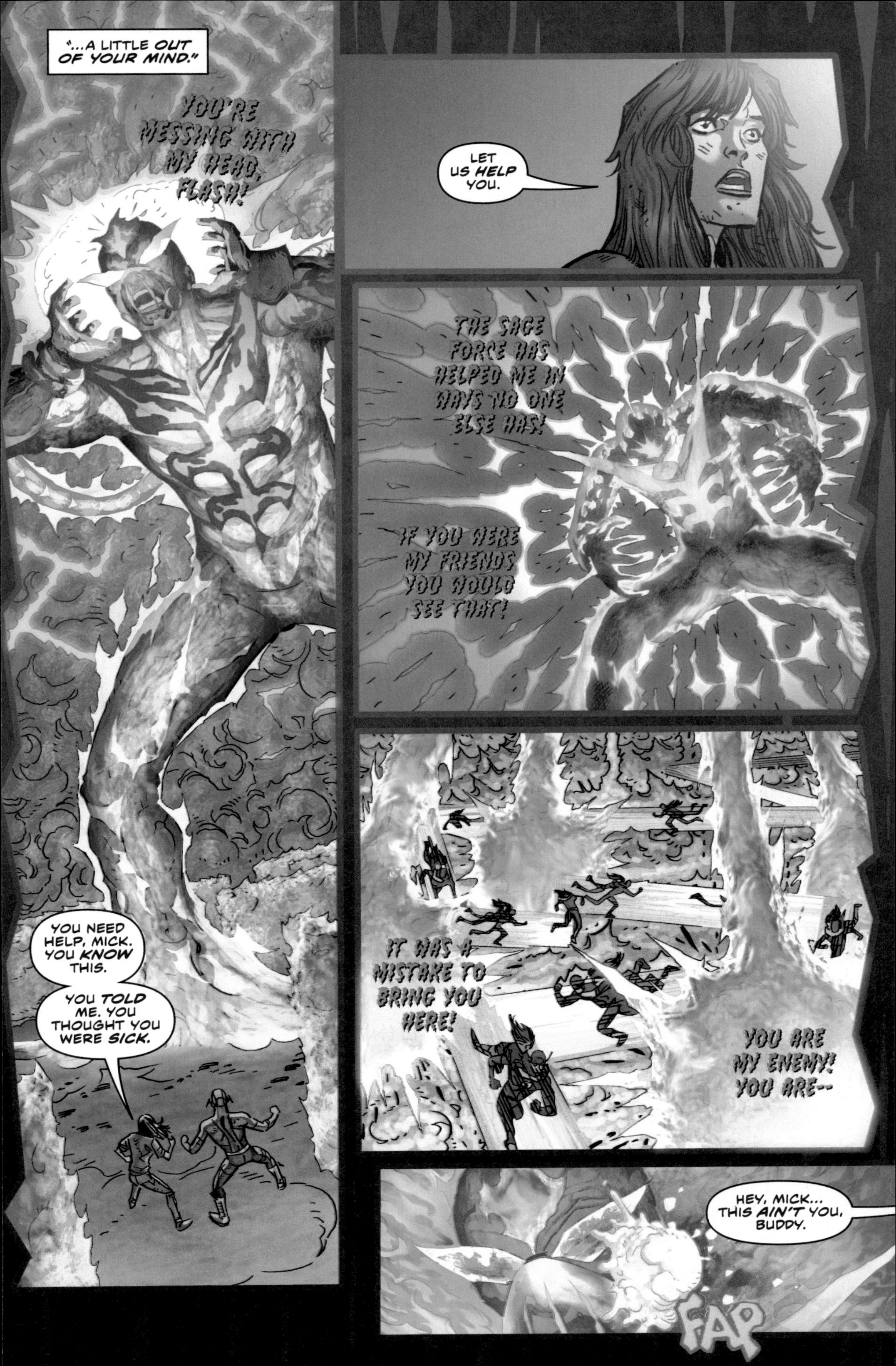

"...A LITTLE OUT OF YOUR MIND."
YOU'RE MESSING WITH MY HEAD, FLASH!
LET US HELP YOU.
THE SAGE FORCE HAS HELPED ME IN WAYS NO ONE ELSE HAS!
IF YOU WERE MY FRIENDS YOU WOULD SEE THAT!
YOU NEED HELP, MICK. YOU KNOW THIS.
YOU TOLD ME. YOU THOUGHT YOU WERE SICK.
IT WAS A MISTAKE TO BRING YOU HERE!
YOU ARE MY ENEMY! YOU ARE--
HEY, MICK... THIS AIN'T YOU, BUDDY.
FAP

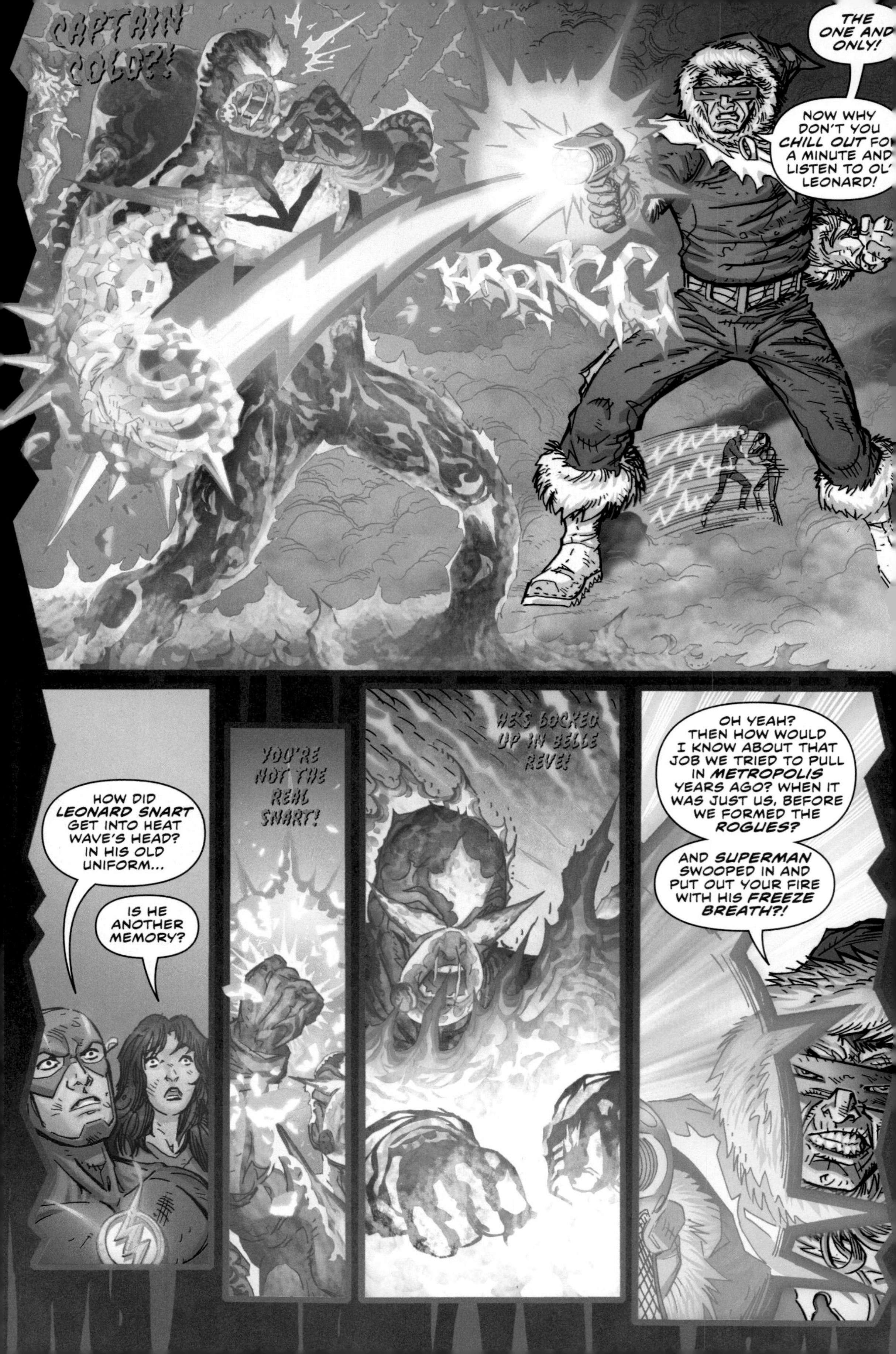
CAPTAIN COLD?!
THE ONE AND ONLY!
NOW WHY DON'T YOU CHILL OUT FOR A MINUTE AND LISTEN TO OL' LEONARD!
KRRNGG
HOW DID LEONARD SNART GET INTO HEAT WAVE'S HEAD? IN HIS OLD UNIFORM...
IS HE ANOTHER MEMORY?
YOU'RE NOT THE REAL SNART!
HE'S LOCKED UP IN BELLE REVE!
OH YEAH? THEN HOW WOULD I KNOW ABOUT THAT JOB WE TRIED TO PULL IN METROPOLIS YEARS AGO? WHEN IT WAS JUST US, BEFORE WE FORMED THE ROGUES?
AND SUPERMAN SWOOPED IN AND PUT OUT YOUR FIRE WITH HIS FREEZE BREATH?!

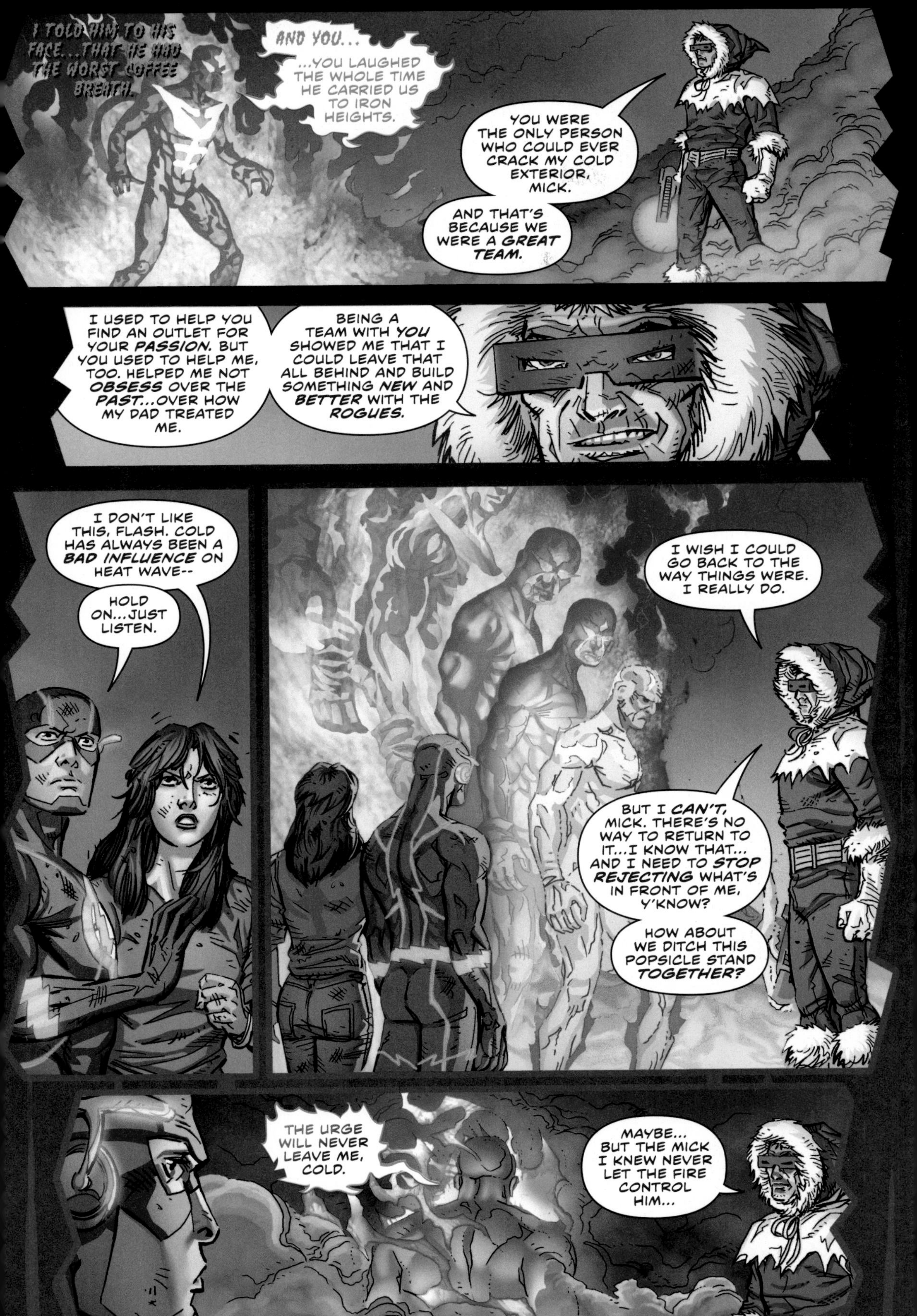
I TOLD HIM TO HIS FACE...THAT HE HAD THE WORST COFFEE BREATH.
AND YOU... ...YOU LAUGHED THE WHOLE TIME HE CARRIED US TO IRON HEIGHTS.
YOU WERE THE ONLY PERSON WHO COULD EVER CRACK MY COLD EXTERIOR, MICK.
AND THAT'S BECAUSE WE WERE A GREAT TEAM.
I USED TO HELP YOU FIND AN OUTLET FOR YOUR PASSION. BUT YOU USED TO HELP ME, TOO. HELPED ME NOT OBSESS OVER THE PAST...OVER HOW MY DAD TREATED ME.
BEING A TEAM WITH YOU SHOWED ME THAT I COULD LEAVE THAT ALL BEHIND AND BUILD SOMETHING NEW AND BETTER WITH THE ROGUES.
I DON'T LIKE THIS, FLASH. COLD HAS ALWAYS BEEN A BAD INFLUENCE ON HEAT WAVE--
HOLD ON...JUST LISTEN.
I WISH I COULD GO BACK TO THE WAY THINGS WERE. I REALLY DO.
BUT I CAN'T, MICK. THERE'S NO WAY TO RETURN TO IT...I KNOW THAT... AND I NEED TO STOP REJECTING WHAT'S IN FRONT OF ME, Y'KNOW?
HOW ABOUT WE DITCH THIS POPSICLE STAND TOGETHER?
THE URGE WILL NEVER LEAVE ME, COLD.
MAYBE... BUT THE MICK I KNEW NEVER LET THE FIRE CONTROL HIM...

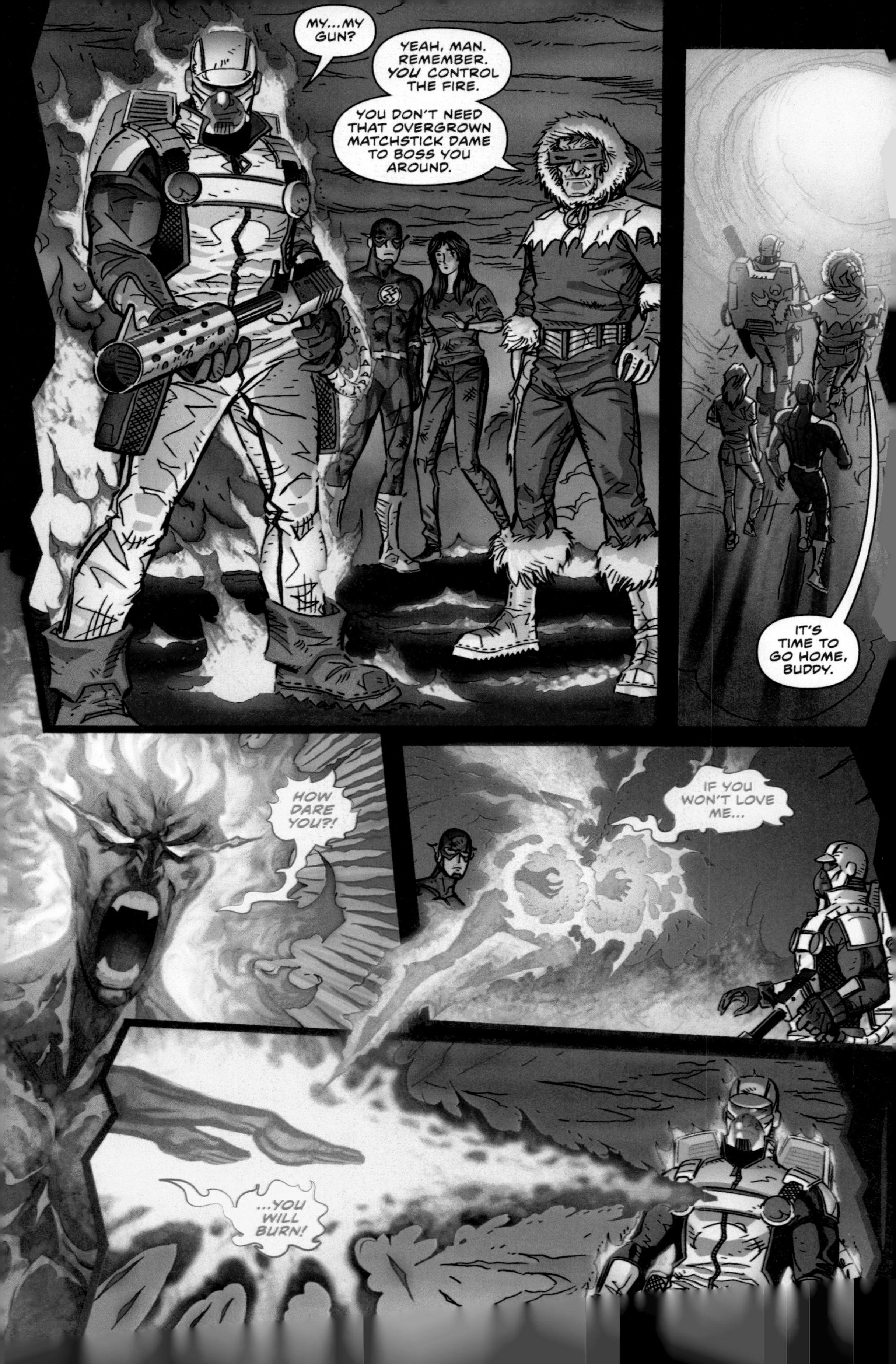
MY...MY GUN?
YEAH, MAN. REMEMBER. YOU CONTROL THE FIRE.
YOU DON'T NEED THAT OVERGROWN MATCHSTICK DAME TO BOSS YOU AROUND.
IT'S TIME TO GO HOME, BUDDY.
HOW DARE YOU?!
IF YOU WON'T LOVE ME...
...YOU WILL BURN!

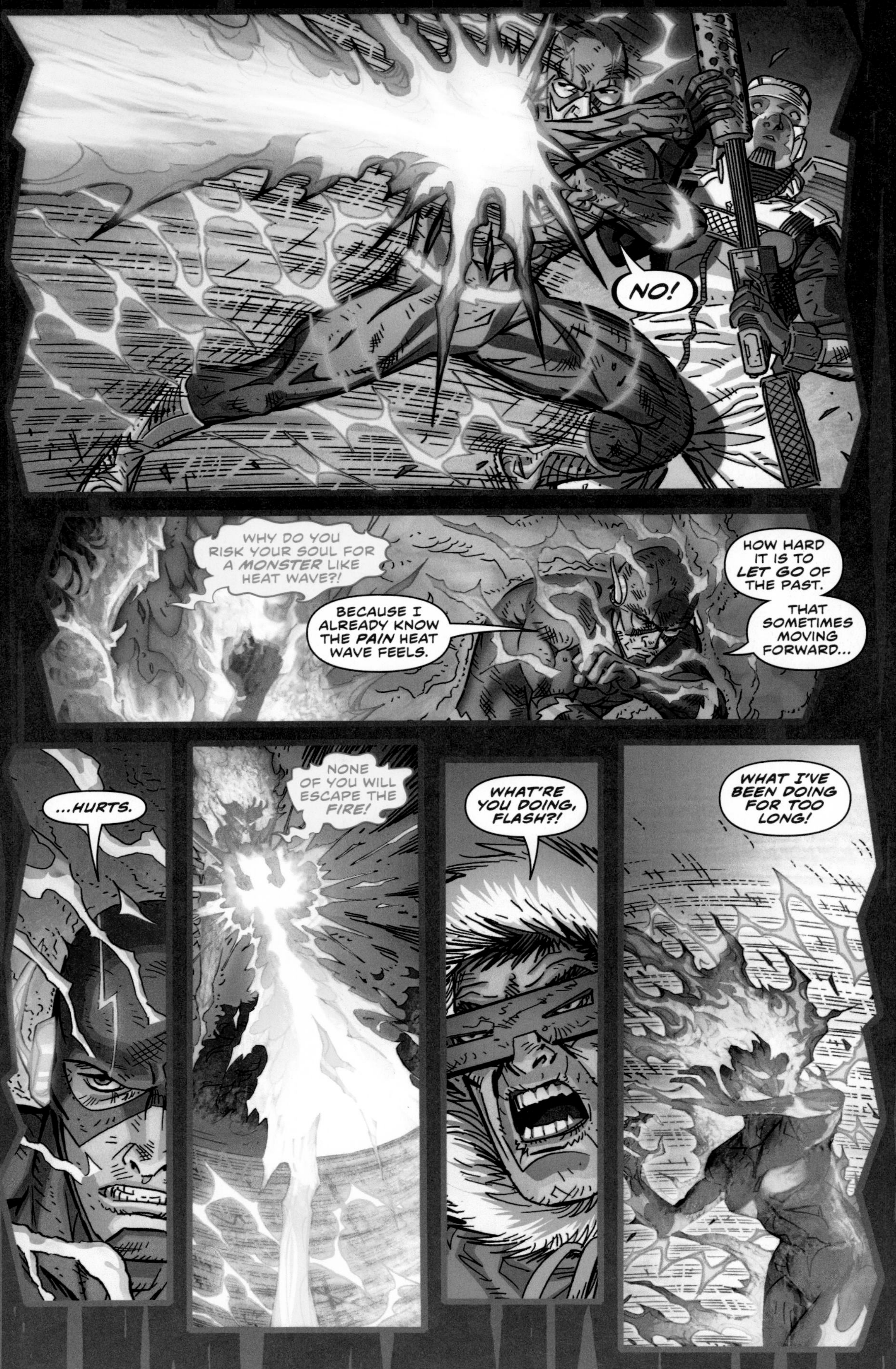
NO!
WHY DO YOU RISK YOUR SOUL FOR A MONSTER LIKE HEAT WAVE?!
BECAUSE I ALREADY KNOW THE PAIN HEAT WAVE FEELS.
HOW HARD IT IS TO LET GO OF THE PAST.
THAT SOMETIMES MOVING FORWARD...
...HURTS.
NONE OF YOU WILL ESCAPE THE FIRE!
WHAT'RE YOU DOING, FLASH?!
WHAT I'VE BEEN DOING FOR TOO LONG!

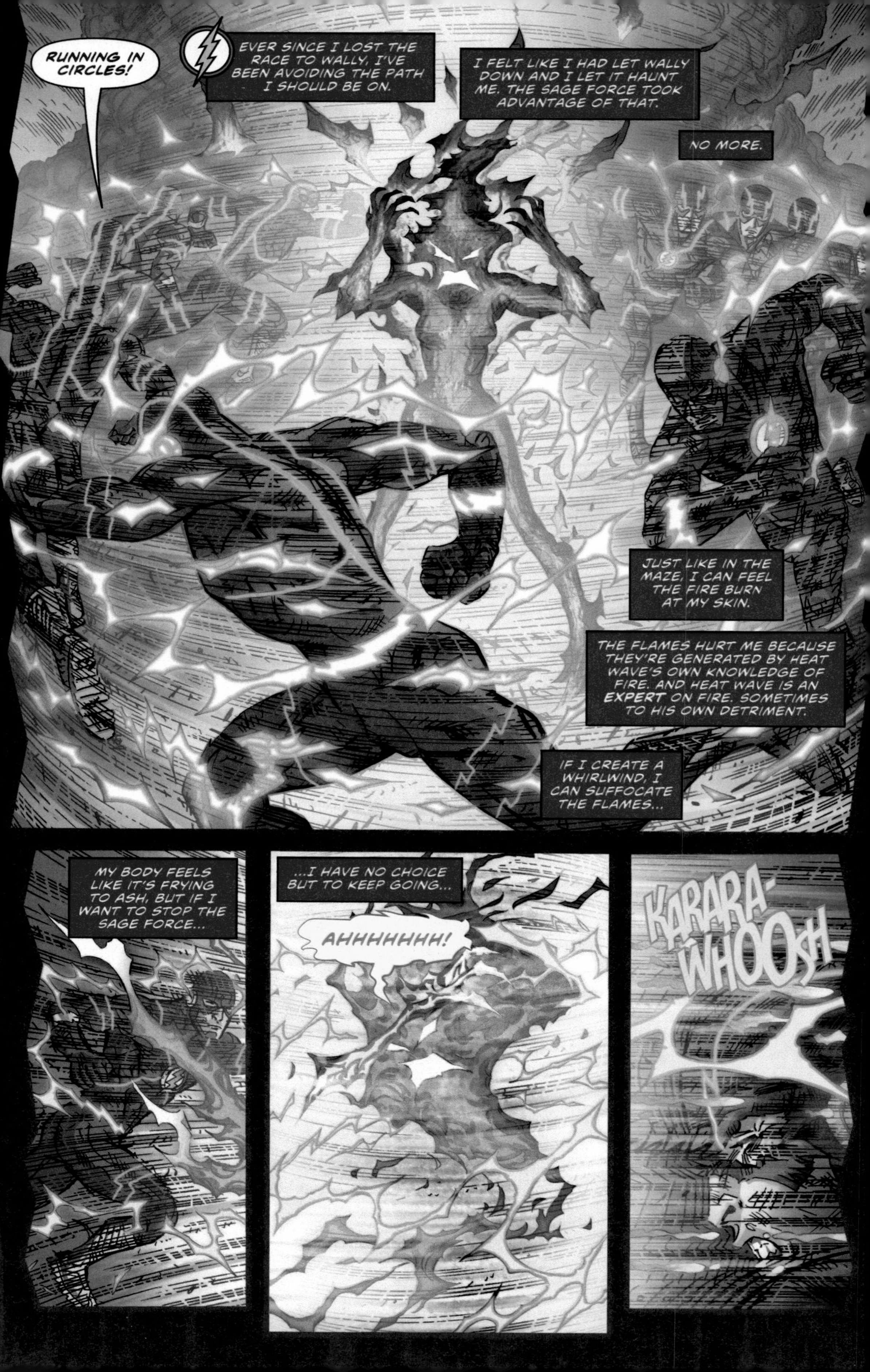
RUNNING IN CIRCLES!
EVER SINCE I LOST THE RACE TO WALLY, I'VE BEEN AVOIDING THE PATH I SHOULD BE ON.
I FELT LIKE I HAD LET WALLY DOWN AND I LET IT HAUNT ME. THE SAGE FORCE TOOK ADVANTAGE OF THAT.
NO MORE.
JUST LIKE IN THE MAZE, I CAN FEEL THE FIRE BURN AT MY SKIN.
THE FLAMES HURT ME BECAUSE THEY'RE GENERATED BY HEAT WAVE'S OWN KNOWLEDGE OF FIRE. AND HEAT WAVE IS AN **EXPERT** ON FIRE. SOMETIMES TO HIS OWN DETRIMENT.
IF I CREATE A WHIRLWIND, I CAN SUFFOCATE THE FLAMES...
MY BODY FEELS LIKE IT'S FRYING TO ASH, BUT IF I WANT TO STOP THE SAGE FORCE...
...I HAVE NO CHOICE BUT TO KEEP GOING...
AHHHHHHH!
KARARA-WHOOSH

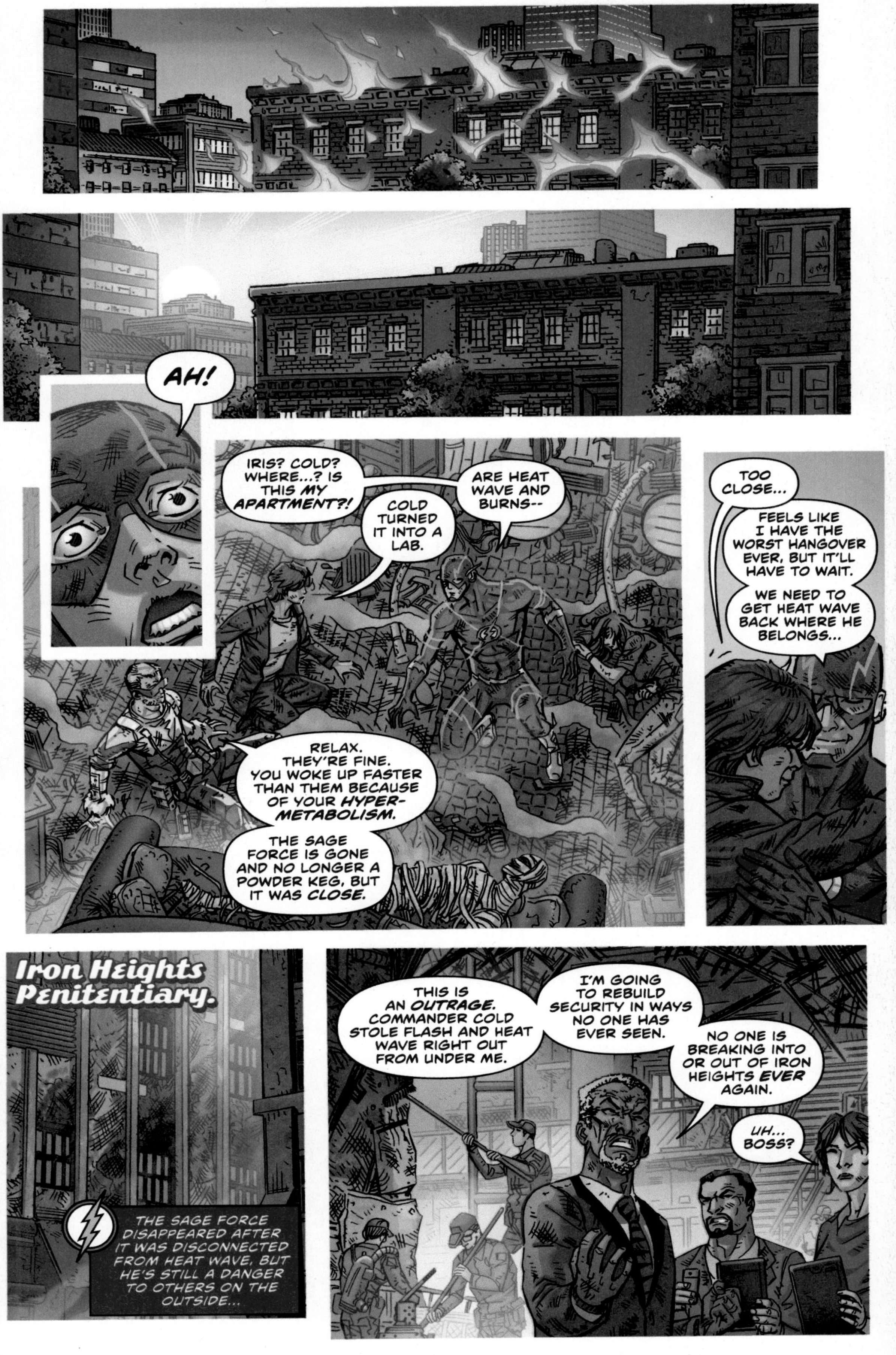
AH!
IRIS? COLD? WHERE...? IS THIS MY APARTMENT?!
COLD TURNED IT INTO A LAB.
ARE HEAT WAVE AND BURNS--
RELAX. THEY'RE FINE. YOU WOKE UP FASTER THAN THEM BECAUSE OF YOUR HYPER-METABOLISM.
THE SAGE FORCE IS GONE AND NO LONGER A POWDER KEG, BUT IT WAS CLOSE.
TOO CLOSE...
FEELS LIKE I HAVE THE WORST HANGOVER EVER, BUT IT'LL HAVE TO WAIT.
WE NEED TO GET HEAT WAVE BACK WHERE HE BELONGS...
Iron Heights Penitentiary.
THE SAGE FORCE DISAPPEARED AFTER IT WAS DISCONNECTED FROM HEAT WAVE, BUT HE'S STILL A DANGER TO OTHERS ON THE OUTSIDE...
THIS IS AN OUTRAGE. COMMANDER COLD STOLE FLASH AND HEAT WAVE RIGHT OUT FROM UNDER ME.
I'M GOING TO REBUILD SECURITY IN WAYS NO ONE HAS EVER SEEN.
NO ONE IS BREAKING INTO OR OUT OF IRON HEIGHTS EVER AGAIN.
UH... BOSS?

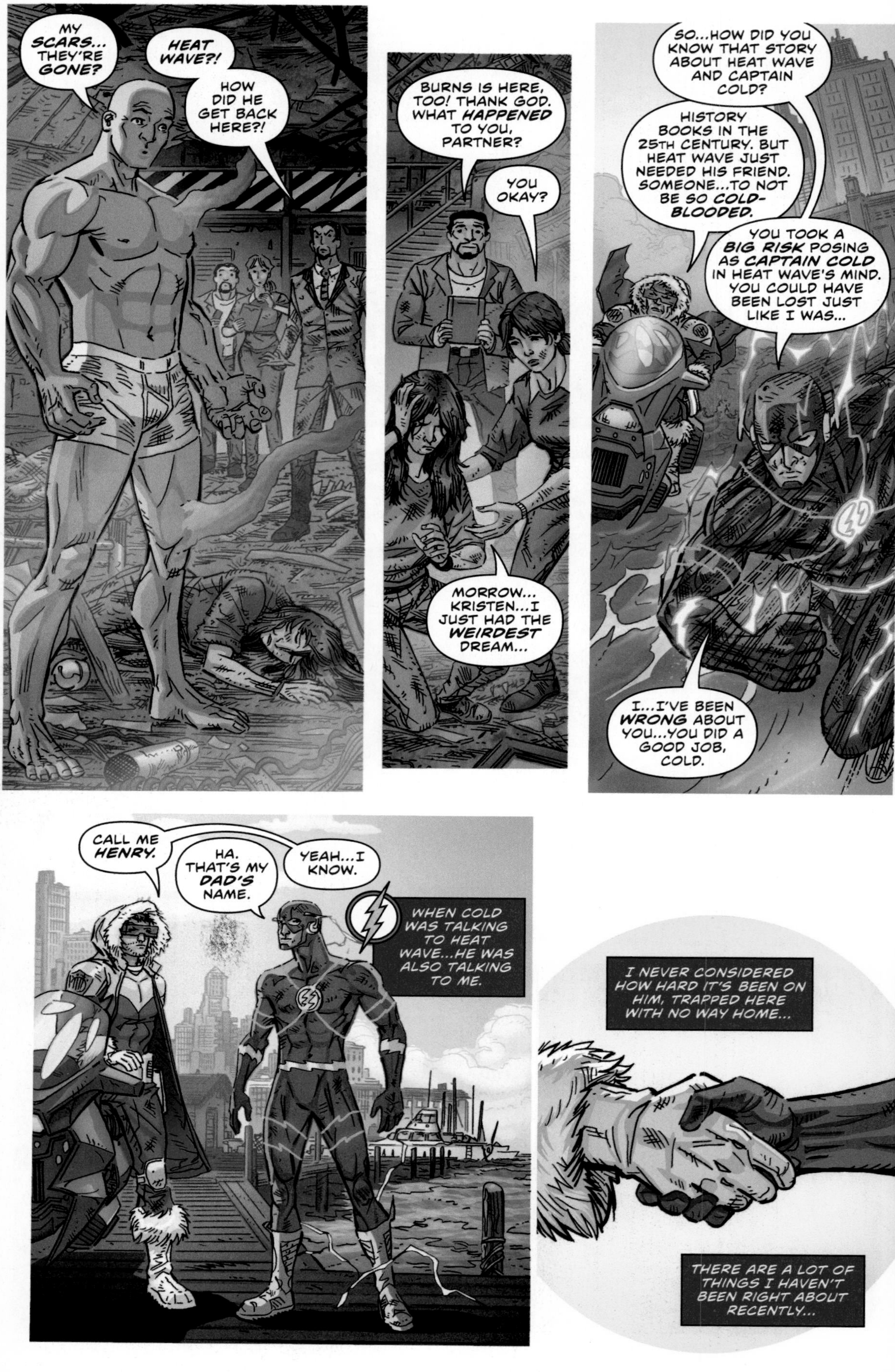
MY SCARS... THEY'RE GONE?
HEAT WAVE?!
HOW DID HE GET BACK HERE?!
BURNS IS HERE, TOO! THANK GOD. WHAT HAPPENED TO YOU, PARTNER?
YOU OKAY?
MORROW... KRISTEN...I JUST HAD THE WEIRDEST DREAM...
SO...HOW DID YOU KNOW THAT STORY ABOUT HEAT WAVE AND CAPTAIN COLD?
HISTORY BOOKS IN THE 25TH CENTURY. BUT HEAT WAVE JUST NEEDED HIS FRIEND. SOMEONE...TO NOT BE SO COLD-BLOODED.
YOU TOOK A BIG RISK POSING AS CAPTAIN COLD IN HEAT WAVE'S MIND. YOU COULD HAVE BEEN LOST JUST LIKE I WAS...
I...I'VE BEEN WRONG ABOUT YOU...YOU DID A GOOD JOB, COLD.
CALL ME HENRY.
HA. THAT'S MY DAD'S NAME.
YEAH...I KNOW.
WHEN COLD WAS TALKING TO HEAT WAVE...HE WAS ALSO TALKING TO ME.
I NEVER CONSIDERED HOW HARD IT'S BEEN ON HIM, TRAPPED HERE WITH NO WAY HOME...
THERE ARE A LOT OF THINGS I HAVEN'T BEEN RIGHT ABOUT RECENTLY...

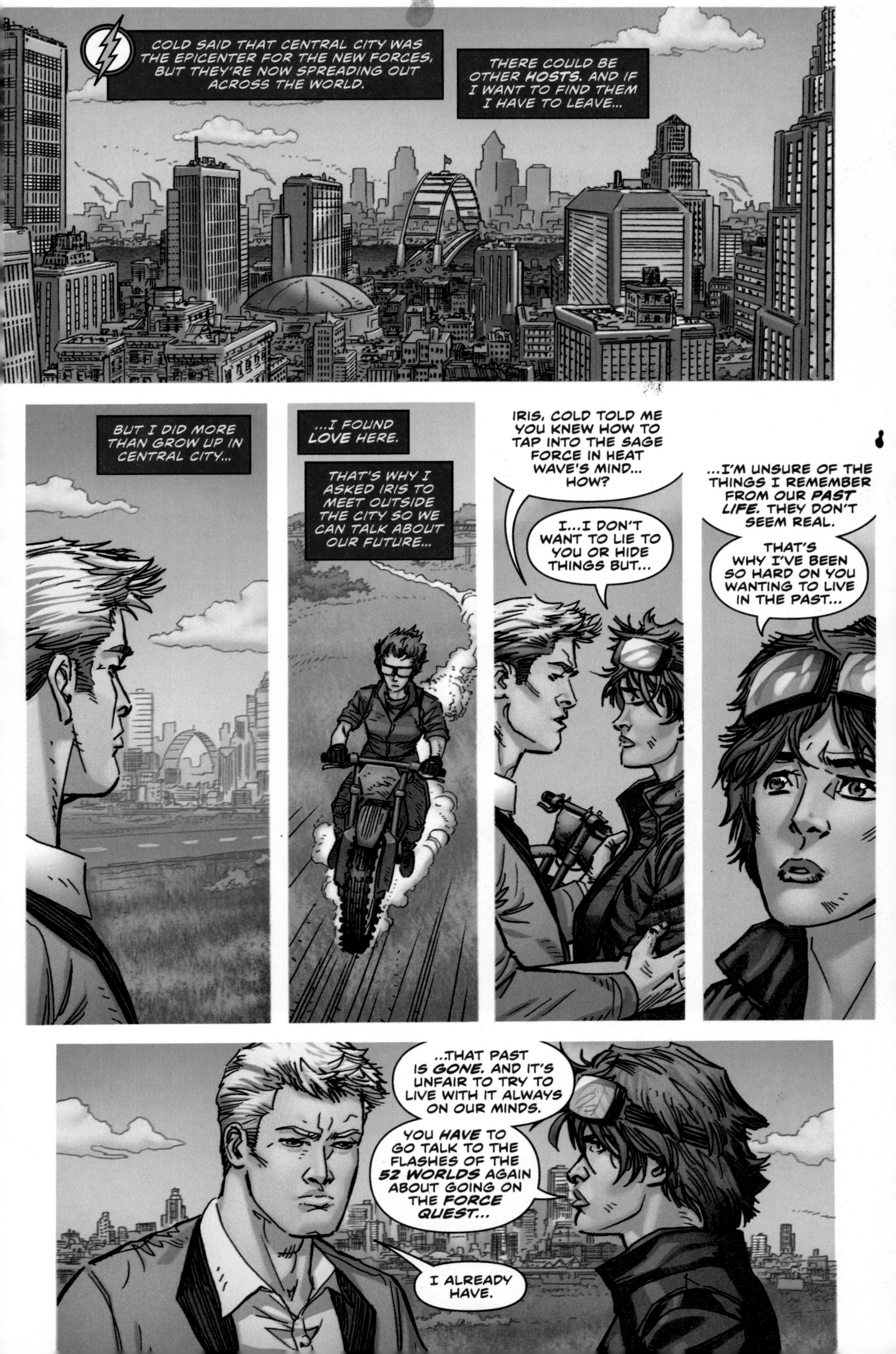

COLD SAID THAT CENTRAL CITY WAS THE EPICENTER FOR THE NEW FORCES, BUT THEY'RE NOW SPREADING OUT ACROSS THE WORLD.
THERE COULD BE OTHER HOSTS. AND IF I WANT TO FIND THEM I HAVE TO LEAVE...
BUT I DID MORE THAN GROW UP IN CENTRAL CITY...
...I FOUND LOVE HERE.
THAT'S WHY I ASKED IRIS TO MEET OUTSIDE THE CITY SO WE CAN TALK ABOUT OUR FUTURE...
IRIS, COLD TOLD ME YOU KNEW HOW TO TAP INTO THE SAGE FORCE IN HEAT WAVE'S MIND... HOW?
I...I DON'T WANT TO LIE TO YOU OR HIDE THINGS BUT...
...I'M UNSURE OF THE THINGS I REMEMBER FROM OUR PAST LIFE. THEY DON'T SEEM REAL.
THAT'S WHY I'VE BEEN SO HARD ON YOU WANTING TO LIVE IN THE PAST...
..THAT PAST IS GONE. AND IT'S UNFAIR TO TRY TO LIVE WITH IT ALWAYS ON OUR MINDS.
YOU HAVE TO GO TALK TO THE FLASHES OF THE 52 WORLDS AGAIN ABOUT GOING ON THE FORCE QUEST...
I ALREADY HAVE.

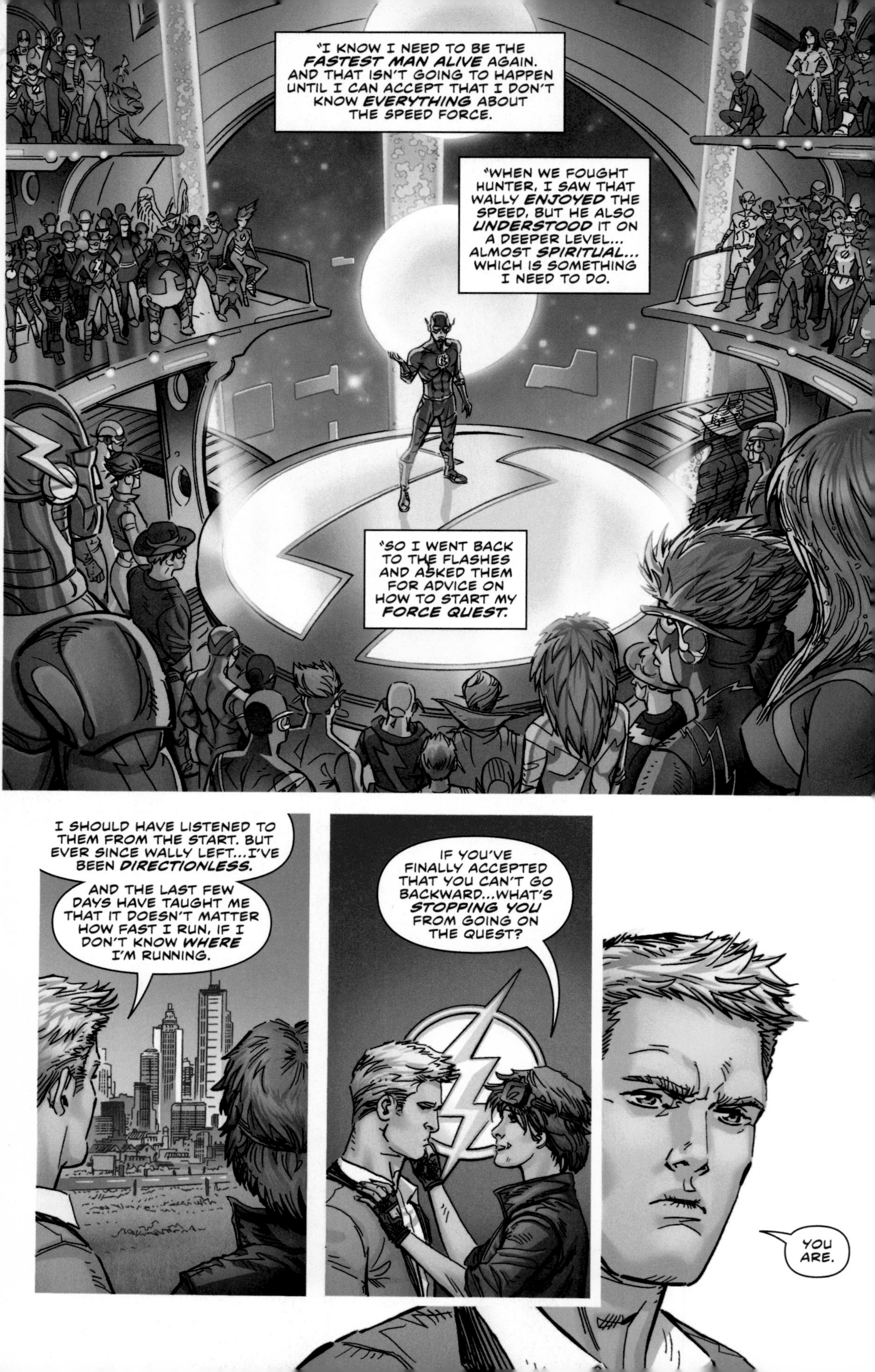
"I KNOW I NEED TO BE THE FASTEST MAN ALIVE AGAIN. AND THAT ISN'T GOING TO HAPPEN UNTIL I CAN ACCEPT THAT I DON'T KNOW EVERYTHING ABOUT THE SPEED FORCE.
"WHEN WE FOUGHT HUNTER, I SAW THAT WALLY ENJOYED THE SPEED, BUT HE ALSO UNDERSTOOD IT ON A DEEPER LEVEL... ALMOST SPIRITUAL... WHICH IS SOMETHING I NEED TO DO.
"SO I WENT BACK TO THE FLASHES AND ASKED THEM FOR ADVICE ON HOW TO START MY FORCE QUEST.
I SHOULD HAVE LISTENED TO THEM FROM THE START. BUT EVER SINCE WALLY LEFT...I'VE BEEN DIRECTIONLESS.
AND THE LAST FEW DAYS HAVE TAUGHT ME THAT IT DOESN'T MATTER HOW FAST I RUN, IF I DON'T KNOW WHERE I'M RUNNING.
IF YOU'VE FINALLY ACCEPTED THAT YOU CAN'T GO BACKWARD...WHAT'S STOPPING YOU FROM GOING ON THE QUEST?
YOU ARE.

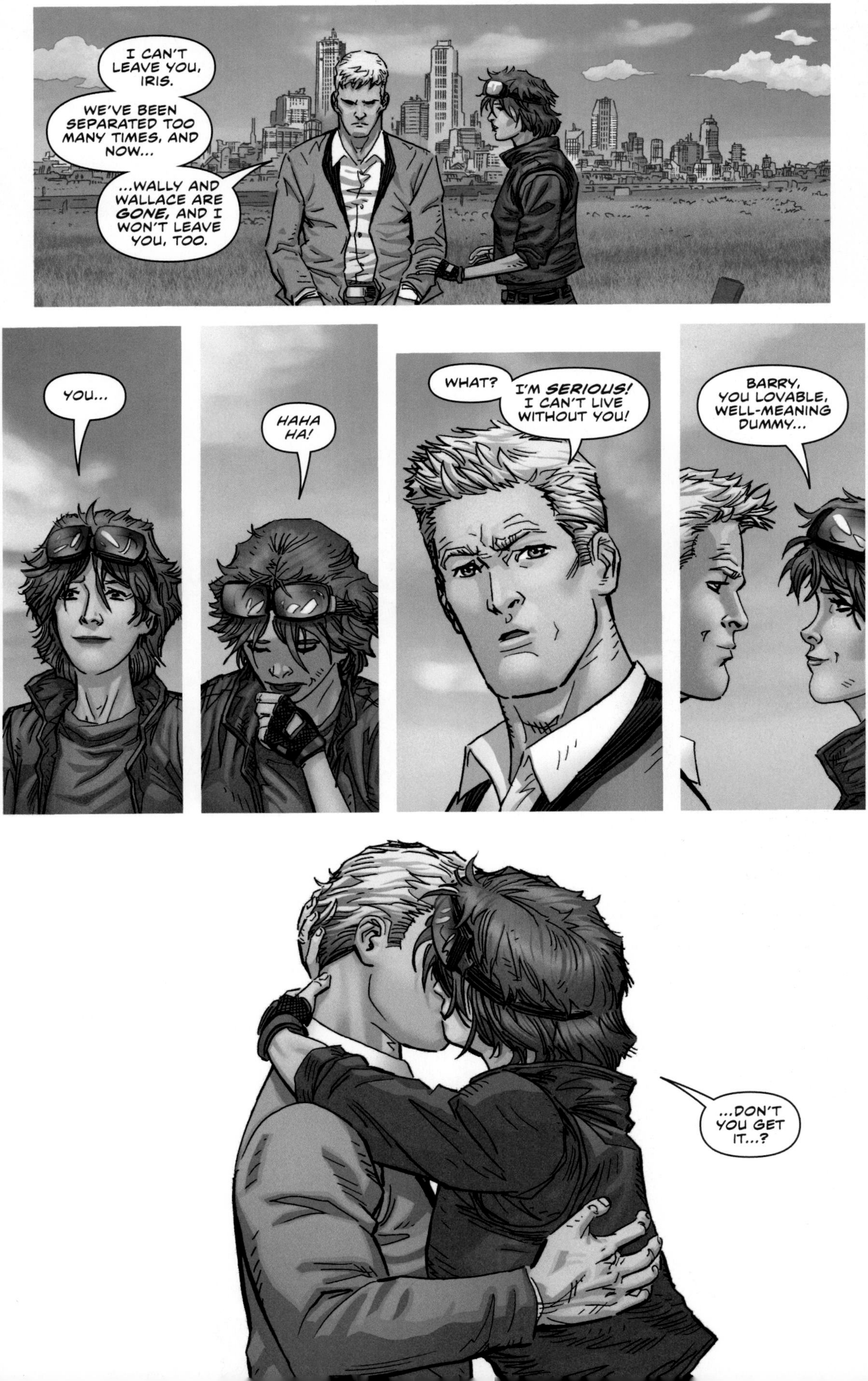
I CAN'T LEAVE YOU, IRIS.
WE'VE BEEN SEPARATED TOO MANY TIMES, AND NOW...
...WALLY AND WALLACE ARE *GONE*, AND I WON'T LEAVE YOU, TOO.
YOU...
HAHA HA!
WHAT?
I'M *SERIOUS!* I CAN'T LIVE WITHOUT YOU!
BARRY, YOU LOVABLE, WELL-MEANING DUMMY...
...DON'T YOU GET IT...?

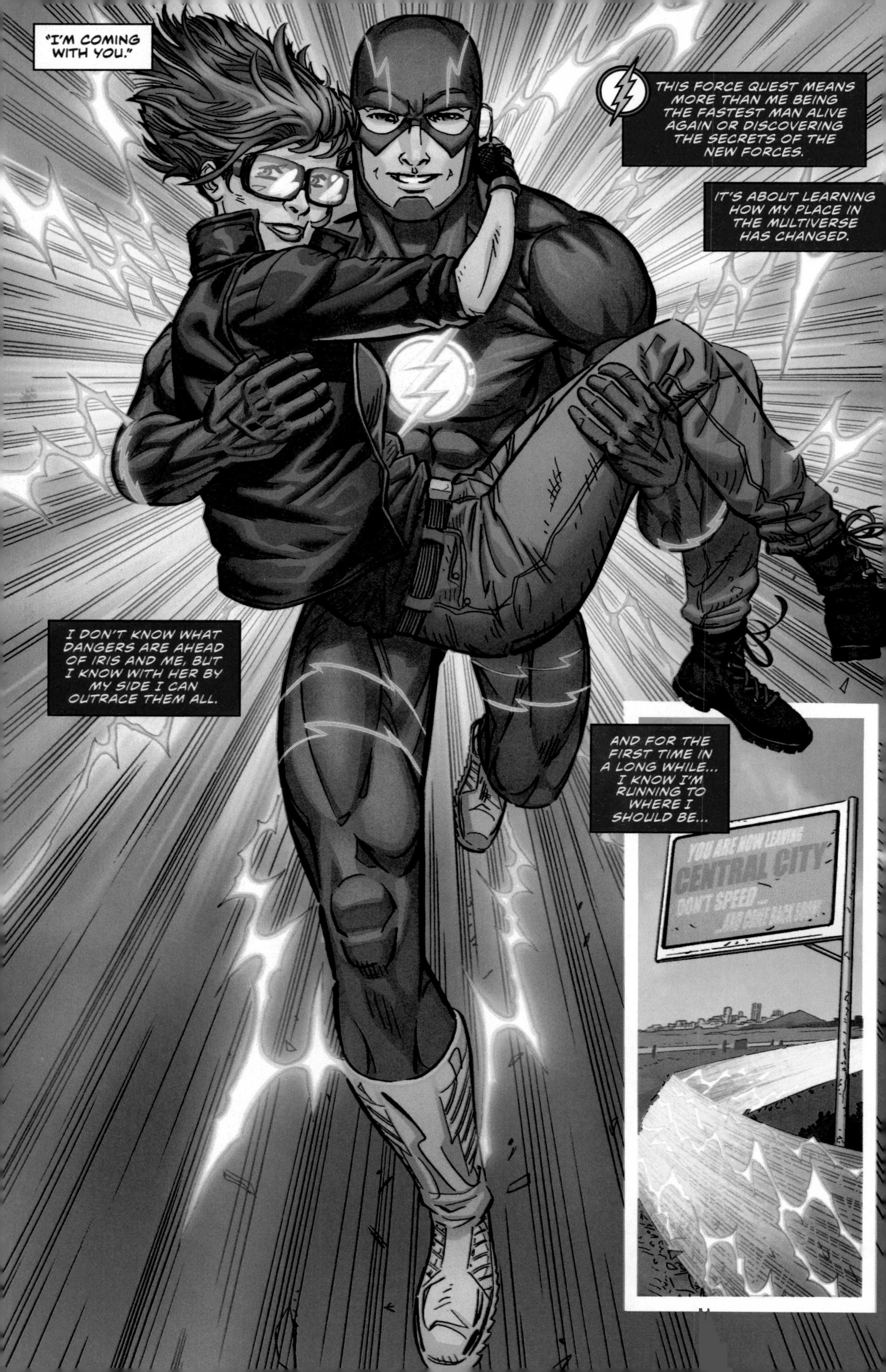
"I'M COMING WITH YOU."
THIS FORCE QUEST MEANS MORE THAN ME BEING THE FASTEST MAN ALIVE AGAIN OR DISCOVERING THE SECRETS OF THE NEW FORCES.
IT'S ABOUT LEARNING HOW MY PLACE IN THE MULTIVERSE HAS CHANGED.
I DON'T KNOW WHAT DANGERS ARE AHEAD OF IRIS AND ME, BUT I KNOW WITH HER BY MY SIDE I CAN OUTRACE THEM ALL.
AND FOR THE FIRST TIME IN A LONG WHILE... I KNOW I'M RUNNING TO WHERE I SHOULD BE...
YOU ARE NOW LEAVING
CENTRAL CITY
DON'T SPEED...

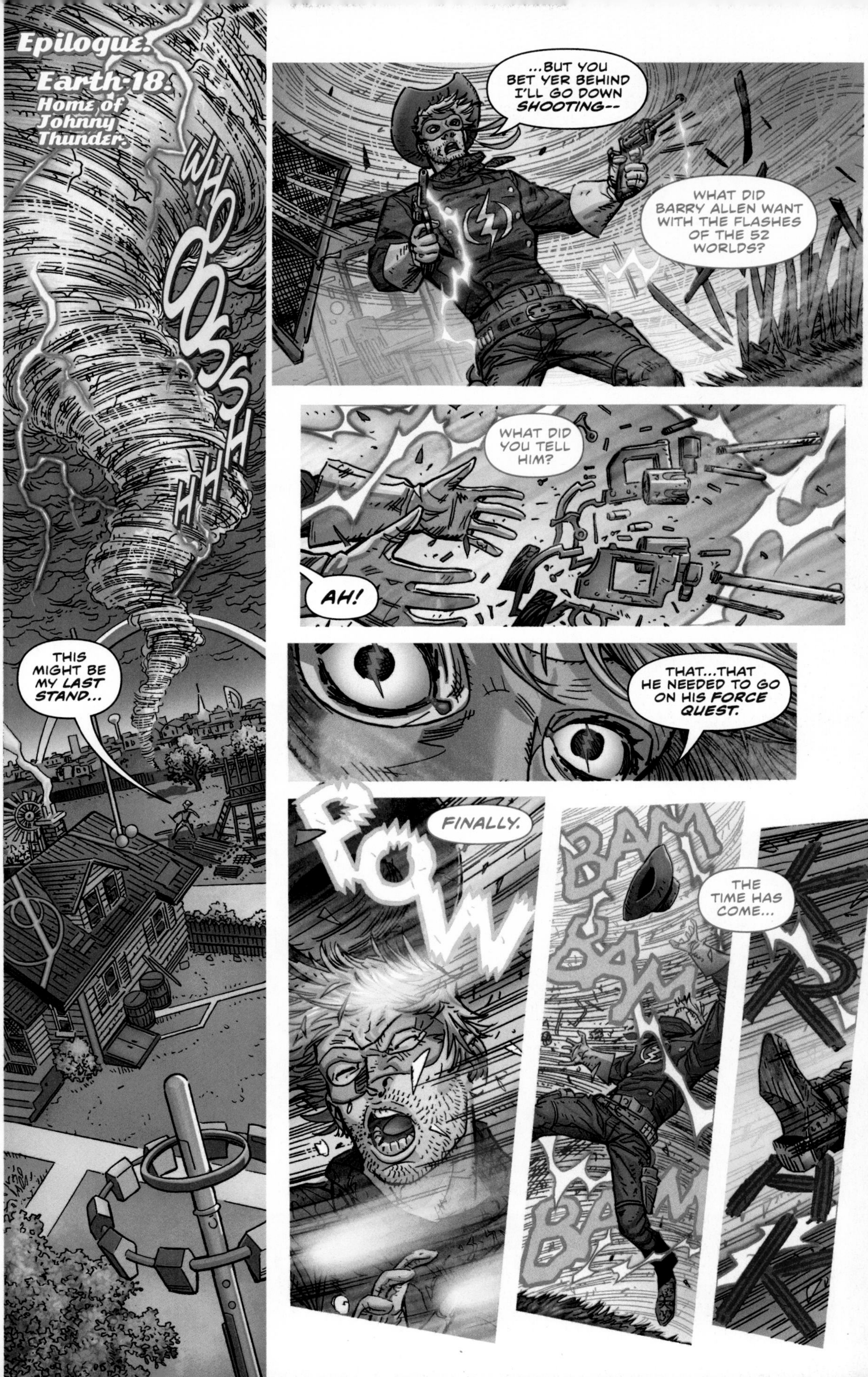
Epilogue.
Earth-18.
Home of Johnny Thunder.
WHOOOSSHHHHH
THIS MIGHT BE MY LAST STAND...
...BUT YOU BET YER BEHIND I'LL GO DOWN SHOOTING--
WHAT DID BARRY ALLEN WANT WITH THE FLASHES OF THE 52 WORLDS?
WHAT DID YOU TELL HIM?
AH!
THAT...THAT HE NEEDED TO GO ON HIS FORCE QUEST.
POW
FINALLY.
BAM
BAM
BAM
THE TIME HAS COME...

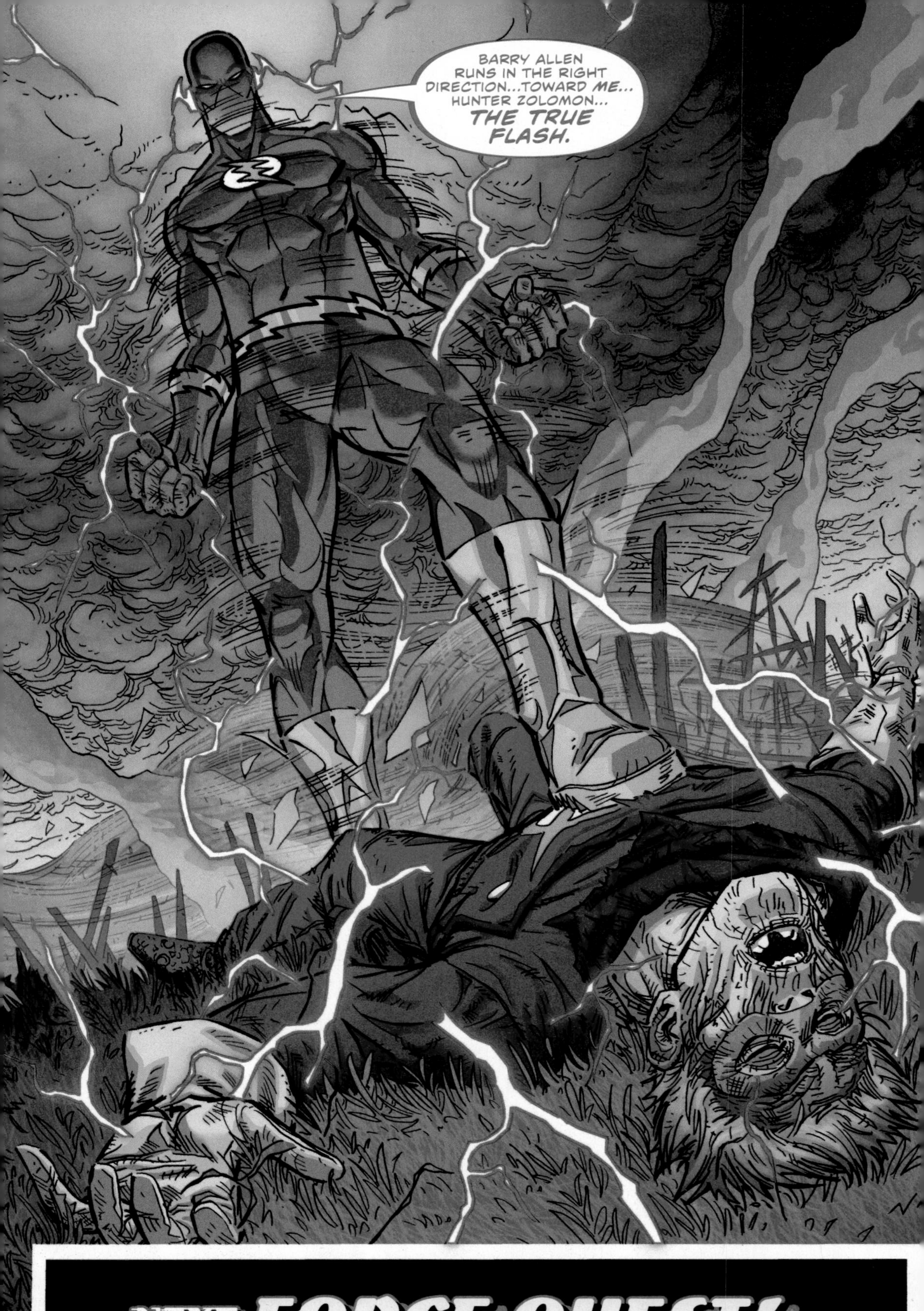
BARRY ALLEN RUNS IN THE RIGHT DIRECTION...TOWARD *ME*... HUNTER ZOLOMON... ***THE TRUE FLASH.***

NEXT: FORCE QUEST!

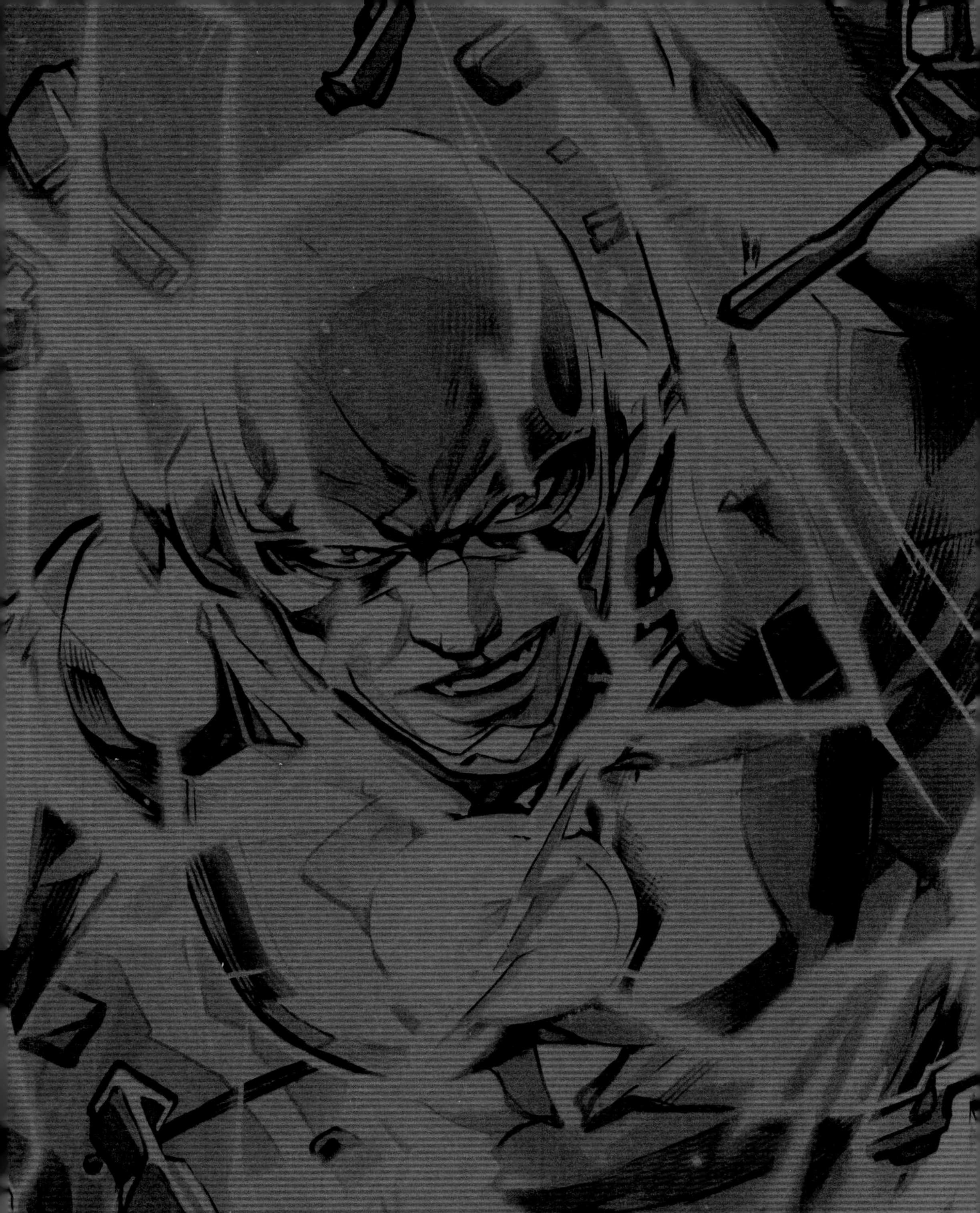

VARIANT COVER GALLERY

THE FLASH #52 variant cover
by GABRIELE DELL'OTTO

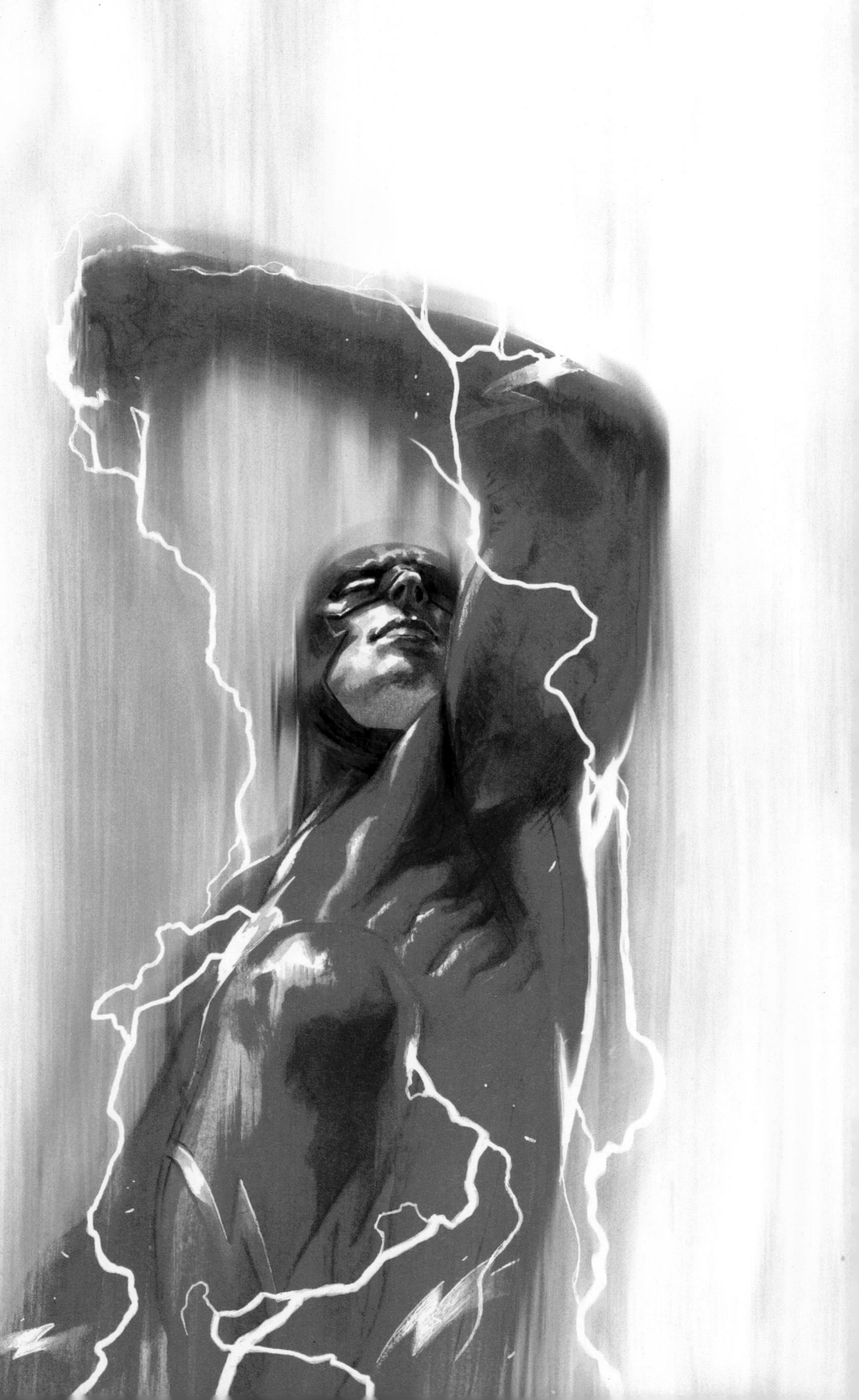

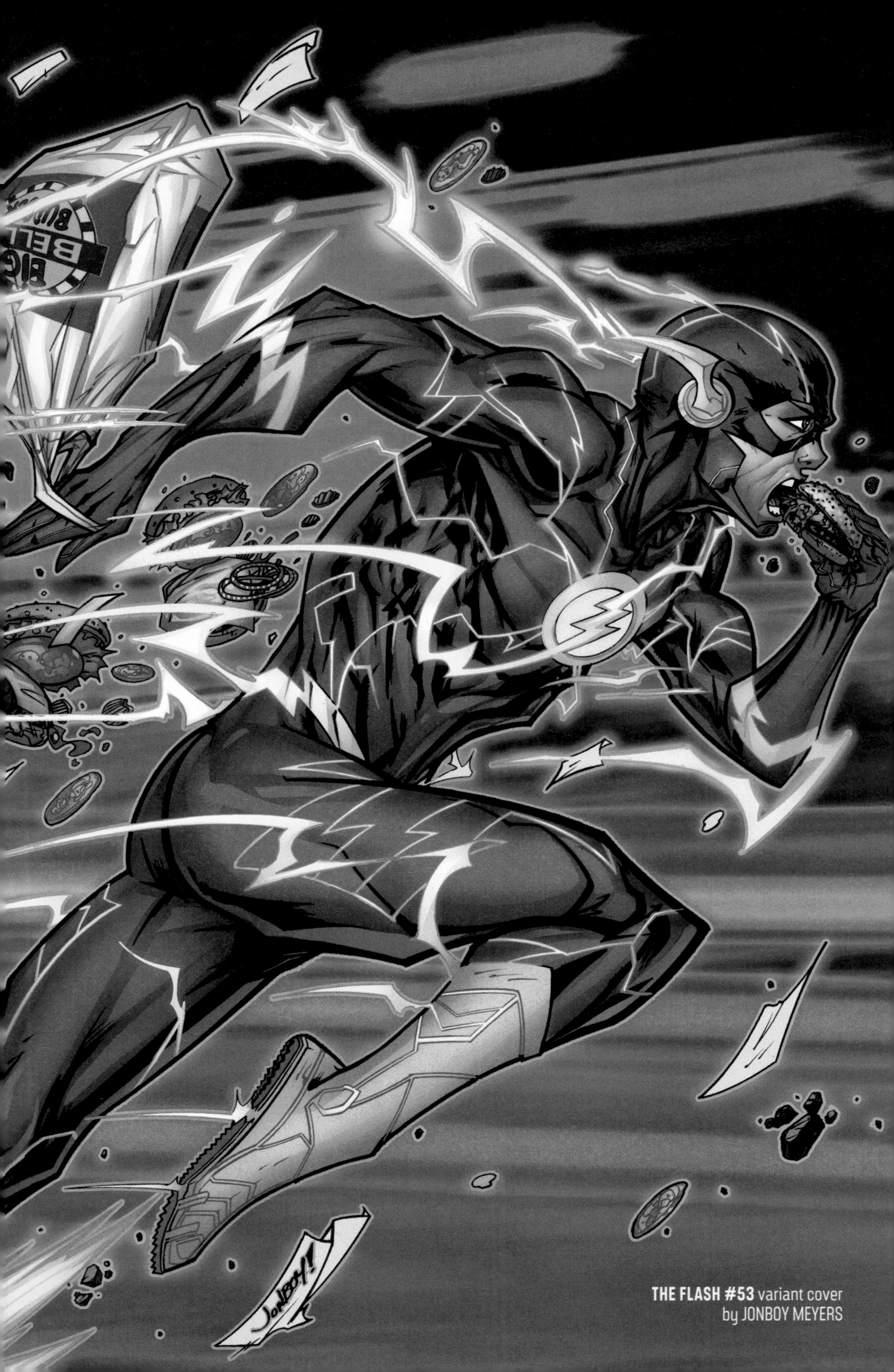
JONBOY!

THE FLASH #53 variant cover
by JONBOY MEYERS

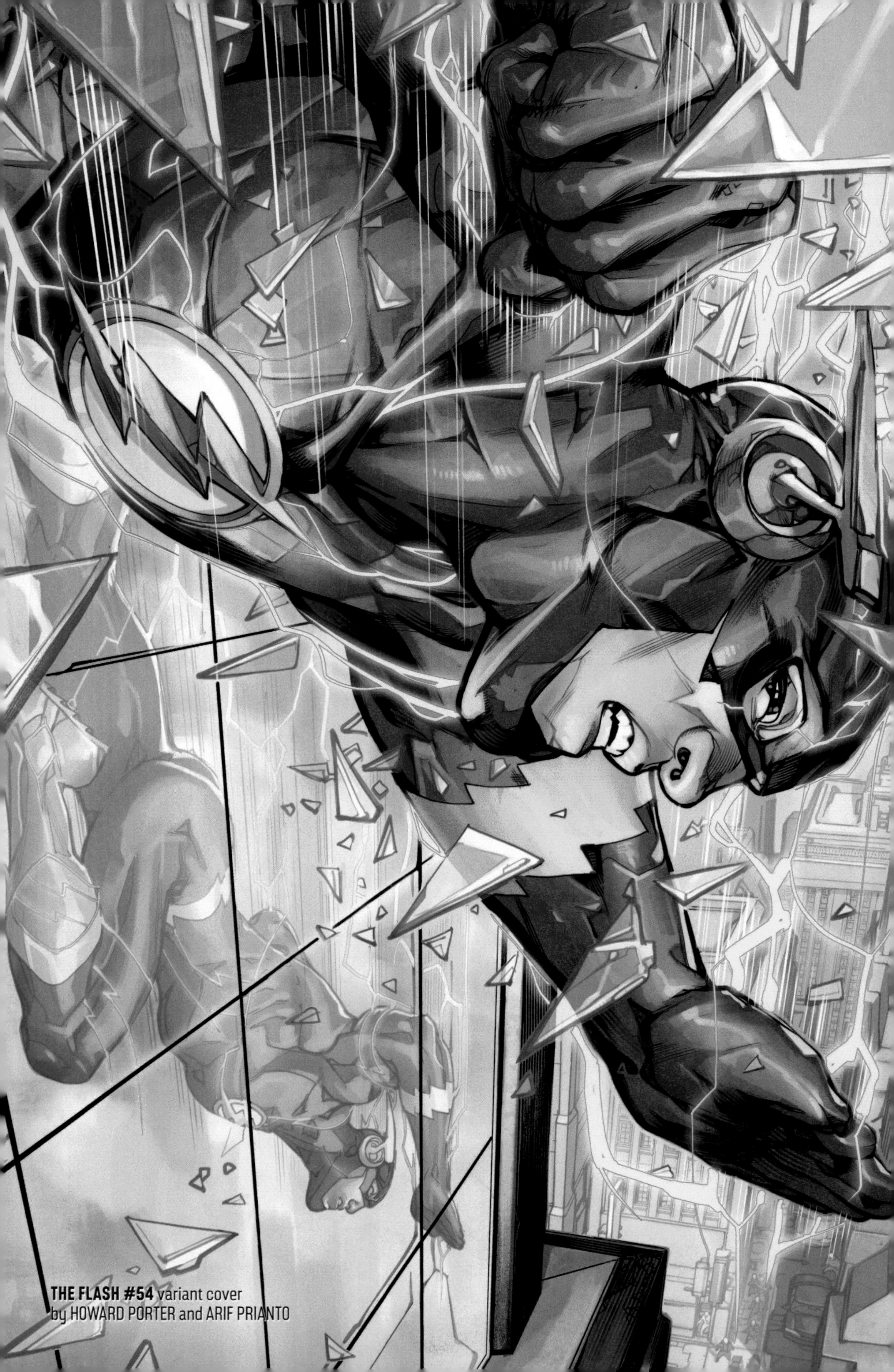

THE FLASH #54 variant cover
by HOWARD PORTER and ARIF PRIANTO

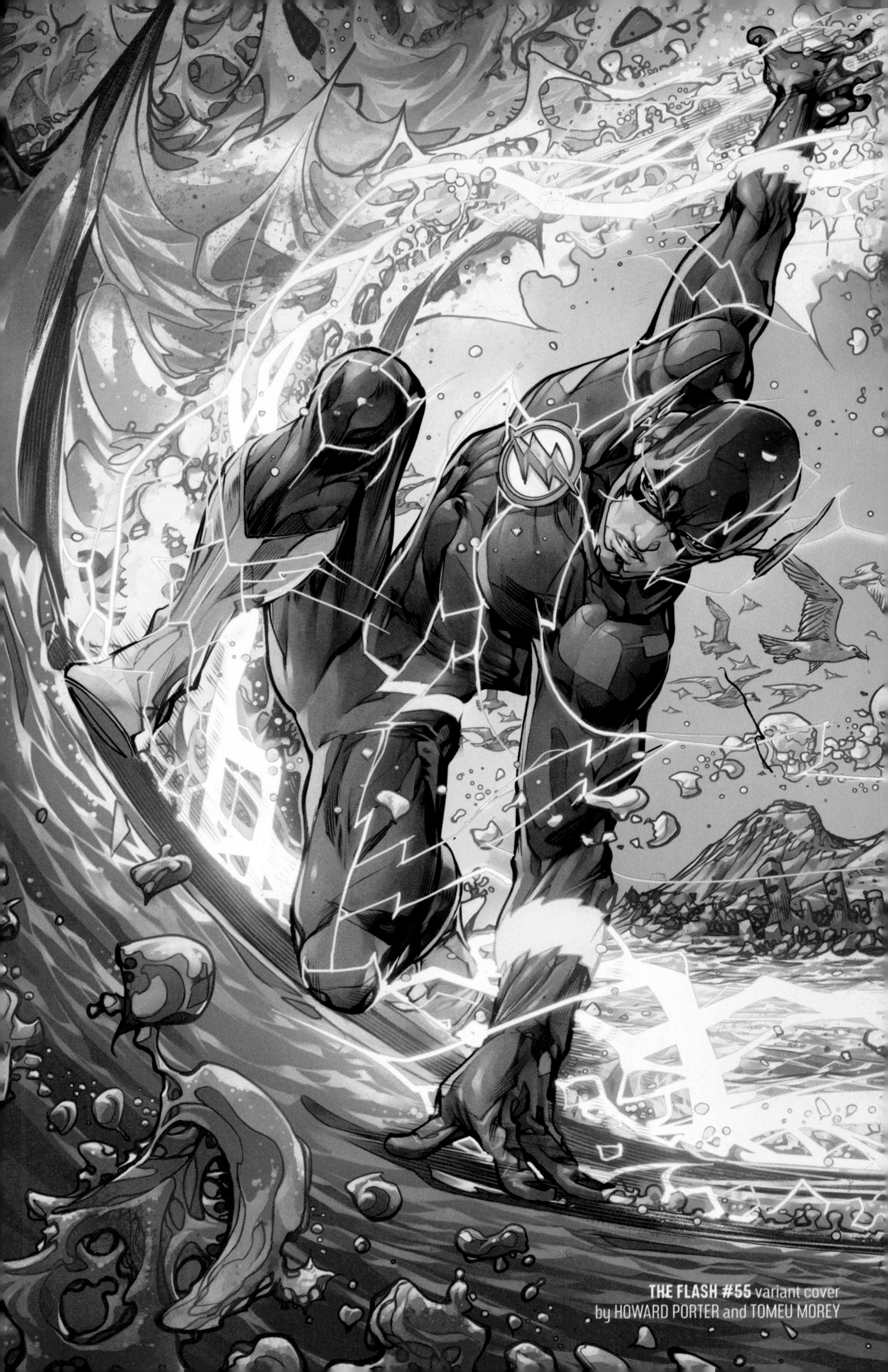

THE FLASH #55 variant cover
by HOWARD PORTER and TOMEU MOREY

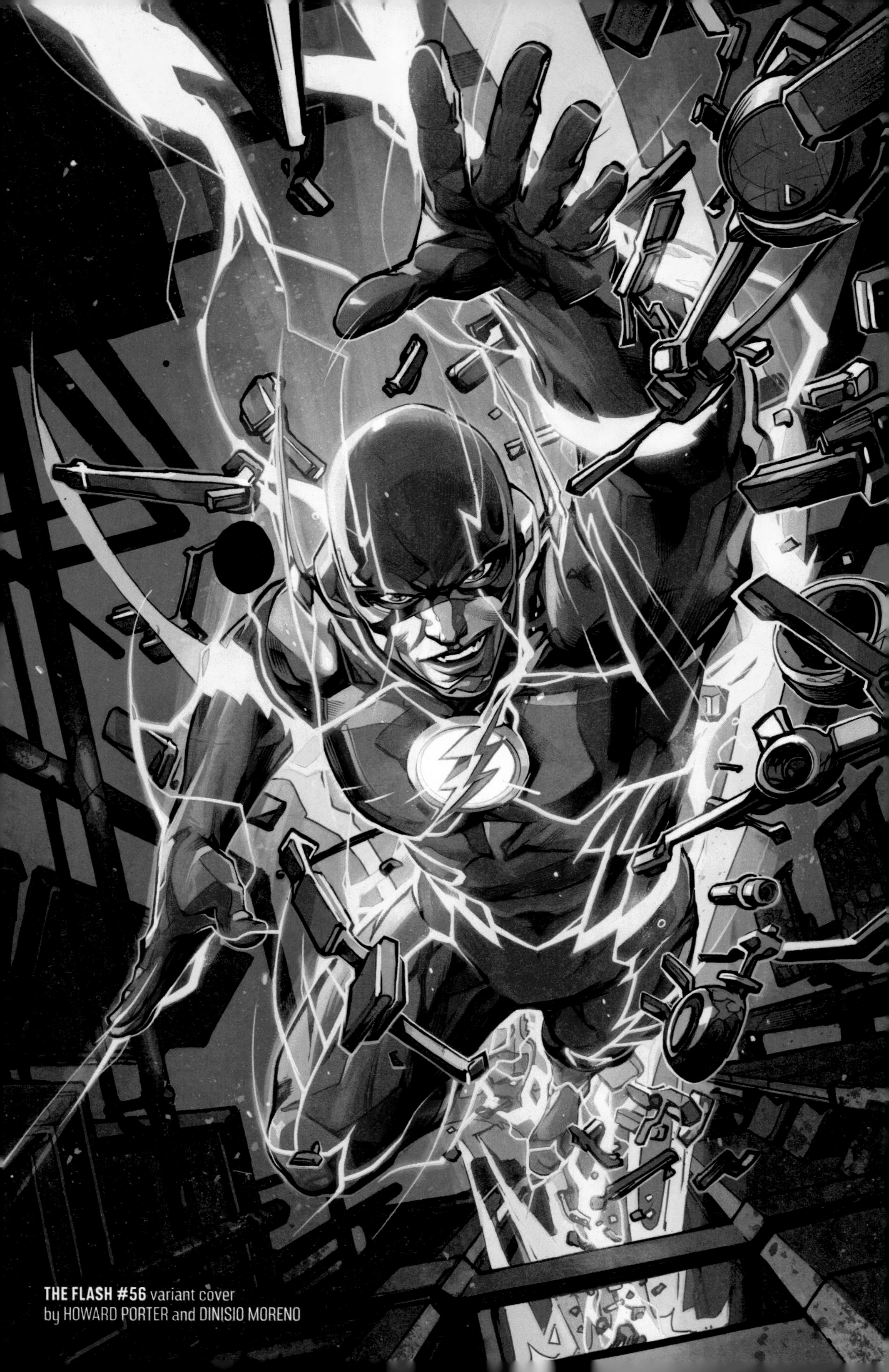

THE FLASH #56 variant cover
by HOWARD PORTER and DINISIO MORENO

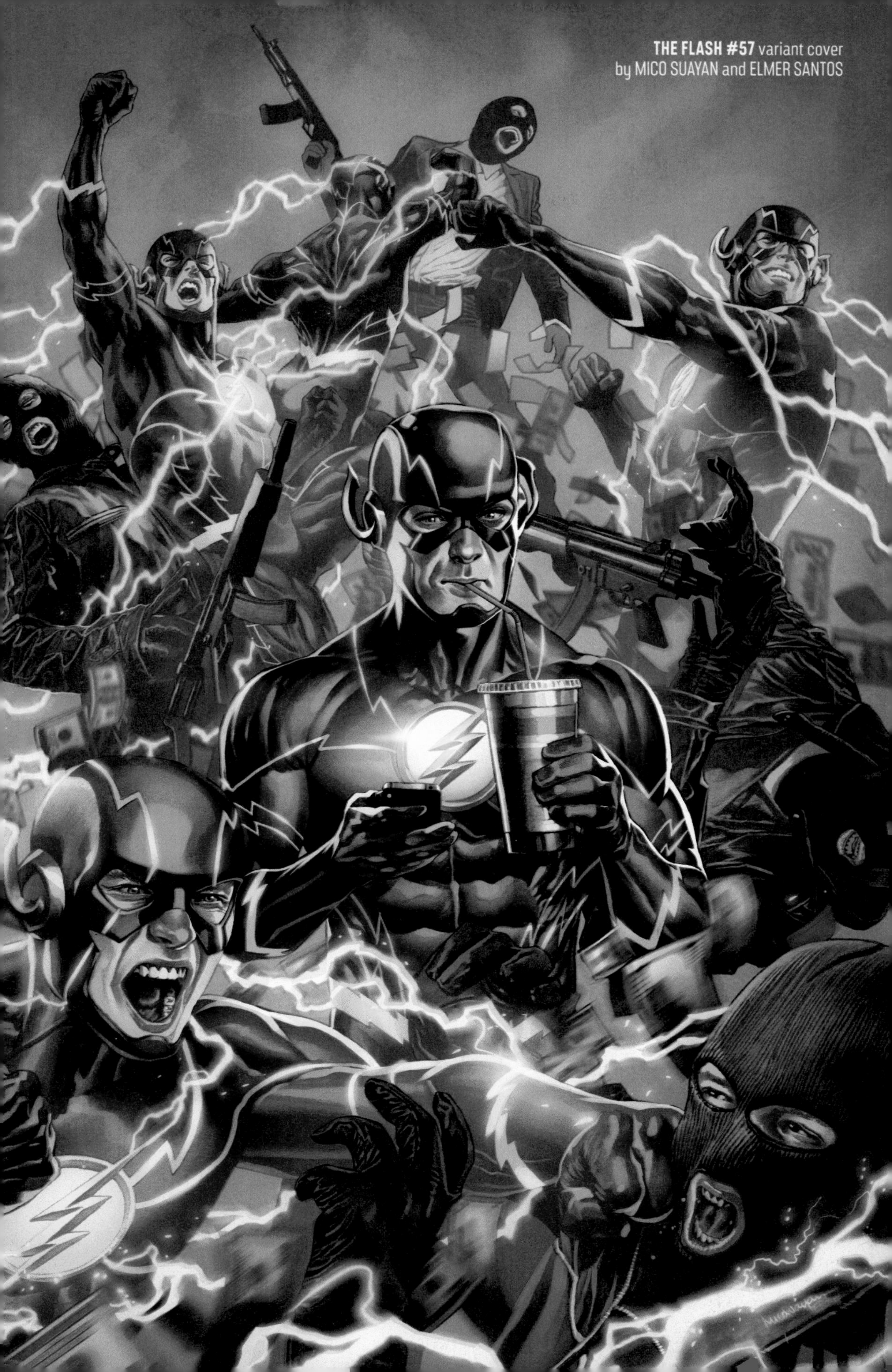

THE FLASH #57 variant cover
by MICO SUAYAN and ELMER SANTOS

"Joshua Williamson's writing is on-point."
–NERDIST

"Plenty of action, emotion, and twists."
–NEWSARAMA

"As accessible as possible to new readers."
–CBR

DC UNIVERSE REBIRTH
The FLASH
VOL. 1 LIGHTNING STRIKES TWICE
JOSHUA WILLIAMSON • CARMINE DI GIANDOMENICO • IVAN PLASCENCIA

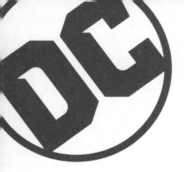

THE FLASH

VOL. 1: LIGHTNING STRIKES TWICE

JOSHUA WILLIAMSON
CARMINE DI GIANDOMENICO

READ THEM ALL!

THE FLASH VOL. 4: RUNNING SCARED
THE FLASH VOL. 5: NEGATIVE
THE FLASH VOL. 6: COLD DAY IN HELL

DC UNIVERSE REBIRTH
The FLASH
"Joshua Williamson's writing is on point." NERDIST
VOL. 2 SPEED OF DARKNESS
JOSHUA WILLIAMSON • DAVIDE GIANFELICE
NEIL GOOGE • IVAN PLASCENCIA

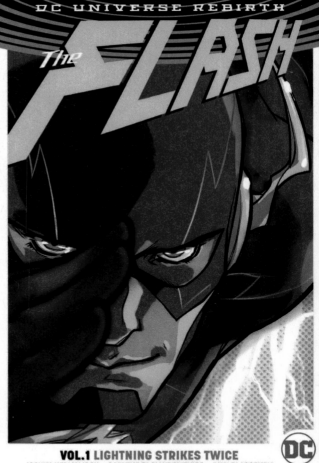

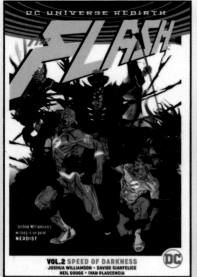

THE FLASH VOL. 2: SPEED OF DARKNESS

DC UNIVERSE REBIRTH
The FLASH
"If you currently are enjoying The Flash on The CW, then you have no excuse left to not read the excellent comic book counterpart." NERDIST
VOL. 3 ROGUES RELOADED
JOSHUA WILLIAMSON • CARMINE DI GIANDOMENICO • IVAN PLASCENCIA

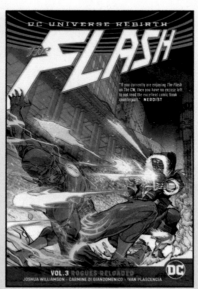

THE FLASH VOL. 3: ROGUES RELOADED

Get more DC graphic novels wherever comics and books are sold!